A GRAND ADVENTURE

A GRAND ADVENTURE

The Lives of Helge and Anne Stine Ingstad and Their Discovery of a Viking Settlement in North America

Benedicte Ingstad

Translated by J.K. Stenehjem

McGill-Queen's University Press
Montreal & Kingston I London I Chicago

© Benedicte Ingstad 2017

ISBN 978-0-7735-4968-5 (cloth)
ISBN 978-0-7735-4969-2 (ePDF)
ISBN 978-0-7735-4970-8 (ePUB)

Legal deposit second quarter 2017
Bibliothèque nationale du Québec

Printed in Canada on acid-free paper.

This English translation is a combined and condensed version of two original books in Norwegian:
Eventyret: En Biografi om Helge Ingstad
© Gyldendal Norsk Forlag AS 2009, ISBN 978-82-05-39064-5 and
Oppdagelsen: En Biografi om Anne Stine og Helge Ingstad
© Gyldendal Norsk Forlag AS 2010, ISBN 978-82-05-39554-1
www.gyldendal.no

Unless otherwise stated, the photographs in the book belong to the Ingstad family private archives.

The author has received funding from the Norsk faglitterær forfatter- og oversetterforening (Non-Fiction Writers and Translators Organisation), from Eckbos Legat, and from NORLA (Norwegian Literature Abroad).

McGill-Queen's University Press acknowledges the support of the Canada Council for the Arts for our publishing program. We also acknowledge the financial support of the Government of Canada through the Canada Book Fund for our publishing activities.

LIBRARY AND ARCHIVES CANADA
CATALOGUING IN PUBLICATION

Ingstad, Benedicte, author
A grand adventure : the lives of Helge and Anne Stine Ingstad and their discovery of a Viking settlement in North America / Benedicte Ingstad ; translated by J.K. Stenehjem.

This English translation is a combined and condensed version of two original books in Norwegian: Eventyret: En Biografi om Helge Ingstad and Oppdagelsen: En Biografi om Anne Stine og Helge Ingstad.
Includes bibliographical references and index.
Issued in print and electronic formats.
ISBN 978-0-7735-4968-5 (cloth). –
ISBN 978-0-7735-4969-2 (ePDF). –
ISBN 978-0-7735-4970-8 (ePUB)

1. Ingstad, Helge, 1899–2001.
2. Ingstad, Anne Stine, 1918–1997.
3. Archaeologists – Norway – Biography.   4. Explorers – Norway – Biography.   5. L'Anse aux Meadows (N.L.) – Antiquities.   I. Title.

DL445.7.I5415413 2017
971.80090909
C2017-900436-0

C2017-900437-9

Set in 10.5/14 Sabon LT with Trade Gothic
Book design & typesetting by Garet Markvoort, zijn digital

TO MY CHILDREN

Ingunn, Kristin, Eirik, and Marit

AND TO MY GRANDCHILDREN

CONTENTS

TRANSLATOR'S FOREWORD

As translator of this book, I am honoured to have been a part of presenting the life stories of Helge and Anne Stine Ingstad to English-language readers. Producing a manuscript of this size and scope feels indeed like a creative birth. In my case, I am merely the surrogate "language mother" to Benedicte Ingstad's creation, but feel just as proud. I admire and am in awe of the story that is told, the beauty and truth in which it is expressed, and the warmth and humour it exudes. Benedicte has done a remarkable job in telling the life stories of her mother and father in a way I believe both of them would also have been pleased and proud.

Whereas Benedicte, the Ingstads' only child, was there in person to witness and experience much of what is narrated in this book, I have had the enviable position of being the metaphorical "fly on the wall," observing and feeling as if I accompanied the people and shared their lives at a deeper level of interpretation and understanding.

In retelling the story in English, I felt as if I hovered over Helge's shoulder, from the time he was born into this world at the end of one century in 1899, following along as he lived a life of adventure and discovery throughout the entire twentieth century before passing away in 2001 in yet another century. I followed his young life as he grew up in the coastal town of Bergen, Norway, and witnessed how much he enjoyed time spent in the mountains and wilderness surrounding his hometown. He loved to ski and hike, was obsessed with playing chess (once against a famous Russian contender), and dreamt of meeting his Native North American heroes. As a young man he studied law and began his own practice, but then could no longer hold back his wanderlust and left home to explore the world. He sailed on an ocean liner from Europe to Canada headed for adventure, then journeyed by railway to Edmonton from where he walked, paddled, and mushed deep into the wilderness of northern Canada. There he lived first as a trapper and then with a group of Chipewyan called the Caribou Eaters. His experiences here became the basis of his 1931 best-selling book called *Pelsjegerliv* (*The Land of Feast and Famine*) and established Helge as a popular Norwegian adventurer.

But this was only the beginning. Helge's fate led him to take on the role of governor as he headed to parts of Greenland and then to Svalbard, a Norwegian archipelago in the Arctic Ocean. From there, it was on to America and to an extraordinary experience of living the life of an American cowboy in Arizona. Mexico was next, as Helge went in search of Geronimo's missing Apache tribe in the Sierra Nevada Mountains. After this, I followed his story as he wandered back to Norway and endured the Second World War and the German occupation of his homeland.

This is where I also began to hover over Anne Stine's life story and watched as she grew up in the small Norwegian town of Lillehammer. It was easy to see how much she loved it there, and how deeply she became connected to the nearby mountains. Her teenage crush and fan letter to the then famous Helge led to their eventual meeting, falling in love, and marrying, despite their great age difference. Initial struggles were a challenge but there was also great joy with the arrival of their only daughter, Benedicte. Wanderlust was one such challenge, and Helge, temporarily leaving behind his wife and young child, once again found his way back to the wilderness of North America and lived for nearly a year with the Nunamiut in Alaska.

Not long after, Helge was drawn to search for traces of Norse people in hopes of exploring a possible settlement in North America. With Anne Stine as his partner and head archaeologist, many years were spent excavating the remarkable discovery they made at L'Anse aux Meadows in Newfoundland, Canada: homes and evidence of the first Europeans in the Americas before Columbus. During these years, I saw how the adversity they faced from scheming fellow scholars and unsupportive government bodies took its toll, especially on Anne Stine. However, eventually, I also witnessed the recognition and appreciation that were finally bestowed upon them from nations, royals, and dignitaries.

As the "hovering" translator, I not only observed what occurred in the lives of Helge and Anne Stine, but also became more deeply acquainted with all the amazing people who filled their lives – remarkable personalities and characters, diverse and vibrant, famous and closely familiar. Many of those "voices" I was able to hear in the incredible number of letters that Helge kept and filed away: almost every letter he ever received and many copies of those he sent. From the time he first left home to study law in the capital city of Norway, he and his father wrote letters to each other nearly every week. The historical details of the times, the fatherly advice, and the prevailing attitudes have all been preserved and provide a wealth of insight into the past for each reader to now experience. Not only did I tune more deeply into the conversations conveyed in the letters, but I also tapped into the words of both Helge and Anne Stine that filled volumes of books. In his life, Helge wrote twelve books as well as one play and several poems. Anne Stine wrote three books, mostly scholarly works but also a narrative of her experience of the people and place of L'Anse aux Meadows.

Besides being the translator following the written life stories of these people, I have also had the unique pleasure of being a part of the actual lives of Helge, Anne Stine, and Benedicte Ingstad. On my own adventure in which I explored my origins in Norway, I lived for a year with Helge and Anne Stine and eventually was persuaded to stay a "little" longer by Benedicte (so far three decades longer). All three have held a very special place in my heart, and as fate would have it, I have translated one book from each. This unique opportunity has meant that, at three various points in my life, I have attuned myself to the "voices" of these individuals. While each was distinct, together they seemed to carry a balanced harmony. Helge's "voice" had the sound of fierce passion for life; Anne Stine's tone was gently vibrant, yet melancholy; and Benedicte's resonance, prevalent in this book you hold, is of deep longing and desire to weave a red thread of understanding through all these stories and events. This book provides an opportunity not only for Benedicte and her family to better see the stunning tapestry created from the remarkable, extraordinary lives of her parents, but also for the rest of the world to experience, and be inspired by, this beautifully woven tale of two unique life stories.

J.K. Stenehjem

PREFACE

When writing this biography of my parents, Helge and Anne Stine Ingstad, I had at my disposal a wealth of material, substantial and unique. This included well over forty shelves of boxes full of archived material, a few unfiled letters, personal diaries and journals from both my parents, and writings from their unfinished autobiographies. During the last two summers of my father's life, I spent numerous hours recording him as he told the vast array of stories and accounts of his life. I have also had access to archives from the National Museum in Reykjavik in Iceland, the University of Alaska in Fairbanks, and from Memorial University of Newfoundland in St John's. I also had access to the expedition journal of Kristiàn Eldjàrn, former president of Iceland as well as archaeologist and expedition member of the 1962 excavations of L'Anse aux Meadows.

But in addition to all this, because much of my own life is woven through the second half of this book, my personal recollections have also become valuable source material: an array of memories, experiences, and perceptions about certain events and situations. I have chosen to include myself in accounts where it is relevant to present a better understanding of Anne Stine's and Helge's lives and/or my interpretations of what unfolded.

In this book and narrative, I also play a role other than that of "just" daughter. As a social scientist, I wanted to present a historical, critical account of events, including the situations and intrigues that surrounded the discovery of the Norse ruins in Newfoundland. These are accounts that, even today, are often misrepresented or erroneously conveyed. For some of these chronicles of events, I am the only surviving witness of the truth. Some of the available archived material cannot be correctly interpreted without the context of an understanding of Anne Stine's and

Helge's reactions and of concurrent events in their own private lives. I hope that by combining all these sources of information, I am able to provide an accurate and true account of what is being told.

No story is ever truly objective, and my interpretation of events is clearly expressed and seen through the eyes of a daughter. But by anchoring this story with extensive references that support the fundamental material, I believe I have come as close as possible to providing true documentation of the historical facts.

Benedicte Ingstad

A GRAND ADVENTURE

INTRODUCTION: THE ASSIGNED TASK

"It's you who must write it." The words came out of the blue, but still as if he had sat and thought long and hard about it. "Write what?" I asked, puzzled. "The biography of course. You will have to write it. And you must write it as if it were your own story, not how I would have. I know you can."[1]

We sat there in the afternoon sun at our island cabin in southern Norway near Kragerø. It was the summer of 1999. Arne Skouen, our old neighbour and friend, and well-known writer, had just strolled down the path towards the dock to row back to his place in his little red dinghy. The two men had played a game of chess and Arne had won; he was very proud when he told me so. But when Arne reached the dock, Helge turned to me, smiled slyly, and said, "You see, I have to let him win once in a while. Otherwise he might not want to come back." This ninety-nine-year-old chess master was not about to admit to being beaten by someone ten years younger.

They were growing a bit frail, those old boys. Helge now made his way down to the dock only when it was time to leave. Except for the one time he suddenly decided to go swimming and then sarcastically scorned the neighbour boy for trying to help him back up the hill saying, "What do you think I am, a hundred years old or something?"

That turned out to be Helge's last summer at the place he loved so much and named after his childhood home in Bergen, called Snippen. Arne at the time was a bit more robust and still managed to row over to Helge to partake in an afternoon game of chess. However, he too didn't have that many more summers there.

The chess games could stretch over several hours. Arne talked the entire time, telling stories from his long, experience-rich life. Helge would sit there in quiet reflection and respond with "hmmm" whenever necessary. Chess was not something to be taken lightly. Helge took great pride in doing it well.

So yes, it was perhaps something that was up to me to write, the biography. My mother, Anne Stine, had for many years jokingly threatened to do so after Helge had died: "Just you wait …" she would say to him. She was eighteen years his junior and, of course, was assumed to outlive him by several years. But now she was gone, passing away before he did. Fortunately, she had always been a wonderful storyteller, so the stories survived as family tales.

It seems to be a tradition in my family to die just before completing a major life's work. My grandfather on my mother's side, Eilif Moe, died just before completing his doctoral dissertation on copyright law. My great-grandfather on my father's side, law professor Marcus Ingstad, sat honing the last of his research until he died, after which my grandfather, Olav Ingstad, published it. Then Olav died right before finishing a large written work on Norwegian clockmakers. Fortunately, the manuscript had come far enough that his son Kaare was able to finish it. My father's sister Gunvor passed away leaving boxes of notes and manuscripts about old national costumes: everything from archaic children's death shrouds to national costumes and leather clothing.

But about the biography. The Norwegian publishing house Gyldendal had been after my father for years to write it. Which he then started, but put away. Why?

I think there are at least two reasons why. The first was that he had other projects he believed were more important to finish, namely a collection of poems and a book about his experiences during the war. The other reason seemed to be that he saw writing a biography as something very final and concluding. Perhaps he thought back on all his family's incomplete major works and that he himself might also die if he were to begin writing his own biography. Even though he was nearing a hundred years old, he didn't talk about death, except for the times he would say, "If I die, you have to remember to …" Most likely, though, towards the end of his life he felt compelled to strongly prioritize the short amount of time he had left. And a biography was decidedly not at the top of his list. No doubt, he also dreaded the thought of having to tackle the enormous job of systematizing and filing all his notes, correspondence, and newspaper clippings.

Why me? Why should I write his biography? Well, as the only child of Anne Stine and Helge Ingstad, I did have all their papers, at least forty shelves of boxes containing their sorted and filed records. Both Helge and Anne Stine had also written various lines and passages in anticipation of writing their own biographies one day, which I too had at my disposal. But in addition to this, I also held an array of Helge's rich correspondence, especially with his father, which has proved to be priceless material. Almost every week, with the exception of the times Helge was deep in the wilderness, father and son wrote long letters to each other. This was how I was also able to follow the detailed progression of my family throughout the years. Unfortunately, Anne Stine burned all her letters before she died.

But perhaps the most important reason for accepting this task my father asked of me is the mass collection of memories I have that are not included in any books or records: all the trips, all the conversations around the kitchen table, and all the times my parents and I spent together, both the good and the more difficult. There will surely be those who write about Helge and Anne Stine after me, but none who have exactly the same experiences as myself.

It has also been quite impossible for me to write just about Helge. He was the first to emphasize Anne Stine's efforts and contributions during the Vinland expeditions, but for me she was there the whole time. And much of the information I have from early years was told to me by her. She was a brilliant and humorous storyteller with an uncanny ability to spot nuances that no one else saw. That is why this biography includes both of them. But since Helge was also eighteen years her senior, many of his adventures took place before she herself was an adult and before they were married. Therefore, the first six chapters of this book tell of Helge's life before he met Anne Stine and the remaining chapters include both of them.

Writing about your parents presents a particular challenge. It's about delving deeper not just into their lives, but also into your own. However, I was presented with a task and I accepted, and have done the best I can – my way.

1   BOYHOOD

The Early Years

There once was a young boy who often climbed to the top of Mt Blåmann, one of several tall mountains surrounding the western coastal
town of Bergen, Norway, where he lived. Even then, at such an early age,
he was a bit of a lone wolf who liked to go off into the great outdoors all
on his own. High from this mountain top, he loved looking out across
the surrounding islands and sea, later in his life saying that "it pulled at
a deep feeling within me – something was so strongly alluring."[1]

When he was about thirteen years old, his parents gave him a sleeping
bag for Christmas. It of course had to be tried out, so he decided that
on his birthday, 30 December, he would climb to the top of Mt Blåmann
and spend the night. After filling his pockets full of gingerbread snaps
and other tasty Christmas cookies, he took off hiking up the mountain.
He reached the top just as the sun was setting, took a look around the
snow-covered summit, and realized it wasn't quite as cozy as he expected it would be. Having no insulating mat with him, he had to lay his
sleeping bag directly on the snow. It was a flimsy, thin sleeping bag, and
he froze bitterly. The entire night he slept with his knees tucked up under
his chin trying to keep warm while munching on gingerbread snaps. The
other cookies in his pocket had long since turned into a pile of crumbs.

Eventually, the early morning light dawned. But for the young boy it
seemed to take an awfully long time. "Enough is enough," he thought.
He flung his sleeping bag over his back and ran down the steep path
towards home. The boy's name was Helge. He wasn't yet ready for wilderness adventures – but he soon would be.

Helge on the Hardanger Mountain Plateau, 1917.

Helge about
two years old.

Born in the central part of Norway not far from the town of Trondheim, Helge moved with his family to Bergen in 1905 when he was
only five years old. His mother, Olga, "a beautiful Tromsø (northern
Norway) girl always quick to smile," and his father Olav, "an engineer
from Oslo of a serious nature,"[2] as Helge described them, met in 1894
on board a Norwegian coastal steamer. After a couple of years in the
north, where Helge's sister Gunvor was born, the young family moved to
the village of Meråker in Southern Trøndelag County, where Helge was
born on 30 December 1899. Born at the end of one century, then living
a life of adventure throughout the entire twentieth century, Helge passed

away at the dawn of yet another century in 2001. Extraordinarily, his life touched three centuries.

Three years prior to moving to Bergen, the young Ingstad family, now also with little brother Kaare, lived on the outskirts of Oslo in Bærum county, where Olav worked as the first county engineer.[3] It was here, in a big red house with a large garden full of apple trees that some of Helge's first memories took root. Once, remembered Helge, when his grandfather Marcus Ingstad came to visit, he and his siblings ran to meet him. "Run down the road, look in the snow and see if you can find anything unusual," he said to the children as they sprinted off to search. There, nestled in the snow, they found a big bag of oranges, a rare commodity in Norway back then. A whole bag of oranges was a precious gift.

And then there was the bicycle, the one he never forgot about, and its sorrowful end. It was a tall, heavy bicycle with no freewheel, so the pedals never stopped spinning as you rode it. Going downhill, a rider had to hold his feet stretched aside the front wheel as the pedals spun faster and faster. Only a feeble handbrake could control the speed, so it was a bit of a risk to take off down a hill. The Ingstad children, however, thought that bicycle was amazing. It even had a name. On a small sign attached to the frame, the word NATIONAL was written in capital letters. Every morning, Olav rode the bike to work. When the young Ingstad family moved to Bergen, the bicycle naturally came with them. As Helge grew older, he too began using the bike. He even took it along to his first legal position at the district magistrate's office in the town of Levanger and used it to cycle all over the district with his briefcase tied on the back rack. When he left Levanger in 1926, the faithful companion was abandoned on the banks of the Trondheim Fjord.

Hometown of Bergen

In 1905, the same year Norway celebrated its independence from Sweden, Helge's father was hired as a municipal engineer and the family settled in Bergen. Since Helge was only five years old at the time, this became his childhood hometown. They first rented a house on Kalfaret Street, not far from the Hansa brewery. It was a residential area just a few kilometres from the city centre and situated a little farther up a hill than the rest of the town. Not long after, Olav found a plot of land a few blocks away at Kalvedalsveien 10. The lot was on a steep slope and

The Ingstad family on the lawn at their house called Snippen.

seemed most unsuitable for building a house. But being the engineer that he was, Olav immediately saw the potential of the property if only a small retaining wall were built. He designed the house himself and called it *Snippen*, or "The Point," due to its steep, slanted position. Another unique feature of the property, at least for the children, was a small creek which ran through – perfect for building a little water wheel. Behind the house, the spectacular and rugged wild mountains sloped straight up, all the way to Mt Blåmann.

The city of Bergen at the time had a population of about 80,000,[4] one of the largest in the country. Situated on the banks of a peninsula and inlet, and nestled between seven mountains, it was one of Norway's most isolated cities – and one of the wettest. The seaways were the only year-round connection with the outside world. Olav, during his time as municipal engineer, strongly advocated and worked for improving inland transportation and access to the rest of the country. On 27 November 1909, King Haakon VII ceremoniously opened the Bergen railroad line, in the pouring rain of course. With this new locomotive connection, isolation ended.

Bergen was also a city with distinct social classes. A few "finer" families, who for generations had owned and operated businesses or shipping enterprises, formed the upper crust. However, an emerging class of corporate leaders from rapidly growing industries also began making their way into the upper class. Civil servants, many of them new to the city like the Ingstad family, created a type of upper middle class, or bourgeoisie. Then there was a middle class, primarily consisting of carpenters and craftsmen, followed by an expanding class of industrial workers who made up the lowest rung in the city's class system. Rapid growth at the turn of the century of both the city and its industries created a huge need for housing. The building and development that occurred to meet this demand in turn reflected the various layers of society.[5]

At first, my grandparents found it difficult to fit in with Bergen society. New residents like Olav and Olga often felt like outsiders to the established group of social elites in the city. Farthest up the hill from their home lived the wealthiest families, but the Ingstads had little to do with them. That my father's family even ended up living in this particular neighbourhood was more coincidence than anything else; Olav's state salary did not offer any great surplus.

Farther down the hill was Fløen, an area where many of the carpenters lived and where a mental institution was situated. "Those boys from Fløen were often treated as if they were from another caste and looked down upon," Helge said as a grown man. "But completely unwarranted," he quickly added, "because they were good people."

As time passed, my grandparents eventually made several good friends whom their own children also befriended such as Professor Vilhelm Bjerknes, a world-renowned meteorologist. Olga got involved with charity work, organizing bazaars for good causes, and participated on the board of directors of a young mothers' home. A place that nobody actually talked about and, at least for the Ingstad children, never knew was for unwed mothers and their babies. Olav was elected chairman of the Conservative Party and even considered a position in parliament. However, in that day and age, it was nearly unthinkable that "westerners" of the country would choose an "easterner" to represent them and their area in such an esteemed position. Yet Olav knew how important it was to maintain his connections with influential people in order to get anything of major importance done. So every New Year's Day, he reluctantly put on his long, double-breasted coat and top hat and headed out for a congenial visit to District Governor[6] Olsen, a man whom Olav didn't particularly like.

However, my grandfather also met some very "unique" individuals whom he *was* interested in, among them a few psychics. Because he himself was able to dowse for water, this made him curious about many other types of phenomena that were not so easily explained. He even became friends with an old monk gifted in the use of legendary herbs who gave him a recipe for a salve made from a distilled concoction of black elderberry. Olav's hands were afflicted with a bad case of psoriasis for which he used this salve to great effect. It was a horrible black goo, but the Ingstad family believed it took "evil to drive out the evil."

Despite Helge's pleasant childhood years in this town, he never really did become a true "Bergen boy." He never played in the Bow Corps, a youth marching and drumming brigade unique to the city, and he never learned the local dialect. He also distinctly hated the rain for which Bergen was infamous. It was absolutely miserable, he had said, to have to take that long walk to school in the pouring rain, day in and day out. He promised himself that when he grew up he would travel far away, to a place where there was far less rain.

Family Life[7]

When my father's family moved to Bergen and as Helge and his brother Kaare grew up, Olav took a great interest in all that the boys did, especially their sports. When they needed new skis, he chopped down a large ash tree in their garden and made the skis himself, clever as he was. Helge had great respect for his father and often used the word "virtuous" when he described him. Olav never forced his will upon his children but rather presented his arguments logically, fact by fact. They generally then followed his advice. He was strict in his parenting and had high moral standards and expectations, but he never laid a hand on his children. A sharp, stern look was effective enough.

In the many richly detailed letters exchanged between my grandfather and father throughout their lives, Olav comes across as both humorous and observant. The letters are long and elaborate, and give a unique account of the times, especially during the war. Things were scarce then, such as tobacco, which the father and son traded information on how to grow.

Olav was also a precise and critical gentleman who said exactly what was on his mind about his son's literary attempts. Helge's poetry was particularly subjected to rigorous critique for precision and rhythm. Olav's motto, which no doubt had a great influence on my father throughout his life, was that a person could do whatever he put his mind to. Helge remembered him often saying, "If someone asks you to climb to the top of a mountain and fly off from there, you don't say it's impossible, but that you will try."

Years after my father died, I found a small note stuck between some of his old papers in a file marked "biography" which read like a declaration of love and admiration for his parents:

He meant a great deal to me. Throughout my entire life he has been in my thoughts. In difficult situations, I have had his admirable and courageous thoughts to inspire me. Mamma, she was always there for us: she was love, a love which I ought to have met with greater warmth. But we were too reserved to show our feelings, and I was also quite self-absorbed.

But embedded in this love for his parents also lay an undertone of obligation to live up to their expectations. The inspiration that Olav conveyed to Helge was perhaps more than just integrity and courage, but also of high expectations of making the family proud.

Olav was master of the household, but it was Olga who created the atmosphere of the family home. They seldom argued. If Olav appeared to have the upper hand in a discussion, his wife still managed to get her own way, especially on issues that mattered to her. My grandmother Olga was a lively northerner: light-hearted, compassionate, and caring with the children, and socially involved with many good friends. Helge said that when she arranged wonderful parties, which she often did, she would always finish the evening with a speech. She often moved herself to tears.

Olga emanated an aura of pleasantness. She baked, canned, and made gooseberry wine, all the skills of an adept housewife of the times. Olav tended to the garden and enjoyed working in it during his free time. He cultivated roses as well as fruit bushes that contributed nicely to Olga's wine and jams. The family also employed a housemaid named Ingrid, but at mealtimes it was the boys who took turns being the "waiter." For this task, they each received a few øre coins, which were officially recorded and collected as savings. Big sister Gunvor, quite remarkably, never seemed to have to do this chore.

When Helge was about twelve years old, Olav taught the boys how to play chess. Helge became obsessed with the game. From the age of fourteen, he began thinking up his own chess moves. He would often get brilliant, nearly triumphant ideas but then a countermove always seemed to end up thwarting the play. Sometimes, if he hadn't manage to figure out a move during the day, he would continue throughout the evening and late into the night with Kaare as his "contender." Up under the attic rafters, the boys sat playing in the big bedroom they shared – Helge's bed on one side and Kaare's on the other. They had a curfew, however, for how late their light could be on. Every night Olav would come to check to see if it was off and say goodnight. So the boys rigged a string to the light switch they could quickly pull and turn off if they heard their father coming up the stairs.

In addition to Kaare, Helge also regularly played against other chess contenders who lived far on the other side of town in Sandviken. Every time they agreed to a match, Helge ran all the way out there. He didn't mind having to go so far to play a good game of chess; it meant less time to have to do his boring old homework.

As the boys grew older and girls began to be of some interest, my father said that he felt they were inhibited by what he called a puritanical aura that lay over all of Bergen. "No one was allowed to let loose. You had to be prim and proper, always. It was a very backwards way of thinking – that old Bergen rule that girls had to behave so properly. Quite a modest treatment of women back then compared with today."[8]

But girls weren't the only enticing thing about town. Movies, the silent kind accompanied by live piano music, cost only a few øre. And every now and again, the circus came to town, bringing exciting wrestling matches between the circus director Karl Norbeck and the Danish Beck-Olsen. These men each took turns winning the match to the great delight of the audience.

Another highlight of the circus was a performing troupe of Ethiopians. A mini-village was set up and brave warriors went about waving their spears. These dark-skinned performers with their unfamiliar features terrified the local public with their wild shouting, war dances, and African chanting. It was Helge's first encounter with people from another culture. Perhaps it even sowed the seeds for future adventures.

During the summer holidays, the Ingstad family often went to the Hardanger Fjord area, about 120 kilometres from Bergen, where they rented rooms at a small guesthouse. The boys would spend the days hanging over the edge of a boat dangling their fishing rods in the water. Those were wonderful summers, that is if it wasn't raining the entire time. Or they spent their summer holidays close to Oslo at Tyrifjord, at an area with old fruit trees and a beautiful sandy beach. Here too they spent most of their time fishing. Helge always had a homemade lure dragging behind a boat. Perhaps not the most modern of fishing equipment, but good enough, thought Helge.

In the fresh water of Tyrifjord, the trout were often large: sometimes great big ones weighing up to 10 or 12 kilos. Once when he was out fishing, Helge suddenly felt a great tug on his line. He jumped up and started reeling in as fast as he could. Seconds later the fish got away: "That was one of the most discouraging experiences in my life. And I still think about it now and again and how big that fish must have been. It was terrible." However, this never seemed to damper my father's love of fishing. On the contrary, he kept at it his entire life and at every opportunity.

"Rieber's Man"

Not far down the hill from the Ingstad house was one of Bergen's finest mansions, home to the Rieber family.[9] Employed at the house was a handyman, a national swimming champion in his earlier years, known to all as "Rieber's Man" but whose actual name was Rusten.

Originally from Sunnmøre, a coastal community north of Bergen, Rusten took to the Ingstad boys and they in return adored him. Helge admired both the man and his northwestern dialect, and did his best to imitate him. The effects of this moulded my father's language and style for the rest of his life. When Helge first came to Bergen, he spoke with an "eastern" dialect. Later, he mixed this with his own version of Rusten's unique district dialect and so was often teased by the city kids for talking like someone from the back country.

Rieber's Man often told the wide-eyed Ingstad boys about the "Wild West" and helped them whittle bows and arrows. Playing "Cowboys and Indians" was soon their favourite game. They hid behind bushes and trees, shooting at targets and sometimes at each other. When Helge was seven, he whittled a bow out of willow and tied it taut with a heavy string. To accompany this he made a quiver out of tree bark to hold four arrows all sanded and smooth. Rieber's Man most likely helped him, but still Helge was mighty proud of the bow and felt as if he had made it all by himself.

At first, young Helge could only shoot the arrows a short distance. But it didn't take long before he quickly improved, which was all very exciting fun for him. He practised by shooting at a tree root, which he actually managed to hit now and again. After several practice rounds, Helge sat down on a tree stump and began dreaming about "American Indians" like those in the big picture book he had received as a birthday gift. He sat thinking about one particularly impressive warrior who was dressed in a leather loincloth and had a big eagle feather sticking out of his hair. The man in the picture knelt before a huge buffalo whose head was lowered and ready to charge. Just as Helge sat there deeply lost in his daydream, a lady came walking by. Helge threw himself down onto his stomach and wriggled his way over to a large rock by the street, readied his bow, and waited. As the lady approached, he shot his arrow through the air and remarkably hit the target. The woman stopped instantly in her tracks, stood up straight, and looked around. To Helge's great dismay, he realized it was none other than old Mrs Rieber. Most likely it didn't hurt her much but still she let out an "ow!" as she stood there holding the arrow and looking quite perplexed before walking on. Helge lay flat and motionless until he was absolutely sure that she was farther down the lane before he ran home.

How Olav ever found out about this little incident Helge never knew, but he suspected his little brother Kaare had something to do with it. Helge was summoned into his father's office, where Olav gave him a hard stare and calmly said, "You go down at once to Mrs Rieber and apologize." With his head hung low, Helge shuffled down the hill to the magnificent house situated so beautifully on the slope towards Puddefjord. He feared the worst when he rang the doorbell with his quivering finger. He was let in, and there, next to window, sat Mrs Rieber in a fine black dress. Helge stood in the middle of the room with his mouth gaping, unable to utter a word. "Well now, how nice of you to come and visit," she said as she got up from her chair smiling. Helge felt uneasy. Nearly in tears, he eventually managed to stutter a few words. "I just ... uhm ... uhm ... sorry." With a pleasant, gentle voice, not at all frightening as he had expected, Mrs Rieber said, "Now my dear boy, there's nothing to worry about. Let me just get you an apple." And then she presented him with a nice big American apple, an expensive gift back in those days. Helge gave a big smile. "Come by anytime," she told him. "It was so nice to have you for a visit." As he was leaving, he ran into Rieber's Man outside on the stairs. "Thanks for helping me with my bow," Helge beamed. "Have you tried it out yet?" the man asked. "You bet I did and it was good," answered the young boy. "You seem quite pleased with yourself. Did you shoot any cowboys with it?" he smiled. "Nah, just old Mrs Rieber," Helge replied.[10]

Sports and the Great Outdoors

Farther up the hill from the Ingstad house was a sports and athletics field. Its location was wonderful: it had a beautiful panoramic view over the fjord and demanded a decent warm-up jaunt to get there. Not many kids nor younger people were involved in track and field back then. The field itself was in poor condition, rough and bumpy, and the only shower was an old iron pipe that managed to squirt out a few sprinkles of cold water. Generally, there were only about eight to ten people out on the field at any one time.

Helge dabbled in track and field; he ran, threw the shot put and discus, but was never any top athlete. He himself thought he was too heavy for it, but even as a boy he liked to keep fit. Younger brother Kaare, on the other hand, was the one who later succeeded in track and field. For years, he was too little to be considered a serious competitor, but once he got started he quickly surpassed his older brother and did quite well competing in discus. Helge found his little brother's sports talents a bit irritating, but their father keenly enjoyed following his sons on the sports field. Olav was very interested in sports and had even been one of the founders and foreman of the Christiania Football Club.[11]

There were also two ski jumps at nearby Ulriken, the largest of the seven mountains surrounding Bergen, where the boys would take their skis Olav had made from the ash tree in the garden. Together with six or seven other kids they would hike to the ski jump and every once in a while spend the night at a nearby cabin. The challenge was getting down the hill again as it was very steep and slalom skiing was not yet a familiar concept. Helge, however, learned to ski down steep hills by quickly swinging around his poles on the curves, even in those wobbly, flimsy bamboo bindings. Sometimes, he would traverse all the way around the mountain and return home down through another valley. At the foot of these hills, grew a spring carpet of yellow primroses, a flower which forever reminded my father of those wonderful ski trips to Ulriken.

Helge also tried a bit of boxing in his youth after an early episode with the sport. A stocky boy in another class, by the name of Fossen, "liked to fight and was a bit gruff, but he was an alright guy," my father affirmed. One day during school recess, Fossen was teasing a much smaller kid. When Helge stepped in and told him to stop, the two boys began to argue. It ended with them agreeing to an after-school boxing match at a place down their street. However, as the day wore on and Helge's initial anger lessened, he realized what he had gotten himself into. Fossen was known to be quite the boxer and my father had almost never boxed in his life. As he sat on the school stairs next to a friend who had his head buried in a book about the Wild West, Helge nudged him for a little sympathy; "I'm going to fight Fossen." Deeply engrossed in the book, his friend mumbled, "Uh huh." Helge blurted, "He's pretty strong, but I'll try to take him," attempting again to rally support. "Okay," his friend muttered as he continued to read.[12]

For Helge, this was a serious situation, but obviously not for his book-loving friend. The boxers met at the agreed spot, each boy with his backup in tow. The two laid into each other. Fighting away, it wasn't long before Helge was so worn out that he could hardly lift his arm. Fossen, however, clearly the better boxer, was also worn out. In the end, an adult came and split the fight up. Since each of the boys was still in one piece, they called it a tie. Fossen later became a well-known boxer.

Laying the First Traps

Rats were a significant problem in Bergen at the time, and city officials paid 10 øre per rat tail, a lot of money for young boys then. Not far from the Ingstad house was the Hansa Brewery, where the father of a good friend of Helge's, Alf Ellingsen, worked. Alf was a more cautious kid and generally not as rambunctious as Helge. The brewery was the world's best playground, and since Alf's father was second in charge there, the boys were given free rein to jump around and play with the large, round empty beer kegs and malt bins. And then there were the rats; lots of rats. Alf had a small rifle and a good aim. He would lay waiting at a rat hole farthest in at the long warehouse. Helge, on the other hand, set rat traps and earned good money – perhaps a precursor of his years ahead as a trapper.

One day, Helge got the idea to catch a live rat. He built a crate trap with a trigger wire that snapped shut when a rat took the carefully placed bait. He set it out one night and, to his horrified amazement, the next morning he found a huge rat staring back at him with scary, yellow eyes. It was, of course, a great catch but how in the world was he going to kill the thing? He hadn't quite carefully thought through his plan. He then figured he could possibly drown the beast. So he took it to a nearby creek and pushed the trap into the water. But the rat just swam around inside the crate. Helge had no idea what to do. Suddenly, the trap door burst open and the rat took off and disappeared down a big sewer drain, to Helge's utter relief. He at least enjoyed the hunt while it lasted.

A Bout of Tuberculosis

In the early 1900s, tuberculosis and leprosy were diseases that were still very much feared. Down the hill from the Ingstad home was a field hospital for lepers. When the Ingstad children walked by it on the way to school, they would hold their breath for fear of catching the disease.

Tuberculosis afflicted mainly those of the poorer sector of society who generally were more susceptible due to living in cramped quarters and not being able to afford proper food. But, of course, others too could catch the dreaded disease. The Ingstad's maid Ingrid, whom the children adored, suddenly didn't show up at their house anymore. Not long after, they were told she had died, and their sorrow was deep. It was the children's first encounter with death. The day after they received the news, the boys were standing by their bedroom window just before going to bed, and the most beautiful butterfly came and landed on their windowsill. They were convinced it was Ingrid who had come to greet them.

A few months later, Helge began having pains in his knee. It was soon diagnosed as tuberculosis, the same disease that had taken Ingrid's life.[13] Because it was socially considered so shameful, tuberculosis was often not discussed. Helge was sent away to the Coastal Hospital in Stavern, over 300 kilometres away from Bergen on the other side of the country, where he stayed for about half a year. He was a mere eight or nine years old, and only once did anyone from his family come to visit him during this entire time, and that was Olav who came on his own. As an adult, my father claimed that he did not mind this separation from his family and thought it was somewhat fun to be in a new place. The hospital was situated by the sea, and since it was summer the patients could go swimming. However, whether young Helge actually took it as well as that is questionable. Maybe he did like being on his own, alone with his thoughts. Or, perhaps it was quite the opposite: his lifelong pull to be off on his own was the result of this childhood experience. After he returned to Bergen from his hospital stay, he had to have his leg in a cast for several more months. At school, the kids teased him and called him "penguin." When the cast was finally removed, he continued to limp for another half a year.

School

In the early years, the Ingstad children went to private schools: Gunvor to an all-girls' school and the boys to an all-boys' school. Helge loathed school. The pupils had to sit with their hands behind their backs when they were not being put to good use. If they did anything wrong they would get a rap on the ear and have to repeat the humiliating line, "I have not done my duty, I have dishonoured my school." If the boys let off a certain "scent" in the classroom, the strict teacher would go around and smell each boy and "graced" the one who was caught. Every so often, the children also had to empty all the items out of their pockets to show that they didn't have pocket knives or other forbidden objects. Even the youngest boys with pockets full of precious personal treasures were subjected to this disgrace. On each desk would lay a small pile of coveted items.

Even in co-ed secondary school, it didn't get much better. Helge wrote poetry and enjoyed language but he didn't find the school lessons especially inspirational. They had to analyze every text and decipher "what this and that meant," which he thought was all quite senseless. Mathematics was slightly better, but German class worse. Helge couldn't understand why the Germans just didn't learn Norwegian. For fear of disgracing his father and grandfather, a professor of Roman law, Helge forced himself to learn Latin to at least earn a decent grade in this subject.

The highlight of his school years was his participation in the student body council, Hugin. First, he was president of the council, then later editor of the school paper for which he also frequently wrote. Hugin was, among other things, a forum for discussion, and one such heated debate during Helge's term as president in 1918 was whether the boys and girls should each have a separate student council. Some of the boys thought that the "young women harmed Hugin and (by having their own group) the girls could have talks on food, home, and childcare which would be of interest to them." The debate was loud and tense, but in the end they voted to let the girls stay and not to divide up the council.

As editor of the school paper, Helge once attempted to compose a somewhat "bold erotic piece that today people would only smile at." When he stood to read it at a Hugin gathering, the audience booed. "It was an absolute fiasco," Helge remembered. He then stormed home and threw the entire manuscript into the toilet.[14]

Nordahl Grieg, famous Norwegian lyricist and writer, was in a class two years under Helge. In a Hugin poetry competition in 1918 Helge won the "Peer Gynt prize" for "best work of a restricted (rhyming) style" with his poem *Hævneren* ("The Avenger").[15] Nordahl Grieg came in second. But then again, Helge was a senior and Grieg a sophomore. Years later Helge met Nordahl Grieg again. "It was you everyone thought was the great poet," he said to Helge. Well, thought Helge, that was safe for him to say now that he was a successful writer.[16]

Despite the poor grades he earned in literature class at school, Helge actually read a great deal. The Ingstad house was full of books, and Olav encouraged his children to read. My father's early favourites were about Buffalo Bill, Sitting Bull, and other Native American stories. He often excused himself from the classroom to go sit in the lavatory to read. As he grew older, he became interested in verse and especially the poetry of the Norwegian poets Herman Wildenvey and Olaf Bull as well as the prose of *Crime and Punishment* by Dostoevsky. It was a huge revelation for him when he discovered that he could borrow books from the library as often as he liked. Perhaps that is exactly why his grades in literature were so poor; he thought he understood more than the teacher.

Chess was another activity that increasingly consumed Helge's attention. At secondary school, he had a World Religions teacher the students liked very much and whom they called "The Bishop."[17] Every so often, this teacher would invite a group of the students to his home to play chess. During one such visit, Helge had his first big win in a chess game, against the one and only Bishop himself. My father remembered this game his entire life. However, his ultimate triumph in chess happened a few years later when the famous Russian chess champion Aron Nimzowitsch visited Bergen and played simultaneous matches against thirty-five contenders. Helge won the first game against the champion and tied for the second. This upset garnered a lot of attention from the public, which somewhat annoyed Nimzowitsch. On 31 May 1921, the following was printed in the newspaper *Arbeidet*:

CHESS
The Russian master plays 35 games simultaneously, wins 29, ties 5 and loses 1 game.
The phenomenal Russian chess master Nimzowitsch, who is currently visiting the city, had his big simultaneous demonstration on Friday. Bergen Chess Club met up with no fewer than 35 of its best players. The results of the matches were remarkable in that the master won all of 29 games and tied for 5. Helge Ingstad alone succeeded in contending him long into the late night hours.

1916 Bergen Fire

In 1914, the First World War broke out. Its effects on Bergen were evident, some even etched in my father's memory, but few were severe. At the outset of war, there was dramatic speculation in the stock market and little regulation. Some hopped on the bandwagon and made quick, easy money. Helge's fellow student, Nordahl Grieg, later in 1935 wrote about this period in a stage play called *Our Honour and Our Power* (*Vår ære og vår makt*); it was a reactive statement to how some could do nothing and earn money while others were fighting for their lives. Helge, however, was never really interested in concerns such as investments and shares. He was careful with his money.

Eventually, the war made it necessary to ration certain foods, bread for example. Helge suspected that Olav gave a large share of his rations to his children. There was little, but the family didn't starve. They heated the house with coal and used a large paraffin lamp during the times they were without electricity. In the evening, the entire family would gather around the table under this light, each doing his or her favourite activity. Helge wrote poetry, Gunvor drew, and Olav worked on his manuscript of the history of Norwegian clockmaking, one of his life's greatest achievements.

About this time in history, the Ingstad family also saw their first car. It stopped right in front of their house. The boys were utterly amazed it could make it up the hill. But in spite of his technical interests, Olav never bought a car.

In January 1916, Helge's school was to hold a formal ball. Despite having had obligatory dance lessons in the waltz, polka, and trot, Helge was still not a very good dancer. He dreaded the thought of going to this event. Due to pressure from his father, however, Helge finally asked a girl to go.

As the gala began, someone came running in and shouted, "The town's on fire!" Somewhat relieved to be able to escape the dance, Helge immediately went to look for his father and ran to his office. By then, the city was engulfed in flames driven by a gusty wind which spread the fire from one house to the next. It was tragic … yet enthralling, my father recalled.

By the time Helge got to his father's office it was empty. As a municipal engineer Olav was out helping to tear down buildings in an attempt to divert the fire. But while Helge stood there, he suddenly thought of all his father's important papers locked in the office's beautiful mahogany cabinet. The fire was closing in so Helge ran to the nearest fire station to get help. No one was there, but he grabbed an axe and some sacks then ran back to the office. He chopped and tore at that fine mahogany cabinet to get to the papers, which he then grabbed and stuffed into the bags, and ran out. Olav's beautiful office building never did burn as the wind shifted just in time. Helge, however, was afraid of what his father would say about the destroyed mahogany cabinet. "Well done, my son," he said, and Helge was as proud as a rooster. The 1916 Bergen fire destroyed nearly 400 buildings and left 2,700 people homeless.[18] Olav estimated that the total damage was nearly 50 million kroner (1916 monetary value).[19]

From the Schoolyard to the Hardanger Plateau

When he was about seventeen years old, Helge and his best friend Odd Martens decided to go to the Hardangervidda high mountain plateau[20] in central southern Norway and stay the entire summer holiday. He later described this time in his life as one of his happiest. Exploring Hardangervidda, the largest alpine plateau in Europe, wasn't unheard of. Each of the famous Norwegian explorers Fridtjof Nansen and Roald Amundsen had taken several winter treks across the plateau, which had been duly described and discussed in their own works. However, at the time, it wasn't as common for people from other parts of the country to visit the plateau, let alone for two teenage boys to spend an entire summer month in this wilderness on their own.

The boys took a tent, which they pitched from place to place, lived on fish, and had the time of their lives. They hardly saw another soul, but every once in a while they would stop in at a *seter*, a high mountain pasture farm, and visit with the farm girls. One in particular caught Helge's eye, but the boys were shy, inexperienced with girls, and raised with such a puritanical upbringing, that there were no summer flings that year.

In a draft of an autobiography, my father wrote of how he first got the idea to take the trip to Hardangervidda:

It was during recess at Bergen Cathedral School. Outside in the schoolyard, everything seemed so much more natural. Everyone large and small were chirpy and full of life, like birds released from a cage. The girls skipped around arm in arm, leaning their heads together and giggling. How anyone could be as happy and cheerful as that during school time was more than I could understand, especially right before German class … I tried to find something to look forward to, but it wasn't easy.

Above and over me loomed the great chestnut tree. There was something reassuringly friendly about it, that sturdy trunk … From that small touch of nature in the schoolyard, it was not a far cry to what was heavily on my mind then; of planning my quickly approaching summer holiday. Where could I find wild terrain with rivers and lakes teeming with trout, big whoppers that eagerly snapped at flies, and a place with hardly any people. The answer came floating in on the wind: Hardangervidda.

Sitting not far from me was my best friend Odd Martens, son of locally-known "Long Martens." Odd was also tall, about 195 centimetres (6 foot, 3 inches) and a fantastic sportsman, when he wanted to be … He was naturally calm and had a witty sense of humour. And I think he even did worse at school than I did, which I found a bit comforting. He sat on the outside stairs gazing off into the distance; he too held a gloomy attitude towards school. "Hi," I said, and he jumped like I had just woken him. "We're taking our tents and going to Hardangervidda this summer. Are you listening? Hardangervidda!" He didn't have to answer – his face lit up with a big smile. The school bell rang and the boys and girls streamed back into the big stone building. I went up to the second floor, sat down at my desk and awaited my fate.[21]

As the summer holidays approached, Helge and Odd intently studied the map of Hardangervidda and got busy organizing their equipment. They would take the train to Haugastøl and from there make their way into the plateau with their backpacks and fishing rods. They had no plan other than to wander about and pitch their tent wherever they felt like it – by any enticing river or lake where they hoped to catch their dinner. Their idea was to survive on fish but also, hopefully, barter a few of their catch along the way for some bread and butter at the mountain farms.

The train ride up through the mountains was new and exciting since the Bergen railroad had only opened a few years earlier. The boys thought it thrilling to watch the forest, birchwoods, and mountains rush by, especially all the rivers where they imagined trout lay lurking in the large eddies. They departed the train at Haugastøl, and as they stood there sorting out their gear, a middle-aged holiday tourist approached Helge. He extended his hand and introduced himself, "Nils Collett Vogt." Helge was startled. Vogt was one of his favourite poets. Here, suddenly, was the man himself and not just as a poem, reaching out his hand to Helge.

"Where are you headed?" asked Vogt.

"In across the plateau," Helge replied.

"Where exactly?" the poet wondered.

"Oh, we'll just pitch our tents wherever we find a good spot," said Helge.

Nils Collett Vogt paused and then sighed, "I envy you," then slowly trudged back up towards the hotel.

Across the plateau they headed. It was like coming to a new world. The plateau rippled with rivers, lakes, and marshes, and the groundcover lit up with splashes of bluish-tinged reindeer moss and colourful alpine flowers. After hiking a good while, the boys stopped at a pleasant spot near a creek. They set up their tent, started fishing, and caught a few trout for their dinner that first night. As they sat around their evening campfire, Odd enthusiastically declared, "It doesn't get any better than this!"

They travelled on, some days walking farther, some days less. The only goal of the trip was to enjoy themselves. In the mornings, they surveyed the map and randomly chose an enticing lake, hoping, of course, that large trout lay waiting. The plateau always offered something new. One morning Helge opened the tent flap and a mother grouse came waddling by followed by her baby chicks. Another morning an arctic fox showed up, then sauntered on. They also came across lemmings that could get so hissing mad they seemed to nearly burst. High in the blue sky, small hawks circled, perhaps waiting for a tasty treat of lemming. The plateau was also filled with its own music from leading musicians such as the European gollen plover, long-tailed snipe, and tiny snow bunting, all accompanied by the wind.

One of the most memorable parts of their journey was an evening they stood fishing as the setting sun glistened across the ripples and eddies of the river they stood in. Suddenly, right before them, the hillside began to rustle and come to life. A herd of wild reindeer![22] Apparently not in any hurry, and not yet aware of the boys, the animals meandered through the brush, slowly grazing as they went. Playful calves gracefully hopped about. It was not until the reindeer were almost to the river that they noticed the boys. Startled, they jumped and scampered back, but not far. Soon they settled down again to graze as though nothing had happened. This was Helge's first encounter with wild reindeer, which years later would have great significance for him when he travelled through Arctic Canada and Alaska together with the "Caribou Eaters" and Nunamiut.

At a narrow channel between two lakes, Helge found a piece of flint which looked like a fragment of an arrowhead. This first find of such an historically old object stirred a great curiosity within Helge, the same that later fuelled his search for Vinland. While he stood there, it struck him that the flint was found right at the narrow channel, which must have been a good place for reindeer to have crossed the water. He imagined Stone Age men lying in wait with their bows, arrows, and spears. The boys also found old, hollowed-out trapping pits used to catch reindeer. Some were completely grown over, but others were still in reasonably good shape, indicating that this hunting technique had been used in the not-so-distant past.

Hardangervidda of the time when Helge was a teenager was not the same as it is today. The plateau had no roads with noisy cars, no exhaust, nor many other hikers. However, lively seter girls were aplenty – young women who lived at the summer pastures to tend to and milk the cows, goats, and sheep and to make cheese and butter. These high-mountain seasonal farms, or seter, have historically been a vital and intrinsic part of the plateau. The boys were always welcome at the seter farms, where they traded fish for butter. If they were lucky, they were also given a plate of sour cream and a good-sized dollop from the big iron pot where the traditional caramelized brown cheese was being made.

Paths of all kinds stretched like latticework across the plateau. First, there were the well-worn paths used by the mountain farm workers. Then, there were those that could be seen, but were quite overgrown. And here and there were paths so completely overgrown that they were barely visible. We know little about the people in the past who have wandered these routes, but at several spots the boys discovered the remains of old turf and stone huts where hunters could have stayed for long periods of time. One day they crossed the Nordmannsslepene, an ancient trail across the plateau linking western and eastern Norway. It dawned on them that at one time it must have been bustling with activity when caravans of horses and people made their way across the plateau to the markets in the east. During the course of the boys' journey, they gained a vivid impression of the uniqueness of the area, its distinct nature and clear signs of ancient use by people dating back to the Stone Age.

One day after a long hike, they threw their backpacks onto the ground and were about to set up the tent when Odd exclaimed, "Gosh it's great to be like a snail and travel around with our home on our backs." My father later wrote in his journal:

> This profound and exuberant comparison, however, shouldn't cover up the fact that some of what was experienced on the plateau would have been much to a snail's dislike. At times, it wore at our sense of humour. Such as when the weather turned sour with pounding rain while we were hiking along or when the air was thick with mosquitos that voraciously attacked us. But, the bad times were quickly forgotten.[23]

One day, they arrived at the River Bjoreia, a pleasant stream flowing through a beautiful landscape. After wading across, they set up their camp in a clearing near a promising pool. They were able to quickly catch some beautiful trout that they cooked over the fire. Life was good. But it had been a while since they last traded for some butter at one of the seter farms, and their craving for it grew. "It's only been fish for every meal," Helge suddenly blurted out. "A little butter with the fish would taste good." Odd was quick to agree and then they had a yearnful discussion about butter. "Butter it will be," said Helge in the end. "Tomorrow I'm going to Maursetseter."

The next morning he took off down a birch-covered hillside headed for the mountain farm. He followed the path and carried on down to the water's edge, where he was met by a discouraging sight. The lovely Bjoreia stream had become a swollen, contentious river. And farther downriver, Helge spotted some wild rapids that he didn't like the looks of at all. He was intent, however, on crossing and aimed his way over. Not long after wading into the river, the current knocked him off his feet. He had no choice but to swim; and swim he did, like he never swam before, desperate not to head for those dreaded rapids. Just in the nick of time, he managed to grab hold of some overhanging willow branches and pull himself ashore. He flopped onto the heather bushes soaking wet and exhausted, heaving to catch his breath. A soaked, dripping Helge arrived at Maursetseter, and was quickly welcomed in by the bewildered workers and given generous amounts of coffee and cakes. They also gave him a big clump of butter and a loaf of bread before they rowed him back across the river. Later that evening he reached the tent and triumphantly called out to Odd, "Light up the fire, buddy! We're going to have butter-fried trout!"

Out of all the boys' many great adventures that summer, fishing at Tinnhølen Lake was what they remembered the best. My father never tired of telling the story. Late one evening, the boys pitched their tent where the Bjoreia runs into Tinnhølen. At dawn the following day, they began fishing, and never before or after did they experience anything quite like it. The full-grown, fat fish, some of them weighing up to a kilo, started biting like crazy. The boys stood in the river wearing their laced canvas sneakers that made it quite difficult to wade to shore every time they caught a fish. Landing nets were a luxury they hadn't taken along. Odd then came up with a brilliant idea. First, he finished off the fish with a rock he kept in his pocket. Then he threaded the trout onto the shoelace of his right sneaker and he threaded the next one onto his left sneaker. When he caught a third fish, he then waded to shore. It was quite a sight! That tall chap wading into shore with a fish on each shoe and one in his hand.

For three sunny, happy days, they stayed at Tinnhølen. One of the evenings, while sitting around the campfire, Helge began to seriously think about other wilderness areas in the world – unexplored areas where little was known about the people who lived there. In his journal, he wrote: "I was fascinated by the unexplored. It wasn't evident then what these thoughts would mean or lead to in my life. But I do wonder if it wasn't that night at Tinnhølen that kindled something within me that later determined my life."

Hardangervidda was a turning point for Helge. Even though his wanderlust and desire to explore had only just taken root, it was the beginning of what would later lead to his grand adventures.

Helge and Odd were so strongly engrossed in their life on the plateau that they forgot to count the days. It felt as if they had oceans of time at their disposal. But the day of reckoning finally came and they realized that their adventure was at an end. They followed the Leiro River and arrived at the beautiful, small community of Øvre Eidfjord in the Hardanger area. On the outskirts of the town, they found a small, green meadow where they set up their tent. It was summer, a warm and happy time for these two boys who were now in great shape and good moods after living life on the plateau. They stripped off their clothes and goofed around with some handmade spears and stone shotputs. Then they discovered a chute with cold running water which they lay down in and let the water rush over them. Female passersby indignantly turned their heads away from these bare-naked boys enjoying life in that beautiful green meadow.

Fishing in the Leiro River had to be tried, despite the murkiness that gave it its name, "Clay River." Helge wandered downstream while Odd stayed farther upstream. In among all of Helge's trout flies was a random salmon fly, which he must have inherited or been given since he could not have afforded such a luxury himself. He used this and cast out his line time and again, but no sign of a fish. He was just about to give up when something dark, about the size of a fist, suddenly started to chase his fly. As a reflex, Helge quickly threw out his line again. Then a miracle happened: a snap, the slap of a huge fishtail, and then a wildly spinning reel. In his journal, my father wrote that he was shaking with excitement. First, the fish plunged deeper as it took off upstream with

Helge running behind it like a madman across the rocks and brush to keep the line taut. Then an abrupt turnabout and they headed downstream. Helge grew tense as he knew the rapids were up ahead and if the fish went in that direction he would most likely lose it. But the struggle continued and the fish leapt high into the air – a big, magnificent, silver-lined salmon glistening in the sun. The fish seemed to be tiring and Helge carefully eased it in towards a small sandy bank. The entire head of the fish was above water when the fly loosened and slipped from its mouth. With a giant leap, Helge threw himself over the fish and pulled it ashore with his bare hands:

> There lay my first salmon, like a miracle, on the grass in between dandelions and forget-me-nots. Odd eventually showed up with a sour look on his face suggesting his fishing hadn't amounted to much. He threw himself down onto the sandy bank and gloomily said, "Fish have to have glasses to see a fly in this despicably murky river. Not a bite. What about you?"
>
> "Oh, I got a bite," I said nonchalantly, then pointed towards the grass. Odd looked down, spotted the salmon, and sat there in stunned silence.[24]

The boys sold it to the shopkeeper for a good sum of money, which came in handy. The size of the salmon was never definitively determined. "When talking about it later, we agreed that it must have been a two-digit number," my father explained, "but I guess that is taking into account that self-caught fish have an uncanny tendency to grow with the years." The shopkeeper told the boys their parents had been looking for them and a rescue party was about to be organized to search. The ferry arrived and it carried them away from the beautiful Hardanger region and home again to Bergen.

Four summers in a row, Helge and Odd lived the free life out on the plateau. Helge often talked about it: the nature, the reindeer, the fish, and especially the feeling of having freedom. No worries other than foraging nature's bounty for their day's meal. It provided a space away from everything he disliked about "civilization," school especially. But it also fostered another distinct characteristic within Helge: restlessness – a personality trait that continued to grow so strong within him that it greatly affected his choices in life. His formative summers on the plateau provided him with knowledge, abilities, and experience that served him well ten years later when he left for Canada to live as a trapper.

Helge and Odd celebrated their high school graduation and the end of school by each buying a cigar. They sat on the school stairs and smoked, right in front of all the teachers and students passing by. Helge comforted himself with the fact that Odd had earned even worse results than he did.

When Helge graduated from high school in 1918, the First World War was coming to a close. He got a summer job as a guard on a boat that watched for smuggled goods arriving from overseas and spies boarding ships into Norway. It was a far cry from living the free life on Hardangervidda.

University

Once it was wonderful to dream and believe
That never a day was in vain.
That sorrow and joy like the stars take leave
To the land where dreams lay wait.[25]
(poem written by Helge at university)

Helge was to attend university; that was almost a given for the men of the Ingstad family. He, however, was not keen on the idea. His restlessness made him antsy, and he longed to take off into the world as soon as possible. However, he finally gave in to the pressure and obligation he felt from his family. What though did he want to study? Engineering was out of the question as he hadn't inherited any of his father's technical skills and could hardly handle any tools greater than a hunting knife, axe, and saw. So it had to be law, in keeping with family tradition. He strongly doubted this choice but decided it was a good foundation to have further in life. With no university in Bergen at the time, he left for Christiania, the capital city (renamed Oslo in 1924).

His first year at university, Helge lived in a tiny room about the size of a closet at his maternal grandmother's apartment in the city. He thought it was wonderful to have his own space out in the big wide world. Once his grandmother, Eilertine, gave Helge two kroner coins – a meagre yet large amount in her eyes based on her widower's pension – an act he never forgot.

Helge's fraternal grandparents also lived in the same area of Christiania. His grandfather, Marcus, had retired from his position at the university and died in September the same year Helge came to study. Helge visited his father's mother every once in a while, but mostly out of obligation. As a child, Helge had had intense respect for his father's parents. In fact, he was actually rather frightened of them. Both Marcus and Dorothea were deeply religious people, and Helge said he always felt like a sinner when he was with them. The family relation whom Helge had the most contact with and enjoyed the most was Olav's brother Emil. Supposedly, Uncle Emil had "applied himself" too hard on his legal studies, causing certain "psychological problems" in which he isolated himself. But Helge and his uncle Emil got along very well. They both liked to sit and quietly reflect, and both had a deep connection to nature that was almost poetic: Emil with paintbrush strokes and Helge with words.

Law school was a four-year program and Helge was determined to finish as quickly as possible. This required an end to his smoking. He was a keen pipe smoker who incessantly puffed on his pipe, but he noticed his memory improved without it.[26] Chess was another problem because it was almost an obsession. "Just as others lapsed into drinking liquor, I lapsed into playing chess," he once said. Helge helped establish the Academic Chess Club, where he was chairman for a time. He soon realized, though, that if he was going to have enough time for his studies he would have to set chess aside.

Halfway through his university education, Helge got completely fed up. He was unsure if he wanted to be a lawyer, or if he was even capable of finishing the degree. His longing to travel grew even stronger. He dreamt of breaking away and escaping to a Pacific island. He approached his father to express his uncertainties, who in return responded with these counter-arguments:

Experience shows that people who leave their studies seldom manage to begin again and finish. Hereto we know nothing about whether the undersigned's future will include any of the necessary resourcefulness on your return … If you consider other facts of the case, I believe that you are too young to reap the benefits of such travel. It is not your intent to travel merely as a tourist. Neither can it be your future intention to work as a labourer … the decision must be to allow a chance to succeed.[27]

Olav believed Helge was still too young to have the necessary social understanding and knowledge to go out and travel the world, and that the older he was and the more experience he gained, the better equipped he would be to handle situations that could arise. Olav promised to contribute 1,000 kroner to his son's travels if he waited until after he graduated. Helge followed his father's advice and as an adult said that he was glad that he did. But at the time, he felt strongly pressured into continuing his studies. He was pulled between his incredible restlessness and a desire not to disappoint his parents, especially his father.

The only break he got during his studies was when he was drafted into the military for a six-month service. He ended up in the King's Guard, and there is much to indicate that he didn't take it very seriously. He did not have much of a liking for marching drills and weaponry. The best about the military, he thought, was becoming acquainted with young men from all over Norway and with all types of people. Many of them had grown up on isolated farms and had hardly ever travelled outside their villages. Having grown up as part of Bergen's bourgeoisie, Helge's circle of friends were generally from the same social class as himself. The men he met in the military made him appreciate the "genuine people from the country." The term "genuine" was meant to be a badge of honour: a people who were sincere and unpretentious and who didn't care about the silly nonsense around town.

When studying law back in those days, students had to take their exams all at once and only at the end of the entire four-year study. It was very tough. Helge systematically went to work and combined studying with spending time in the outdoors. He believed it would help ensure the good results he felt his family expected. Every day he had free, he took off on his skis across Nordmarka, the northern woods on the upper side of the city. Two days before the exams, while everyone else sat with their noses in their books, Helge took off and went hiking. An encouraging letter arrived from home: "My dear Helge, Just a short greeting. We are all suffering from examination anxieties. Yes, God bless and help you my dear boy. Relax and I'm sure it will go fine. Your very own Mamma."

Examination results were released on a November day in 1922. A professor came out into the vestibule of the old university building and read the results aloud: "I was very satisfied when I heard that I had received an 'Honours,' but many others [upon hearing their results] heaved a few sighs and moans. Then I left and went to a café with Gunvor to celebrate."[28] She was living in a small apartment in Christiania then. They ate sandwiches with an Italian mayonnaise spread, something they considered a great luxury. His father had sent him a letter of congratulations:

Bergen, 27 November 1922
Dear Helge,
Thank you for your last letter. We have been thinking of you with great interest when at six minutes before three [o'clock] you lit your first cigar and with that returned to leading life as a civilian again. Yes, whatever the results of your exam we would like to congratulate you on a tremendous, completed achievement: it must have been difficult. Even I have been in a state of examination fluster.

Now, without delay, you must send me a message concerning the amount you need to get you well on your way to your yet lingering posts.

Beautiful skies here. Haven't heard anything from Kaare. We are well and send you a thousand greetings.
Yours O. Ingstad
PS – I have stopped smoking. It is dreadful.

Little brother Kaare moved to Christiania two years after Helge, also to study law. Several years later when considering a career in journalism, Kaare spent time studying in Munich during the fall of 1932. There he was given the task to meet, interview, and write an article about "the new leader of the National Socialist Party, a Mr. Hitler who has appeared to have taken it upon himself to reign over Germany."[29]

Practising Law in Levanger

After graduation, Helge faced a new dilemma. Should he leave and travel the world or should he first establish his career? He wanted to do the first. His good friend Odd had been hired as a doctor on board a whaling ship in the Antarctic. After returning, he wrote Helge an enthusiastic letter dated 23 May 1923 telling about various wild animals, fish and penguins, and his experiences. "Any chance of getting away?" he asked. Counsel from Helge's father was to first establish himself as a lawyer, which Helge reluctantly heeded.

For many students, it wasn't easy to find work right out of law school, but because of his good grades Helge fared well. In 1923, he was hired for the position of clerical officer at the Magistrate's Office in the town of Levanger, about 50 kilometres north of the city of Trondheim, where he ended up living for three years. Helge had a sense of belonging to both the area and the people, perhaps because he was born in the same district. He rented a room at a family-run guesthouse where the son, Kristian Salater, was the same age as Helge and a master at fishing at a spot where the tides ran rapid and washed up over an embankment. The two of them would often stay there late into the evening, at least until 9 p.m. when Kristian's fiancé returned from work and requested her share of attention. Fishing was certainly a priority, even sometimes on the way home from the office. When a huge fish nearly slipped away, Helge leapt into the water, blue suit on and all, to grab the fish with his hands. Rabbit and bird hunting was also on the agenda, which Helge enthusiastically joined in with Kristian and his foxhound.

Even though the Salater family warmly included him, it took time for Helge to feel settled in Levanger. In a somewhat melancholy letter home he wrote, "It is quite peculiar that we people, at any given time, could possibly die and yet have to be content with that." On 8 July 1923 his mother answered, "It sounds as if you are lonely in the big town of Levanger. You should try to go out and visit folks. A young gentleman is always welcome." Helge replied, "I understand that the town is congenial and that I can be a bit of a recluse. People encourage me to come visit. But to the contrary, I enjoy my time at home. Now and again, I chat with the family's son about fishing. I have ways of making contact with people if needed. Sunday I am going out hunting again."

It was also clear that Helge's mother was concerned about his involvement with women at that time. On one hand, she hoped that he would find a suitable wife, but on the other, she was a bit anxious thinking of what following his own heart could lead to. On 5 March 1923 she wrote:

I know you are thinking of taking a trip to Trondheim. You must then finally stop in to visit Chief Justice Flock. You can imagine his two girls have grown beautiful now and well-brought up. But I won't say more on the matter ... Have you gotten to know any other young people in Levanger? You must not just spend time on your own and grow lonely and older ... Helge my dear, you must also be careful about writing to young women. Before you know it, they will consider themselves attached. I know such things have happened and you had a difficult time getting away. This is just a little motherly advice between the two of us. Women aren't always easy to understand.

In a later reply to his mother, it appeared that at least one of the Flock daughters, Karen, stirred a certain interest and was the reason for a few of Helge's visits to Trondheim:

I am well. Have recently been to Trondheim and fostered my acquaintance with the Flock girls. They are pleasant ladies. But Gunvor and mamma can rest assured; it is out of the question for me to indulge in any love affairs. I simply don't desire it. I cherish my independence. Danger could be lurking anywhere, so I withdraw my attention in good time. I try for a happy medium, but I thoroughly enjoyed my time with Miss Flock. We were both involved in the student society among other things. I liked her.

It was the "happy medium" that surely broke a few young ladies' hearts. However, his affections for Karen Flock could possibly have been more than what he had admitted to his family. In a letter, she thanks him for a poem, but does not mention which one. It was about this time Helge wrote his poem titled "My Sweetheart," but we will never know if this was the poem he sent to Miss Flock.

Despite the good advice from his mother, Helge was a bit of an elusive charmer throughout those years in Levanger. He realized that his plans to travel the world conflicted with establishing any kind of steady relationship. Nor had any woman captured his interest enough for him to relinquish his freedom.

Along the outskirts of Levanger lay a mountain range called Skjøtingen, a favourite place for Helge and his friends to spend time and hunt grouse, but a good distance to ski from the town. Two local legendary skiers, the Lian brothers, were part of a group of Helge's friends who often hiked and hunted together. But Helge would also often ski alone to Skjøtingen and spend the night in his sleeping bag beneath the open sky. Once, while on his own, he fell through the ice on a lake near a local farm. He was able to make it out of the water and then walk to the farm. He wrung out his clothes in their washbasin and carried on, soaked to the bone.[30]

Another time, he was with a friend hunting in the mountains when they got caught in a horrendous snowstorm. In order to survive, they had to break into a cabin. To this day, the skin of a wolverine that Helge shot hangs on the wall at that cabin.

There were only a few lawyers in Levanger at the time, and after a year at the Magistrate's Office he decided to establish his own law practice. Every Tuesday, a small ad appeared in the upper left-hand corner of the local newspaper: "Attorney Helge Ingstad, Levanger." The somewhat rocky start of his business was confirmed in his father's letter dated 23 October 1924:

> Thank you for your last letter. I can see by its breadth and content that you have much to do. That is, of course, both good and bad. That you have certain difficulties and adversary are to be expected; that is part of and not to be excluded from a young man's work if he is to acquire thick skin and understanding.

The advice was general and not focused on any particular case, and the exact problems are unknown since the letter to his father was not saved. However, soon Helge's business began to flourish and several big clients, including the city bank and land estate offices, began using his services. "Had I stayed there, I most likely would have settled down and grown rich," he said tersely several years later – a fate he feared the most.

According to the various letters exchanged with his father, it is clear that after only a year Helge began thinking about selling his practice. However, times were difficult and it wasn't so easy to find a buyer. His father again advised him:

> to develop your practice, earn money and then go travel. It does not hurt to have to wait a little, especially now that Norwegian currency is so low and everything is so unsettled overseas … Not setting out to travel the world right away isn't to worry about. You are still young and it is only good to acquire a little experience before going. As for business, you cannot expect to succeed so soon. I believe you have got a good start.[31]

Moving On

The nature surrounding Levanger was beautiful, but the climate not necessarily so; it was almost always windy and rainy. Helge longed for sunshine and warmth, but mostly to experience what he called "the wild." Where exactly, he wasn't yet sure. As soon as he sold his law practice, he departed Levanger. He was twenty-six years old at the time. His parents took it well, realizing that they couldn't hold him back any longer, and therefore did not protest. Besides, he had done what his father had advised and finished his studies first. On 15 October 1925, Olav wrote:

> We have not been completely unprepared for what you announced in the letter we received today. Recently, we heard that you sold your practice to a man named Harstad. We correctly assumed plans were in the making, but did not feel we should interfere in the matter. As you know, I have always thought that if you were to travel that now is the time. I agree with the initial steps that you have taken. However, I would have rather not seen you completely part with your business, but it is not for a third party to judge. I hope all works out for the best. It seems that everything has been taken care of. All of us wish you a time of many positive and valuable memories to live on during your old age. And remember that we want you back safe and sound.[32]

Olav too had dreamt of travelling out into the world when he was younger, but was never able to do so. Helge was now mature enough to take responsibility for his own life, Olav thought, and therefore he realized it was time to support his son's big adventurous dream. His mother was more concerned: "I will have many anxious hours thinking of you … It was so safe to have you in Levanger where hunting consisted of hares and grouse."

Helge's initial desire was to go to a dry, warm climate. After selling his business, he used some of the money to buy a train ticket to Paris. From there he travelled to Nice, where he ended up spending eight months. He stayed in a nice guesthouse, enjoyed the sunshine, and generally had a pleasant time. His main objective, at least according to the letters he sent to his parents, was to learn French. He advertised for a private French tutor, and after receiving over seventy inquiries, he chose a young female teacher from Avignon. Every day, he sat on a park bench for an hour conversing with this young woman in French. The rest of his time was spent with other young Scandinavians – girls sent to learn the language and art, and young men who also aimed to enjoy freedom and live life.

After a while, however, Helge again grew restless. One cold and gloomy October day in Nice, Helge decided on perhaps going to a warmer country. A few days later, he happened to meet another Norwegian at a bar who had just returned from living several years in Mozambique. He inspired Helge with his vivid images and stories. Helge then went to a travel agency and bought a ticket to exactly the same place. Back in his room at the guesthouse, however, he began to intensely regret his purchase. Where he actually wanted to go was to northern areas, not Africa, he realized; he had always dreamt of trout fishing and hunting. Distraught, he returned to the travel agency and asked for a refund. To his great surprise, it was no problem. In a letter to his parents on 26 October 1926, he explained:

> I pulled out my pocket atlas and studied the four continents for the thousandth time. I was cold and feeling a bit miserable. Nothing in particular urged me to favour that specific part of northern America. However, quite unconsciously, I suddenly found myself outside the shipping office of the White Star Line to Canada. And again, without any conscious participation from my part, I arranged for my ticket to Canada which is now in my pocket. I am now delighted with my choice.

An old dream of his was to travel to northern Canada, a country where white, unexplored spots still marked the map. He bought sea passage on the ship SS *Doric* sailing to Montreal the following week. At the departure dock, a physician checked everyone for lice and eye disease. Helge arrived donning a flat cap and pipe in his mouth but was sharply warned to put away both before boarding. The *Doric* was filled with emigrants all sharing a similar dream of a new and better country for themselves and their families. A few came from Scandinavia but most were from Central and Eastern Europe. The ship was divided into three classes – Helge was in third class on the lower decks. Many other young adventurers were also on board, but he was the only one heading towards the continent's most northerly areas. During the voyage, a "lively and attractive" young female passenger caught Helge's eye. But "I decided to be careful with that." He had bigger plans in store.

In his last letter home directly before departing, dated 28 October, he wrote:

> There is nothing more exhilarating than being an emigrant. Here we are a group travelling together to an unknown land. Most have committed their fate to this country forever. All of us Scandinavians pull out the map to see where each of us is going. The Dane, who is 20 years old, wants to go to Winnipeg, a prairie area, and take to farming. He is bursting with hope and eagerness to work and almost ready to begin on board. I too feel like I am beginning anew, and that my [relinquished] law degree and practice belong to somebody else. However, I am not saying that I in any way am planning to stay. That is out of the question. But in many respects, this is the beginning of a dream I have held ever since I was very young.

Land was sighted on 5 November 1926: Newfoundland. Little did Helge know that this would be the place of his life's most important discovery thirty-four years later, and where another ancient adventurer, Leif Eiriksson, had landed and settled. The *Doric* followed the mighty St Lawrence River upstream and on 7 November they landed at the quay in Montreal, a city of a million but where he didn't know a soul. As soon as he arrived, he boarded the Canadian Pacific Railway headed west. As the train stopped at various towns along the way, Helge often got out to have a look around. He thought it was important he should talk with people who knew the area and who could advise him well. Canada was huge. Yet he remembered well a place along Lake Superior where several Norwegians and Icelanders had settled. There he made a number of friends but decided to continue on to the wilderness of the north, because "it was so legendary up there." He was told the best city to begin his adventure was Edmonton, a place in northern Alberta where all the big rivers flowed north to the Arctic Ocean. That's where he needed to be.

2 THE LAND OF FEAST AND FAMINE[1]

Standing on the platform at the Edmonton railway station, Helge watched as the train pulled out and rolled down the tracks. There he stood with nothing more than what he had in the bag on his back, no definite plans, and next to no money. Edmonton, a city of about 65,000 back in 1926,[2] got its start as a fort and major trading post for the Hudson's Bay Company. With the building of the Canadian Pacific Railway (CPR) and the Calgary and Edmonton (C&E) Railway a century later, the railway townsite enticed a great number of people from eastern Canada, Britain, Europe, and the US, as well as from many other parts of the world. The rich, fertile earth surrounding the area drew many settlers, and the city as a hub of supplies attracted hordes of adventurers on the path to the Klondike Gold Rush. In Helge's words:

Here is a city to which a man may come straight from the wilderness, an overgrowth of beard on his face, moccasins on his feet, the seat of his pants blazing with patches, and walk down the street without having a single soul turn round to stare at him …

Hither come the wild and restless souls who have found civilized society too tame for them and who have therefore come to seek adventure in the wilderness. Here they congregate: trappers from the Barren Lands and the great forests, gold-diggers from Alaska, river captains from the Yukon, cowboys from the prairies, men with furrowed faces and unflinching gaze. Their varieties are many, but their type is one. All express the same spirit of swashbuckling independence, the same unshakable feeling of self-confidence, found in men accustomed to doing for themselves.

To these fellows, Edmonton is the "City."[3]

Helge, then a young man of twenty-six, dreamt of becoming one of these wild frontier men. He finally had the freedom and now the chance to experience adventure. He longed to go and explore the uncharted areas on the map where few, if any, had ever been before. This was the land of his childhood heroes, the indigenous North American people, whom he so wanted to meet and learn from. He had no idea how long he would stay, he just knew that this is what he *had* to do. He also realized he was a bit of a greenhorn and that his summer experiences from Hardangervidda were not enough. What he needed most was an experienced trapper willing to be his partner and mentor.

After wandering around Edmonton for a few days, he eventually ended up out on the town one evening with some Norwegian and Swedish railroad workers. Sitting in one of the bars was a man by the name of John Sellie, clearly quite drunk, who had been a trapper for over twenty-two years. Sellie was about to head back to his cabin far off in the forest. There he had all the essential trapping equipment, but no partner. The previous fellow had left and he was now looking for another to join him. Helge jumped at the chance. The man's drinking was of some concern, but Helge assumed that everything would be fine once they had left the city.

After a twelve-hour train ride, they climbed aboard a horse-drawn postal coach. Four horses pulled the two-compartment coach: half the wagon was for mail, and the other half was for passengers. On the third morning, they arrived at the trading post town of Grouard by Lesser Slave Lake, "little brother" to Great Slave Lake. Helge and Sellie woke a Chinese innkeeper, got a room, and sacked out. The following day, the men purchased winter clothes and equipment for close to $100 on credit at the Hudson's Bay Company, a debt expected to be paid in full with furs in the spring. Donning their new mukluks, they carried on by foot. By evening they reached another post called Moore, where they spent a pleasant evening with a bunch of other rugged souls who talked about hunting elk, moose, and weasels. This was Helge's first taste of the real Canadian wilderness.

Early the next morning they journeyed on, still by foot, until they arrived at White Fish, a small trading post where the temperature dropped to a chilling minus 30°C. They stayed at a small lodge belonging to the

Helge in the forest at Bat Lake, 1927.

Hudson's Bay Company and waited three days for arranged transport that would take them farther into the wilderness. They spent their time visiting with Sellie's friends, fellow trappers, and the indigenous Dene people,[4] It was Helge's first encounter with his childhood heroes. He wrote detailed journal entries about his impressions of both the people and everything they talked about. Helge's journey became not only a wilderness adventure, but also something similar to an anthropological field study.

After a strenuous ten-day journey, on 4 December 1926 the men finally reached Sellie's cabin situated on the shores of Bat Lake. The cabin was a little log house with two bunks, a table in the middle, and a small stove. It lay beautifully by the lake, nestled within that immense forest. Moose, elk, caribou, snowshoe hare, and weasel provided good hunting as did beaver in the rivers and large fowl in the woods. But before they could start trapping, they had to chop enough wood for the winter and cut a hole in the ice to get water. They went to collect Sellie's dogs from some Dene who had been taking care of them during the summer. The animals were thin and ragged and looked quite unimpressive, but proved to be good sled dogs.

It soon became apparent that this partnership was not going to be what Helge had expected. As a novice trapper, he had hoped to be mentored and to divide their catch fairly between them. But it became clear Sellie had no interest in teaching, nor in sharing. After getting settled in the cabin, the first thing Sellie did was to change their original agreement. He would take the dog sled out on his own for longer trips into the territory while Helge, who was without dogs or equipment of his own, would stay at the cabin and make do with day trips on skis. There was no talk of sharing in this partnership; each man would hunt for himself.

According to what he wrote in his journal, it seemed that Helge did not dare or think it wise to protest these changes. He was then left on his own and his trapping produced little. With others also trapping in the same area around the cabin, the competition was tough for the best hunting grounds. Sellie was away with his dog sled most of the time, only stopping in every once in a while to replenish supplies and drop off his furs.

On Christmas Eve 1926, Helge sat alone in the cabin. What he wrote in his journal hinted at the homesickness of a young man celebrating his first Christmas away from home: "To be honest, despite it all, it has been a nice Christmas Eve. I didn't get up until 9:30 this morning, something

I've never done before. No hunting today. The camp needs to be prepared for Christmas."

He got to work chopping wood and splitting thick logs that sent chips flying in every direction. Hot and sweaty, he stripped off his clothes and rolled in the snow. He lathered up with a bit of soap and gave his body a thorough Christmas wash. Then he headed out into the woods to find a Christmas tree, a task not evidently so easy. There were plenty of tall pines in the woods, but few small ones. At last, he noticed a cluster of small spruce that were nearly all covered with snow:

> After close consideration, my choice was between a straight, thin spruce or one that was thick and scraggly. Since the latter was more like the ones we have at home, I chose that one. I fetched some water and washed the table, something that hadn't been done since we had arrived. Then I started cooking my dinner of bacon and beans. A superb meal! Afterwards, I whittled a stand for my simple Christmas tree and found a candle to put on top. And then I filled my pipe with tobacco and smoked throughout the evening. Not much more to tell other than that I watched the clock and followed Christmas time back home, and sat thinking a great deal. I have missed Mamma's cakes. Sellie is somewhere west of here. His only focus is hunting.[5]

In March, Helge decided to end the partnership. The following winter he wanted to be farther north at Great Slave Lake. So he headed off to Edmonton in hopes of finding a new trapping partner. In his book *The Land of Feast and Famine*, Helge never mentions a word about this first winter as a trapper. Nor did he talk about it much any other time in his life, most likely because it was such a great disappointment.

Hjalmar Dale

Helge met Hjalmar Dale[6] during his first visit to Edmonton during the fall of 1926. Dale had just come down from the north and was on his way to Norway to visit family for the first time in twelve years. The two men found out about each other through other Norwegians in the city as the community was small and news spread quickly. They hit it off straight away. Helge wrote home to his parents and asked them to invite Dale to dinner if he came to Bergen: "He is one of the most fearless men I know, as well as amiable and helpful. I am sure that pappa, who himself is a bit of an adventurer, will be very interested in spending an evening with him."

Dale, in his early thirties, was a few years older than Helge. He had spent the last seven years as a trapper in the Mackenzie River area and eventually became one of the best. He was a good, sturdy canoer and a tough, skilled musher. He knew the explored areas well and the uncharted territories even more. Helge described Dale as "a little stout bear of a fellow with fearless eyes. He was also quick and confident, befitting of an immigrant who for years had forged his way in a new country."[7]

Dale came from the western part of Norway, not far from Helge's hometown, from a community also called Dale. As a young boy, he was not able to walk for several years after suffering from what was diagnosed as polio. He had to crawl around on the floor. "That's why I have such strong wrists," he used to say. When he was eighteen and immigrated to Canada, he still walked with a cane. He systematically and methodically trained up his body and eventually ended up in the wilderness of northern Canada, where he lived the rest of his life. "*There's always a way out*," Dale used to say. This too became Helge's motto. Perhaps what attracted these two to each other was their shared experience of being seen as different from their peers as children: Helge with his tuberculosis and Hjalmar with his polio. Both had to overcome physical impairments caused by illnesses and both had ventured out into the world in search of challenges that stretched their boundaries and tested their endurance to the utmost.

When they met, Dale had already been in Canada for twelve years. His immigration was, as for many others, fuelled by a combination of a desire for adventure and a dream to become rich. He began by taking on repair work on the railroad, farms, and other places where his skills were needed. Then he settled on the prairie, where he single-handedly cleared the land for his own small farm. But as soon as the work on it was finished, he grew restless. He sold the farm, bought a canoe, and travelled north to live a free life as a trapper in the wilderness.

A Collaborative Partnership

Helge again met up with Dale during the spring of 1927. The seasoned trapper had just returned from his visit to Norway and Helge had just ended his partnership with Sellie. Dale related greetings to Helge from his parents. Then he asked if he would be interested in joining him on his way north and becoming his partner. Helge didn't hesitate a second. As an experienced trapper, Dale had not only the necessary skills but also the needed equipment to endure life in the Far North. The man's abilities and expertise impressed Helge as well as his reputation with the other trappers for being "the toughest guy in the North." He couldn't have had a better mentor than Hjalmar Dale.

After Helge's first incredibly disappointing winter with John Sellie, he must have had a thought or two about returning home. Later in life, my father said that it was thanks to Dale that he stayed in Canada as long as he did.

So the two joined forces: Helge the greenhorn and Dale the "veteran" trapper. "[He was] a reliable and fiercely self-disciplined man," Helge said.

When there was a choice between lying a little longer in a warm sleeping bag or having to run out into a raging snowstorm to do whatever needed to be done with the dogs or anything else, he never hesitated. There was also so much about him besides the wilderness. Like one evening when we lay in our sleeping bags, he suddenly said, "I strive to think positive thoughts." He often voiced his perspectives on life and death. He believed completely that life didn't end with death but we return to Earth and live again as another person.[8]

The two men obviously had something in common, as Dale was used to being on his own and most surely wouldn't have taken on the role as mentor for just any young kid from Norway. Exactly what Dale saw in Helge is rather uncertain. Perhaps it was Helge's summers spent on Hardangervidda that gave him an air of being more prepared than he actually was. Or maybe Helge's introvert tendencies made an impression. He wasn't the type to talk all the time and could sit for long periods puffing on his pipe lost in thought. In that case, he was a welcome companion for someone who wasn't used to anyone but himself for company. Dale knew exactly where he wanted to go and Helge wisely let him choose. It didn't matter to him where they went as long as they ended up as far into the wilderness as they could go.

Dale had a refreshing sense of humour that helped take the drudge out of the heavy tasks. But he could also be stubborn and sometimes opinionated. Still, only once during the course of a year did the two have any kind of a serious disagreement, and that was resolved within a day.

Life in the wilderness is demanding, which Helge already knew from his experience in the forest the winter before. But during the next few years in the Far North, Helge would learn this to an even greater extent. His experiences from summers spent on Hardangervidda would not get him very far; here it was either make or break. You were on your own. A number of tasks had to be done quickly and precisely, despite minus 50°C temperatures, raging snowstorms, or swarms of mosquitoes surrounding you like a dark cloud. You had to know how to handle an axe and be quick to find wood, set up camp in all kinds of weather, bore holes in the ice, chop wood, handle dogs, repair sleds, sew moccasins and mukluks, chase caribou, and tan animal hides.

Into the Wilderness

Helge and Dale's initial plan was to "paddle and portage our equipment as far north into the treeless plains as we could before the waters froze."[9] They would canoe down the Slave River to where it runs into Great Slave Lake by Fort Resolution, the oldest permanent settlement in the Northwest Territories and a fur-trading hub for the area. A few Dene lived here year round but the majority only during the summer months to fish. There were others, too: settlers who set up shop to trade and peddle their wares, as well as the Royal Canadian Mounted Police (RCMP).

From Fort Resolution, Helge and Dale intended to cross the lake's eastern extremity and continue farther east along the coastline there. They would then follow the waterways that led to the tundra, travelling as far as they could before winter set in, hopefully as far as the mouth of the Coppermine River. Most likely, they would meet other Dene as they made their way eastward but otherwise only a few lone trappers here and there – that is, if they limited their trips to "civilization" to only a few weeks at the trading post every summer. They would have to paddle their canoes nearly 1,800 kilometres to reach the land of caribou, which they eventually did. However, where they ended up was not where they originally intended.

Before leaving Edmonton and with the little money remaining after purchasing his share of equipment, Helge sent a telegraph home. He informed his family of their plans to reach the mouth of the Coppermine River that winter. Then the men bought two nice but very expensive dogs. One was timid and had the markings of a wolf, so they aptly named him Wolf. The other, named Prince, was white, beautiful, and more trustworthy, though it had a tendency to pick fights with stray dogs and get miserably thrashed. To keep their load as light as possible, Dale and Helge intended to survive on what they could catch.

Early in May 1927, the men headed north by railway. "There was something quaint and naïve about that north-bound train ... After a full day and night on the train, we arrived at Waterways, the end of the line, on the banks of the Clearwater River."[10] In the nearby settlement of Fort McMurray, Dale managed to get them hired for work on the paddle steamer *Northland Echo* headed north on the Athabasca River. They had plenty of time, but little money, so it was a good arrangement. Every day, they got up early and worked long and hard. The *Echo* first needed scraping and painting, and wood needed to be chopped. All the other hands were Cree, except for one Chipewyan – free-spirited souls who would suddenly leave work to go off hunting. Cleaning a boat seemed to be beneath their dignity. At first, Helge was annoyed with such a work ethic. Later, however, he acquired a greater understanding of their longing and need for freedom when he himself experienced living with the indigenous peoples of the north.

Once the *Echo* was scraped clean and ready for travel, the captain and the crew still had to wait for the ice to disappear farther north on Lake Athabasca. When it finally did break, it was quite a sight:

> One day the river began to growl. The ice was breaking up and had begun to flow downstream. Block crashing against block, they would both leap into the air and collapse as one, only to continue their feuds up over the riverbanks, where they would sweep away earth and rocks and trees. For twenty-four hours, the battle raged and then it was over; there flowed the river, like yellow grease, through the forest.[11]

Finally, the day came to launch the steamer into the waters and head slowly up the Athabasca River. It was a strenuous journey. With the disappearance of the ice, the water level had sunk several metres. The boat ran aground numerous times on large deposits of tar sand and they had to struggle for hours to get it loose again. It was difficult knowing where these shallow spots were because every year they developed in new areas depending on the currents and ice conditions.

When the *Echo* finally reached the remote community of Fort Fitzgerald, they could hear the droning of tremendous falls in the distance. In Fitzgerald, surrounded by a wall of mosquitoes, the men unloaded the cargo. Here, they ended their work on the steamer and collected their salaries. The combined amount of their wealth, including what they earned on the *Echo*, was a total of $90. They used much of it to pay for transport across the sixteen-mile-long dirt road to Fort Smith, where again the river became navigable.

Now as broke as ever, their next challenge was to find a way to earn $150 for a trapping licence for Helge. Dale still had his from the year before. They needed to find more work, but where: Fort Smith or Fort Resolution? Then quite unexpectedly, they met an owner of a sawmill by the name of Dick Winn. "He asked if we knew anything about mill work. We replied that we were both pretty handy with a saw, and it was lucky for us he didn't ask us what kind of saw he meant."[12] The mill was only 64 kilometres away, but due to car trouble their travels slowed to a snail's pace. Rather than the usual five hours, the journey took five days.

At the sawmill, they worked hard, long days for three weeks, always surrounded by hordes of mosquitoes. In the end, they had chopped, sawed, and planed about seven hundred timber planks. It was tough, but good training for the life that awaited them. Floating the logs along the river down to the sawmill was the most dangerous part of the work. Helge had never done anything like it before, and so ended up falling into the river several times a day. "I eventually got pretty good at driving logs, but I was in no way ever a lumber jack."

The boss himself stood watch over the workers, yelling and screaming that they had to pick up the pace. Any spare time Helge and Dale had, they went hunting and net fishing, often spotting signs of bear and wolf at the water's edge. "The place is so beautiful nestled in among the trees that it is difficult to describe," Helge wrote in his journal on 21 June 1927. Then one evening, after spotting a beaver in the river and feeling that "the wilderness beckoned," Dale and Helge agreed it was time to move on. They collected their wages, $62 each, then loaded their goods and dogs into two canoes and struck off down Slave River. Near the mouth of the Salt River, they picked up three of Dale's dogs who had been in the care of a Dene while the trapper had been south in "civilization." After four days of paddling the two fully loaded canoes, they reached the trading post of Fort Resolution at the edge of Great Slave Lake.

> Yesterday we made only 30 miles due to a strong headwind; today is going well. Sitting relaxed with my dogs on each side. The river carries us four miles an hour. Every once in a while, we see a trapper's cabin. The river is currently swollen. Full of drifting logs.[13]

Fort Resolution was warm and the air full of mosquitoes. Dogs seemed to be a part of the place; they were everywhere, howling and fighting day and night. Helge and Dale were in need of three more dogs but found that the prices for these, along with everything else in the north, to be sky-high. People selling dogs demanded anything from $100 to $150 for animals that were no better than those they bought for much less farther south. This was because at these northern outposts demand was high and supply low; trappers bought all they needed for the coming trapping season here, and experienced dogs were scarce.

Despite the high prices in the north, Helge and Dale had to find a way to buy what they needed, which included an extra canoe to haul their equipment. Not an easy task with not much more of value than Dale's watch and Helge's tailor-made suit from France. In the evenings, Helge would attend the dances in town to show off his suit in hopes of bartering it for a dog. Meanwhile, they hired three Dene women to sew moccasins, mukluks, and caribou parkas for them.

When the men had arrived at Fort Resolution, a cheerful, encouraging letter from Helge's father awaited him. Olav wrote that he was following Helge's travels on a map and would surely have enjoyed making the same journey if he were a young thirty-year-old man. Skepticism about Helge giving up his career to take off for an adventure in the wilderness seemed to have vanished completely. Olav stressed the importance for Helge to take pictures and to keep a journal as he might want to write a book when he returned home. Perhaps Olav began to sense an alternative way for Helge to bring honour to the family. He also suggested that Helge contact a large American media agency: "Write with audacity and lavish it up. Mention that the journey will be 3200 miles and to places where no white man has been in the last hundred years."[14]

But this was not actually true and there is nothing to indicate that Helge chose to follow his father's advice. However, there is little doubt that his father's repeated encouragement to create some type of literary work from his experiences was a major influence. Helge kept detailed accounts of his life in his journals:

Fort Resolution   1 July 1927
Still here. The squaws are late in their work after having been paid in advance. We have bought a wide, 18-foot canoe. The boat dilemma has now been solved; the dog dilemma unfortunately not. "Prince" disappeared yesterday. He was sick and probably disappeared into the woods to die. My great, beautiful dog. I have managed to acquire three other dogs. Most likely will start Saturday morning.

The tailor-made suit from Nice was exchanged for a pair of beautiful dogs. Other small objects were traded for the remaining needed dogs, five in total. Wolf, who kept running off, was bartered for the much more loyal Tiger: "It feels like that dog and I are committed to each other. He absolutely obeys me and after only a day I could let him run loose," Helge wrote in his journal. Dale had his own team.

And so they headed off along the coast of Great Slave Lake, each in their own canoe and with a third in tow. It was hard work but Helge was thrilled to be in the long-anticipated wilderness and he welcomed the chance to get fit again. Apart from the side winds that could tip the canoes, the big lake was beautiful. In pleasant, sunny weather it shone like a jewel, full of ducks swimming peacefully around. The lake seemed more like an ocean as the opposite shore was barely visible in the distance.

Helge and Dale paddled for several weeks, the dogs running loose along the shoreline with packs on their backs. Sometimes the hounds would run farther inland following the scent of a moose or bear but the weight of the packs and the denseness of the forests always kept them from going deeper into the woods. They would always return to the shoreline to keep up with the men. Once, Trusty and Spike disappeared into the woods and the men heard horrible, pitiful howls. When Helge went ashore to see what had happened he found both dogs full of porcupine quills. It took several hours to remove all the quills with the dogs howling like mad. Sometimes one or both of the dogs were allowed to sit along in the canoe as a kind of reward.

In the evenings after they had set up camp, Dale would often go in search of precious metals. He still had a touch of gold fever. Once he returned with his hands full of what he thought to be gold, but Helge explained it was only copper ore mineral. Every now and again, they also met a few Dene people along the shores of Great Slave Lake catching the seasonal fish. Helge and Dale also fished along the way, dragging their fishing line behind their canoes. Luckily, they often caught trout big enough to feed both themselves and their dogs. It soon grew evident that the men would not be able to reach the mouth of Coppermine River before winter. In his journal on 12 July, Helge explained:

Big news. Coppermine plans have been scratched and we're headed towards Thelon. Reasons for this are many: We started out too late [from Edmonton]. Our canoes are not suitable for heavy winds and we have to account for delays when the autumn storms begin. It takes time to paddle with three canoes and it won't be possible to reach the Great Barrens by the Coppermine River. We also heard at Fort Resolution that parts of the area have now been designated as a muskoxen reserve which certainly means no trapping there. The risk is, therefore, too great and so we will head for Thelon. We now intend to find a way across the east of Snowdrift River.[15] A small channel to the Thelon is there which we can follow down to the main river. All the country around Thelon is practically unknown. We should find white fox there.[16]

From the trading post at Fort Reliance on Charlton Bay, Helge wrote to his parents on 29 July 1927 telling them about their change in plans – that they now aimed to reach the headwaters of the Thelon River:

The Indians we waited for at "Narrows" left to go hunting for caribou, so the letter lay waiting too. Its fate was quite uncertain until we came here and ran into four "bughunters." Bughunters is

Hjalmer's term for insect collectors (biologists on a summer exped-ition to study insects) and is pronounced with contempt. They are two women and two men. Nice people by the way.

He goes on to tell them about everything that happened along the 480 kilometres they had just travelled. They had reached the end of Great Slave Lake, and he explained how wonderful it was to see the moun-tain range ahead of them with the tundra, caribou, and white fox just beyond. The posing challenge was to find a passable route:

As many lakes as possible is what we would like.[17] The country here is supposedly filled with lakes. We should reach Eileen Lake, but in the worst case we'll pull our stuff together for the winter. As mentioned before, we will return by boat over Great Slave Lake. I am younger and stronger than ever before. Many greetings from Helge.

Pikes Portage, known as "the gate to the Barren Lands," was histor-ically the most used trapper route on the eastern end of Great Slave Lake and the path they had been recommended to take. After a steady climb, it led to a series of narrow lakes reaching all the way to the Arctic tundra. However, Helge and Dale met a Dene man who could speak a little English. He told them about an old, more easterly canoe route that began farther upstream of Snowdrift River, beyond its last steep descent into the lake. They chose this route tempted by the idea that few trappers knew about it and therefore possibly offered virgin hunting ground.

However, they quickly understood how little the route was used. In many places, it was hardly visible and it was a demanding, slow strug-gle to move ahead. Sometimes they found the path, but much of the way they had to fight through the scrub or walk along the riverbanks. They portaged their equipment and canoes and each dog carried a pack, which helped.

The men didn't always know where they were but easily found their way back by following the river in the opposite direction. They soon realized that this easterly route had not been the wisest route to take to the tundra. They finally had to accept that they would have to stay in the forest until the snow fell, and then they could use their dogsleds on the ice-covered river. As fall wore on, the mosquitoes faded but the gnats grew worse. Eventually, night frosts killed the little beasts. Water buckets froze and they knew that it was time to find a place for the winter. The entire time, they provided for themselves and their dogs with food they hunted or fished.

Before winter set in, they shot the last moose by a beautiful little lake which they dubbed Moose Lake. They decided to make it their winter home, as it was too late to reach the headwaters of Thelon. They threw their gear onto the ground and were elated not to have to continue their drudgery, at least for a while. It was good to have the summer's travels behind them. They had been on the move for nearly two strenuous months. However, there was still plenty of hard work ahead to prepare for winter.

The main advantage of coming to such a remote, untouched area was that it increased their chances of better trapping. The plan was to use the cabin by Moose Lake as a base, then set up a camp farther east to lay a trap line. Over Christmas, they would travel towards Eileen Lake and from there to the tundra, setting traps along the way.

Helge and Dale built a roomy, notched log cabin. Applying a trusted Norwegian method, they stuffed moss into the crevices, "but not nearly as elaborate as the experts," Helge later said. It was hard work. Dale was very resourceful and made a small stove out of a tin plate he had brought with him. On cold nights, they would sit on a couple of log stumps by the stove warming themselves. Beside the cabin, they built a "cache" to protect their fish, meat, and hides from other animals.

To Helge, the place felt like a small paradise. "If signs of human life were few, the signs of a rich animal life were many. Here was a world belonging solely to them – muskrat, beaver, lynx, fox, moose, mink, and all the many others."[18] Surrounding the lake were small hills that provided good vista points. One of the hills was covered with lingonberries and they duly dubbed it Lingonberry Hill. Dwarfed birch trees and dense spruce forests grew all the way down to the water's edge. A nice clearing in front of the cabin would make it easy to pull their sleds up close to the door. They caught fish and hung them to dry. Now all they had to do was wait for snow and winter.

The lake froze, snow fell, and it was time to set off hunting and trapping. Dale knew almost everything there was to know about caribou, which they now eagerly awaited. Thousands of the animals would soon start to migrate in large herds. But the area was so immense, and where exactly the caribou would go was always uncertain. Everything depended on the weather and wind. Helge was eager with excitement.

Then the caribou came, like a small miracle. They poured out of the woods and across the frozen lake. It was an amazing sight: thousands of the animals! The dogs went wild when they caught their scent. Helge and Dale shot as many as they needed to feed themselves and the dogs for the rest of the winter. Caribou meat, marrow, and blood were on the menu morning, noon, and night. They could not have had it any better.

Becoming a strong, skilled musher didn't happen overnight, as Helge expressed in his journal on 22 November:

> The worst is getting out of the sleeping bag in the dark and cold and having to start the fire. The next worst is the wind that can billow around the fire from every which direction. It can drive you crazy! In addition to this are the particular problems I have with my dogs. It's difficult to get going from the cabin. Actually, I like it just fine around the campfire so getting started is always difficult. It's easier for Hjalmar who starts with good dogs and full speed. I have a world of trouble with mine until I get across Moose Lake. If we set off together, my dogs do well following his. If I'm on my own, the dogs want to turn back home again. The whip is the only thing that works. But it's improving now.

Dale set trap lines to the east; Helge followed the river to the south, "for thus have we divided the country between us."[19] Each trap line was a pathway through dense forest only wide enough for a dogsled and its musher. Cutting a trail through the woods along the routes was hard work and they were glad when the job was finally done. Setting up a camp when working the trap lines took a couple of hours, partly due to the scarcity of dry kindling. Temperatures were now reaching minus 10°C during the day and often minus 20°C in the early mornings.

Helge for the most part heeded Dale's expertise, whose strengths also included a gentle humour and an array of interests. The man also pondered over questions of life, death, and existence. In the evenings, all burrowed up in their sleeping bags, he would often lay very still staring up at the ceiling and meditating. A unique man he was.

During daylight, there was never a lack of work to do. When they were not out hunting or checking traps, something always had to be done around the cabin. Dog harnesses and sleds needed to be repaired, clothes and moccasins had to be patched. They were never bored. Helge had with him a small box given to him by his mother containing thick needles and thread. It was good and handy, and he held onto it his entire life.

They didn't bring any liquor with them into the wilderness. That would have to wait until spring when they visited the trading post near the community of Snowdrift, where trappers would gather after the long winter in the wilderness, often spent alone. Here they would all indulge in a great party and collect their longed-awaited letters from home. Helge's pipe, on the other hand, was good to have in the wilderness, if for nothing else but to keep away the mosquitoes.

Most of their day trips went fine. But once when Helge went off on his own, it nearly ended badly.[20] It was an icy-cold winter morning with a temperature of minus 50°C when he left. The dogs had caused some trouble so he had left them behind at the cabin. Because of the extreme cold, it was incredibly important to keep moving all the time. Helge soon reached a precarious spot where he had to cross a river. At very low temperatures, snow can sometimes insulate underlying water, preventing it from freezing, and in turn create dangerously thin ice. Sure enough, farther out on the river, Helge suddenly fell through a pile of snow and straight into the freezing-cold water. He managed to hold tight to the edge of the ice but his legs kept being dragged under by the water's current. A willow branch hung over the river not far from him. He jammed his freezing fingers into the ice, heaved and crawled until he could reach the branch and pull himself up. His ordeal, however, was not yet over. He now had to keep from freezing to death.

Helge rolled in the snow like a dog trying to press as much water out of his fur garb as he could. Then he quickly snowshoed back to his last camping spot about twenty minutes away. Luckily, the coals in the campfire were still glowing and he was able to rekindle a roaring fire. He grabbed a change of undergarments from the sled and dressed as close to the fire as he could. When he removed his stockings, he discovered that his toes had stiffened and turned a strange colour of white. They were frozen solid! He struggled to warm some water over the fire to soak his feet. He managed, and as soon as his toes looked reasonably better, he packed up his things and took off back to the cabin at Moose Lake.

When he saw the cabin, smoke was rising from the chimney. What a relief. Dale had arrived before him. As he walked in, a newly shot wolf lay on the floor and Dale was over at the stove making food. Helge told him what had happened and that he was happy to have survived. However, when he took off his stockings and began walking across the floor there was a distinct clicking sound. His big toe was still white and rock hard.

Not long after, Dale had to go to Fort Reliance, about a four-day journey by sled, to get more supplies. Helge was left on his own at the cabin. He hobbled around with his painful foot packed in wool blankets and canvas. Once he tried to shoot a caribou standing out on the lake but couldn't manage to get close enough to bring it down. Luckily, Dale had shot four caribou before he had left so Helge and the dogs were well supplied with fresh meat. The next day, Helge again tried to go out to hunt. This time proved to be more successful. On 12 December 1927, he wrote: "I shot one but it disappeared into the bushes. I crawled in after it with great difficulty and was able to make a final shot to its head. I then pulled it back to the cabin on the toboggan. My poor toe!"

Dale returned from Fort Reliance with coffee, butter, fruit, bacon, and a cigar for each of them. The plan now was to travel eastward towards Artillery Lake the day after Christmas. There were plenty of beaver and muskrat around Moose Lake, but not much more than that. The white fox out on the tundra was what the men were most interested in now. But Helge's toe was still causing him serious pain. The colour had changed from white to red, then yellow to violet. There was no doubt gangrene was setting in. Helge realized he needed medical assistance as soon as possible, so they left earlier than intended. He wrapped his foot in a wool blanket and took off on his sled, Dale following behind on his. The idea was to backtrack over Dale's path to Fort Reliance, where they could get medical help. They would then continue on to Artillery Lake and in towards the tundra.

It was a strenuous trip. On the way, they passed a camp of Dene hunters who had a good laugh when they saw Helge's toe. Only idiots managed to get so frozen in the wilderness. An old woman gave him some bark salve but it didn't help. Another person offered to chop it off with an axe, but Helge politely said no. The two men moved on hoping to find someone with more sterile equipment. One of the Dene men from the camp accompanied them and in the evening sat by the fire sharpening his axe.

Suddenly the three of them heard a gunshot and spotted two men with a dogsled a short distance away. Corporal Williams and Officer Trundle of the Royal Canadian Mounted Police, whom Helge knew from Fort Resolution, were out on inspection duty and happened to be carrying medical supplies. Talk about luck. The Corporal claimed that he was an expert "toe remover" and was thrilled at the prospect of something to contend with. The two Mounties explained that there had not been much to do – no crazy people or criminals to catch. They had been looking for a trapper named Blackey but found him dead in his tent with dog meat on his plate.

The Corporal, in fact, offered to amputate the toe to where it connected with the foot. Helge hesitated and managed to negotiate having only the outer tip removed. The Corporal strongly protested and in quite dramatic detail explained how the gangrene would spread up through Helge's body and kill him. He was already almost as good as dead. But Helge insisted and in the end got his own way. The tip of the toe was removed with only a few splashes of whiskey used as a general anaesthetic. Helge later joked that the Corporal never forgave him for denying him a bit of fun in cutting off his entire toe.

Helge and Dale headed on to Fort Reliance, where Christmas was now over but New Year's Eve celebrations were in full swing. Dogsleds cruised around with bells jingling on their harnesses. Helge's toe was healing, and as soon as the New Year's celebrations were over, the men headed for the tundra. This time they took the well-used route over Pikes Portage that led to Artillery Lake. It was a long, bitterly cold journey and the hunting was poor. Storms whipped about them day and night. The same hard winds drove the caribou deeper into the forest, as Helge noted in his journal on 6 January 1928:

> The tundra!! Only a few bushes and trees here and there. Travelled 15 miles and found a beautiful, small valley by Burns Lake. Have got a wonderful fire burning now. We pushed across the last stretch by lovely moonlight. Only about six miles to go to Artillery Lake. Traces of Indians everywhere. Little dog food left and only porridge for dinner. No trace of caribou.

Several days later, the men found a dead caribou left as bait in a fox trap. It stank horribly but it was something to eat. "We cut off as much of the meat as we thought we would need and, as payment for this, we hung on the antlers of the dead beast a little pail containing the last of our sugar."[21] Hunger started to seriously gnaw at them. They had counted on shooting game for food along the way. One evening, after setting up camp near the waterfalls of Lockhart River, the men suddenly heard dogsled bells. An old Dene man they knew, Lochard, came walking towards them smiling and sat himself down by the fire. He had some dried meat and fat that Helge and Dale devoured. Lochard sang and then told them about muskox hunting in the "promised land" by Thelon. Helge responded with a few lines of a Norwegian folk song.

The next day, Helge and Dale followed Lochard to his family's camp. They arrived late at night after a strenuous trip through deep snow and minus 50°C temperatures. The women dished up fresh moose meat and all sorts of tasty treats. Helge later reflected on their hospitality: "As soon as someone sticks their head into camp, food is brought out, no matter what time of day it is." They spent several pleasant days with Lochard and his family. It was still bitterly cold outside and both dogs and men needed rest. Helge used the opportunity to have a new caribou parka made.

On 14 January, they were finally back at their cabin by Moose Lake. It was wonderful to have their own roof over their heads and a full cache of fish and meat awaiting them. The previous day, they had travelled through deep snow, freezing temperatures, and darkness. It was especially tiring for Helge, who could not yet use snowshoes because of his semi-amputated toe. But it was difficult too for the dogs, whose eyelids nearly froze shut from the cold. After only a few days back at the cabin, the men realized they needed to head for the trading post at Snowdrift to get professional help as Helge's toe continued to worsen. Dale mushed and Helge rode on the sled. It turned out that the frozen toe required much more time to fully heal. Dale returned to the cabin at Moose Lake and Helge stayed behind in Snowdrift until the beginning of April.

In late winter, the folks back home in Bergen began to grow anxious. The letter from Charlton Bay written back at the end of July was the only sign of life they had received. They had no idea where in the wilderness Helge and Dale were or whether or not they were still alive. On 29 February, Olav wrote a letter to the Department of Interior, Northwest Territories, carefully inquiring if anyone had seen his son and friend. It is easy to imagine their growing concern when they didn't receive a reply until 27 April. A letter from the Department of Interior, Northwest Territories, told them that a patrol from the Royal Canadian Mounted Police had run into the men in February near the community of Snowdrift and that they had helped Helge with a frozen toe. Then they were given information, not entirely unexpected, that confirmed it could be a while before they saw their son back in Bergen again: "Your son seems to be doing well and plans to spend at least two more years in the North-west Territories."

Dale returned to Snowdrift on 14 April, and together the men headed towards Fort Reliance in search of beaver and muskrat. As the spring thaw began, the heat of the sun made it more and more difficult to travel by dogsled or snowshoe. The quality of the animals' winter fur was also quickly diminishing so they were running out of time. Soon it would be impossible to get anywhere by snow and then they would have to return to Snowdrift and wait for the ground to go bare.

In the late spring, Dale and Helge parted company. The apprenticeship was over and now Helge had to make it on his own. No disagreement led to the parting, just a realization that each had different ambitions for the following winter. Helge wanted to learn more about the Dene people. North American indigenous people had interested him ever since "Rieber's Man" had taught him how to shoot a bow and arrow back home in Bergen. He would like to find a group he could live and hunt with for a time and have a chance to experience their culture first-hand.

Dale had seen enough of this area during the years he spent on the tundra and was more interested in going farther north. He wanted to travel alone over the tundra to Inuit territory near Chesterfield Inlet by Hudson Bay. He figured it would take him two years to make the journey, quite a risk for a man on his own. Few believed he could do it, because others had not and ended up dying alone in the middle of nowhere.

But Dale smiled and headed off. Two years passed before anyone saw any sign of life from him. Then one day he came paddling down the river at Chesterfield Inlet in a makeshift canvas trough. Helge never saw him again, but remembered Dale his entire life as an honourable man and one of the greatest masters of the wilderness. "He was a fur trapper by profession, but an Arctic explorer by nature."

Not long after parting from Helge, and before his trip to Chesterfield Inlet, Dale made a quick trip to Norway to visit his aging parents. He relayed greetings from Helge to Olav and Olga in Bergen when they spoke on the telephone.

In 1932, while Helge was in East Greenland, Dale was again on a visit to Bergen. He was disappointed to learn that Helge was not in town. He told Helge's parents about his adventures after the two men had parted and Olav wrote them down.[22] After leaving Reliance, Dale told them, he paddled down the Thelon to Baker Lake. He eventually ended up at Beaverly Lake, where he stayed two years with the Inuit, living in an igloo like them. Then he travelled north to Chesterfield Inlet where he lived for several more years.

Many years later, on 10 February 1968, Helge received a message saying that Hjalmar Dale had been found dead in a cabin near the Mackenzie River. Eighty per cent of his body had been burned. They suspected his gas stove exploded and his clothes caught fire. Yet he still had the will and the strength to write on a piece of paper all the names and addresses of his closest kin so that when he was found those people could be notified. This time, *there was no way out* for Hjalmar Dale.

Living with the "Caribou Eaters"

Here is my canoe, here are my nets, my guns, and my dogs. The forest and lake are at my disposal. I sit in my shirt-sleeves in front of my tent and feel like a millionaire.[23]

Such were Helge's sentiments as he sat at the edge of Great Slave Lake near Snowdrift one beautiful summer day in 1928. He had parted company with Dale and was now spending his time netting whitefish for which he was paid good money at the trading post. The lake was brimming with fish, real whoppers. He cleaned and filleted the fish, and hung it to dry. He also had a wood chopping deal with the Hudson's Bay Company for $17 a cord that was very hard work. Much of this was just waiting for winter and for ice to cover the rivers so a dogsled could make it across. During the summer, waterways were the only means of getting anywhere since the forests were too dense to wander through.

Snowdrift[24] was a small trading community located on a peninsula only a few kilometres west from where Lutselk'e lies today.[25] The place had two trading posts that competed with each other in buying trappers' furs for the lowest possible prices. One of these was the Hudson's Bay Company. The posts sold equipment to the trappers, often on credit, which in turn committed them to selling their furs to the same post again. The community consisted of a few log houses, a church with missionaries, and a cluster of tents. The Royal Canadian Mounted Police also had an office in Snowdrift and were responsible for medical treatment since there were no doctors or nurses. During the winter, only a few people remained in Snowdrift. All abled trappers and Dene people left to go hunting caribou, wolf, and white fox. However, during the summers, the population swelled to a couple of hundred when they all returned to fish and sell their furs.

During the summer, many Dene stayed out on the islands near Snowdrift and fished. Once, Helge paddled out to visit them and he found it strangely silent. They had all been infected with an influenza epidemic. Two of their men had gone south and brought the infection back with them. Many lay dying or were already dead. Only a single old woman was sitting outside her tent looking incredibly forlorn. Her husband was dead and she expected to suffer the same fate. Helge helped to bury the dead and was urged by the woman to carry the sick over to another island, a place not affected by "evil spirits." When Helge was about to leave, the woman came to him with a scraggly dog she wanted to give him in appreciation for his help. It had belonged to her dead husband. Helge thanked her but said no, he did not need nor want anything in return for helping. But the woman insisted and said "good dog." Rascal became a faithful companion for the next two years. Helge too became infected with influenza and felt miserable for a period of two weeks. But unlike the Dene, he was more immune to such illnesses and soon recovered.

The fishing was lucrative. He caught about 150 large fish every day, but soon tired of it and longed to go hunting again. He moved his camp to the other side of Snowdrift River, where he met another group of Dene, which he wrote about in his journal on 18 October:

> This evening I visited the Indian camp. The best hunter, Antoine, had returned. He had shot two caribou and the people in the camp were thrilled and excited. He had seen many (of the animals) and there were signs of them everywhere. Tomorrow I too am going off hunting. No more fishing!

Several days later Helge packed up camp and paddled eastward into the headwinds and high waves along the southern shores of Great Slave Lake. The dogs followed, running along the shoreline. Helge shot a caribou at one spot and as "evening approached I saw yet another herd of about 20 animals. Those standing in front had magnificent antlers. It was a beautiful sight in the setting sun."[26]

Camp on the tundra. Frozen wolf carcasses on the sled.

Winter came, covering the rivers and lakes with snow and ice. Helge journeyed alone, mushing his team farther in across the country until he came to the foot of a mountain. He set up camp, tied up the dogs, then set off on foot to look for caribou. His female dog had just had a litter of pups and, not wanting to rile up the team, he left them behind at camp. After walking a fair distance, he came upon a herd, shot three animals, and returned to his camp carrying as much meat as he could manage on his back.

One day, a few visitors suddenly appeared and pitched their tent nearby. It was a group of Chipewyan, part of the Dene or Northern Athabascan nation,[27] called the "Caribou Eaters," including Antoine, whom Helge had met earlier that summer. They were headed the long distance back to their home. Since they had not yet caught any caribou themselves, Helge offered them the meat he was not able to carry if they would return and collect it with him. They all set off by dogsled to where Helge's game still lay, made camp, lit a large fire, and then gorged themselves on large pieces of caribou meat. Afterwards, they laid their sleeping bags atop the snow around the campfire and crawled in.

Silhouetted in the light of the campfire's fading embers, Antoine looked over at Helge and asked if he would like to join them to where they were going. They were headed back to their home near a large, very distant lake called Nonacho, a place where they lived when they were not following the caribou. The invitation was unexpected, and perhaps prompted by Helge's assumed good luck in hunting. But it now offered him a unique chance to learn from and about these Dene. Antoine spoke a little English and seemed to represent the group. His wife, Phresi, Helge described as "a heavyweight. Standing beside her, Antoine, her husband, seemed hardly to exist at all."[28]

Helge suspected he knew why he had been invited. Not only because of his presumed luck in hunting, but also for his stockpile of coveted supplies like sugar, tea, and other goods. Eventually this would be shared with all, as is the Dene way. However, as Helge later wrote, "this interested me, not so much because of the hunting possibilities, but because it would give me the opportunity to live with the Caribou Eaters. With them, I could journey farther into the country that had obsessed my mind ever since I had come to the North; the country lying at the source of the Thelon River … It is known, of course, that the Caribou Eater people annually make long journeys by dogsled to the upper Thelon, but jealously guard the secrets surrounding this part of the country."[29]

The following morning they all headed out towards the Caribou Eaters' home. They first returned to Helge's camp at the foot of the mountain to collect his dogs and equipment. From there they journeyed on for several days until they reached Nonacho Lake, a beautiful, large expanse of water filled with small islands. Here, the Caribou Eaters had built several simple log cabins along the shores to live in when they otherwise were not traversing the land. Helge was given lodging in a cabin together with a couple, a man named Albert and his wife, and provided with all the food he and his dogs needed. In the evenings, many of the group would often sit around listening to an old wind-up gramophone they had bartered for at the trading post. Helge once took the liberty of asking one of the young girls to dance, to everyone's great amusement.

Helge slowly felt more at home with this small group and integrated with their way of life as much as he could as an outsider. While living here, he was also able to repair his equipment and have a new caribou parka sewn. After several days, all the hunters left for a long hunting trip. Helge stayed behind with the women and relegated himself to wandering around the surrounding area. From his journal on 8 December:

> I went out to hunt but didn't have any luck. Saw 12 caribou on the lake but didn't manage to hit any of them. My reputation as a hunter is in serious danger. All the women teased me when I returned. They had watched me from their houses. Antoine's wife said that I didn't get any caribou because I was "too hot with the women." When I threw my hat and gloves down by the door, she said that I would not catch any caribou if I left my equipment by the door.

This was to be known as the year of no caribou. The wind blew in the wrong direction. But the Caribou Eaters were very good at providing for themselves, by ice fishing and small-game hunting. They did not go without, but it certainly was not a winter of plenty.

Helge learned much from his new friends, of their history and legends and, most importantly, their techniques for surviving in the wilderness. The Caribou Eaters were people who lived in keeping with their traditions, as their ancestors had always lived. Antoine and a couple of others who could speak a little English acted as Helge's interpreters and teachers. He learned from the women how to treat hides, repair moccasins, and butcher meat correctly for hanging and drying. For Helge, however, his main intention was to get to know these people as friends. He said it himself years later, "I got along very well with the natives. And to a large degree, they liked me."

Towards December, the Caribou Eaters began to prepare for their journey eastward to the headwaters of the Thelon. The trek would be an incredible test of strength and endurance. Snow lay deep within the pine forest and ice covered the rivers and lakes. The area they were heading towards was uncharted territory, still considered a "blank spot" on the map. According to legend, the river supposedly originated from some great seas and was surrounded by a strange forest country, like a green, wooded island far inland on the tundra plateau.

The Caribou Eaters anticipated a fantastic catch of white fox and wolf. But before they could leave, there was much to do and prepare. Meat had to be hunted for the women and children who would remain behind at camp and caribou parkas and footwear had to be sewn. The men also made new snowshoes and collected wood. Firewood had to be taken along since it was difficult to find on the tundra, but it made travelling heavier and more strenuous for both man and dog. Thelon lay at least seven full days away, four of those across barren terrain.

The evening before they left, all the men gathered in the largest tent to discuss the trip. They reviewed their plans in detail and recounted experiences from previous trips. They stressed the importance of everyone having a double-length towrope trailing behind the sled; it would be a dire situation to lose a sled. One element of the trip they failed to discuss, however, was the mention of food supplies. It was assumed that they would hunt for food along the way. On 12 December 1928, everything was finally ready. Helge described the scene in his book *The Land of Feast and Famine*:

> One clear starry morning, eight dog-trains turn out across Nonacho Lake and proceed single file; in the sleds are huddled figures of men wrapped in their sleeping-bags. At the head of the expedition, a little fellow is running along on snowshoe. He moves forward with a swaying rhythm, his arms swinging briskly at his sides. There is a faint jingle of bells which keeps time with the even trotting of the dogs. Hour after hour passes. At length the sky above the eastern ridge pales, and soon the sun is shining brightly over the white expanse of the lake. The huddled forms in the sleds begin to shake themselves. Men sit up, blink their eyes in the light, call back and forth to each other, and begin lighting their pipes. Dogs wave their plume-like tails in the air and quicken their pace, whilst their steaming breaths trail back on either side of them.
>
>   Thus began the expedition of the Caribou-Eaters to the land of the upper Thelon.[30]

At night, they all slept in one tent. It was cramped, but it kept them warm. Each had their own designated spot determined by rank and age. Helge's sleeping bag stuck halfway out the front flap of the tent and his head was pillowed on the legs of the young boy, Isèp. Early in the morning, shivering with cold, the younger men had to crawl out over the other sleeping bodies to light the fire and put on the kettle of meat. The pattern was repeated daily: eat breakfast, pack up camp, harness the dogs, and take off long before the sun rose. They took turns breaking the trail by running ahead of the first sled on their snowshoes and felling trees with their axe when the forest grew dense.

At first, they periodically spotted a lone caribou and were able to hunt what they needed. They chose not to carry more food than would last them a day or two. Speed was important and the meat would weigh the sleds down. Then, the unthinkable happened; all the caribou disappeared. The animals seemed to have changed their course of migration. The men fervently scouted but didn't find a single track. This was a serious lack of planning for their food supply. Hoping that the situation would soon improve, they continued their eastward course towards Thelon. They eventually arrived at a lake called Satin-tuè and set up camp. Without a morsel of food, both people and dogs began to feel a gnawing hunger. Everyone took off to hunt, but all came back empty-handed.

The forests thinned as they neared the Barren Grounds, and soon great blinding waves of white stretched to the east: "The eye loses all sense of proportion, everything flattens out into a deceptive whiteness … Suddenly my dogs and sled avalanche down an invisible precipice and we are buried deep in snow. I crawl frantically around, look in all directions, and catch sight of Antoine. He is standing up on the brink, slapping his thighs and laughing boisterously."[31]

Then a storm came blowing in over the Barren Grounds. Antoine ordered everyone to keep the sleds together, because, as he said, "Big wind, nothing see." He became the compass.

The day before Christmas Eve they set up camp near a lake called Natel-a-tuè – "lake where the tent blew over."[32] The storm continued to blow and the dogs hunkered down and refused to move on. There was still no food, for man or dog. When the winds settled slightly, the men went to hunt for snowshoe hare. Caribou were still nowhere in sight. Helge and Antoine found other animal tracks, but the hare hid well. At the very end of the day, they managed to shoot a single hare. The other hunters' combined efforts totalled one ptarmigan. This was Helge's third Christmas in the wilderness and the meal was not exactly a feast. There they sat, eight men in quiet anticipation, staring at the pot. With painful precision, they divided the fowl and hare between them and ate everything but the bones and feathers. Afterwards they sat and smoked their pipes, no one really wanting to talk: "And then the realization that it is Christmas Eve sinks in. I linger contemplating that thought then think about my loved ones so far away on the other side of the ocean: Christmas tree in the warm living room, roast pork and ... I achingly hold on to those feelings, but then my thoughts return to the same old chilling issue: Will we find caribou?"[33] The thirty-two skinny sled dogs lay in the snow. They had not been given a single piece of food despite the expected heavy load they would have to pull for the next few days.

On Christmas Day, with the storm still raging, hunting was out of the question. They had to go another day without food. That's when Antoine quietly went to his sled and came back with an entire caribou stomach he had hidden in case of extreme need. It was frozen solid but they chopped some of it into small pieces and threw it into the pot. The mixture turned into a kind of green soup that the men greedily drank. The remaining stomach sack was then divided into equal portions, which they slowly chewed bit by bit.

The caribou stomach proved to be their last meal for three days, and eventually their gnawing hunger turned into a lethargic drowsiness. But since the wind had settled a little, they continued their eastward trek. Still no caribou in sight. They were getting close to Chizi-ta-tué (now called Lynx Lake), from where the Thelon flows, and could see the contours of a forest ahead. They set up camp on a ridge by a watershed divide and agreed that each of them would go in a different direction to find food. Helge went to hunt ptarmigan, but only managed to wound a wolf. His dog team took off after the wolf with him hanging helplessly behind on the long steering rope. He nearly lost his sled. The dogs ran fast and far until the sled capsized and they came to a screeching halt. On their trek back to camp, the snow and wind grew worse and Helge barely found the tent again as it was covered in a pile of freshly fallen snow. Nothing to eat on this day either. The situation grew critical.

The next day the men decided to head south. After mushing for several hours, Helge suddenly heard the driver of the first sled yell "*E-then*" (caribou). They all took off on a wild chase and the anguished dogs came alive. They downed a caribou buck, which provided a feast for both men and dogs.

Continuing south, conditions grew even harsher with temperatures dropping to minus 50°C. They came upon some dogsled tracks in the snow and followed these, which led straight to a trapper's cabin. Clark and McKay, whom Helge knew from his summer in Snowdrift, were surprised to say the least to see this starving group of men come mushing up to their cabin. The trappers dished up the best food they had to offer, despite not having any excess themselves. After three days in the cabin, where they did nothing but eat and sleep, the hunters headed back to their base camp at Nonacho Lake. Helge managed to set sight on the headwaters of the mighty Thelon, but only from a distance.

Kajàse – "Little Hare"

She stood tall and grand
was agile and spry
like a prancing caribou across the barren land
When she passed by
it could startle a man
With her raven black hair waving behind
A bird to catch and caress
She was yes the finest girl in the woods my eyes ever did find.[34]

Several years after Helge returned to Norway from his life as a trapper, he wrote the above lines in a poem titled "Squaw Man." The words described not just any girl, but a girl by the name of Kajàse, the young woman he felt he had to escape or otherwise forever be married into the Caribou Eaters' way of life.

Kajàse, or Little Hare, was the daughter of Antoine and Phresi and was seventeen winters old. She could speak a little English since she had spent time at the Roman Catholic mission in the south and had also learned about religion. Every evening she would kneel by her bed and pray to the Virgin Mary. A certain connection developed between Kajàse and Helge, but he insisted that they were never a couple. He wasn't the only one who thought she was beautiful. Kajàse was generous with her compelling glances to other young hunters and her beauty affected more than one. Helge likely had feelings for her, although he never completely admitted it.

Every culture has its understanding of how to initiate a marriage. The Caribou Eaters presumably took Helge's talking kindly to Kajàse as a sign of more serious intentions. A white fur trader, despite being as shabby and as poor as he was, was considered a good match. It would guarantee the entire extended family would be cared for in the future.

It began with Phresi, who suddenly began showering Helge with unusually kind treatment and attention. Once she surprised him with a brand new pair of moccasins, and on another evening she took his caribou parka without his knowing and edged it with beautiful wolverine fur. Sometimes she presented him with a marrow bone or bit of meat even though there was little extra food in the camp. Helge began to suspect something and kept his eyes and ears open. Then he noticed that whenever he entered a tent, the women would lean their heads together, whisper, and giggle. The hunters, meanwhile, constantly razzed him with innuendos. The entire tribe clearly assumed Kajàse and Helge were going to marry. Helge, however, was the only one who clearly did not assume this.

Then one day a young hunter came into Helge's tent and asked him directly when he was going to marry Kajàse. Helge then realized something had to be done, but what? As an outsider, he really didn't want to say straight out that he wouldn't marry the young woman. He wasn't sure how they would react. They could cast him out of the group and leave him to his own foodless fate, a possibly fatal situation. It was a long way back to Great Slave Lake and the snow was too deep to break trail on his own. With currently so few caribou and no provisions, he felt he was in a sticky situation. "'Mother-in-law' treated me with ever-increasing familiarity. Kajàse, in the meantime, spent her entire day at work upon the most charming pair of moccasins imaginable, embroidered as they were with red and blue flowers. Judging by the size, there was no doubt whatsoever as for whom these were intended."[35]

Helge felt trapped. He could not leave on his own without food, so he searched for caribou to provide what he needed to escape. When caribou were finally spotted, he asked Antoine if he would follow him a short distance to help break trail. Helge explained that he wanted to go west to visit some trappers at Great Slave Lake. Antoine agreed and then asked Helge when he would return. He replied that he was not sure. They would surely meet again soon, said Antoine, or at least at the trading post this summer.

When the day came for Helge to leave, he ceremoniously said goodbye to each and every one in the camp. As he approached the tent where Kajàse was standing, she turned and fled into the woods:

> She was wearing her new caribou parka, edged with wolverine fur and embellished with broad red fillets. As she ran, her hood fell back from her head, and the last I saw of her was her black hair

flowing out behind her ... At the very moment we were round-
ing the point, a fraction of a second before it shut off my view, it
seemed as though someone appeared at the edge of the woods,
someone who waved. But of course I couldn't be sure.[36]

Helge and Antoine took off, the camp slowly fading into the distance
behind them. Antoine accompanied Helge for three days, then left him
and his dogs to carry on alone. The deep snow was heavy going and
Helge's snowshoes sank with every step. After several days, he arrived at
a narrow lake formed by the Snowdrift River. To his great surprise, he
met two trappers who he quickly recognized from his previous summer
at Snowdrift. They too had been far in on the Great Barrens and had
exactly the same experience: no sign of caribou. The trappers were
nearly out of provisions. Helge shared with them what little he had and
together they continued on the long trip to Snowdrift. None of them
were actually sure of the way, but they found it in the end.

Helge, in his ninety-ninth year, reluctantly admitted that his departure
from the Caribou Eaters was not the most gracious way of leaving a
hopeful young woman. But what else could he have done? He wasn't
planning on spending the rest of his life in Canada, nor did he consider
ever bringing Kajàse back with him to Norway. And he was not the kind
of man to abandon a wife and child when it no longer suited him.

When Helge arrived at Snowdrift in the middle of February 1929, he
quickly wrote a letter to his parents telling them about his adventures
and future plans. He was struggling with whether to remain in Canada
longer or to leave. His parents' expectations for a legal career hung over
him, but he was not yet ready to abandon the wilderness. In the letter,
he wrote that he would stay in Snowdrift for a couple of months "and
gorge myself with bread and the like ... fire up the stove and live like
a prince, eat bread at every meal and porridge with sugar." Delicacies,
no doubt, after such a simple, meagre diet. He planned to hunt martens
near the edge of the woods, fish, wander about with the dogs, and hunt
caribou to sell to the trading posts. After that, he planned to spend one
more winter in the wilderness.

It took three months for the letter to reach Bergen. Olav replied immediately, relieved to receive a sign of life earlier than expected. "After
now experiencing such a life as a trapper, you must put efforts into

writing a book," he insisted. "Don't make it too sombre, but tell that you suffered." A book, he emphasized, would be much more important than earning good money from trapping. He ended by saying, "I'm not against your being away another year or two. I understand that a certain process within you must run its course. I stress that I am not worried in any way for you. I know that you are reasonable and level-headed enough not to take any risks."

Between June and August, other letters were exchanged.[37] While still in Snowdrift, Helge learned of the growing excitement about precious minerals and the rush to find them. The tranquility of northern Canada was starting to disappear. From around the world, people came in search of fortune. Even as close as Pine Point, near Fort Resolution, rumours spread about discoveries of zinc and lead. There were also whispers of gold in other places. A new time was surely coming. Would it be like the rushes to the Klondike or Nome, Alaska, at the end of the nineteenth century when thousands of prospectors came rushing north only to die or return empty-handed? Helge certainly hoped not. But he knew that it heralded a time of great change and that he was lucky to have experienced the wilderness and its indigenous peoples before "civilization" came and wreaked havoc and destruction.

Helge, however, was not completely immune to a little "mineral fever" himself. Persuaded by a fellow trapper, he bought a claim (mineral rights) at Pine Point for $50. That was a lot of money for Helge then. However, a claim also demanded that the holder oversee its gradual development in order to retain the mineral rights. Unable to see himself doing this, the next day Helge talked his friend into buying the claim back. This nearly caused a serious conflict between the two men because it was interpreted as deep distrust.

At about the same time, Helge received a letter from his father:

It was fun to hear about life in Snowdrift and about the rush towards the new discoveries. I admire that you are taking it so calmly. I'm not sure if I could have done the same. But of course, rumours can be exaggerated and their claims less substantial. No, it is safer with the book ... I must tell you one thing though and that is I fear that if you are too long in the wilderness you may get caught up in getting married there. That would be complete ruin for a civilized person.[38] The telegraph inspector mentioned one of his friends whom this happened to and he completely lost himself. I hope you are laughing at me.

No, Helge was not exactly laughing, not with the beautiful Kajàse still fresh in his memory.

Alone on the Barren Grounds

Helge's last winter as a trapper was spent alone on the Barren Grounds. It was not a conscious choice to go on his own; he just had not found anyone else with whom he wanted to spend the winter. Dale had gone his own way and Helge could not live with just anyone under such tough conditions. He did try partnering with a Canadian by the name of Fred for a while. They paddled up Snowdrift River into the rough waters and nearly lost their canoe, equipment, and their lives several times over. One day during this time, Helge came across something that stirred his imagination and hopes. From his journal on 21 August 1929:

> I was out walking looking for stones. And I found one that I truly believed was gold! It looked so real. I climbed to the top where I could see into the distance, as far as to the other side of the lake. A beautiful little river ran below. I thought about all the riches buried beneath my feet and already felt like a millionaire. There I stood on top of my gold mine thinking it was worth an enormous sum. Back at camp, Fred ruined everything. He laughed at my gold and said it was called "zinc."

The camaraderie between Helge and Fred was not the best, not even close to what Helge had experienced with Dale. The men built a nice log cabin, which Fred preferred at the edge of the woods. But after an argument about Helge's dogs howling all night they decided to part ways.

Helge didn't want to spend the winter there at the edge of the woods. He wanted to travel farther in on the Barrens and hunt white fox. On his way, he stopped at a camp on the second lake by Pikes Portage. A man by the name of Bob offered him work floating logs, which also allowed Helge time to fish. However, as it can happen when a trapper returns from the wilderness to "civilization," he often lets off a little steam.

Helge wrote on 4 October 1929: "Started the job with Bob by drinking up our entire rum ration (12 bottles between two men). We were drunk for five days. Ended up getting into a fight with a French man."

Despite the rough start, Bob must have been happy with Helge's work since he asked him to be his partner for the winter on the tundra and they soon departed. The caribou had started migrating and there were great herds of them, in the hundreds. The dogs went crazy. They had more than enough meat but were limited by how much could be loaded onto their sleds and transported. Enough snow had fallen and the rivers began to freeze. The weather, however, deteriorated with a driving wind that kept them weather-bound in their tents for several days at a time. At one point or another, Bob must have given up because any mention of him disappears from Helge's journal without further explanation. Helge carried on to the Barren Lands by himself.

Helge was perhaps better suited than most for life alone on the tundra. He was not an especially social person. He had no strong need to sur-round himself with people and was more than happy to be on his own for long periods of time. Despite this, it was still a great challenge to go it alone for such extended periods and under such difficult conditions. But Helge liked challenges and he had the dogs to keep him company. So he took off across the Barren Lands, without direction or detailed plan of where he was headed. Wherever there was plenty of white fox was where he wanted to be. Then out there in the middle of nowhere, he happened upon a little haven in the naked landscape: a small grove with about a hundred fir trees, a river, and a lake. He pitched his tent, tied up his dogs, and ended up staying there for the rest of the winter.

Helge and his dogs were not the only ones in that sheltered dale. Ptar-migan lived in the marshy willow thicket and calmly dawdled about, quite uninterested in him or his dogs as they came rushing by. Out on the ice, caribou had made indents in the snow to sleep in and to return to often. An arctic hare with his large family lived on the hillside. "But there was plenty of room for us all. By tacit agreement we remained good neighbours, each with respect for the domain of the others … Thus the valley was in reality fully populated and the snow-birds and squirrels were almost considered extra boarders."[39]

The animals kept him company, and he was surprised how quickly they got used to him and his dogs. But then again, he didn't hunt his "neighbours" either. The dale provided enough wood for the winter's fuel and the caribou were abundant. To catch white fox, Helge made a trap line along a two-day, eastward course across the tundra and spent the night in his small canvas tent. No doubt, it was tough going in the storms and cold. Once when he took off across the tundra without his dogs to check the traps, he got lost and barely found his way back again.

With the company of all the animals, especially his dogs, Helge was never lonely. When spring came, however, he felt a strong pull to return to life's comforts that he had gone without for so long. This time though it was not Snowdrift or Fort Resolution that tugged at him, but home.

He felt that he was at a crossroads. He either had to stay and perhaps end up like one of those many "old-timers" who never returned to their homeland, or leave now before the love of a life in the wilderness made it too difficult to adjust to "civilization." He considered staying, but thoughts of his parents back in Bergen undoubtedly tipped the balance in favour of leaving. Besides, the book he wanted to write was now more fully developed in his mind and he was ready to get started. Helge knew it was time to return to Norway.

In Snowdrift, he met up with other trappers, all returning from the solitude in the wilderness to sell their furs. The prices were good and everyone was in the mood for a long-awaited celebration. Not long after, however, Helge and a few others decided to head south, to Edmonton.

Before leaving, Helge sold all of his equipment. He was not coming back. The dogs were the most difficult to part with as they were now dependable friends. He sold them to people he thought would treat them well. He could not, however, bring himself to sell Rascal, that shaggy dog given to him by that old Dene woman for helping to bury victims of the flu. "No one else shall ever drive him," Helge wrote in his book.[40] Instead, he shot him.

Helge and his travelling companions made their way first to Fort Resolution, and after much deliberation the group decided to buy tickets on one of the first airplanes ever to fly from Fort Resolution to Edmonton. The plane ride was expensive, but worth it. This was Helge's very first experience in the air. In his book *The Land of Feast and Famine*, he described what he felt as he looked down across the wilderness that had been his home for four years:

> Staring down at the steamer as she splashes her way along, awkward and old-fashioned in every detail, I see two different ages

closely contrasted. The Northland has been given her warning; civilization, expanding from the south, is seeking new fields of activity for her sons. Today she is still groping, but another day will come when, with full majesty, her will shall prevail: factories, smoke-darkened cities, milling humanity.[41]

In Edmonton, modern life met Helge with all its hustle and bustle. Cars zoomed by, neon lights flashed, and people rushed about as if life depended on it. On his fourth day in town, the old trapper named Klondike Bill came up to Helge and said, "Lighting out for the north tomorrow. Got to get home to my tent, it's too lonesome here."[42]

Coming Home

Four years in Canada had passed quickly and Helge's contact with Norway had been sparse. The only times he had been able to send and receive letters were when he had been at the trading posts to sell his furs and buy new equipment.

By the beginning of July 1930, Helge was home again in Norway. He felt a strong contrast between his life in the wilderness and the noise and activity of "civilization." "Being surrounded by people brings on loneliness," he wrote in a poem several years later. No doubt he felt this as he walked along the streets of Oslo[43] while thinking of his time in remote northern Canada. In a letter on 25 September to his friend Jon Rye Holmboe at the Norwegian Consulate in Montreal, he wrote it was good to be back in his beautiful country, but it felt all too cramped and quiet. A lot had changed during the four years he had been away. Friends had married and had children, and those who had been teenagers when he left were now young adults.

In a letter he sent during the summer to his childhood friend Odd, Helge told him a newspaper had interviewed him for a story and after it was printed people treated him with the most "amazing politeness." He was continually stopped on the street by people telling him that he had done what they had always dreamt of doing when they were young. Odd replied, "That's easy to say. Currently, I know of no person other than yourself who really would have done it, circumstances allowing."

Changes in Helge's family had also occurred. His sister Gunvor had married Halvard Trætteberg and Kaare had been stationed with the

Norwegian delegation in Shanghai. Helge wrote to Kaare commenting on Gunvor's new marriage:

> It's nice. Half the purpose of a woman's life is to get married and have children, not to wander about like me and be a vagabond who never settles. I now have the wilderness in my blood and there's nothing I can do about it. But I am also aware that certain things are inevitable and that there may come a time [for a different life.] I have begun studying geology at the university here in town. It could come in handy if I choose to go out again next year. Someday, I will no doubt find a gold mine.

However, more important than finding a gold mine just then was the question of what Helge was going to do now. He had irrevocably sold his law practice in Levanger, not that he wanted to go back to it anyway. A routine job was no longer to his liking; he was used to living freely and being his own boss. Then he mentioned to Kaare he thought about going to East Greenland to trap the following year. But a few obstacles stood in the way. One, no doubt, was the debate between the Danes and Norwegians about rights to East Greenland, and the other was getting the necessary money.

It was to Olav's credit that Helge carried through with plans to write a book about his adventures in Canada. Equipped with an old typewriter, Helge took off to the beautiful Hardanger fjord. He stayed at the guesthouse where his family had spent the summer holidays during his childhood, and worked on the book until it was finished just several months later. It was easy to write. Helge was so full of impressions and experiences that he could have written several volumes. Olav, who was his strict but well-meaning critic, read through the final draft, editing and making suggestions.

Helge received a letter from Harald Grieg at the end of July, the publishing director of Gyldendal Norwegian Publishers. He had read the newspaper article about Helge which mentioned his plans to write a book. Greig asked Helge, quite formally even though the two had known each other as children in Bergen, if he would like to send his manuscript to Gyldendal: "I would think that such a book, if properly engaging, could generate great interest."

Helge's reply was equally as formal. One would think that such a young and unknown debut writer would jump for joy to receive such an offer from one of Norway's most established publishers. But no, he clearly wanted to play his cards wisely:

Glydendal Norwegian Publisher, Oslo
I respectfully send appreciation for your gracious request dated 30 July, which I only now have received after returning from a long journey. With reference to the book that I am currently working on about my experiences living as a trapper with the Caribou Eaters of Northern Canada, I regrettably cannot at this time give a decision. Permit me to return with an answer at a later date.
Sincerely and gratefully yours,
Helge Ingstad

Offers also came from Cappelen and Steenske Publishers. But it was Gyldendal that published it in the end, marking the beginning of a lifelong relationship between author and publisher. Helge used Harald Greig and Gyldendal not only as a publisher, but also for assistance with tasks such as holding or rerouting his mail, paying bills, or other similar tasks when he was away on expeditions – services over and above what anyone could expect from a publisher today.

On 3 October 1930, the manuscript *Pelsjegerliv blant Nord-Kanadas indianere*, later titled in English *The Land of Feast and Famine*, was delivered to the publisher. The book was dedicated "To my father," and in a letter to him Helge wrote: "This is both my book and yours for I would not have managed it without your help." The book would go on to become one of Gyldendal's greatest successes of all time and received several good reviews. The first was from his university friend, Gunnar Larsen, who was now editor of the daily newspaper *Dagbladet*, who wrote that "everyone should read it!" Knut Hamsun, who was awarded the Nobel Prize in literature in 1920, sent a letter which said: "You are a masterful observer and descriptive writer and you support it all with knowledge. Yours sincerely, Knut Hamsun."

Not long after, Helge and Hamsun met by chance at Oslo's fashionable Theatre Café. They started talking about logging as they walked together down the city's main street, Karl Johan, with Hamsun swinging his cane to demonstrate how to chop a tree so it falls in the intended direction. Both men had been loggers at one time. In retrospect, Helge would smile at the thought of a meeting between two prominent authors and the most important thing they had to talk about was logging. It was the only time they ever met.

The Norwegian publication of *The Land of Feast and Famine* was quickly sold to publishers in Sweden and Denmark as well as translated into English, German, and French. Helge became an overnight sensation, at the age of thirty-one. And even though he was pleased with the success of the book, it was also all a bit overwhelming for him. *The Land of Feast and Famine* must have touched something within the Norwegian psyche. Helge was practically considered a national hero and people came from every city and town to hear him speak. He spoke to crowds and drew full houses wherever he went with his captivating tales. Without any film footage or slides at the time, he just stood and talked about what he remembered. He had so much to tell about his experiences.

Norway had long been proud of its polar traditions, and rightly so. Roald Amundsen, who led the first-ever expedition to reach the South Pole and the first to navigate the Northwest Passage, died in 1928 while Helge was in Canada. Fridtjof Nansen, explorer of the North Pole and Greenland, died only a few weeks before Helge returned to Norway. Quite possibly, Helge filled this sudden, vacant void for the Norwegian people. The admiration and enthusiasm that came streaming in were perhaps not only about what he had accomplished, but also what he had touched in the collective national psyche.

The Land of Feast and Famine was mostly a tale of adventure, but also included keen observations of the indigenous cultures and their way of life. Helge was especially interested in how the native peoples could survive on a single-source diet: the caribou. When European polar explorers tried to survive on meat alone they died of scurvy. The answer, he thought, must lie in the fact that the Caribou Eaters ate most everything of the animal: meat, marrow, fat, and most importantly the contents of the animal's stomach. In that way, they got the necessary vitamin c.[44]

The Land of Feast and Famine was a turning point in Helge's life in many ways. Not just because he became famous and fairly wealthy at such a young age, but mostly because he now knew that it was possible to follow his dreams – and earn a living from doing so. It was not necessary to relinquish those dreams for a conventional job, nor did he feel that he had to follow his father's advice about finding a career.

About a decade after *The Land of Feast and Famine* was first published, the book played a vital but little-known role in events of the Second World War. The story was presented in 2003 by British survival specialist Ray Mears in his book and BBC television series *The Real Heroes of Telemark: The True Story of the Secret Mission to Stop Hitler's Atomic Bomb*. Mears talked about a group of young Norwegian men who made a courageous raid on a hydroelectric plant in the Telemark region of German-occupied Norway. The plant was producing heavy water, a prerequisite for building an atomic bomb. Military leaders in the US and Britain feared that if the Nazis managed to collect the amounts needed for such a bomb, the consequences could severely tip the balance of the war.

Mears explained that this young group of Norwegian saboteurs had to hide for months on the Hardangervidda mountain plateau in the middle of winter until they were able to sneak down and successfully destroy the plant. The key to their survival, he said, was their diet of reindeer. "Most young Norwegian boys of the time had grown up reading the books of legendary Helge Ingstad ... and his descriptions of Indian eating habits and survival techniques were well known to [the group of saboteurs]. It was from reading Ingstad that they knew they could eat the moss in the reindeers' stomachs and how best to cook it," explained Mears. Special Operations Executive team leader Jens Anton Poulsson added that "if we hadn't been able to [survive on] reindeer I don't think we could have accomplished what we did."[45]

Mears concluded by saying that, after the many months these men hid in the mountains, "their beards grew long and their skin became sallow, but thanks to the reindeer, Helge Ingstad, their own survival skills and the strength of their spirit, they were still alive."[46]

3 EAST GREENLAND

Helge grew restless and longed to return to Arctic regions. He could easily have lived off his book royalties and lecturing income for several more years, but that's not what he wanted to do. No particular girl held his attention for very long, though many were drawn to the handsome, famous young man. He shared a small apartment for a while in Oslo with Kaare, who wrote a letter to his parents in Bergen bemoaning his older brother:

> Helge has met a dancer by the name of Schultz, but doesn't appear to be all that interested. He's becoming a bit blasé about women. He needs to get a little wilderness in him again. His clothes are beginning to hang on him, his back is getting crooked and that fine hat is getting covered with dust. He's a bit of a lost cause right now.[1]

Nor was he especially good at tending to the few relationships he did have with women. An unknown Gerd wrote to him from France thanking him for his invitation for a possible dogsled trip that winter. She replies that most likely she will be married by then, "so I guess another young girl will be lucky to get that chance. At least Helge, those few ski trips we had together at Easter were so wonderful that I will always remember them."[2]

His friends had long since gotten engaged or married and it was certainly clear from those around him that he too should follow suit. Of

Helge in East Greenland. Seals had to be hunted to feed the dogs.

course moving about the world didn't exactly help the matter either, but his thoughts were focused elsewhere.

The Struggle for East Greenland

It was about this time that Helge seriously began to dream about new adventures in East Greenland. During his years in Canada, a serious conflict between Norway and Denmark had steadily developed concerning the rights to Greenland's eastern coast, where Norwegians had a long tradition of fishing and hunting. This debate affected him two ways. The first was that it had to do with an Arctic wilderness similar to the one he had become familiar with in Canada. The other was that he, like many others, was aggravated that the Danes were allowed to keep the old Norwegian possessions of Greenland, Iceland, and Faroe Islands after the dissolution of the Denmark–Norway union in 1814 with the signing of the Treaty of Kiel. The treaty severed these dependencies from Norway, leaving them under Danish rule.

Yet another agreement was signed in 1924 allowing Norwegians access to the Danish areas of Greenland for hunting and fishing, and was irrevocable for twenty years after this time. This treaty also stated, "and for the occupation of land by those subjects for their own use."[3] East Greenland, however, was almost uninhabited at the time, and some, particularly a few Norwegians, believed it to be a *terra nullius*, or no man's land, and therefore open to anyone. They asserted that a country could hold sovereignty over an area only where a person had built his house and set out his trap lines.

As this debate unfurled and eventually led to an international court case to decide who had dominion over the eastern part of Greenland, the Danes began to move certain settlements of Greenlanders from the western to the eastern side of the island in order to populate the area. They chose a spot called Scoresby Sund, located in the middle of the eastern coastline of Greenland. Norwegian trappers also attempted to mark their presence on this same easterly rugged strip of land in East Greenland by raising the Norwegian flag at points north and south of the settlement. This 1930s conflict over East Greenland escalated to the point of setting off a race between the Danes and Norwegians to see who could first get a foothold in the area before the case came before the

International Court of Justice at The Hague. A qualifying importance was to show that whoever was occupying the land was putting it to economic use.

The Norwegians encouraged trappers to put up as many small cabins as possible along the trap lines to mark their presence. Many of these buildings were just symbolic structures and not practical places to live. In the spring of 1931, Helge began planning an expedition to this part of Greenland and realized he had best hurry to secure a position.

Today we can shake our heads over this dispute thinking that the question was not whether the island "belonged" to either Norway or Denmark, but that it of course ought to belong to the Greenlanders themselves. Fridtjof Nansen took that stand when at an early stage of the debate he wrote an article in *Tidens Tegn*, an Oslo newspaper, on 22 February 1924:

> The country's rightful owners are the Eskimos; and their interests are what should be the decisive factor. The best and rightful that both Danes and Norwegians, and other nationalities, can do, if possible, would be to keep away and let the Eskimos live in peace without European involvement.

Like other Europeans out to claim land areas as their own, Helge was caught up in the influences of his time. The dispute over Greenland was for him of national importance rooted in the Vikings' voyages and discoveries of Iceland, Faroe Islands, Greenland, and Vinland. As much as he was interested in the political issues of the Greenland dispute, however, Helge didn't engage himself politically. The most important issue for him was to return to the Arctic so he could once again live a free life in the wilderness.

Not long after his return to Norway from Canada in 1930, Helge already began mentioning plans for a trapping expedition to East Greenland. In a letter dated 28 August to Consular Officer Holmboe at the Norwegian Consulate in Montreal, he wrote:

> My plans of going to Greenland next summer are still not yet organized but I am hoping to go. I truly long to get going. I can handle civilization for shorter periods, but I find it all a bit strange.

I also get the impression that some consider me an odd creature ... and for the time nothing of great importance is happening in this country. The parliament and the newspapers only focus on all sorts of silly issues. Ongoing trivial things.[4]

Helge struggled with resettling into his homeland and even considered emigrating. During this time, he closely followed the situation in Greenland and dreamt of travelling there to what he heard were even better trapping opportunities than in Canada. His initial plans were purely for trapping, which he indicated in a letter on 24 July 1930 to his fellow trapper in Canada, the Swede named Joe Nelson, only two weeks after his return from North America:

> I arrived in Bergen just a few days ago. Worked as a deckhand from Canada to France. I'm doing well, but my thoughts often return to the north country there. I'll get to the point about trapping in Greenland next year. All of Greenland's eastern coast is open to Norwegians. No license is needed. This also includes Swedes. Just recently, 15 Norwegians have begun trapping there. It's good. They haven't caught any wolf, but are catching white and blue fox as well as muskox and are shooting a few bears, all of which has been paying well. There are also a good many walrus and seal.

The letter indicates that these two talked about trapping in Greenland even before Helge left Canada. Helge's old trapping buddy, Hjalmar Dale, was at the time deep in the Canadian wilderness and could not be reached. Joe, however, was known to be "the best trapper in the Northwest Territories." Helge explained to him they could take a research ship over to East Greenland the following year and that hopefully the government would offer free, or at least cheaper, transportation. Where exactly the ship could take them was unclear, but Helge said he thought as far north as possible, away from the other trappers. Since both Helge and Joe were unfamiliar with the country, he said it would be best if they stuck together, "so you have to be prepared to be partners."

About a month later, Joe sent a reply from Fort Reliance addressed to "My Friend Mr. Helge Ingstad. Yes, I would like to come and agree to a partnership." He planned to arrive at Fort Resolution by the middle of May the following year and from there fly to Edmonton. On 25 October, Helge wrote back to Joe thanking him for his letter and said how pleased he was that Joe was willing to join the planned expedition. He also told him he had talked to people who knew the conditions of East Greenland:

> I have gotten the impression that Greenland is "fine trapper country." And I understand that there are plenty of fox in Greenland. I've also heard that it's possible to make a stake. It certainly won't take many blue foxes before making a profit. In some of the districts there are as many blue as there are white fox, in others about 20% blue fox ... Trapping is almost only done by poison. Nobody makes a fuss about it. We can get the poison here in this country. If it isn't too difficult, you can also take some along ... There are also a lot of polar bears. But we absolutely need traps. I leave it to you to buy these when you arrive.

That nobody made a "fuss" about the use of poison was not actually true. Norwegian trapping methods, including the use of strychnine, was exactly one of the arguments the Danes used against Norway to create conflict over East Greenland. Danes also claimed that hunting muskox, as the Norwegians did, was "exploitation."

In his letter to Joe, Helge also talked about meetings he had had with several significant people in the Norwegian Council of Arctic Administration, including the geologist and Arctic researcher Adolf Hoel, who had become a key figure in the Greenland case.[5] This meeting clearly influenced Helge's expedition plans and his possible role in the political game being played out:

> I seem to be in good standing with the man on the State Board[6] who is of great importance in this strife over Greenland. He absolutely agreed that I should go to the fjord (in East Greenland) that I had decided upon and would support me in anyway. I would also be given Norwegian police authority. The Danes won't like that, but we give a damn about them.

Which particular fjord he was actually referring to is not mentioned in the letter, but other sources indicate that it could have been Scoresby

Sund. This was a bold move since this was the same area that the Danes were attempting to populate with a community of Greenlanders.

Helge initially told Joe they would take supplies to build one base cabin; otherwise they would use tents. However, he later wrote to say that they would build as least ten cabins evenly spaced by a day's journey between them. The reason was to quite simply occupy "no-man's land." Helge wanted to build the cabins in Norway and transport them by ship to more easily (and quickly) set them up: "This way we have a better chance at taking possession of the largest possible amount of land."

Helge suggested using skis with "Finnish shoes," or reindeer skin boots, for hard snow and Canadian snowshoes for deep snow. He also bought some moose hide to sew moccasins. In the end, the elaborate plans indicated that Helge was once again seriously thinking of living life as a trapper for many more years to come: "After first getting our house set up we'll have a trapping ground for the rest of our lives."

Helge also wrote to his friend Odd Martens on 26 July 1930 about his Greenland plans:

Next year I will shed my previous two titles, lawyer and trapper, and will assume the title of landowner in Greenland. I have in fact been informed that over there one can simply take possession of land and own it. In the treaty with Denmark, East Greenland is considered no-man's land. The result has been a race between the Danes and the Norwegians in getting over there to stake out the largest possible amount of land. The Norwegian government will supposedly assist. In other words, a regular old brawl – just to my liking.

Helge then went to work to acquire funding for his Greenland expedition. He wrote to the Meteorological Institute suggesting they contribute to the establishment of a new weather station, but they declined. On 14 October 1930, he wrote to the Ministry of Trade and Industry requesting 15,000 kroner in government support for the expedition. He had heard they were granting money for such purposes and based his application on the importance of establishing Norwegian interests in East Greenland. He emphasized that the main goal of the expedition was to trap, primarily fox and bear, but that he also had plans of other financial utilization of the land. He intended to study the geological conditions, and if he were to find minerals or coal, he would attempt to begin operations: "In addition, I will as much as possible explore conditions considered to be of scientific interest and in the event of finding anything will collect natural historical material."

It was quite ambitious and stretched his areas of competency, but it looked good in the application. He was well aware that the conflict with Denmark needed to be used for all its worth in order to serve his main interest: a trapping expedition to Greenland.

During the spring of 1931, Helge wavered between being hopeful and doubtful about receiving the expected funding for his Greenland expedition. His contacts first told him "most likely" then "perhaps unlikely." So Helge wrote again to Joe telling him that he had managed to earn a bit of capital for equipment and was still hoping for a "large contribution of money" but that it was still uncertain. If Joe chose to come home (to Scandinavia), he had to do it at his own risk. On 27 June 1931, Helge received word that he would not be getting any funding. He sent a letter, but Joe was already on his way. The trapper then spent the winter in Sweden and returned to the Northwest Territories the following year.

Eirik Raudes Land

At the same time Helge was trying to get to East Greenland, another trapper, Hallvard Devold, was already there. He and members of his expedition hoisted the Norwegian flag at Myggbukta on 27 June 1931 and claimed possession of the area on behalf of King Haakon VII. A few days later, the Norwegian government proclaimed it theirs and called it Eirik Raudes Land.[7]

The occupation of the area first appeared to be by private initiative. But it was clear that stronger forces were also at play, such as Adolf Hoel and his Arctic Council, which received full government funding that year. Since Hoel was interested in getting as many expeditions to Greenland as possible, there was again talk of planning an expedition for Helge, but to a less politically sensitive area in East Greenland than Scoresby Sund. However, after much deliberation, it was again put on hold. Meanwhile, the question of sovereignty over East Greenland grew exceedingly more conflicted. The Norwegian government clearly saw the need to both strengthen the administration in the area and reinforce Norwegian rights by building many more trappers' huts.[8]

Helge did not give up on his Greenland plans, but instead set them aside while he attended to his book and lecture tour for *The Land of Feast and Famine*. In the spring of 1932, he was again busy trying to gather support for his own private expedition. This time, however, he was considering more easterly areas he had wanted to explore, Siberia. He contacted Aleksandra Kollontaj, a Soviet politician and the world's first female ambassador,[9] to Norway and then Sweden.

While Kollontaj was a diplomat in Sweden, Helge was there giving lectures at the Swedish Society for Anthropology and Geography at Stockholm. He boldly invited the ambassador, twenty years his senior, to dinner at a fancy restaurant and then turned on the charm. She encouraged him to send his expedition ideas in writing, which he did on 4 March. He wrote a long letter where he discussed his experiences in Arctic Canada and his success with his published book. He then explained his plans for an expedition to Siberia and his intentions to explore the wilderness, and to learn about the land's nature, animal life, and "primitive groups" as well as any possible financial opportunities. He was especially interested in exploring the unique characteristics of the Siberian people's culture. He planned to write a book including beautiful photos, and to present lectures in various countries. "I dare say that with this in mind, I consider it a given that I would be able to get my Siberian book published in various countries where my currently successful book is known." He writes further that his observations of the "unexplored" areas will of course be at the disposition of the Soviet government. He hopes that this kind of collaboration would be of interest to a country as a sign of development and that they "would grant me a favoured position with the various Siberian authorities. I do hope Mrs. Minister doesn't find this too forthcoming."

This was a very different tune for the man who only a few years earlier stood and gave a rousing speech in his community town on Norwegian Independence Day warning against unrestrained admiration for communism and the Russian Revolution. But for Helge, it was all about beginning a new adventure in the north. This was far more important to him than the political views of the time and he was willing to formulate his requests in any way that would best help him to achieve his goals.

On 12 April 1932 a message came from Kollontaj thanking him for the copy of his book and saying that he should take contact with "the Soviet Union's minister in Oslo, Mr. Beksadian, and explain to him your plans. He will do his utmost to help you with your travels to Siberia." At the end of the letter she wrote, "I've already notified Moscow about your plans and I am sure that you will be very welcome in my country."

Another Attempt at East Greenland

Helge's Siberian plans seemed to drag on and his Greenland plans continued to progress, mostly due his contact with Adolf Hoel. On 28 April 1932 Helge wrote to Hoel: "I am [now] willing to take on the previously mentioned winter expedition to Scoresby Sund. The expedition will go under my name which will also be used in conjunction with raising funds in Norway."

The plan was to begin from Norway the following summer with the goal of staking claim to as much land as possible in compliance with the previously mentioned East Greenland Treaty of 1924. Helge, however, had one condition: the rights to the land and housing would fall upon him or other expedition members, to whom he would eventually hand over the use. The requirement was that the land had to be in Norwegian hands: "The administration of these lands will be according to … a firm assertion of Norwegian interests."

Hoel was again pushing for an expedition to Scoresby Sund, which was only to Helge's advantage due to the good trapping in the area. It was important, however, that the expedition appeared to be a privately funded venture. In that way, the Norwegian government could not be accused of contributing to the occupation of land near a Greenlander's colony.

At about the same time, another opportunity emerged. Leaders of three Norwegian trapping expeditions, who were already based in East Greenland, had been given police authority. A new position was now needed to assume full police authority over the entire occupied area. With his combined judicial and Arctic background, Helge must have seemed the ideal candidate. For him, this was an opportunity to earn a salary, gain status and authority, and still have the opportunity to finally fulfill his trapping expedition plans.

The first sign that something extraordinary was in the works came from brother Kaare, who on 1 June 1932 wrote home to his parents from Oslo: "The heat is tropical here. Helge will surely be glad to leave. He is busily engaged with his expedition, which from what I have heard in the Department includes all chances that he will leave as Governor. A good title, yes?"

In a letter to the Greenland delegation dated 2 June, Helge presented his plans. He reiterated what the cancelled expedition to Scoresby Sund in 1930 cost him in terms of money and disappointment, outlined his expedition plans for the upcoming winter, then argued against moving the expedition farther north into Eirik Raudes Land. Trapping was considered poorer there and he would not be able to acquire the same rights to the area if he did not occupy new land by Scoresby Sund. He said that he would, however, be willing to alter his plans if he were compensated with a fixed salary and an official position, as well as be financially allowed to conduct his own trapping during the expedition.

On 10 June 1932, Helge was appointed governor of Eirik Raudes Land effective 1 July of the same year. However, the appointment came without a salary; otherwise the case would have to be subjected to a parliamentary decision, resulting in an uncertain outcome. Costs of transportation would be covered for him and other expedition members. The rest of the equipment, including telegraph equipment, he would have to fund himself through donations and sponsorships. The day after the announcement was made, Helge's father wrote to congratulate him. He pointed out that it will surely be an interesting time to remember: "You risk becoming a part of the history of Greenland. And now you must see to getting the family name Ingstad placed on the map, in one spot or another." As usual, he ended the letter with some good advice: "When facing your own people, it is of greatest importance to never relinquish your leadership. Of course, one has to be good-natured, forthright and friendly. A certain dignity, however, must be maintained. Otherwise it will not work, especially under daily subjection to such conditions."

Helge's primary duty as governor was to represent Norway in the occupied area, but also to ensure that Norwegian law was followed. Direct confrontations with the Danes were also expected. In that case, he was to follow the protocol of the 1924 East Greenland Treaty between Norway and Denmark to the best of its understanding and compliance.

"Of course, violation of any Norwegian authority must not be allowed nor any foreign state authority practiced in the area."[10]

Helge was also expected to secure Norway's presence in the area by building as many new huts as possible. In addition, and this was to Helge's delight, he was to study the animal life and make suggestions for conservation and hunting regulations. For the most part, he was to get to know the land. He could carry out his own trapping, as he so desired, but not with strychnine. The Justice Department banned this, most likely to avoid criticism from the Danes.[11]

Despite the fact that Helge now had an official position, that the occupation of Eirik Raudes Land was indeed established, and that the borders of this area were roughly marked out, there were some who were still secretly scheming behind closed doors concerning the area. Gustav Smedal, a lawyer actively involved in procuring Arctic areas for Norway, sent a letter to Helge on 6 July, marked "CONFIDENTIAL." The letter encouraged him to, as soon as possible and in secrecy, occupy an even greater area which "when all is taken into consideration it can be said to be included in Norwegian operations or will be in the near future."

Wherever Helge's trapping expedition went, Smedal wanted the men to claim land on behalf of King Haakon VII and specifically mark the area by raising the Norwegian flag. Immediately afterwards, they were to send Smedal a telegram saying, "The trapping prospects are good." The trappers were further advised to keep the occupation secret until the court decision at The Hague was made in favour of Norway. After this, a telegram about the occupation would be sent at once to the Norwegian government and newspapers. The telegram would also further explain that the reason for the occupation was to impede Danish possession of this land, which would make it impossible for any Norwegian business to operate there. If the International Court of Justice at The Hague ruled against Norway, the private occupation would remain a secret. Smedal insisted that his letter was not be shown to anyone and delivered back to him when Helge also returned to Norway.

Why so secretive? To keep the Danes from getting there before them? Or because Helge, who now officially represented Norway, was not initially (nor formally) instructed to expand the occupied area. However, he was never told *not* to. Most likely, though, such expansion would not have been taken lightly while the case was still in deliberation at The Hague.

Helge's life grew hectic. Several hopeful young men wrote and asked if they could be a part of his expedition. Requests asking for contributions to the expedition, in the form of money or goods, were sent to all imaginable and unimaginable agencies. In addition to all the necessary equipment and supplies, Helge also asked for items that would make the stay extra pleasant for the men. The Norwegian chocolate company Freia donated 100 kilos of "arctic chocolate," a number of publishers and bookshops were asked to donate books, and the state-owned liquor store received a letter asking for ten bottles of cognac and twelve bottles of aquavit, which "were partly considered medicinal, partly for special occasions such as Christmas Eve." It was emphasized to all potential supporters that "the expedition was of strong national character."

Helge's forever strategically thinking father had more advice in store before his son departed: "It is possible that you may have to make a visit to the King. I think that is the general rule when appointed to an office … In any case, it appears to me that a visit up there would be highly recommended. It could be good for the King to know you for another time. You don't necessarily need to criticize the Danes during your conversation."[12]

There was just no time for such a visit. Helge had a thousand other things to think about. Besides, it was very possible that King Haakon VII was careful not to show any great engagement in the conflict due to his own Danish background[13] and the great political implications the case could have. However, a telegram was sent from the Arctic vessel *Polarbjørn* to commend King Haakon VII's sixtieth birthday on 3 August 1932:

> From Eirik Raudes Land allow me to send Your Majesty my honourable congratulations on the occasion of your 60th birthday.
> Governor Helge Ingstad

The next day a reply was received:

> Thank you for received congratulations.
> [King] Haakon [VII]

And with that, the *Polarbjørn* chugged along on its journey northwards, towards new land and new wilderness adventures.

East of the Great Glacier

> The first musk-ox is following the line of the shore which rises by terraces to the foot of a steep mountain wall. Machine-like he barges along, up and down over sand dunes, straight through stream beds and formidable falls of rock. All these he treats as nothing, being himself such a mountain of rugged flesh. And old, no doubt, he is too; yes, a veteran. He is shy one horn, his neck and shoulders are heaped high with an enormous welter of mane, while his shaggy belly-hair trails like a fringed rug and almost grazes the ground. Beneath this surging tide of hair and wool, head and legs are so well submerged that the creature most resembles a black boulder overgrown with moss.[14]

This opening paragraph from Helge's book *East of the Great Glacier* conveyed not only his first impressions of the East Greenland coast, but also set the theme of his entire book. Along with his expedition crew, he arrived there in late summer 1932 on the *Polarbjørn*. Helge did have duties as governor, but more importantly, he was there to explore the land. Once he had departed for Greenland, he put politics behind him and took up the role of trapper and nature lover.

In addition to Helge, four other men were part of the expedition group. Sverre Røstad was a farm boy from near Levanger, where Helge had practised law, and who possibly could have known Helge from before. Then there was Arne Jacobsen from Tromsø who had two years' trapping experience on the Arctic island of Jan Mayen. Sverre and Arne, both twenty-one years old and good workers, were planning to trap on their own farther in near King Oscar Fjord by Kap Petersen. Bjørn Western, a nineteen-year-old Oslo boy who had only recently graduated and received his radio certification, was responsible for sending all messages via radio and telegraph. Many of the messages were sent in code; it was all very secretive.

We hear very little about these three men in Helge's book. It was mostly Norman Andersen, from northern Norway, who came to be Helge's trusted trapping companion on the many strenuous sled trips. Andersen was a seasoned Arctic man experienced in seal hunting, mining, and trapping on Svalbard. This particular Greenland expedition was initially planned to last for two years, although Helge was formally appointed governor for only the first year, awaiting judgment from The Hague.

On board the *Polarbjørn* were three other Norwegian expeditions, fifty-four men in total who were all going to various places along the

Members of Helge's East Greenland Expedition. From left: Helge, Sverre Røstad, Norman Andersen, Arne Jacobsen, and Bjørn Western.

eastern coast of Greenland. Two were summer expeditions including a number of scientists: zoologists, oceanographers, botanists, and archaeologists, plus two journalists. The third was a winter expedition headed for Myggbukta that planned, among other things, to raise blue arctic foxes to import to Norway. This team had their own doctor.[15]

Helge's expedition needed a long list of equipment, and it helped to have had spent time in the Arctic to know what to take. Obtaining dogs proved to be the greatest challenge. There were few experienced sled dogs of suitable breeds in Norway, and the owners were reluctant to part with them. Not only were Helge and Andersen each planning a team, but Røstad and Jacobsen also needed dogs. Western, who would be more stationary, could make do with females and puppies. The year before, Helge had bred dogs specifically for the Greenland expedition, but after his initial plans were thwarted he sold all the dogs. It was just as well; it was doubtful the breed combinations he chose would have had thick enough fur to handle an Arctic winter. The only dog he took with him in the end was an Alsatian blend named Bobby whose sire had been on an expedition to the South Pole. Three Greenland dogs were borrowed from a factory owner in Trondheim, but two got very ill and died soon after. Fortunately, Helge was able to buy six full-bred Greenland dogs from a previous expedition to East Greenland. These were offspring from the dogs Roald Amundsen had taken to Svalbard, and were shipped to Greenland from there.

Røstad and Jacobsen were the first to disembark at Kap Petersen with equipment and dogs. Next stop was Myggbukta. Two planes and their pilots were also on board the *Polarbjørn*. During the summer, these were going to be used for aerial surveys and charting maps. When the boat arrived at Myggbukta to unload the planes, the winter residents came climbing over the railing in hope of receiving mail from the homeland, and perhaps a bit of whisky. One of them was "old-timer" Gustav Lindquist, a quick-witted northerner. After much struggling, the planes were finally unloaded. The first one took off from a patch of land along the beach used as an airstrip and headed north towards the Danish area. Shouts and hoorahs rang out, and old Lindquist waved his whisky bottle, yelling, "If you fall, fall on a Dane!"[16]

Western and a total of seventeen dogs were put ashore at Antarctic Havn, and on 1 August Helge sent a telegraph to his parents from the *Polarbjørn*: "Arrived Antarctic Havn ... stop ... muskox outside cabin door ... stop ... beautiful landscape ... stop ... I like."[17]

Helge and Andersen first planned to familiarize themselves with the area and then build huts at Flemming Fjord and Nathorst Fjord farther out towards Davy Sund. They would then return to Antarctic Havn to collect the dogs before winter. As they were put ashore at Nathorst Fjord, they watched the *Polarbjørn* sail off and disappear into the distance. There they stood with that vast unknown territory before them waiting to be explored.

The first task was to build huts, an important part of marking the Norwegians' presence and use of Eirik Raudes Land. The first to be built was a hut they dubbed 'Kaare's abode,' named after Helge's brother, at the base of what they called Raven Mountain. Then they chugged along the coast in a little motor boat and set up similar small huts along the way. They were simple structures of prefabricated sections that were quick to put together.[18] The most important thing was to erect a building.

From the top of the highest mountain around Nathorst Fjord, they had a magnificent view. Far out to sea, the drift ice lay like a long, white stripe along the coastline. Helge glimpsed the top of a mast out on the water and thought about all the many Norwegian polar vessels that had for generations sailed along these coasts.

From Nathorst Fjord, they planned to head along the coast towards the west to Fleming Fjord, but the drift ice proved to be difficult and dangerous. The east wind had packed the ice tight in the fjord and the men couldn't see a channel through anywhere. Finally, they spotted a small opening and agreed to give it a try. But before they knew it, they were completely surrounded by ice again and began drifting out towards Davy Sund. It was a desperate situation. Arctic ice has crushed many a boat throughout the years, causing several people to die. The two on this little expedition boat slept in shifts that night. At first light, Anderson woke Helge, having discovered an opening in the ice not far away. With a lot of struggle and strain, they were able to pull the boat across the ice and move onward.

They built their winter home base at Fleming Fjord and quite appropriately called it *Heimen*, "Home Sweet Home." From here, they planned to venture out by dogsled to the surrounding areas to hunt. One of the most important things they had to do before winter set in was to secure a decent supply of seal meat for dog food. They dug a deep depot into the ground and secured it well with a cover of driftwood logs to keep out polar bears and foxes.

Farther inland they also set up a tent to be used as a stop-over station during their winter sled trips. They found a good, suitable spot, pitched the canvas tent, and supported it with turf and stones. While they were building a framework for a cache, a huge herd of muskoxen wandered by on the other side of the river. They shot one of the bulls, and with that the cache was full. Now they could safely move onward, or so they thought.

First they returned to Heimen. The plan was to motor the boat up along the coast to Antarctic Havn, but the ice lay too thick. They had to pull the boat ashore and take the long journey over the mountain by foot, which took three days. When they finally arrived, they looked so ragged that only one of the dogs recognized them. The others growled or took cover in their doghouses. Western, on the other hand, was thrilled to see company.

The first thing they did was build a hut for the radio and communications equipment and raise a 30-metre-high mast. This was Western's first real job after receiving his official diploma and he was eager to get started. However, "that ancient [telegraph] motor of ours, a pathetic contraption which had seen service in the German trenches, would sputter, heave a sigh, and stop dead … For a long time there was only one thing about the motor that was up to scratch, and that was the exhaust. It happened on more than one occasion that the entire wireless staff would lie stretched full length abed, overcome by the noxious fumes."[19] Finally, the apparatus surrendered and contact was made with the outside world. One day Helge received a "wireless message" from his old trapping buddy from Canada, Hjalmar Dale, who was in Norway visiting and had stopped by to see Helge's parents in Bergen. On another day, he heard his brother Kaare's voice on the radio delivering a lecture on China.

Snow began to fall, and with it began the long dark season. The foxes' furs had begun to grow full and beautiful, and trappers Helge and Andersen grew impatient to take off hunting. They had used their time in Antarctic Havn well and had sewn much of what they needed to journey inland: tent, dog harnesses, and mukluks. Then came time to leave, and at the beginning of November the two men took off across the dark winter landscape, each mushing their own dogsled. Their plan was to first stop at Heimen to collect dog food and then push farther east across the land.

The first challenge they faced was a long stretch of loose snow. The dogs sank so deep that the tips of their noses were barely visible and they had to hurdle their way forward. Helge and Andersen took turns breaking the trail on dogsled, their skis sinking a metre into the snow. Neither had taken along a pair of snowshoes.

As they approached Heimen, however, a distressing sight caught them utterly by surprise. Despite all their efforts to secure their depot of seal meat, polar bears had gotten in and ravaged their supply. It was supposed to have lasted them the entire winter, but now nearly everything was gone. Hunting in the dark of winter was not an easy task. There was nothing else to do but to make it to their inland tent as soon as possible; at least there they had part of a muskox carcass. They struggled on through more loose snow, then fog came rolling in. Arriving at the tent, all they found was a pole with a piece of canvas on it. The foxes had taken the rest. Luckily, the animals had not taken the main cache so the men at least had food for themselves and the dogs. Still, the situation grew serious. They pitched a second tent they had brought along, but the howling wind piled the snow up around the sides making their sleeping area smaller and smaller. On the inner walls of the tent, a layer of frost formed so thick that if one of them accidently touched the canvas it created a downright avalanche. A solution presented itself one day when the wind was blowing at its worst and the men found an abandoned bear den. After several unsuccessful attempts to set up the tent again, they decided to crawl into the den. It was the best night they had had in a long time, sheltered and warm. After this, they started building igloos Inuit-style as often as snow conditions permitted.

Helge and Andersen were completely dependent on catching a muskox. It seemed, however, that the place was now empty of the big beasts, even though the expedition team had seen large herds of them in the fall. Out hunting one day in a heavy fog, Helge and Andersen nearly didn't find their way back to the tent. Had they not heard their dog Storm barking in the distance they might have ended up missing their camp entirely. Just as their meat supplies were nearly depleted, they happened upon a lone, old muskox bull. Its meat was hauled back to Heimen, where there was a feast for both man and animal.

As they grappled with the worst of the darkness and the storms, Helge sat one night in his wet sleeping bag skinning a frozen fox and later complained:

As I slave away at my task, it dawns upon me what a driving force is woman. I think of the hundreds of worthy men who, year after year, endure no end of hardships in the frozen wastes of Siberia, Canada, and Spitzbergen [Svalbard] – for the sake of her personal adornment. Here I sit in the winter darkness in a narrow tent off in the mountains of Greenland, struggling to pull a frozen fox-skin inside out over the poor creature's head, my toes meanwhile frozen and aching – for her! And she – sailing along on high heels, she enters some brightly lighted shop, demands a fox fur, and acquires it. She drapes it over her shoulders, twists this way and that in front of the glass, and smiles with pleasure. Then on her way she gaily trips, out into the thronged street, where there are other women draped with fox, and men who turn to stare. And as she nestles her cheek into that fluffy embrace, a rapturous breeze fans her feminine heart, knowing herself to be captivating and having the thing she wants. But otherwise – why, damn this frozen fox-skin that never seems to want to come off![20]

The men's next venture away from Heimen was to the areas around Nathorst Fjord and along the coast way out to Davy Sund. A hard struggle, no doubt, against the storms, ice, and fog, but they caught several foxes. By Christmas, they wanted to reach "home" at Antarctic Havn, and see Western once again. But then the heaviest fog either of them had ever experienced rolled in. Their compass stopped working and they were left to their own sense of direction, not always as accurate. As they were crossing a river, the solid, slippery ice sent both men and dogs sliding a great distance.

They finally arrived at Antarctic Havn on Christmas Eve to the great delight of Western and his puppies. They hadn't been there since the beginning of November and it felt good to sit in a warm, sheltered cabin again.

Their Christmas Eve dinner, prepared by Western, couldn't have been better. On the menu, listed as five courses, was:

1
A light portion of lamb & cabbage stew (for tradition)
A bottle of lime juice with a generous portion of cold snow water
A bottle of aquavit
2
Cured sausage of Norwegian horse
3
Lingonberry jam with whipped cream
Cakes from Western Bakery
4
Coffee and cakes (telegrams distributed by telegrapher Western)
Liquor
Cigarettes (pipe for Hooded Seal Andersen)

5
Cigars
Whisky[21]

Telegrams were handed out and read, a whole pile of them from friends and family. Two telegrams,[22] however, stood out from all the others and must have surely surprised and pleased the fellows. They were both addressed to "The Trappers at Antarctic Havn":

Best wishes for a Merry Christmas
[King] Haakon [VII]

Merry Christmas and Happy New Year. Next year we can meet in Greenland.
Hope you catch many foxes.
Crown Prince Olav and Märtha

A few days after the holidays, the men departed from Antarctic Havn on their longest excursion towards Scoresby Sund, the largest and longest fjord system in the world.[23] The upper branch of this tree-like inlet system, Nordvest Fjord, extended into the Norwegian-occupied area, Eirik Raudes Land, the same area where Helge and Joe had planned their expedition that never was, "the land where everything flows of milk and honey." It must have been quite special for Helge to have finally made it there – particularly in his role as the Norwegian governor of an occupied territory. In his book *East of the Great Glacier*, he wrote:

Our opponents at the Hague would be anything but elated were it ever to become known that we had cut across the mountains with houses on our sledges and that we had made ourselves at home on the shores of that far-famed fjord … But never mind! The project was formally and practically in order, and other than that, the responsibility was mine and no one's else.[24]

What the Danes actually knew or thought about the Norwegian governor travelling well beyond the Norwegian territory carrying loads such as these was never mentioned. But the chance of meeting any Danes was small, and Helge was a practical, experienced Arctic man who just chose the best route. Besides, he wanted to see as much as possible of what that fjord had to offer. Those secretive words of Smedal, no doubt, were also in the back of Helge's mind.

They stopped and loaded up at Heimen and headed out again one day in February. With the housing materials heavily loaded onto two dog-sleds, Helge and Andersen travelled inland, up the mountain ridge, and down along the river that led to Scoresby Sund. Transporting a house was no easy task, even if it wasn't much of a luxury home.

As the men travelled along the steep, narrow, winding river path, three huge muskoxen suddenly appeared in front of them blocking the entire width of the ravine. "'Hey, there!' I yelled at length at those three. 'Go on and get out of the way!' They coldly snubbed my request. Whereupon I gave them blue blazes, making no effort whatever to conceal my opinion of them," Helge wrote. The beasts refused to budge and contemplatively lay there chewing their cud.

I howled and waved my arms ... Pausing for breath, I was relieved by Andersen who took up my cause and for five full minutes abused them roundly in his singsong north-country Norwegian. But not even that made the slightest impression upon our friends up ahead ... Thereupon I spread full sheets to the wind and let fly with the very quintessence of the English language ... Rich and juicy expressions I had picked up as a trapper in the Canadian Northwest flew to mind and these I spat fair in the teeth of the enemy. And that worked![25]

The beasts finally moved and the men were able to travel onward. They soon arrived at the bottom of another valley. While camping there one night, the men heard the howl of a wolf nearby. At first, they thought it was just the dogs, but gradually a chorus grew between the dogs and wolves, a sing-song exchange that pierced through the dark Arctic night. The men later dubbed the area Wolf Valley.

As they continued south, the land opened up and soon they spotted something glimmering white in the distance: "Scoresby Sund! There lay the fjord like a revelation of splendour as we rounded the last bend in the river. Of all I have seen in the Arctic north, nothing has ever produced so deep an impression upon me."[26] An endless forest of icebergs loomed up from the frozen fjord, some shaped like mighty cathedrals, others like "vaulted portals or glistening spires. And over all, shone glittering sunshine reflected in the myriad mirrors of snow and ice."[27] Behind this was the bluish inland ice with its sloping glaciers and dark crevasses.

They carried westward over Jameson Land and farther towards Nordaust Fjord, seeing more fertile ground here than anywhere else: carpets of heather, grass, spring flowers, and small willow trees scattered in patches, along with numerous signs of fox tracks. "I visualized the scene as it must appear in summer: the land, framed between ice-capped mountains and a blue fjord ... Ah yes, here was the place at last where one could settle down, live and die, and leave the world to take care of itself."[28] Just like what Helge had imagined when he wrote to Joe: "a trapping ground for the rest of our lives."

Here too marked the boundary of the Norwegian-occupied area farthest in on Nordvest Fjord. Spurred on by Smedal's secret letter, Helge's expedition claimed a private occupation on 27 February under Andersen's name. The triangular area covered a good portion of Jameson Land from an east point in Davy Sund farthest out in the Carlsberg Fjord, to west along the northern boundary of Eirik Raudes Land, and south to "Wolf Valley" extending from Scoresby Sund. (See map pg 262.) In other words, the area they claimed included a large upper portion of Jameson Land but was still a good distance away from the Greenlanders' colony at Scoresby Sund on the farthest southern tip of this peninsula. Whether they used Andersen's name to make the claim because of Helge's position as governor or whether Helge himself later withdrew from being included in the claim is unknown.

Following their map, the small expedition team eventually ended back up in Eirik Raudes Land. They caught sight of a valley, headed towards it, and continued inland to explore what this part of Norway looked like. They were not disappointed. The vegetation was lush and covered with tracks of both fox and muskoxen. The territory looked promising in every way, a dream spot for Norwegian trappers. They unloaded their materials with the intention of returning and setting up the hut after they collected more supplies from Heimen. However, the journey to their base became a tremendous feat in a heavy snowstorm. The men dug a snow cave, where they stayed for three days. The storm packed so much snow around the entrance of the cave that many nights they were in danger of suffocating and only barely managed to dig themselves out in the morning. Their small Primus stove functioned poorly due to so little oxygen and caused quite a risk with its poisonous fumes. All they had to eat was raw polar bear meat.

After a rough two months, the men were thin and bearded by the time they made it back to Antarctic Havn. It was only after they saw themselves in the mirror that they understood how difficult their journey actually had been. But as soon as they arrived back in Antarctic Havn, Helge sent a telegram to Smedal: "Regarding trapping prospects refer to 'svalis.' Ingstad."[29] "Svalis" stood for Norway's Svalbard and Arctic Ocean Survey, who in practice was Hoel, to whom Helge also sent a long, coded telegram:

> With Norman Andersen on month-long excursion to Scoresby Sund … February 27 Andersen occupied Nordaust Fjord country as well as inlet of Nordvest Fjord … I acted as summoned witness … entrust sealed occupation document to my radio telegrapher for disclosure of key words from Svalis … If key words absent, document is to be returned me unopened … kindly notify view of the matter and provide any key words … quick reply very important.
> Ingstad[30]

The International Court of Justice Decision

The international court ruling from The Hague concerning the territorial dispute between Norway and Denmark over East Greenland was scheduled for the beginning of April 1933. For Helge and his men waiting in that far north telegraph station, anxious anticipation grew despite their feelings of a sure win for Norway. On 5 April a message came ticking in from the south. Western slowly, quietly walked into where all the men were sitting in the cabin with a telegram from the Justice Department in his hand. He laid it down in front of Helge without saying a word. It read: "Unfavorable verdict at The Hague … Governor position is revoked by first minister; police authority also recalled … question of your desired continuation of the winter is being considered; further notification later."[31]

Not a word was spoken, but one man after the other got up and walked out. They stood there looking out across the land that glistened white in the spring sunshine: "all that we have made so much a part of ourselves and reckoned as our own."[32] That evening Helge wrote in his journal: "Today is my last day as Governor of Eirik Raudes Land. Well, I have long learned to take things as they come."

Norway had lost on all counts. The Court found the Danish arguments more convincing despite historical evidence from the Norwegian side and despite the fact that the Danes' only presence in Greenland was confined to the southwestern coast. Reactions in Norway to the decision from The Hague were many and varied, and a political dispute ensued between those who had been for a negotiated settlement and those who had supported the occupation. When the case was brought up for discussion in the Norwegian parliament, the majority of those in the foreign ministry blamed the ruling party government, Bondepartiet,[33] for allowing itself to be blindly led by the experts. The Labour Party raised the question of impeachment of the minority government but let it go with a particularly sharp statement.[34]

The same day the court decision was announced, a telegram from Stockholm arrived for Helge's parents from their son's old trapper friend: "I am with you in mourning the decision at The Hague. Hjalmar Dale." Fridtjof Nansen's widow also telegraphed Helge saying, "Every cloud has a silver lining, welcome home, sincere greetings, Sigrun."

No one had heard from Helge yet. He sat in Greenland wondering what he should do. He was no longer the governor. However, there was no reason why he couldn't stay for another year as a trapper. The East Greenland Treaty of 1924 still allowed for Norwegians to live and trap in the area for at least another twenty years. It was only a sovereignty issue of the country that had been settled. Helge wanted to stay, as did his companions.

Another telegram came from the Norwegian Foreign Ministry asking whether he would be interested in taking an administrative position at Svalbard. Before he replied, he telegraphed home to his father asking him to find out more about the position. Olav wrote to Carl Platou, the director general of the Ministry of Justice, and inquired. He seemed to be particularly concerned with finding out what effect such a position would have on his son's further legal career. Platou responded immediately: "The position is titled Governor Attorney, but the person will in fact be the Governor Representative as it will be of a very independent character."[35] He explained that this would be of importance for appointment to future legal positions, but it would by no means guarantee any future county governor seat.

Helge contemplated the offer and decided to accept. In a letter to a friend, he explained his reasoning: "Svalbard is now one of the last Arctic areas that Norway has left." No doubt it was also because his father wanted him to take the position with thoughts of a future legal career.

When the first boat arrived at East Greenland with mail, Helge more clearly understood the reactions back home. In a long letter from Olav dated 23 June 1933, he reassured Helge and said that his time as governor must have been an interesting period, an experience he certainly would not have wanted to be without: "I don't think your youthful experiences could have culminated any better." In other words, he assumed Helge's longing and desire for travel and adventure were coming to an end and that it was now time to plan more seriously for the future. From Olav's point of view, the appointment at Svalbard was both an ending and a beginning in this regard.

Olav then reminded Helge that the last boat to depart from Bergen for Tromsø (and further to Svalbard) was to leave on 15 October. Time was short. At the end of his letter, he commented on the continuing debate over The Hague court decision in which both Smedal and Hoel fared poorly: "self-willed directives are excused and praised if they succeed, but are a serious affair if they fail. And now both Hoel and the Council of Arctic Administration is very unpopular."

Olav took on the responsibility of both organizing and shipping equipment to Greenland for the remaining expedition members there, and to Svalbard for Helge. He also dealt with inquiries concerning the publication of Helge's book *The Land of Feast and Famine*, which was being published in various languages and countries. These were not simple tasks that Olav took on, and Helge could hardly have left so freely on his expeditions had it not been for his father's help. The letter from Olav ended with a heartfelt plea:

> You know that I have never tried to hinder any of your excursion plans since you achieved your diploma. But now I think there is no harm in setting roots. You've led a rich life filled with experiences that you can look back on with many fond memories. You have also supplied yourself with a financial basis. Now we hope to see

you pulled together and in one piece ready to face your next stage. If you don't like a governmental position, you can always find new opportunities when the time arrives. In the meantime, you can write a book at Svalbard.

Farewell then. A thousand greetings. Welcome home.

Pappa

Helge also received some letters from his mother telling him that she wept when the verdict from The Hague was announced on the radio. Nevertheless, she congratulated him on his new position at Svalbard. She also had some news about Hjalmar Dale: "He's been to see us several times. He was so nice and fit. It seems he is travelling around [and] has a good amount of money. He mentioned he was thinking of a trip to Italy or Egypt, but not at the moment. He was disappointed that you weren't here this time either. We served him a reindeer roast for dinner. It was supposed to be a Canadian dinner. He is a very handsome fellow."[36]

Helge was unable to leave Greenland until there was a relatively open passage in the ice large enough for the *Polarbjørn* to get through. Andersen and Western, still in Antarctic Havn, and Røstad and Jacobsen at Kap Petersen, all planned to stay in Greenland. They had decided to try their luck at trapping for one more year. Officially, Helge was also responsible for the expedition that second year. He wrote a long list of instructions on how each of them should collaborate in terms of responsibility and equipment.

Waiting for the boat to arrive was a period of increasing restlessness, but not idleness. There was enough to do, and muskoxen migrating through the area made for a few hunting trips. On 22 July, the men received word that the *Polarbjørn* had finally arrived farther north at Myggbukta after a long delay due to the ice conditions. Meanwhile, down at Antarctic Havn the men worked at getting everything clean and tidy, and Andersen and Western even painted the outside of the cabin white. They wanted it to look nice for the boat's arrival. On 23 July, Helge wrote in his journal that it was incredibly warm and windstill, almost unbearable for the dogs, who dug holes into the dirt to escape the heat. "We've got everything organized and prepared," he wrote, "just the floor left to wash. Strange to think the boat is coming. A year of my life has passed, amazingly too fast. Greenland has been a good area to where my thoughts will often return."

Helge with his typewriter on a dogsled.

A day later the ice broke at Davy Sund and message came by radio from the *Polarbjørn* that the boat would arrive the following afternoon on 24 July, with Adolf Hoel on board.

Helge took four of his dogs from Greenland with him to Svalbard: Spot, who was now a lead dog, Ulrik, Norbeck, and Laila, all of East Greenland descent. Once on board the *Polarbjørn*, Helge sent a telegram home to his father telling him of his expected arrival in Norway on 29 July at Ålesund, where he planned to stay for three days: "Send pin-striped clothes, hat, shoes, raincoat, etc. as well as 400 kroner to Hotel Scandinavia."

Helge's arrival back in Norway caused quite a stir in the media. At the Palace Theatre in Oslo, newsreels showed clips from the expedition every day for an entire week. There was great excitement, despite the defeat at The Hague.

Later, Helge spoke little of his time in East Greenland, perhaps for several reasons. One being that he did not like to dwell on a lost case, but rather preferred to look ahead to new challenges. He remained convinced that Norway's loss of East Greenland was a great injustice. However, he also witnessed that times change, and that the Greenland case eventually became just an interesting curiosity in Norwegian political history. He also wanted to disassociate himself with the attitudes of some of the key Norwegian figures involved in the case when the Second World War broke out. What was once an ideological and patriotic fight for Norwegian Arctic interests became, for some, a movement towards extreme-right politics that led to their joining the Quisling Party and supporting the German occupation of Norway.

Because of the war, new negotiations over the East Greenland Treaty were postponed until the year 1947. The agreement was then renewed, with a few modifications, for an additional twenty years. In 1967, the agreements of the treaty were terminated.

Helge's book, *East of the Great Glacier*, about his year in Greenland was first published in 1935, just two years after The Hague court ruling was declared. It was written while Helge was living in another Arctic area with strong Norwegian traditions: Svalbard. The political issues of East Greenland that were such a heated topic the year he was governor are hardly mentioned in his book, except for the passages in which he wrote about the dogsled journey to Scoresby Sund and when he described the expedition members' reaction to the verdict from The Hague. "You shouldn't cry over spilt milk," he used to say. Instead, the book is primarily a descriptive narrative of the nature in Greenland – of the animals, mountains, flowers, ice, and Northern Lights. It was a book in which some of Helge's most poetic sentiments were best expressed, perhaps his way of saying, *Look at what we lost.*

4   SVALBARD

The land arises from the drifting ice
Glaciers and mountains hazed in the misty white
The cool summer sun dreams it into a lull
On the border of the freezing pole.[1]

In October 1933, Helge was again headed towards the polar north on what was to be the last boat of the year going in that direction. This time he was going as the Governor Representative of Svalbard, a Norwegian archipelago in the Arctic Ocean located about halfway between continental Norway and the North Pole. After he had sailed a few days northwest from Tromsø, these Arctic islands appeared to rise up from the sea like a crown of steep weathered mountains, treeless valleys, and glaciers stretching all the way to the water's edge. This was Svalbard, the most northern place on earth where people lived and worked.

The coal boat carrying Helge chugged along in the heavy seas. It travelled north along the west coast of Spitsbergen, the largest of the many islands of Svalbard and the one that has historically attracted the most commercial interest. For centuries, the people here made their living by whaling and coal mining.

The waters were open as far as Helge could see, with only an occasional iceberg slowly drifting by. The relatively open ice conditions were due to the warmer currents of the Gulf Stream that flows north up the western coast of Spitsbergen. This was quite different from the packed ice conditions Helge had to sail through to reach the coast of East Greenland. Sailing up along Spitsbergen, Helge glimpsed stretches of fjords that cut deep into the coastline. At a latitude of 78° N, the boat reached the mighty Isfjorden, an area rich in coal deposits. Svalbard's layers of coal testify to a time when pre-fossilized life abounded on these islands, when strange reptiles ran around in magnificent ancient forests and fertile plains in a climate more similar to that of today's southern Europe.

Entering Isfjorden, Helge's coal boat made its way around a small headland where he glimpsed several houses dotting the landscape. It was Kapp Linné, where the Norwegian government had built a lighthouse and the Isfjord radio station. As the boat sailed farther down the fjord, flanked by majestic mountains on either side, the sky filled with flying sea gulls, terns, eider sea ducks, and guillemots. Close to land, a steep cliff seemed to move and come alive as a million birds took flight. They sailed on past the Russian mining facility of Barentsburg and not long after another Russian plant, Grumant, where they spotted a small cluster of houses just below the steep mountain and piles of coal. The boat then entered the smaller fjord called Adventfjord, where at the very end lay a fleet of boats moored at the dock, mostly coal boats waiting to be loaded. Farthest in and up the shores lay the coal mines along with some small houses and barracks – this was Longyearbyen.

Helge was no doubt aware that life in a mining town, in that narrow valley surrounded by steep mountains, would be completely different from life in the open Arctic. But then, he wasn't planning to stay in this valley, Adventdalen, more than necessary.

Hallvard Devold, one of the first trappers who occupied and planted a Norwegian flag on Eirik Raudes Land, was now in Kapp Linné, the headland at the entrance of Isfjord. When he first heard that Helge had been appointed governor representative, he wrote and congratulated him, then asked him to bring an extra case of Black & White whisky when he came. "I can make up for it with fox furs," he offered Helge. In his letter, Devold also gave what must have been quite a daunting description of Longyearbyen: "several nice people, many from Bergen, but a certain 'temperament' is maintained in the halls that not everyone is equally enthusiastic about."[2] The trapper had also recommended Helge to bring sled dogs from Norway since they were scarce in Longyearbyen and difficult to obtain. Helge heeded his advice and brought along his lead dog Spot, a striking white and black Greenland dog, and three more of the same breed.

After returning home from East Greenland in early September, Helge had not had much time to prepare before the last boat sailed to Svalbard in October. Equipment had to be arranged and ordered for both Svalbard and for the remaining expedition members on Greenland. The furs from Greenland had to be transported to Norway in proper packaging and then shipped to England, where they would be sold at the fur auctions in London. Even though the Norwegian expedition to East Greenland had not been a success in terms of annexation, it had been a financial success for the trappers. Their 248 white fox furs and 35 blue fox furs earned a total of 23,000 Norwegian kroner, which was divided equally among the expedition members. In a letter Helge wrote, "It all worked out in the end, despite not ending up as capitalist trappers. The camaraderie between my men was first class and I am particularly satisfied with that. They were all robust, determined fellows."[3]

Helge was still officially regarded as leader of the trapping expedition in East Greenland and therefore had to arrange for both equipment and instructions to be sent to the remaining members. In a long and detailed letter, he instructed which equipment should be transported home, sold, or abandoned when the men left Greenland the following spring. From the sounds of the letter, he didn't completely rule out the possibility of returning as a trapper *in a few years*. Even though the country was now definitely Danish territory, the 1924 East Greenland Treaty still gave Norwegians the right to use the cabins they had built and the trapping lines they had established.

In order to manage all these necessary tasks and arrangements before leaving for Svalbard, Helge was able to marshal help from family and friends. Olaf managed most of the issues concerning finances and correspondence, a heavy workload in addition to his own job and affairs, as well as contributed good advice. Helge's childhood friend Odd handled the Tax Office in Askim, outside of Oslo, where he was a practising physician at the time. Helge had reported residence there before departing for Greenland, but hadn't paid particularly close attention to his tax returns while away. The amount he owed was based on a taxable income of NOK 5,000 after Odd had sent a letter to the Tax Office explaining how impossible it was to determine income when you were a trapper in Greenland. "You certainly got off cheap there!" he wrote to Helge.

Another who helped organize the equipment for Greenland was Herman Mehren, to whom Helge wrote and possibly, for the first time, conveyed a clear impression of his interests in conducting scientific studies in the Arctic region. Helge thanked him for his help and then ended the letter by saying, "It will be nice to talk with you in Oslo ... would you mind reserving one of your lovely ladies for me."[4]

Kaare, who was in the middle of preparing for his final exams in French at the Foreign Ministry in Paris, still found time to help by organizing some of the equipment and providing advice for his older brother: "I hope your heart's not taken away too quickly in Oslo. You are a pure amateur when it comes to women and can be ridiculously gullible at times. You can get as many of them as you like so just take it easy, you have plenty of time. Yes, that's the advice I can give you.[5]

Helge must have been quite the hit with several young Oslo ladies judging by the number of letters that arrived for him with the first boat to Longyearbyen that following spring. No fewer than five "hopefuls" clearly expressed, to varying degrees, how much they missed him and that they hoped to see him again when he came south for the summer holidays.

Land of the Cold Coasts

The coal mine cableway, hanging 600 metres overhead and running right through the middle of Longyearbyen, played its monotonous tone. They called it the Mountain Harp. This was a busy community where despite the short shipping season, from May to October, they still managed to export 300,000 tons of coal a year.

Coal boats, and a few other Norwegian Arctic ships, were moored alongside the quay seeking shelter and fuel at Longyearbyen. Two boats, however, stood out from the others: one French tourist boat and another Norwegian vessel called *Lyngen*. Both of these had sailed as far north as 80° where the polar ice bathes in the midnight sun.[6]

Svalbard had officially been under Norwegian sovereignty since 1920. When Helge arrived there in 1933, he came as "governor representative," as there was no resident governor position then. The official governor, and Helge's superior, was John Gercke Bassøe, county supervisor of the country's most northern county of Troms. He resided on the mainland and in the winter could only be contacted via telegraph. Helge's new position was governor with adjunct responsibilities and duties: the Norwegian government's representative in the archipelago. Both Helge and his father had hoped that the title would be full governor. The Svalbard position was actually a step down from Helge's previous post in East Greenland, but they assumed it would change when a permanently based governor position was created. And then, they presumed, Helge would be the most likely candidate.

Longyearbyen when Helge lived there.

A residence was not yet provided for the governor representative. Instead, Helge had to move into a barracks-like building he rented from Store Norske Spitsbergen Coal Company. He had a small room with a couple of office machines. The office manager was an old polar skipper, not exactly a speed demon on the typewriter, but kind and good in every other way.

Longyearbyen, at the time Helge first arrived, was a simple, small community with low, weathered houses and about 650 inhabitants in the winter. Some had lived on Svalbard for twenty to thirty years and had only been to the mainland on a few short trips. They seemed to belong on that island in the same way as the wild reindeer and grouse did. Around twenty-five to thirty trappers were also spread across the island and two Russian mining communities supported about two hundred people.

Longyearbyen was a class-divided community with two halls where the people would gather in the evenings. One hall was for the officials and the other for the workers. The officials' lodge was old and worn;

small openings pierced the walls here and there – evidence of strong storm damage. People would stuff their handkerchiefs into the holes to stop the wind blowing in. The furniture was also a bit shabby with a few springs sticking out of the upholstered chairs in one place or another. But it was here that people would come to play cards or practise target shooting and, on rare occasion, be served cream cakes. The other hall, for the workers, was even more worn and sparse.

Another quite noticeable difference was the relationship between private company leadership and the representative governor's position. "Initially, when I arrived," said Helge, "Spitsbergen Coal Company had taken charge of Svalbard, you could say. They were the powerful element up there which wasn't always quite right, and one I had to take authority over because there were things under Norwegian jurisdiction that had to be accounted for. It was an interesting experience."[7]

A third distinction between the workers, rife with potential conflict, was the scarcity of women in Longyearbyen at the time. Some of the officials had taken their wives and children along. The coal company workers, however, were there on their own. Many of these men were often from small places along the northern mainland coast where the women stayed at home to care for the farm and children while the husbands worked on Svalbard or hunted and fished the Arctic Ocean. This shortage of women in Longyearbyen made for fierce competition over the few who worked as waitresses in the canteen or as nurses. In order to maintain the peace, Helge proposed that only men be hired as waiters, but the majority rejected this idea.

In Helge's play *Last Boat*,[8] the first piece he wrote about Svalbard after his return to the mainland, Helge vividly describes how the differences between people in a small, isolated Arctic community play out in conflict, intrigue, and love after the last boat has gone and how a person fears starving to death in the Arctic darkness. In his old age he said, "There were experiences, very intense experiences, from Svalbard and the period of dark and people's shifting moods that the play was based upon."[9]

How much of what he wrote in the play was taken from real life is unclear. It is, however, striking how little he tells of Longyearbyen's social life in the documentary book he wrote about Svalbard, *Land of the Cold Coasts*. It was probably easier to write of such conflicts without directly referring to people who were still living. But he does write about how the isolation affected the people and made it difficult to form close friendships:

> So we begin to know each other. Know what we're told before it is told and what will be answered before it is answered. And we know exactly what the tone and smile mean. This is not to say that we know each other well, far from it. What often happens is that the innermost is hidden and the past blotted out ... forces are at play and walls erected between people.[10]

Helge's duties as governor representative on Svalbard were very different from those he had conducted as governor of East Greenland. While in Greenland, his primary duty was to establish a Norwegian presence in the area but otherwise hunt as he so desired. At Svalbard, he had a number of specific official duties to deal with, ranging from enforced salary deductions for child support, paternity cases, bankruptcies, and help in filling out loan applications for a farm on the mainland, a dream of many of the miners. His law degree and experience from his law practice in Levanger were quite useful. Serious crimes were not much an issue, but he did have to deal with a few small conflicts. Generally these were resolved by talking to each party involved, such as when one of the waitresses accused a colleague of stealing a pair of her shoes. It nearly became quite the drama in the women's quarters.

The part of Helge's work which interested him most, without a doubt, was contact with the hunters living on the various islands in the area. These men were not used to being visited by the governor representative. His predecessor never had a dogsled or a boat. So they were all a bit amazed when Helge suddenly showed up at their cabins.

Lead dog Spot and the other wonderful dogs from East Greenland had all been placed in a large dog kennel near Helge's residence. Their numbers grew quickly, and soon there were several dogs to make a team. Every evening after work he would take off on his dogsled, even in the dark of winter when the only light was from the stars and the flickering aurora borealis. He preferably drove with six or seven dogs with Spot in the lead. It was such a beautiful and powerful dog team that people talked about it throughout the town.

One of his first long sled trips was to the northern tip of the main island of Spitsbergen. He first followed the coastal ice northwards then headed up into the mountains and across the inland ice. He spent the nights in either a tent or a snow cave. Along the way, he stopped in at a few of the trappers' cabins before making it all the way north of the island.

This was really how Helge learned the country. Svalbard reindeer, smallest of its kind, were protected, as was the small herd of muskoxen that had been introduced from Greenland. Every once in a while he saw an Arctic fox or a polar bear, but he wasn't interested in hunting. It was not part of his assignment this time. He wanted to study the wildlife, in hopes of possibly providing a few ideas and suggestions for conservation.

Seasons of the Year

Christmas at Svalbard could be one of the most challenging times of year for this isolated community. Many longed for their loved ones back home. For Helge, he was not only thinking of his family in Bergen but also his fellow trappers still in East Greenland. Although he had met several nice people in Longyearbyen, he had not experienced a camaraderie similar to the one he had with Andersen, Western, Røstad, and Jacobsen. The East Greenland expedition was formally considered Helge's as it was he who had organized and financed it. But his interest in it was based on much more than just practicalities; he felt a strong connection to the land that Norway had lost. Just before Christmas, he sent a telegram from Longyearbyen to his pals in Greenland: "We wish you a pleasant year and a Christmas celebrated with Western cake and muskox steak ... 'Spot' and I send greetings especially to 'Bella' and 'Peik.' Ingstad."[11]

As the weeks passed, the long, dark nights grew shorter. The sun slowly returned and with it a more vibrant life compared to the quiet times during the dark period. Green started showing along the valley floor and hillsides and melting water gurgled in between the stones. People came out of their homes nodding and smiling to each other when they met – it was, without a doubt, spring. Helge took great pleasure in the flora of Svalbard, which greatly resembled that of East Greenland. He didn't know much about plants, nor was he inclined to learn more as his main interest was in the Arctic wildlife. However, he still marvelled over the vegetation and enjoyed the tufts of colourful plants that clung to that barren ground so far north. They became the friends he lovingly described in his books and poems:

Small tufts of blushing saxifrage, a few mountains tinged with blue and some lovely yellow wild roses along a river. The colourful, fragrant flowers brighten in sharp contrast over the land, a graceful touch against the naked gray. Along with the pleasure of seeing them is the admiration of their hard life. Even as few as they are, or perhaps for that very reason, they seem stronger than the richest floral displays in the south.[12]

In the summer of 1934, Helge travelled home to the mainland for vacation. One of his most important tasks that first year had been to plan and build a governor's residence, which he did, beautifully situated on a small ridge by the white church overlooking the fjord. While in Bergen, he needed to advertise for a housekeeper since the residence would be ready to live in when he returned. When his mother Olga got wind of this, she immediately took over the hiring process. She didn't trust her son's understanding of what was needed to run a suitable official residence, nor did she feel secure in his choices of women he might be charmed by. When he returned to Longyearbyen after his summer holidays, Miss Kristine Lund, whom he described as "a little older and harmless lady," accompanied him.

Sled Trip to the Russians[13]

According to the Svalbard Treaty of 1920, which awarded Norway sovereignty over Svalbard, other countries were allowed to keep their commercial rights but were subject to Norwegian jurisdiction. The Swedes had sold their mining rights to Norway several years earlier and now their mines lay empty and deserted. The Russians, on the other hand, had two mining communities in full operation: Barentsburg, the headquarters, and Grumant, a smaller operation.

Towards the end of January 1934 – in the midst of the darkest period on Svalbard when only a faint strip of sun appeared on the horizon at noon – Helge decided to inspect the Russian mining communities. Both of the mines lay farther out along Isfjorden; Barentsburg was about 40 kilometres from Longyearbyen and the Soviet settlement of Grumant about halfway between the two. Had he had his own boat, and if the fjord had been passable, it would have taken only a few hours. But since a boat wasn't an option, Helge had to travel by dogsled. This made the trip a little longer but was a good excuse for a nice excursion. A telegram was sent to notify the people at the mines of his expected arrival.

Visiting the mines was a part of the duties as governor representative. The distance wasn't great, but crossing the area by dogsled in the long, dark days and changing weather conditions could create difficulties for the journey. Just to be safe, Helge took along a fellow from the Longyearbyen mining company who not only was supposedly an expert, but also claimed to be familiar with the territory and with mushing.

Departing Longyearbyen was not without drama. On a dark and windy morning, the harnessed dogs stood about on the river ice. A small crowd of people had enthusiastically gathered to watch the preparations, which Helge noted in his journal:

> Those who show up when a man is about to take off on a dogsled are hard, spiteful people who don't come there to show kindness to those leaving, but to take delight in his misery. They know from experience that a pack full of polar dogs about to take off on a long journey, after being cramped up for ages in a dog kennel, are capable of almost anything. And [the spectators] also know there is good chance that these rascal dogs can cause quite a scene in which suddenly the driver finds himself playing the lead role in a chaotic comedy.

And quite right! The entire team lunged into a massive fight and Helge had his hands full in sorting out the tangle of harnesses, straps, and growling dogs. "The Expert," "a little fellow with a face without space to smile," as Helge described him, didn't lift a finger to help. "Life is full of messes," was his only response as he stood leaning over the fence watching intently. Eventually order was restored, Helge's fingers were frozen stiff, and the dogs eagerly pulled through the dark towards Adventdalen and up across the glacier. It was a wonderful team, eight dogs in all, loosely tied together with Spot, now a fully trained lead dog who obeyed Helge's every command, leading the way.

Higher up, the snow grew deeper, making it difficult to keep moving. At the entrance of a valley called Colesdalen, Helge stopped to wait for "The Expert," who was lagging far behind. When he finally caught up, he explained that he had just worked two straight shifts at the mine without any sleep. Helge gave up on any hope of making the trip without stopping and instead decided to pitch a tent to let the guy sleep. Helge did all the work tying up the dogs, but when he crawled into the tent exhausted, he saw that nothing else had been done. "The Expert" sat there on his rolled up sleeping bag with a cold primus stove in front of him and his hands tucked up under his chin: "I've been thinking of things," he said. "Obviously not the cooker," quipped Helge, who lit it and made dinner. Later while lying in their sleeping bags, the men's chat turned to the subject of women. Mentioning a mutual acquaintance back in Longyearbyen, "The Expert" said dreamily, "She reminds me of a girl I once met in France." A philosophical francophile miner up there in the cold north? Life was full of surprises, thought Helge.

The next day they continued across Colesdalen towards Isfjorden. In a deserted cabin at Kapp Laila they came upon a snoring Russian with a vodka bottle at his side. He had been sent by the Russian director to escort the Norwegian "gubernator" to Barentsburg. Helge, who was used to travelling alone, suddenly had two companions with him. However, unlike "The Expert," the Russian proved to be a valiant skier.

The last stretch along the west side of Isfjorden posed major challenges. The entire hillside was covered with a sheer layer of ice and only a few patches of snow. The dogs struggled to get from one snow patch to the next. Every now and again, they lost their footing, slid down the ice, and scrambled to regain their foothold. Visibility was difficult and the men could only sense the valley and fjord with its drifting ice lurking below in the dark. Suddenly, Helge's sled took off, sliding down an icy slope. The dogs didn't have a chance and the sled skidded closer and closer towards a dark cliff. Helge, who had been sitting on the load to brace it against the slope, threw himself onto his stomach in front of the sled and was able to grab hold of a rock frozen in the ice. Spot sensed the danger. He stood very still, looking at Helge as if to say, "What now?" Helge caught sight of a patch of snow a little farther across the hill and gave the command, "march, left." Spot heaved hard in his harness, slipped, struggled to get his footing, and slowly led the others safely to the patch of snow. This was the first time Spot saved Helge's life in the wilderness.

The Russian now led the way along Grønnfjorden to Barentsburg since he knew this territory well. The wind and snow blew hard, and every once in a while Spot would stop to rub a paw over his eyes and give a yelp. Helge would have preferred pitching a tent to spend the night as

"The Expert" was still trailing far behind, but the Russian was relentless. He wanted to get back – to warmth, fellow comrades, and vodka. "Not much farther," he said for the hundredth time. Eventually they stood at the top of a steep slope, where the Russian motioned to Helge that he and the dogs should head down first. Plummeting down in the pitch dark, Helge didn't have a clue what was beneath them. The sled toppled but he was able to right it again and after an intense struggle eventually reached the bottom of the valley that led to Barentsburg. From here the going was easier and they finally arrived at midnight – after fifteen hours of strenuous mushing. The dogs were put into an empty stall next to a small barn full of black-spotted pigs. Helge and "The Expert" couldn't wait to crawl into their sleeping bags.

However, that was not to be. In Barentsburg, there was great excitement about having the Norwegian "gubernator" arrive, and Helge and "The Expert" were quickly ushered into the director's house, where festivities had been arranged and waiting. Helge could not believe that anyone would be up waiting so late for them especially since he had been quite vague as to when they would arrive. At the director's residence, they were greeted by a woman named Marusa, "who was dark, voluptuous and smiled impishly." Then Helge greeted the director, a friendly and likable Ukrainian, and once again indicated that it was time for him to retire for the evening. But again, Helge was mistaken. The director gestured towards the living room, where Helge spotted a generously laid table. "How he ever knew so surely of my arrival that night and for food to be prepared and the table set remains to be one of the greatest mysteries."

The table was filled with a variety of delicacies: grapes, apples and oranges, jars full of finest caviar, huge hams and smoked Siberian salmon, jams, apricots, candy, vodka, bubbling wines, and large, elaborately decorated cream cakes – enough to feed a regiment. It was now two o'clock in the morning. Since "The Expert" and Helge had not eaten since earlier that day, the extravagance was well received, though short-lived. After three servings of Russian cabbage soup followed by caviar, several portions of salmon plus large chops from the black-spotted pigs, followed by potent cream cakes, they excused themselves from the table and wandered up to their rooms. Neither of them felt particularly well.

Helge spent the next two days inspecting the facility. People were friendly and hospitable everywhere they went. The place, however, had a strange, unnerving atmosphere. Large pictures of Lenin and Stalin hung on the walls, and Helge thought it peculiar to walk through this miniature Russia. More than two thousand men, women, and children from all across the vast Russian empire, from the Siberian tundra to the fertile Black Sea regions, were clustered together on this far northern windswept island. Long-bearded men dressed in homespun coats, tall felt boots, and wolf-skin hats trudged by in the snow. They were like figures in a Tolstoy novel that Helge read so eagerly when he was younger. In this Arctic Russian community, every little detail was like an exact replica from Lenin's country. Helge even noticed a "home" where children were put during the day so their mothers could work. Production in Barentsburg and Grumant was not as high as in Longyearbyen despite the fact that there were several more workers. The Russians, however, were relatively new to the field and it took time to master Arctic mining.

When it came time to leave Barentsburg, Helge tried to explain that they could return to Longyearbyen on their own. But the director would hear nothing of it and sent eleven men to escort them back. Their sleds were heavily loaded with all sorts of gifts: four large cans of caviar, a large supply of red apples, and an enormous cream cake decorated with a large bouquet of lifelike flowers made of fondant – not a very suitable load for a dogsled.

The dogs were in good condition after having rested for two days and they took off at a swift pace towards the foot of the mountains. Spot had one ear pointed forward and one back, which he usually did when he was most eager. When Helge turned to look, his escorts were far behind and he soon lost sight of them. Up over the mountainside the dogs kept pulling and the sled kept tilting. All went fine for a while, but then the entire sled flipped onto its side, landing on top of Helge's legs. He couldn't get loose from under the sled without having to unload the cream cake and the entire lot, so he decided to wait for "The Expert," who wasn't far behind. The man soon pulled up next to Helge's sled, then just stood there staring and surveying the problem: "'Hurry up,' I said. He jumps as if startled. Then just continues to stand there in an apparent daze; his awareness seemingly miles away while I lie there with my head pointed down the slope. I then quite forcefully say, 'Lift the sled man!' A light bulb suddenly seems to switch on in his head and he says, 'Oh, that,' and helps me get loose."

They decided to spend the night at a cabin near Kapp Laila to see if their entourage of escorts was still following in their tracks. After a few hours, they showed up. Inside the cabin, the Russians reached into their sacks and pulled out some large loaves of dark bread, caviar, and vodka. They fired up the small wood stove until it was glowing warm, put candles in a few bottlenecks, and dug into their food and drink. The discussion was loud and lively, in Russian, German, and Norwegian. Later in the evening, the Russians went to their sleds and returned with their instruments: a balalaika, flute, violin, and two guitars. They took off their shirts and sat bare-chested in the steaming-hot cabin. Soon the sounds of "Volga, Volga" and other well-known Russian tunes echoed through the winter night air. The party continued on into the wee hours of the morning. At some point, Helge grabbed a reindeer sleeping bag and crawled into a snow cave to get some sleep.

The next morning, they all headed for the second Russian mining community, Grumant. They took a shorter route along the edge of some ice at the foot of the steep mountains rather than crossing over the mountain. The slab of ice, however, grew smaller and smaller until at the very tip they were splashing in surface water, to the dogs' great dismay. Although they were able to see the lights of Grumant in the distance, they could go no farther as they were surrounded by open water. They had no option but to turn back and take the heavy route over the ridge.

When Helge and "The Expert" arrived at Grumant, their escorts were lagging far behind. But since these two were terribly hungry after a long day without food, they found their way to a hall where people sat eating dinner. Using their best sign language, Helge explained who they were and that they were hungry. A smiling man who seemed to be of some influence invited them in and put them alongside the others. The meal was excellent, but Helge was a bit baffled by the difference between the two mining communities when it came to receiving guests.

Full and satisfied, Helge came out of the hall to see his escorts standing talking to a man. Helge went over and greeted him using the few words he knew in Russian, which included "*thanks for dinner.*" The man, who turned out to be the director, looked shockingly at his guest. With the help of a German-speaking doctor, Helge was informed that the "gubernator" had mistakenly had a meal in the workers' mess hall. The director looked dismayed but Helge assured him that the food had been wonderful. The Norwegian "gubernator" and his assistant were then led to the Russian officers' mess hall where a feast lay waiting of the same calibre as the food orgy they fought their way through at Barentsburg. Once again, Helge and "The Expert" ate and after the meal were entertained

Summer training of the sled dog team with helper Per Barkost. Spot is the lead dog.

with Russian music and dance. The next day, it was a straight route back to Longyearbyen and to the waiting dogs back at the kennel. This time, though, without an escort.

The trip to the Russian mines did little to change Helge's skepticism of communism. But in meeting the people behind the political facade, he experienced the Russians as friendly and hospitable people. There in that Arctic country, it was possible to enjoy each other's company despite political divides.

Risking Life and Health[14]

Later that winter, a message arrived at the governor's residence: a hunter on the east coast of Spitsbergen needed help. Mental problems due to loneliness and the long, dark winter had put his life at risk. Waiting another month for the sun to return was not an option. However, it was not easy to find someone willing to make the trip with Helge across Spitsbergen during the dead of winter, so he had to go alone. He and the dogs were used to it, and he hoped to find a trapper along the way who could help him get the patient back to Longyearbyen.

The necessary equipment was loaded onto the sled, and on a cold and windy morning Helge and his dogs took off inland towards Advent-dalen with the faithful Spot leading five powerful male dogs. The lights from Longyearbyen soon disappeared behind them, and then all was dark – not even a star in the sky shimmered through the snowstorm. All the maps to where he was going were incomplete, so on his way Helge stopped at the cabin of trapper Hilmar Nøis, about a day's journey from Longyearbyen. Nøis had spent about twenty winters in the area and knew where the sick man's cabin lay and marked it on Helge's map and said "just by a river and a valley." Another Norwegian living in Nøis's cabin, Sverre Skoglund, agreed to accompany Helge to help.

The men had been travelling for two days when suddenly they got caught in a violent storm. The wind swept both dogs and men sideways and there was nothing else to do but to set up camp and wait it out. For three days they were weather-bound with temperatures fluctuating between freezing and melting. On the fourth day, the weather improved and they hurried on.

They finally reached the coast and the area Nøis had marked on the map. But his description of "just by a river and valley" didn't match up. For four days, Helge and Skoglund scoured the area, first north and then south, down every valley and bay looking for any sign of a cabin. Their supplies were running out, and if they did not find the cabin soon they would have to turn back. Through snowstorms, rain, and fog they carried on farther south. Finally, the contours of a cabin appeared in the fog and they anxiously approached. Was the man dead? There was good reason to fear the worst, but no, he was still alive. He looked puzzled and distant as he stared at the first people he had seen in a long time.

It was agreed that Skoglund and the trapper would take the shortest route back to Nøis's cabin where the man would stay until spring. Helge would take another route back to Longyearbyen over the mountains and glaciers.

After spending a night in the cabin, Helge headed inland towards the steep slopes and deep valleys. In the winter dusk, it was hard to determine just how steep some of the slopes were. Once he had to send one of the dogs ahead to see if it could reach the valley safely, then Helge slid down with the sled and rest of the team. They continued on with the dogs running in the dark at a galloping speed when all of a sudden, man, sled, and dogs disappeared out of thin air into a several-metre-high snowdrift. Helge managed to get to his feet, check to see if he was still in one piece, then started to dig the dogs and sled out of the snow. Amazingly, none was hurt and the sled was intact, so the only thing to do was to carry on. The wind picked up and soon it became a raging storm. Helge had no choice but to stop and set up camp. He was feeling a bit limp but assumed it was due to that incredible tumble in the snow. Then he discovered he had lost a bag of seal meat, direly needed for himself and the dogs, and now only had a bit of seal blubber and a few rusks to live off. If the weather improved, however, he could quickly make the last part of the journey.

But the weather did not improve. The wind continued to blow, and Helge and his team struggled daily to cover ground. Finally, they reached a glacier Helge thought they could cross and more easily make their way to Longyearbyen. Helge divided what little food he had into small portions for himself and the dogs, then continued through the deep snow towards the top of the glacier. The weather held at first, but dark, threatening clouds came blowing in as they neared the top and then a great storm let loose. The danger of sliding off a cliff was now too great, and Helge had no choice but to dig a snow cave and crawl inside like he did on East Greenland. There he lay for two days in his damp sleeping bag "like a mummy in its tomb." After a while though, he realized that the melting snow inside the cave was making his sleeping bag even more wet, creating a lack of oxygen. He decided he had to set up his tent, and after much struggle, he finally got it up and assembled. Although the tent was protected by a wall of snow, the wind blew in and soon everything was covered with an inch-thick layer of snow. For four days, he lay at the top of the glacier like this, in a wet reindeer-skin sleeping bag with his food supply quickly running out. Helge was completely exhausted, had a rising fever, and knew that if he didn't do something drastic, things could go extremely wrong.[15] He had no other choice but to rely on Spot.

With the last of his energy, Helge hitched up the dogs, ripped down the tent, and tied himself to the load on the sled with his sleeping bag over him. "Go home," he commanded Spot, and that clever lead dog again seemed to sense the seriousness of the situation. He headed towards the valley, down along cliffs, and in between deep crevasses. The sled tilted a few times and sailed down the hill sideways, but Spot found his way and they finally reached Adventdalen, and from there the journey was quick and smooth. "And there in the darkness shone a cluster of golden lights, Longyearbyen. With my mind full of images of the barren, harsh wasteland, it struck me odd to come upon a human community in this mountain hollow. When the dogs caught wind of the mining camp, all fatigue and toil was forgotten and they took off running towards the Governor's place. Here we ate to our heart's content and the world was once again light and friendly."[16]

Helge did not recover as quickly as expected after his hardships travelling across Svalbard. His body continued to fight a fever, and he had to spend much of his time in bed. Longyearbyen's excellent doctors could not determine what was wrong and suggested it might be best for him to get to the mainland on the first boat that spring. Helge had little desire to do so. Much was occurring concerning his position and rumours were spreading that a resident-based governor of Svalbard was going to be appointed. Naturally, Helge was interested in this position and wanted to be in Longyearbyen when Prime Minister Nygaardsvold and the Foreign Affairs Committee, under the leadership of C.J. Hambro, and several members of parliament came to Svalbard with the boat *Bergensfjord* in July. It was clear, however, he wouldn't be able to wait that long. He made a compromise with the doctor to stay until Bureau Chief Lund arrived with the first boat to prepare for the prime minister's visit. Helge would then return home on the second boat, the *Inger 6*.

Somehow, the media on the mainland got hold of Helge's story about his gruelling journey to the east coast of Svalbard. The Norwegian Business and Maritime newspaper (today *Dagens Næringsliv*) published the

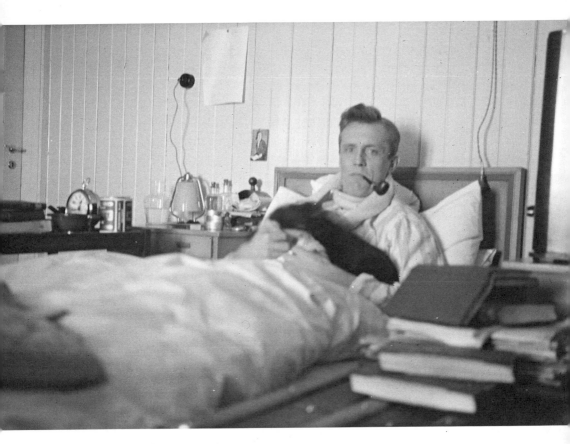

Running the government from bed – with a sled dog puppy on his lap.

story of the rescue expedition and wrote that Helge had gotten sick, returning in serious condition. This of course caused a great deal of anxiety for his parents in Bergen, who knew nothing of what had happened. Helge's reply to their telegram was intended to calm their concerns rather than reveal the full truth. He was also convinced that the story would all blow over in time:

No reason to be concerned for me. I am well. Have sent in health certificate as requested. Bit of a negative at first mention but emphasize that the negative aspect was due to having to travel on official duty to the rescue of human life … stop. Despite unfavourable timing, I have applied for holiday leave from the end of June for a two-month period on the grounds of rest after mentioned trip … stop. Come what may, I'm calm about the matter … stop. If you were to see me now at the time of this writing, you would be wholly reassured. Journalists exaggerating, all of passing insignificance. In good spirits. Regards, Helge.[17]

As the telegram mentions, the "unfavourable timing" was that it had now been decided to establish a full governor's position with permanent residence in Longyearbyen. Helge wanted to apply and thought his chances were good, but the required health certificate concerned him.

The first boat of the season arrived at Svalbard and with it the mail everyone so eagerly awaited. This time, however, there were no love letters for Helge. He must have greatly neglected the ladies the summer before. However, he did receive a fan letter from a very young, unknown admirer from Lillehammer by the name of Anne Stine Moe.[18] His brother Kaare had also sent a letter from Paris: "I spoke the other day with a young woman who, when she received your book [*The Land of Feast and Famine*] had clipped out your picture and kept it on her nightstand. You see, you have much to live up to."

A Twist of Fate

Following his father's advice, on 12 June Helge submitted his application for the position of governor of Svalbard. If he were to pursue a career in the civil service, then Svalbard was a good choice from Helge's perspective. On 1 July 1935, parliament decided to establish a full governor's position based in Svalbard, and Helge was immediately appointed temporary acting governor until the position was officially recruited. The first thing he did as governor was leave Longyearbyen for what was supposed to be a two-month holiday and recuperation, arriving in Bergen on 9 July. He had little baggage with him and the dogs stayed behind in Svalbard since he was planning to return in the fall as the new governor. A judge by the name of Irgens was sent to Longyearbyen to fill in during Helge's absence.

In Helge's suitcase when he left Svalbard that spring were two manuscripts: his completed work about East Greenland, *East of the Great Glacier* (published later that November) and a draft of his play about Svalbard, *Last Boat*. Helge had not been idle during his two years in Svalbard as far as literary works go.

Immediately upon returning home, Helge was admitted to the regional hospital, where tuberculosis was diagnosed in one of his kidneys. The contagion in his knee as a child had flared up again due to the serious hardships he had endured during the storm and rescue mission. The doctor recommended surgery to remove the kidney as soon as possible, but Helge hesitated. He pictured a life of being a perpetual patient and feared that his days in the Arctic wilderness were over. In despair, he consulted a kidney disease specialist recommended by his friend Odd to see if there were any other options or cure. The physician replied that he agreed with his colleague: surgery was the best option. But he also reassured Helge that a person could live a long life with only one kidney without any physical problems. Helge took it calmly, underwent the surgery, and thought of his grandfather's words: "Everything will work out, because life always finds new forms – the transitions, however, can be trying."

Helge's hospital stay was long. He was admitted on 8 August but not operated on until January 1936. He was also very secretive about his illness. Tuberculosis was still considered shameful, and those closest to him were not allowed to tell others what ailed him.[19] Typical of Helge, he actively explored and researched the cause of the disease. In a letter to the local paper, he suggested they interview renowned nutritionists about the possible link between Arctic people's simple diet and the high incidence of tuberculosis among them. He proposed that this would be of great importance in understanding the high tuberculosis rate in northern Norway.[20]

Prior to Helge's lengthy hospital stay, the final decision regarding the full governor position was announced: it was not in his favour. By Royal Decree on 23 August 1935 a state geologist by the name of Wolmer Tycho Marlow was appointed governor. Marlow was no novice to Svalbard and had actually held the same position as Helge the year before him.[21] The government's justification for the appointment was that they wanted a mining engineer who could also function as a mine supervisor. In other words, they wanted to do away with the division of power in Longyearbyen between the Store Norske mining company and the Norwegian state.

Helge took the defeat calmly, perhaps was even a bit relieved, as he needed more time to recover from his illness and to ponder why it all happened. As usual, he looked ahead and thought about what to do next. He no longer felt he needed to heed his father's advice about taking a permanent position, and instead began his search for new adventures.

Helge's book about Svalbard marked a clear shift in his style of writing that would continue for the rest of his life: from the adventurer's narrative stories to the researcher's thorough exploration and study. The book also showed a new focus, most likely influenced by the East Greenland case: an interest in Norwegian discoveries and settlements in faraway places. In conversations we had during his last summer at our cabin, he said:

> One thing that then fascinated me greatly was the reason for it all; Svalbard was one of the most integral parts of our old history. The past has to be seen in context of Norwegian expansion during Viking times, partly towards the east, partly to Svalbard; it has to do with expansion over to Finland and all the way to the Soviet Union. There are sources that show the discovery of Svalbard in the early 1100s. This was all part of the great expansion that strongly grew towards the west across the ocean. It is certainly one of the most remarkable elements of our history, how Norwegians traveled to the Faroe, Shetland and Orkney Islands, to Scotland and Ireland where there was a Norwegian king continuing on across the ocean to Greenland with Leif Eiriksson and Eirik the Red. I began [to explore] this a good deal in the Svalbard book, but not in great depth; I started it … and continued with it for the rest of my life.

5   OUT WEST

Helge refused to be defeated by his illness, so quite determinedly began his road to recovery. With exercise, lots of fresh air, and a good swig of cod liver oil every day he slowly began to feel better by Easter 1936. The months recuperating gave him plenty of time to contemplate his future. Meanwhile, his book about Greenland, *East of the Great Glacier*, was published. Although it received good reviews from both critics and readers, it didn't draw as much attention as *The Land of Feast and Famine*.

As spring returned, so too did Helge's restlessness. The Norwegian Ministry of Foreign Affairs offered him a position with responsibility for Arctic issues, but he declined – no doubt to the great dismay of his father, who had now clearly stated that it was time for him to settle down and think about a career. As spring turned to summer, Helge decided to rent a place on the Myrstad farm in Engerdalen to continue his recovery, including fattening up on sour cream, and to finish his play about Svalbard, titled *The Last Boat*.

Around the same time, the political issues regarding Greenland once again drew the public's interest. Rumours circulated that Denmark was planning to sell Greenland to the United States, which patriotic Norwegians considered an ultimate violation. On 6 May 1936, a group called the Norwegian-Danish Plan was formed to "work for a revision of the injustice that occurred when Greenland was separated from Norway in 1814. The alliance will also work for just resolutions of other issues related to the dissolution of the union between Norway and Denmark which also hinder genuine friendship between the two countries and thus understanding within the Nordic region." Announcements for the meeting were marked "confidential" and sent out. Despite the assumption that the group was bipartisan, a large majority of the members were involved in far-right-wing Norwegian politics. These included government ministers and members of parliament as well as farmers, polar explorers, and northern residents. However, one of the directors of this group petitioning for "old wrongs to be righted" was the Norwegian politician Vidkun Quisling, who later betrayed his own country during the Nazi occupation of Norway. Helge's name was on the list of supporters of the Norwegian-Danish Plan, but there is nothing to indicate he was more involved than signing his name on the petition. Instead, he had other adventures on his mind.

Initially, Helge tried to revive his old plans and re-establish his connections for travelling and exploring Siberia. The lack of reply from the Russian government about a possible travel permit, however, put his plans on hold once again. Helge then decided to set course for New York and Washington, DC, to promote the English version of his book *The Land of Feast and Famine* and to find an American publisher for *East of the Great Glacier*. He hoped to hold a few lectures and then make his way across America for a few months. He would head for the west coast, from where he could then travel to the Soviet Union if his permit ever came through.

America

In the fall of 1936, Helge walked off the ship *Stavangerfjord* onto the dock in New York. In complete awe, he walked around the largest city he had ever visited. He watched all the busy people hurrying about, nobody taking much notice of one another. Spending time alone on the tundra, Helge had never felt lonely, but here in the big city of skyscrapers, he did.

Eventually he made a few contacts and didn't feel quite so alone. He was able to arrange some lectures at the Norwegian Seamen's Church as well as at a number of other Norwegian organizations, but received little pay. This improved though when he was invited to speak at the prestigious Explorers Club. Dressed in a tuxedo, Helge delivered his first lecture in English in front of several thousand people in an enormous hall. After his talk, many of the club's better-known members came up and thanked him for an interesting lecture.

The Great Depression had left its mark in the United States: workers at General Motors had to strike to get higher wages, and President Franklin D. Roosevelt struggled to get his reform program, the New

Deal, accepted and implemented. Helge wrote home in detail about these events thinking that his father would be especially interested.

From New York, Helge continued on to Washington, DC, where he was invited to stay with his distant relative, Norwegian minister Wilhelm Morgenstierne (later appointed Norwegian ambassador). A highlight of his stay was a lecture he gave on 17 December in connection with the National Geographic Society's prestigious Christmas lunch. In an elaborate room in the Society's building, about thirty "fine" people attended, including the president of the Society, multi-millionaire and son-in-law of telephone inventor Alexander Graham Bell. Helge wrote:

> We ate well and afterwards President Grosvenor held a speech for me in which he said something to the extent that I was an outstanding explorer and a worthy successor to Nansen and Amundsen. Oh well, I suppose they felt they had to say something nice. Personally, I think it was pointless having all these esteemed gentlemen sitting there for my sake when they could have been doing much more useful work during that time. However, they had to eat lunch and this way they got it for free. After the meal, we went down to a smaller lecture hall and I held my talk about the [Caribou Eaters of Northern Canada] and showed some slides. I spoke as I usually did without a script and it went well. They told me I was a hit. Afterwards I spoke for a while with the great men.[1]

Helge's lecture led to a request to write an article about the Caribou Eaters for *National Geographic* magazine, where he was also offered an office space in which to work.[2] He hoped the magazine would also be interested in some articles about his stay in Greenland and Svalbard.

At the same time, he attempted to coordinate a countrywide tour with an organization called Norwegians Worldwide (Nordmanns Forbundet) but received an apologetic reply that their program for the coming year was already fully booked. But he had more encouraging news to share a few days later, which he shared with his parents on 29 December 1936, the day before he turned thirty-seven years old:

Dear Mother and Father,
Just a few, quick words. There is a slight chance that I can get my name on the map of Canada in relation to some of the great lakes

Helge's parents Olav and Olga followed their son's travels through a frequent exchange of letters.

at the headwaters of the Thelon River[3] ... Tomorrow I will finish my article about Canada for National Geographic Magazine. I think it will be good ... the question, however, is whether they will want my Greenland article afterwards ... the entire article is written in atrocious English.

There was much to see in Washington. The White House did not impress him much but he thought the Capitol was magnificent. However, "the Norwegian painting by Krohg titled 'Leiv Eiriksson Discovers America,' was placed in a most inopportune place. In fact, the history books here hardly mention earlier Norwegian discoveries of the country." Helge bought an American history book and had great pleasure reading about the country. He was interested in everything that had to do with the pioneer period: cowboys, wars, and indigenous people. Reflecting on that period of history, he said, made my blood rush and wish that I were there myself."

From the 169-metre-tall Washington Monument, he wistfully looked out across the populated land and thought of how *"the free Indians"* had once lived here. The notion suddenly struck him that people who had fought in the wars between the white settlers and native nations, as well as people who had once been slaves, were still alive. "The entire culture wasn't more than a couple hundred years old."

The intention of Helge's visit to America was to promote his books. So one day he boldly went to the editors of the *New York Times* and said it was about time they interviewed him. They sent a journalist, and Helge dictated an article and provided a few pictures to be included when the interview was published. He also tried his hand at screenwriting, penning a film manuscript about the lives of people living in Arctic regions with the working title, *Flight from Fame*. Helge was quite pleased with the somewhat autobiographical manuscript: "I myself think it is quite good, but then that could be a bad sign. For now, I'll just work on a rough draft and send it to an agent. I will also suggest they put me to work during the filming; perhaps try me as an actor. But here I lack faith in myself."[4] The reply from the film company was discouraging. They said he no doubt had many exciting stories to build upon, but recommended he contact a professional writer to further develop the manuscript.

Life in the big American cities was radically different from existence in the Arctic, but he still enjoyed it, at least for the four months he was there. He bought a tuxedo and courted many beautiful young women. Helge had no lack of confidence or ambition. When he did not receive word from the Soviet Union about a possible Siberia expedition, he set his sights on travelling out to the American west and possibly to California. On 5 February 1937 he took the train to Chicago, but did not care for the city and its miserable wind. He thought the people were in too much of a rush. Sometimes they ran down the street so fast he almost yelled out "Stop thief!" but then realized they were just in a hurry.

Helge gave a few lectures at the Chicago Geographical Society and the Adventurers Club. His first lecture was held after a large lunch, which Helge later described in a letter to his parents: "Irritating that they have to pester the speaker with food right before a talk. I didn't eat much."[5] The lecture hall was filled to capacity with three thousand people, and in the middle of the stage stood two chairs and a microphone. Helge bowed, then sat down on one of the stools. "I was obviously nervous as I could hear my own heart beating … (because) I was going to talk and lecture off the top of my head without a manuscript in this confounded English language that not only do we have to understand, but also accurately pronounce so others understand us." Helge approached the microphone and launched into his presentation, and everything went much better than expected. "The man who worked the sound said 'very fine' and the lecture brought in 150 dollars."

At the end of this long letter home, Helge shared his thoughts about the life he led: "I can't very well continue to aimlessly travel around like this forever while all sorts of people struggle with serious situations. But it's so rotten hard to decide on a steady job in Norway, which I may end up not even liking, but for the time being I'm not worried … It is so great to be able to explore the world. A person should be given two life cycles: travel during one and devote himself to society during the second."

After a while, he grew tired of Chicago and realized it was not the place for him. He bought a $35 train ticket and headed for Denver, then on to Colorado Springs, Albuquerque, and the Grand Canyon in Arizona: "I quickly understood that this was good country because I almost immediately spotted jack rabbits and rattle snakes. I got off in a town called Phoenix and soon found out that I was among decent people. They smiled and asked how I was doing and were only moderately in a hurry."[6]

Phoenix had about fifty thousand[7] residents and lay on the upper edge of the Sonoran Desert surrounded by massive, scorched-dry mountains. Cacti of all shapes and sizes grew on the stony, reddish-brown desert floor and beautiful flowers sprouted up after an infrequent rain, up through the sand almost overnight. The original inhabitants, the Hohokam peoples, were followed years later by pioneers in the 1800s, who discovered that the land was quite fertile if it were only watered. Cattle drivers, missionaries, gold diggers, and the cavalry all left their mark on the city. This was, to Helge's wholehearted delight, a quintessential "frontier town."

Cowboy Life in Arizona[8]

What was it that made this Arctic enthusiast decide to go south to Arizona and Mexico? The landscape and climate were so different from the

Arctic region, but perhaps this was exactly what he needed at the time. Helge had been quite ill not so long ago, and that dry, warm climate in Arizona was good for recuperating. Helge was perhaps also searching for that old pioneer spirit he felt was so sadly lacking in the larger cities. However, the strongest pull to this area was his desire to search for a link between the indigenous peoples of Arizona and those in Arctic regions. During his winter nights spent in Canada, when he had sat around the fire with the Caribou Eaters, he listened to stories of their ancestors who left their land and journeyed southward a very long time ago. Later, he also learned Apache and Navajo tribes spoke an Athabaskan language, similar to that of the Caribou Eaters, and that they originally came from the north. This piqued his curiosity. He wanted to discover if there were any traces of the legends and stories of the Caribou Eaters in stories of these southern tribes.

In Phoenix, he got to know a man by the name of Vic Householder, a widower with three sons, who was a driving force behind many of the local volunteer activities. Vic was an avid outdoorsman, and one of his hobbies was collecting rattlesnakes in the desert. He had a big heart and a large group of friends. Vic took Helge under his wing and began introducing him to everyone worth meeting in Phoenix. Helge was presented as the previous governor of Svalbard and East Greenland, which opened up several opportunities to hold lectures for many organizations there, albeit free of charge. In a letter to his father, Helge wrote: "I have absolutely fallen in love with this country. Friendly people and sunshine. A strange mixture of cactus-filled deserts and majestic blue mountains. The only thing missing is water. Just a tad bit of water would transform the entire desert into a fertile garden."[9]

Eventually, though, Helge wanted to leave the city. The mountains in the distance pulled at him, so he asked around and got a job as a cowboy on a ranch – the Rail S Ranch in Dripping Spring Valley. After he had been provided with a horse, the next big challenge for Helge was actually riding it. He had never been on the back of a horse in his life. He wrote in his journal:

27 March
Tomorrow I'm going to ride for the first time in my life. I'm anxious. When I told them that I had never ridden before the cowboys had a good laugh. It was almost like saying a man couldn't read.

28 March, Easter Sunday

At sunrise, we were up. Buggy rode out to herd the horses into the corral, one intended for me. I got the nicest horse, jumped into the saddle and tried to appear calm. First, a couple times around the corral and then out into the woods. It went well, though terribly bumpy when trotting. The whole time I had the impression that the horse had a deep disdain for my incompetence.[10]

Eventually, he grew more confident and wrote home to his parents: "At the start, my butt was really sore from the riding, but I've made great strides ... We are 1,000 metres above sea level and the air is so fine, we can really breathe it in. I'm not overexerting myself in any way. Riding is easy, enjoyable, and actually jolly good fun ... Had you seen me here you probably would have envied me. The valley is incredibly beautiful and I couldn't have come to a more enjoyable place."[11]

Helge gradually grew more confident with his riding, until one day a rattlesnake rustling in the bushes spooked his horse and sent him flying onto a cactus. The long needles from the prickly pear cactus, about 230 of them, pierced their barbed ends deep into Helge's backside. The pain was one thing, but quite another for him to stand there with his rump in the air having bawdy cowboys plucking those cactus needles out of him. They managed to remove only 55 of them; the other 175 spikes dug deeper in with every painful bump on his horse. The other cowboys laughingly reassured him that, "after a while they just rot away."

Helge eventually learned to master the art of riding and enjoyed the freedom a horse gave him to move about the terrain. Every morning at sunrise he left to hunt the ever-abundant jackrabbits. But despite how much he enjoyed this lifestyle, restlessness came creeping in. Helge wanted to take off farther up into the mighty Superstition Mountains. Just as their name indicated, a certain sense of mystery surrounded these mountains and not many dared to venture there. Rumour also had it that people died up there searching for an old Spanish gold mine.

Helge found work with a bunch of cowboys at a ranch located about 1,500 metres high tending to a large herd of cattle and over a hundred horses. Every day at five in the morning, two of the men gathered in the horses and herded them down to the camp. Several of the cowboys would then trot off to the working field. Once they got to the herd, the pace picked up with horses galloping and cattle scattering. Helge gradually became more adept as a cowboy and even learned to throw a lasso, although perhaps not quite as impressively as the others. He tended to be more cautious after his harsh encounter with the cactus.

Helge really enjoyed his time and the semi-solitude at the ranch. He lived in a beautiful house with grapevines growing up the walls and had a bunch of puppies to keep him company in the evenings. During his free time, he rode around and explored the wild, isolated landscape. He wrote to Kaare saying, "I am in good condition. Up early every morning, exercising and drinking cream every day; no alcohol."[12] It was important to reassure the family that he was healthy, living well, and taking his convalescence seriously.

A highlight of Helge's cowboy days was a cattle "round-up," where the calves were branded and yearling bulls were separated from the herd. Eight cowboys came to help: Heavy, a chubby Yugoslavian who was always cheery and helpful; Shorty, the joker; Bob, the old cook who called himself a "drifting man"; then Charley, Billy, Val, and George. Foreman Bill, a calm, confident cowboy who the others looked up to, led the operation with simple but firm orders.

They began by riding down into a deep gully to round up several hundred animals. Then the cowboys spread out along the hillside and systematically chased the large herd towards the river. If an animal darted off, a cowboy would follow in hot pursuit down the steep hillside and through the thickets of cacti and chokecherry trees. They threw their lasso over its head and pulled it into the corral. One by one, the calves were roped in, flung onto their sides, and held down to have their hides branded with a red-hot iron.

In the evenings, the worn and weary cowboys would arrive at their camp under an old mesquite tree, starving hungry. They would eat then sit around the brightly burning campfire, smoking and chatting. The frogs croaked down by the river and the coyotes howled off in the hills. Later, they lay by the fire and slept. Helge looked up at the starry sky and thought about the many nights he had slept out in the open in the Arctic. The stars were the same, but somehow in all the wrong places.

Once they gathered up the cattle, the cowboys drove the herd through the desert, a very different landscape from where they came. Saguaro cactus, some reaching 10–20 metres tall, grew everywhere, and in the twilight, they looked almost ghost-like with their thick branches sticking out, like the arms on an octopus. In daylight, white flowers adorned the end of each "arm." Helge also noticed mesquite trees, cottonwood trees with their bits of cotton-like bulbs and that strange, dry tumbleweed bush that breaks free from its roots and tumbles about blown by the wind. Rattlesnakes hid in the bushes and shook their rattles if anyone got close, and the cowboys warily passed the large, venomous lizard called the Gila monster. At times, it was especially slow-going as they carefully dodged the many prairie dog holes covering the ground.

With his feet nearly dragging the ground, Helge rode a small, white horse called Mike. Foreman Bill said that the horse hadn't been treated well by a previous owner and that's why it was a little slow and sad.

Eventually, the cattle drive reached a pool of water built in the middle of the desert by sheep farmers to collect rainwater. There was a corral surrounding the pool and the cowboys drove the cattle in. Three hundred thirsty cows took off running to drink, then walked around splashing in the water to cool down. The horses came next. Beneath a few mesquite trees, Bob the cook set out a lunch of cooked meat and baked bread on the tailgate of his wagon. After a hefty meal, the men all fell asleep in the shade of the trees; they had slept little the previous few days. When they awoke, two wild horses and a small foal stood quietly looking at the men but quickly became startled and took off.

Later that night, the cowboys set up another camp under a new grove of trees. The men mumbled something about rain and then all settled in under a tarp. Helge, who had not seen a drop of rain since he had arrived in Arizona, thought they were all just kidding and as usual climbed into his sleeping bag out in the open – a decision he later regretted. During the night, it started to absolutely pour, a torrential rain with forceful winds that soaked him to the bone. The following morning, after the worst of the storm subsided, the cowboys carried on. They told each other how that kind of weather was quite refreshing; a few even claimed they liked it. However, they were soaked through and the air began to chill. Soon they were utterly freezing, right there in the middle of the desert.

They set up camp once again, even though the ground looked more like a mud hole than the dry, dirt floor of the desert. They took shifts during the night to keep watch over the herd, riding in pairs for a couple of hours at a time. They could talk and sing, but they were not allowed to smoke. The slightest flicker of a match or sudden sound could cause a stampede. The night watch was tiring to ride, but also quite incredible:

listening to the night birds sing and coyotes wail out in the desert and looking up at the stars shining as brightly as they did in the Arctic. One cowboy named Heavy had a wonderful singing voice and entertained them in the evenings with songs from Yugoslavia and Russia, as well as a few traditional cowboy songs. He once had been a bookkeeper in Chicago. Now, he wouldn't trade the cowboy life for anything.

The next day, the animals flatly refused to go any farther. The cowboys tried all their usual calls to get them going, but nothing seemed to work, not even Helge's Norwegian "*hipp, hipp, hurra.*" It wasn't until they shook a few cans filled with stones that the cattle quickly took off.

They kept up at a good, steady pace until they reached a place called Florence. When they arrived, they drove the cows into an enclosure, set up camp, and lit the campfire. They had been on horseback for fourteen hours straight. The foreman brought them each a cigar, but Helge had already crawled into his sleeping bag and was fast asleep. The next day, they herded the cows farther up to the ranch where the owner lived. Once the animals were put out to pasture it was wonderful to see them all standing in fields of metre-high alfalfa with tall stacks of hay bailed up behind them. The landscape was quite different from the barren mountain pasture where the cattle had to scrape out tufts of grass from in between the rocks and sometimes settle for leaves from the trees.

The end of the round-up called for a large celebration for over a hundred cowboys and their women. Beef that had been slow-cooked over a bed of hot coals was now ready to be served, lanterns hung by the stables, and a blazing bonfire roared in the middle of all the festivities. After everyone finished the meal, they danced. The very traditional square dancing was not much different than old Norwegian folk dances, Helge thought. To his amazement, no one was drunk and everything "was good-natured and fun." The party lasted until six in the morning; Helge finally found a bed and fell asleep in between two other snoring cowboys. They didn't sleep long though as they were awake again an hour and a half later. "A party is no excuse for a cowboy to sleep in."[13] But for Helge, this was the celebratory end of a month-long adventure living the life of a cowboy in the Superstition Mountains.

6   THE APACHE NATION

After experiencing life as a cowboy, Helge decided he wanted to travel farther north – to Apache territory. The Apaches were among the last native tribes to succumb to reservation life and had fought their last battle with the encroaching white settlers only forty years earlier. Several of the cowboys Helge had worked with were Apache whose ancestors had ruled over Arizona, New Mexico, large parts of Texas, and northern Mexico. Now their people were forced onto two reservations: San Carlos in the lowlands southeast of Phoenix and Fort Apache in the highlands farther north. Helge's hope was to meet some of the elder warriors so he could hear stories from the old days.

Early June 1937, Helge departed for the San Carlos reservation. His friend Vic Householder had written a letter of introduction for him to give to Pastor Francis Uplegger, who, along with his family, had lived on the reservation for years and had become a recognized expert of the Apache language. Originally a minister from Denmark, Uplegger was now a seventy-year-old widower cared for by his two spinster daughters, Gertrude and Dorothea. In addition to ministry work, they also ran a school and a modest health care service. They warmly welcomed Helge, especially the preacher's daughters, who rode around with him and helped write the notes of old songs the Apaches sang for him.

Uplegger taught Helge about the Apache culture and much about the language. Helge eventually began to recognize several familiar words he had learned while living with the Caribou Eaters in the north.[1] This fuelled Helge's enthusiasm; as he wrote home to a friend, "I have found several interesting similarities which strongly suggest an emigration

Apache girls.

from the north. Most probably, these Apaches are none other than my wandering Caribou Eaters in just another form."[2]

Helge spent several evenings in an old medicine man's wickiup listening to the Apache warriors tell their old tales and legends. Here too he found similarities with the stories he had heard from the Caribou Eaters. Helge then shared with the Apaches the tales and customs of the people in the north. He found it a very effective way of connecting with them.

After spending time at the San Carlos reservation, Helge decided to travel onward to Whiteriver at the Fort Apache reservation. Wanting to become even more acquainted with the Apaches, Helge once again took up the life of a cowboy. Up in the mountains, about 25,000 head of Apache-owned cattle grazed across the lush green meadows. The herd was tended to by a foreman and sixteen Apache cowboys. Helge ventured up there one day, saw all those cowboys sitting around a roaring campfire, and decided to stay.

It was beautiful country: forests of tall, mighty pine trees; rivers full of beavers and their dams; vast sweeping green plains; a colourful array of flowers and a scatter of wild sunflowers. Several types of birds, ducks, and wild turkey lived in the woods, all of which tasted exceptionally good after being cooked over the evening campfire. Cougar, black bear, and wild boar roamed the mountains.

One time, the cowboys took a couple of days off and rode all the way up to the top of the highest mountain, Mount Baldy. The view was magnificent: an impressive expanse of land stretching as far as the eye could see, all the way to "old" Mexico, New Mexico, and Colorado. At the top of the mountain, they found arrowheads and several handmade beads among some old Apache ruins.[3] Helge's companions told him their ancestors used to come to this summit and pray to the spirits for rain.

At the time, the Whiteriver community wasn't more than a trading post, mission station, small church, and a couple of white houses with picket fences. These were pretty much the only buildings. The Apaches lived in wickiups – domed, round dwellings made with frames of arched poles covered with hides, brush, bark, and reeds, or any other suitable and accessible material.

To the east of Whiteriver, about 10 kilometres, was a smaller mission station at East Fork. To the south was Fort Apache, the old US Army cavalry post where the last Apache warriors were taken, held prisoner, and assigned an identification number they used for the rest of their lives. Helge was very interested in interviewing the few remaining people from this era and was able to talk with two of them, George Goklis (A8) and Taipa (A100). Both of them told him the stories of their lives.

George told him a creation myth of how the Apaches began: A group of people wandered the earth looking for a land without illness or death, a place of eternal life. They sent a scout to follow a light they spotted in the distance. He returned saying he found a place that was better than where they were now, a place where corn grew. They went there and were welcomed by corn-growing people. The group, however, still wanted to find the land where there was eternal life. They continued onward but left behind a girl and a boy, and these two gave birth to the Apache tribe.[4]

Helge could not help but wonder whether the people who farmed corn were of the Pueblo nation of northern Arizona and if the wandering tribe in search of a paradise without illness, hunger, or death were the Caribou Eaters, who lost many to starvation after a hard winter. For them, a land with enough food would have been a land of eternal life.

Helge wrote down the myth and his thoughts about it in a letter home. Both his father and brother immediately replied, fearing that his book about Arizona was going to be too scientific and sombre, and urged him to write fiction. Helge replied:

I have a lot of good material based on what I have seen here. It's not just about cowboys, but also about the Apache Indians and [how I want to write it]. Pappa will get his chiefs and he'll get them so wild that Cooper's Indian stories will pale in comparison, and all without me exaggerating. I don't want to put together a bunch of sloppy stuff that sells just because it is dramatic and sensational. I want to write something that is worthwhile; timeless. In addition to the cowboy life, I will try to give a vivid account of these Apache, a most remarkable people; wild, wise, full of humour and with a history of battles with the whites and an interconnection like no other in all of American history. I have it in me to create something good, my own way. Fiction will have to wait until next time.[5]

Helge explained in his journal how he was able to win the trust of some of the Apaches. He sat down under a tree with his pictures of the

Apache sunrise ceremony, 1937, celebrating the coming of age of young Apache girls.

Caribou Eaters and began talking about these northern people. Several others gathered around, and soon an attentive, interested group sat with him under that tree. They especially liked his story about the man who lassoed the sun, which they wanted him to retell several times. When he finished, he intentionally let the Apaches tell their stories. He wanted them to feel that if they received a story, they should give one in return. He was seldom wrong: "When I finished, one of the old women said that it was as if they had been on a long journey and had lived for a while with the Indians of the North. I will come another time and stay the whole day, she said."[6]

Helge disappointedly realized, eventually, that despite the similarities in language and other cultural elements, there was little in the Apache legends he heard that indicated any migration from the north.[7]

One day in August, Helge and two other men, Chester Gatewood and Bid Giles, took a trip over to East Fork. He hoped to talk with one of the elders there, an Apache by the name of Taipa, or A100. The old warrior came out of his tent and sat down cross-legged in front of a small campfire. He was between seventy and eighty years old and had long, grizzled hair down to his shoulders. "The look in his eyes was strong and incredibly vibrant, but something sly hid lurking in his gaze. When he spoke, he made direct eye contact and acted as if nobody was better than another."[8]

Taipa's camp was situated on a beautiful, open clearing with a view across the White Mountains. He knew exactly what he wanted: compensation for his stories – and Helge paid. First, Helge tried to get him to tell the Apache creation story. But he replied that it was a much too long and complicated story and if he told it he risked being punished by wind or lightning. Besides, such a story was so expensive that he would have to receive a huge pile of money if he were tell it. Helge gave up and let Taipa choose the subject. He chose to tell about life in the old days:

> His voice was something else. Melodic and clear, as if it testified
> to the land from where the Apaches had once come, Northern
> Canada. There was a sense of cascading rivers and a fresh breeze
> in his speech. When he spoke, he came alive. He gesticulated in a
> most amazing way. Sometimes I could understand what he was
> saying just by his gesturing. A dramatically gifted man. It was en-
> joyable to sit there and watch him talk so confidently and engaged
> in his topic. At times, he laughed hard when he thought he had
> said something funny. All the while, he was straightforward, strong
> and natural. As he sat there, I had a feeling of how that strong
> little character of a man had emerged from the land just the same
> as a tree emerges from the earth.[9]

Taipa told about his youth when he was a scout for General George Crook, whose troops defeated the Apache in 1872 then forced them to live within the reservation's boundaries. Crook wanted to make them self-sufficient so provided them with cattle and encouraged them to farm the land.

To a degree, there was freedom on the reservation. It was also Crook's idea, however, to assign each Apache a number to wear around his or her neck. He provided them with paid work and gave them jurisdiction over minor cases. The scouts, like Taipa, acted like a police force that assisted in tracking down and catching the "free" Apaches, those who had not yet conformed to reservation life. The scouts also tracked down warriors from other tribes who ravaged the Apaches' cattle herds and attacked pioneer settlers.

A few years later, however, the situation Crook had created disintegrated after he was transferred to another regiment. His absence opened the way for unscrupulous traders and deceitful officers to exploit the Apaches. The agreements Crook had signed on behalf of the government with several tribal chiefs were violated when large numbers of Apaches were relocated from the beautiful mountain forests down to the scorching desert landscape of San Carlos. The Apaches reacted strongly to these injustices and turbulence grew in San Carlos. The scouts from Whiteriver, including Taipa, were sent along with two hundred soldiers to sort it out.

This resulted in several groups fleeing from the reservation and heading south towards the mountains of Mexico. Among them was the well-known chief Be-do-ja, also called Victorio, of the Mescalero Apache tribe, who for years were enemies of the White Mountain Apaches. Scouts were sent south to Mexico to track down and capture the runaways. Victorio and his people left a trail of damaged property, frightened farmers, and killings all the way from southern Arizona to Mexico. In 1880, Victorio was captured and killed.

Taipa explained that even after Victorio was killed, some of the Mescalero tribe refused to surrender and return to the reservation. They hid in the mountains, saying that "everything here is ours and this is where we will stay." Other Mescalero were taken back to the reservation, then fought with the scouts an entire night; twelve were killed and seventy-nine held prisoner in an enclosure of cacti. "Now almost everyone is dead," Taipa said to Helge. "The Great Chief in Washington has thanked me for what I have done and gave me a pension. Everyone knows what I have done and everyone knows me. When they see me they say: There is A100, Taipa."

Neither Helge nor Taipa seemed to consider the idea that famous Apache scouts were most likely perceived as traitors by their kin who escaped to Mexico's mountains and elsewhere. They both were influenced by the prevailing view of the time: that it was best for Native Americans to live on reservations with access to schools and health care and under the protection of "The Great Chief in Washington" and his long arm of the law, Bureau of Indian Affairs.

Helge also spoke with a few past members of the US cavalry who had participated in the fights with the Apaches. One such war veteran was seventy-three-year-old Henry, who came to Arizona in 1883 to fight the Apaches, and now lived in a small house by the river at East Fork. Helge went to visit him along with Pastor Guenther. A smiling "Sergeant Henry" welcomed them into his militarily clean and orderly cabin. He began talking and continued for seven hours. He told of how he fought against the Apaches and of all the horrendous killings and torture carried out by both sides. Along with his troop, he rode down to Mexico in 1883 to bring Geronimo and his people back after one of their many escapes.

Helge questioned some of the details in Henry's stories. There was no doubt that both sides committed atrocities, but how much and to what extent was unclear. For Helge, it was important to understand these stories within a context of a long oral heritage: history told and passed on through the generations; stories that heavily shaped and influenced the relationship between indigenous tribes and pioneer settlers.

Helge was especially fascinated by the incredible story of Geronimo and his people, their plight and struggle for freedom. Initially a medicine man, Geronimo was a Chiricahua Apache who led his people in several battles to defend their homeland against American and Mexican military powers. Numerous times he and his tribe were forced back to the reservation from which they would escape again and again. They would always flee to the Sierra Madre Mountains, a couple of days' ride from southern Arizona across the border into Mexico. Reportedly, there was a time when about four hundred to five hundred free Apaches lived in these mountains they knew so well. In the summer of 1886, after years of war, Geronimo surrendered. The American government then separated his people and scattered them across states and prison camps. Geronimo never returned to his homeland, despite his several pleas. Confined as a prisoner of war, he died a bitter and beaten man. On his deathbed with his nephew at his side he said, "I should never have surrendered. I should have fought until I was the last man alive."[10]

Helge was interested in the story of Geronimo and his tribe not so much because of its dramatic events, but mostly because it was about a group of people who sought freedom and the chance to live the life he had experienced with the Caribou Eaters in Canada. He imagined how difficult it must have been to be forced to settle on a restricted piece of barren land, to be governed by others, and be forced to live a completely different lifestyle. But what also excited Helge even more was the idea that there were people still alive and living in Arizona who could give first-hand accounts of these times.

One day, Helge visited Jesus Velesquez, a Mexican married to an Apache woman, who had lived with the Apaches for about fifty years. Once the "chief scout" of the Apaches, Jesus told Helge that all that had been written about Geronimo was inaccurate; he was no warrior but instead a medicine man. Chato was his general and it was he who had commanded the difficult battles.

Helge also met an eighty-year-old Chiricahua Apache woman, one of the many who followed Geronimo into the mountains. She had been given the number G-26, but her new name was Anna Palmer. She talked about life on the run in Mexico's mountains before she married a White-river Apache, settled there, and thus avoided being sent to captivity in Florida. Her story indicates that there must have been regular contact between the runaways in the south and people on the reservation. When Helge met her, she was a wrinkled old woman whose clothes hung loosely on her thin, frail body. She had a piercing gaze and waved her hands wildly while she talked. She said to Helge, "I have lived during a difficult time. Now when I think back, it is as if it were a dream. I was always running. I always had to duck the bullets … we were like wolves being hunted down by many. Once there was a big battle in Mexico. The whites surrounded us and nearly all the Indians were killed. They were going to kill me too but I crawled between the campfires and ran to the woods."[11]

She explained to Helge that the women fought alongside the men, sometimes with rifles and other times with just clubs, while the children hid in the mountains. They often had very little food and had to steal from the farmers. "Many men were killed," she said, "But our own people turned against us, that is why we lost."[12]

Anna Palmer was never captured; she always managed to get away. "It's as if I can see the old woman galloping away on her horse, a shotgun in her hand and throwing herself into battle,"[13] Helge wrote about her in his book *The Apache Indians: In Search of a Missing Tribe*. Later he also said, "they were dangerous women, and strong, self-sufficient and resourceful. They knew the land just as well as the men."

Helge also befriended a medicine man by the name of Tenijieth, who one day began talking with him about the Apache Wars and notorious

Helge together with Anna Palmer, who had been with Geronimo's people in the mountains of Mexico.

warriors such as Victorio and Geronimo who had fought and fled south to Mexico. Their conversation grew quiet and then Tenijieth said:

> Geronimo and some of the Chiricahua Apaches surrendered and were taken prisoner, but not all of them … Some of the Chiricahua Apaches hid in the mountains and the Americans didn't know. Today they still live in the Sierra Madre. They are a free people, but have a difficult time. The Mexicans are always after them and there are many fights. One of their women and several children have been captured by the Mexicans. But the Chiricahua Apaches are clever; nobody finds them.[14]

Tenijieth could not, or would not, say more. But a plan took root in Helge's mind. He wanted to search for those last remaining free Apaches living in the mountains of Mexico. The idea of being the first to meet these people since their isolation was exciting in itself. But perhaps more important to Helge was the hope of finding Apaches who had preserved many of their old cultural traditions and characteristics, and who could shed light on what interested him most: a possible link identifying migration of the Caribou Eaters from the north many generations earlier. Lost myths and traditions could possibly still exist with the "free" in Mexico.

Helge mentions his plans about a trip to Mexico in a letter to his parents. However, a reply from his father, dated 10 October 1937, was less than encouraging:

> I cannot help but add that your plan seems to me quite un-reasonable. I am not just thinking of the incredible distances, the unpredictable and treacherous terrain, or your lack of knowledge of the natural environment, living conditions and language, among other things; but that you will also need a large, well-equipped expedition for an extended period of time. More importantly is the serious illness you have had followed by major surgery. I have never before advised you against taking a journey, but here I must do so. I have nothing more to say. You are your own master.

This was one of the few times Olav did not agree with his son. But Helge was his own master and he obstinately continued with his plans. On 22 September, he wrote to his parents saying he had arrived in

Medicine man Tenijieth.

Douglas, Arizona, near the Mexican border and was about to begin his expedition to search for the "free" Apaches. He again briefly explained his reason for the expedition and emphasized that two Apaches who spoke the language and who could recognize any sign of their kinsmen would be joining him, minimizing any risks. Financing this expedition was still unclear: "I have written to a few wealthy individuals in New York. Hope one of these comes through."

Helge must have convinced his parents as the next letter from his father arrived with a very different tone:

Yes, now it starts to get exciting. We generally are not dismayed by your elaborate plans for Mexico and with the Indians. It is your stay with the Caribou Eaters that has given us faith that you will manage. Perhaps you yourself have a certain primitiveness to offer. Yes, it is unfortunate that I am not 40 years younger and [thus] could have joined you … We are, however, prepared for discouragement. It is very unlikely that you will find an authentic, living past left behind … [but] we are happy that now there is no longer any talk of any outrageous plans for a trip through Asia.[15]

Financial support for Helge's expedition, however, was impeded by the general economic state of 1930s America. He did receive some funding from wealthy Norwegian Americans he had met on the east coast and in Chicago, but the newspapers and National Geographic Society were reluctant to provide support before seeing any finished articles. Helge then took the heavy decision to secure a loan from the bank. Expedition expenses were fairly low as their main means of transport, for the most part, was horseback.

Information about the Apaches who still lived in the Sierra Madre was sketchy. However, it was common knowledge that the Apache of the Sierra Madre had contact with their kinsmen who lived on the reservation. Helge couldn't get any more information from old Tenijieth, who only worriedly said, "You are a young man and many times the sun will rise for you. But if you follow the trail of the Chiricahua Apaches, I fear too much. They are like cunning animals. You do not hear them, you do not see them. Then suddenly, an arrow comes flying in."[16]

Helge searched for people who had any substantial, relevant information, and in the town of Douglas he got lucky. He met Jack Harris, an American who had lived on a ranch in Nacori Chico at the foot of the Sierra Madre Mountains for twenty years. Harris confirmed that Apaches still lived in the mountains by his ranch and that he himself, just a few years earlier, managed to capture a young Apache girl about six or seven years old. His relatives later adopted her and she was living in California. Harris promised to assist Helge with horses and other equipment.

Helge also wrote and asked for advice from Grenville Goodwin,[17] a self-taught anthropologist, who had lived on the San Carlos reservation from 1928 to 1936, shortly before Helge arrived there. Goodwin was also interested in the connection between the northern and southern Athabasca Tribes (the indigenous people from Alaska and northern Canada and the Apache in the south) and had written a monograph titled *The Social Organization of the Western Apache*. In 1930 and 1931, he had organized similar expeditions to Mexico[18] to register old Apache camps, but he never saw any people living in the mountains. He wrote to Helge wishing him good luck and said: "It was my fond hope to someday tackle the Sierra Madre Apache, attempting it in the same manner as you apparently are; that is, taking only two or three Chiricahua Apache along, men who spoke the language, had relatives among the Sierra Madre Apache group and knew the country. However you seem to have gotten there ahead of me and I can only wish you the best of luck and offer you what help I can."[19] Helge and Goodwin never met. The anthropologist died only a few years later at the age of thirty-two. His work and writing on the Apaches are considered a major contribution to American Indian ethnology.

Another anthropologist interested in the Apaches, Morris Opler, who had worked with Goodwin, sent a more candid letter to Helge saying he shouldn't expect to find any Apaches living a traditional way of life. After having been chased for so long and forced to live a life of thieving from the area's settlers, it was doubtful any such way of life still existed for them.[20] The Museum of Natural History in New York also sent a letter (via the Norwegian Consulate General) stating they themselves were planning an expedition to the same mountain area and therefore could not grant Helge any funding. They added that it would be extremely difficult to get permission from the Mexican authorities; they had tried for a long time, with no results.

Despite all this, Helge did get permission and financial support. His friend Vic Householder was able to pull strings and managed in the end to get Helge support from the governor of Sonora in Mexico. About the same time, a permit arrived from the central authorities in Mexico with several recommendation letters instructing public authorities along the way to provide Helge with all possible assistance.

Helge then hitched a ride with a truck driver headed to the Mescalero reservation in New Mexico to look for a couple of men to join his expedition. He met the local administrator of Indian Affairs, Director McCray, a nice man of Scottish descent who immediately offered Helge help in finding a team. The first Apache they visited was Yahnozah, a seventy-year-old man who in his youth had been one of Geronimo's people in the Sierra Madre Mountains. He fought in battles there, knew the area well, and was more than willing to come along. His eagerness to join though was not prompted by his desire to find lost kin, but to find a lost Spanish treasure of gold and silver, supposedly hidden somewhere in those mountains. This was his big chance. Helge stressed that in no way was hunting for treasure the goal of the expedition. If the opportunity arose, however, they could perhaps briefly search for the treasure at the place Yahnozah was told it might be hidden. And just in case, the two men signed a contract agreeing to split any findings fifty-fifty.

Finding a third expedition member proved to be difficult. Helge spoke to several of the elders who had fought in the Apache Wars, among them the son of the famous chief Victorio as well as the son of Chief Juh. For various reasons,[21] Helge didn't choose any of these men but decided upon a younger man by the name of Andrew Little, who spoke fluent Spanish. Andrew's mother had been a member of Geronimo's tribe and fought in several battles, until she died in a last fight. Only an infant at the time, Andrew slid off her back and down a slope, which saved him. His father was a Mexican who as a child had been captured by the Apaches in the Sierra Madre and adopted into the tribe.

Helge wrote a Christmas letter home to his parents and apologized once again for not being home for the holidays. For the first time he admits longing for home and says that, only a day earlier, he considered cancelling the expedition. But when he awoke the following sunny morning, he thought of the Mexican treasure of gold and silver Yahnozah was so sure could be found, and of all those who had helped organize the expedition. He decided to go after all:

> Regarding the wild Indians, there aren't many of them left. Perhaps a few, maybe between 10 and 20. It is of course not at all certain that I will find them. A hunted people. But deep within the mountains they have their protected spot where the Mexicans don't dare venture. My Indian companions feel quite confident about coming into contact with their kin. If we come across a trail we will surely find them, they say. At every camp they will leave their Apache

Helge with his expedition members Andrew (left) and Yahnozah.

sign ... I have also brought along a few photographs from the Apaches on the reservation. I will put up a picture of our camp, hang a white rag with it and an arrow pointing to our direction.[22]

What if Helge were to find them? What would he do then? In a letter to a friend in California he says very clearly: "It is my intention to join them and study them."[23]

Early in the morning on 4 November 1937, Helge's small entourage crossed the border at Douglas, Arizona, into Agua Prieta, Mexico. Their first stop was a small town called Bacerac, where the little expedition team created quite a stir; they didn't seem to get many strangers there. The people's bewilderment, however, turned to apprehension once they realized what "type" of people Yahnozah and Andrew were. The villagers were taught to fear Apaches as if they were the devil himself, Helge later explained. The two Apaches, however, wandered peacefully about the square and ignored the others' fearful reactions to them. Helge again writes home to his parents: "Could not have had better people than those two I am with. We are good friends."[24]

When Helge presented the letter of recommendation from the governor of Sonora, the town mayor suddenly became profusely pleasant. He asked Helge to take pictures of the entire city council as well as a prisoner accused of murder who sat in the jail cell. The townspeople confirmed that at least six free Apaches still lived in the mountains, perhaps more, which was encouraging information for Helge. They also told him that they had shot at a few over the course of the last few years when the mountain Apaches came down and were caught stealing cattle.

In Bacerac, Helge was offered assistance from a couple of Mexicans who helped equip him with horses and mules. They suggested the expedition team head south to the Sienequita ranch, which lay at the foot of the mountains. From there they could begin their ascent and hire more people if needed. The Mexicans could accompany them as far as the ranch.

Riding south, Helge made a note of all the wonderful nature, rugged mountains, and abundant wildlife. "We travelled across a rolling landscape with semitropical vegetation. On the hillsides, acacia trees were in full bloom, and in small forest clearings patches of yellow and red flowers glimmered in the sun. Now and then we wandered by the crystal-clear Bavispe River, which flowed under the shade of poplar, walnut and sycamore trees."[25] Yahnozah pointed out old, familiar places he knew of his time with the free Apaches, and where he and Geronimo were captured the first time. He also identified the mountaintop where he thought the Spanish treasure was hidden.

The next day, they journeyed closer to the mountains and towards the mighty pine forest covering the hillside. They spent the night at a cattle ranch owned by Gildardo Moreni, who treated them like royalty and provided them with useful information. Moreni's beautiful wife dished up the best they had: tortillas, wild honey, brown sugar, dried meat, and Mexican cheese.

Having recently had a few skirmishes with the Apaches, Moreni confirmed they were up there in the mountains. He recommended the men continue their journey higher into the mountains and stop at another cattle ranch where a Yaqui Indian by the name of Isidro Mora lived with his family. Mora, known to be a keen tracker and a mountain man, knew every inch of the area. But he also had the reputation of a brute who had shot at a few Apaches. In Helge's words, "When I first saw Mora, I quickly realized he was a sly devil and a rough fellow who had no regard for the Apaches. A completely different type from the Mexicans I had met at the foot of the mountains … He was a descendent of the Yaqui people who dominate large parts of Sonora and are known to be the most ferocious and fearless of all [indigenous peoples] in Mexico."[26]

The trail to Mora's place was steep, rugged, and clearly difficult for the lowland mules and the accompanying Mexicans not accustomed to the mountains. But they finally reached the farm situated on a 2,000-metre-high plateau. Contrary to the Mexicans, Mora had a team of mules conditioned for the mountains and knew the area better than anyone else. Helge decided that the Mexicans and their mules should turn back, then made an agreement with Mora to continue with the expedition. This proved to be a disastrous decision.

The expedition team searched the western parts of the Sierra Madre, zigzagging their way while heading south. They were in the "great and mysterious" part of the Sierra near Nacori, the wildest and most inaccessible area. Deep, jagged ravines cut through the mountains, leaving few valley floors to ride in. It was either straight up or straight down. Mora's mules climbed like goats and showed an endurance that reminded Helge of his Arctic dog team.

One day, the team found an abandoned Apache camp under some large pine trees, high on a summit with a panoramic view. It appeared that one or two families had once lived there in a small, grass shelter, but it must have been some time earlier. Another day, Mora showed them a cave where he said he knew Apaches had lived, but again it was empty.

The place was not far from where Mora said he shot and killed three Apaches who had stolen his mules. On the ground lay a skull which Mora held proudly as Helge took a photograph. Yahnozah stood quietly in the background, slowly scanning the camp where his kin had been slaughtered.

There was no singing in the camp that night, as there had been on previous evenings. The flickering fire burned intensely from the oily sap of the pine, casting a crimson shadow of smoke into the sky. The old Apache sat by the fire, quietly staring into the flames.

Reflecting on what he had seen and was told, Helge wrote:

This is the way that the Sierra Madre Apaches are compelled to live, since they are constantly being pursued. No other group of people anywhere in the world is so mercilessly chased to death as these last, free Indians of the proud and previously powerful Apache nation. They don't lack courage, only weapons. The only thing they can do against their mighty enemy is to hide and flee. So they set up their humble grass huts in places where they believe no pursuer would imagine anyone could live. On a steep mountain ledge at three thousand metres – an eagle's nest.[27]

After scouring the western parts of the mountain range, they headed towards the small town of Nacori Chico. From there they journeyed eastward, with Mora still guiding them. Once again, they found themselves having to climb massively high cliffs. To the east, north, and south lay endless rows of rugged mountains draped in green pine forests. Somewhere in there were Geronimo's Apaches. But would they find them? It would take a great deal of luck.

One day, Helge sat looking through his binoculars scouting the top of a mountain on the other side of a narrow ravine. Suddenly, he spotted "something alive, moving upright at the edge of the forest, hurrying between the trees. It had to have been a human!"[28] They hurried to investigate, but the path was long and difficult, and before they reached the area, the rain came pouring down, erasing any tracks. The men looked around but couldn't find any signs or traces of humans. Yahnoza, Andrew, and Mora were skeptical and suggested that it might have been a deer. Helge, however, was certain about what he saw: "It could have been one of the Apaches' scouts I had caught a glimpse of. They would have watched and known about our travels in the mountains, so this probably wasn't the first time they had been close to us."[29]

While Mora briefly returned home to see his family, the other three spent four days scouring an area of the mountains where Yahnozah was convinced the Spanish treasure was hidden. In and out of caves and crevices, he believed they were close. But the more they searched, the more uncertain Yahnozah became. In the end, Mora returned and they had to give up. Three tired and disappointed treasure hunters sat by the fire that night. Yahnozah was the most discouraged. For years, he had dreamt of the day he would crawl into one of those caves and retrieve bars of gold and silver.

With Mora back, they headed south through the mountains and into more difficult, almost inaccessible terrain. Gradually, however, the land opened up to lusher green clearings where deer grazed. This was the Chihuahua district of the Sierra Madre where the Chiricahua Apaches once based their main camp, a nearly unreachable area whose conditions alone would have safeguarded them from attack. It was quite possible the last free Apaches continued to use this place. Andrew suggested he and Yahnozah ride up into the mountains and try to make contact by singing old Apache songs and yelling out that they were there as friends. Helge and Mora followed them halfway up the mountain, but then remained behind in an open clearing so as not to frighten off the elusive Apache. After four days, Andrew and Yahnozah returned without any apparent contact.

With Christmas approaching, the expedition team decided to head down from the mountains. Large, white flakes of snow began to fall, reminding Helge of home, and soon the men were soaking wet and freezing. After an eleven-hour ride, they reached the small village of Nortenia located several miles north of Chuichupa. Mora had friends here where the men could roll out their sleeping bags and enjoy the heat from a fireplace.

The next day they carried on towards Chuichupa and soon arrived at a clearing with a cluster of houses, larger than those in the other villages. It turned out to be a colony of American Mormons who had moved to the area after polygamy was banned in the United States. The Farnsworth family welcomed the men and offered them an empty house to stay in as long as they wanted. Once they got settled, the first thing

Helge did was to fire Mora. He no longer felt he could trust the man. Mora had started talking behind Helge's back and was creating dissension within the expedition group, growing more quarrelsome. After he had been drinking, Mora came and demanded immediate full payment in cash and equipment for his part of the expedition. The original agreement was half cash, half cheque and part of the expedition equipment after Helge had returned to Douglas. Helge was furious, but in the end decided to give in as he didn't want the expedition to end with an argument, even if it cost a little.

Helge went to get the supplies in a shed along with Jess, the eldest Farnsworth boy. As the two of them stood there, Mora walked in. Before either of them could react, Mora grabbed a rifle and ran out. Helge and Jess stormed after him. Outside, standing in the dark shadows, Mora was pointing the rifle at them. They heard him load and then cock the rifle: "This Mora had fought and gunned people down and three years earlier had shot down a group of Apaches. And there he stood roaring drunk with his finger on the trigger. Strangely enough, I wasn't afraid. I said to myself just stay calm. Shooting a man who isn't attacking or running away isn't easy."[30]

Andrew, whom Mora had unfortunately gained influence over, stood nearby with his hands in his pockets enjoying the predicament. Eventually Jess said, "I guess this is about enough," and he and Helge turned and slowly walked back up to the house. Mora and Andrew then slowly sauntered off to go drink some more with the Mexicans. Yahnozah at the time was in bed, passed out drunk.[31]

Clearly, Andrew was now on Mora's side. As Jess also found out, Andrew hadn't been translating correctly, and that was at the core of the conflict. Helge felt he had no other choice but to send Andrew back. He didn't trust him any longer. Helge then went to tell Andrew that he too would have to go and agreed to arrange for transportation back to the reservation for him. Andrew, however, was very angry and said, "Fine, but I'll tell the entire Indian reservation that the expedition was absolute crap." Helge didn't respond, turned his back, and walked away.[32]

The next day, Mora was still feisty and confrontational. In addition to the rifle, he had also gotten hold of a hunting knife. Helge and the Farnsworth boys had to keep an eye on him to keep him from taking any of the other supplies.

Deciding to include Mora in the expedition proved to be a big mistake. Not only because of his dramatic antics at the end, but also because his presence could actually have prevented any of the free Apaches from making contact. Mora was notorious for having ruthlessly shot Apaches. There was no reason for the mountain Apaches to expose themselves when he was around. Helge should have considered this, but he felt pressured into taking someone familiar with the land, the terrain, and who had suitable animals. He also had few others to choose from. There were indications that Yahnozah and Andrew actually did make contact with the free Apaches when they had gone off by themselves into the mountains to sing their Apache songs. Later, Helge realized that it was because of Mora they did not reveal this.

Helge would have liked to have continued the expedition with just Yahnozah, but Andrew persuaded the old man to return to the reservation with him. And with that, the search for Geronimo's missing tribe was ended.

Over forty years later, in the early 1980s, Helge received a strange letter from a university in California. It was from a professor who allegedly said he was an Apache Indian. He explained that he had grown up in the Sierra Madre, but was captured and later educated among white people. He remembered how, as a child, they kept watch over Helge's expedition in the mountains. They did not make contact because Helge was together with a man they feared. Whether this was true or not, by the time Helge received the letter he was very old and never followed it up. However, the letter arrived long before Helge's book on the Apaches was ever published in English. So how could this man have known about all this if he had not experienced it?

Helge's dream of finding "Geronimo's missing tribe" was never fully realized. He did, however, experience so much more than expected: more than he ever dreamt of and more than enough to write a new book.

Back to "Civilization"

Helge's return to Phoenix spurred a media frenzy. He wrote home to his parents: "When I came back, wildly eager reporters gushed over me and the Associated Press published a long article and then another with pictures. These articles have spread across America, supposedly to 3,000 newspapers. There is a lot of nonsense in the articles, but it is essentially not my fault."[33]

But the damage was done. The articles included sensational details and stated Helge had met the "free" Apaches. One had even been reprinted in a couple of Norwegian newspapers with the title, "Ingstad Back from Three-Month Expedition to the Wild Apaches: The Expedition Presents Amazing Results." Not long after, Helge received a stern letter from his father:

Dear Helge
We have read the enclosed articles in Dagbladet and Bergens Tidende and are not pleased about the stories of your meeting the Apache tribe ... When writing a travelogue of fiction and to entertain, the writer has the right to take a certain "licentiae poeticae." But when presenting reports about an expedition, encountered discoveries and other scientific results, no such freedoms apply. The author must be fully and unconditionally trustworthy. The enclosed articles without a doubt belong under that last category ... one of the worst things is to risk your reputation ... under all circumstances, and especially concerning any further newspaper reports or potential lectures, you must omit everything about your and Yahnozah's meeting with the tribe. And if it is otherwise asked about, you change the subject and say that there was no meeting. We miss a tone in your articles from that humble and solid journey of discovery in the Arctic Canada. It must be America that has wrought this change; we hope that it is not wedged deeply ...
Many greetings from Mamma and me, Pappa[34]

To what extent Helge himself contributed to the newspapers' sensationalism, or whether he was tempted to let the exaggerations pass and be credited as the one who had "found" the free Apaches, is not known. At any rate any such intentions were dismissed after he received his father's letter. There were no other views which Helge regarded more highly than his father's.

After several days, Helge travelled to Los Angeles. First, he visited the Apache girl named Bui who, in May 1932, was captured high in the Sierra Madre Mountains after her grandmother had been killed. The girl had been adopted by a family in California and was now about twelve years old and was going to school. Helge met her as well as her fair-haired sister, and deemed them a very cute pair. Bui, somewhat reluctantly, talked to him about life with her grandmother. When asked if she liked living in the mountains, she replied, "I was scared a lot and I don't want to go back." Her grandmother had been very strict and she

Apache girl, Bui, right after she was captured by Jack Harris.

was almost never allowed to speak or run around for fear they would be discovered. One thing she did remember from her life as a free Apache was the small deerskin outfit she was wearing when she was captured.

Helge's other purpose with his trip to Los Angeles was to see if that old dream of his about making a film could be realized. In Hollywood, he was given an "audience" with a reputable company that worked with screenplays. He presented his old idea about a film about life in the Arctic. In Arizona, he had taken a bit of footage and also wanted to explore the possibilities of making this into a documentary. He had earlier written to an acquaintance in Los Angeles asking for help in arranging an introduction to such prominent people as Douglas Shearer, director of MGM, movie director Clarence Brown, and the actors Clark Gable and Gary Cooper. Clark Gable was a friend of Norwegian-born pioneer aviator Bernt Balchen and Helge believed that he "surely would like to see pictures from a country where you have to sleep with a loaded shotgun by the side of your sleeping bag."[35] But no meeting with the stars transpired, nor did anyone show interest in his film ideas. Any dreams he had of succeeding in Hollywood were abandoned then and there.

Helge still had heard no word about a possible travel permit to Russia. He had originally wandered this far west in the country in hopes of travelling on to Russia if the permit was granted. But now, Helge felt there was no point in extending his visit on the west coast. He boarded a train heading east and arrived in Washington, DC, on 18 April. He wrote home to say that he had held a lecture at the National Geographic Society and had received an invitation to speak and show his film footage at the Explorers Club in New York on 22 April.

Helge was given free passage back to Norway on the ship *Bergensfjord* in exchange for giving lectures to the passengers. The boat left New York on 4 May carrying Helge's newly acquired pride and joy: a 1937 Plymouth. Helge had failed the American drivers' test miserably but hoped he would do better in Norway.

Home Again

When Helge returned home in May 1938, he had been away for nearly two years and had acquired a wealth of experience. Home, however, was much the same. His father had turned seventy and retired, and his mother was still busy with husband, family, and religion. Younger brother Kaare, like Helge, was still single and free, but most other friends were either engaged, married, or had a bundle of kids.

Horrible unrest was brewing in Europe. The Spanish Civil War was in full force and crucial events were about to unfold in many other countries. Near Christmas, Helge wrote a letter to the Uplegger family in Arizona detailing concerns of war and disgust over Hitler's conduct regarding the Jews: "It looks bleak for Europe, it will be difficult to avoid war … It is terrible how Hitler treats the Jews. In one night he destroyed all they possessed."[36]

For Helge, life after an expedition took on a familiar pattern: giving lectures and writing books. His first lecture about his experiences in Arizona was held in the theatre hall in Bergen on 23 May 1938. It was titled "In Search of the Missing Apache Tribe in the Mountains of Mexico," and was the first showing in Norway of the film footage he had taken. In August, he went on a lecture tour arranged by the National Academy, and by December he had toured all the way up the coast from Bergen to Trondheim. He spoke to full houses everywhere. "Cowboy and Indian life" was a popular subject. At the university auditorium in Oslo he lectured to full houses on 13 and 14 October. He also talked about his experiences on national TV. Professor Hans Wilhelmsson Ahlmann in Stockholm, whom Helge had met in Svalbard, managed to get him an invitation to the Swedish Society for Geography and Anthropology.

Helge's writing went smoothly, most likely because he had taken such careful notes and made detailed journal entries during his time in Arizona. His book *The Apache Indians: In Search of the Missing Tribe* was published in 1939. Although the subject matter varied from his earlier works about the Arctic, the tone was much the same: lyrical descriptions of nature and a keen interest in the indigenous peoples and their way of life.

Helge lived in a time when the theory of evolution was strong. One believed that human development and adaptation progressed from "primitive" to "civilized," the latter of course ranking highest. For many, this was also connected to race, with "white" assumed to be superior to all others. Helge, however, perceived this quite differently. He fully admired "primitive people," their ability to manage with simple tools, and their myths and legends tied so closely to nature and the environment. He was also convinced that they were better off in their "primitive" existence than in the modern world. "Civilization," he believed, could devastate indigenous people, with its emphasis on a monetary economy, alcohol, and a competitive mentality (valued more than sharing and collaboration). His views also adhered to the romantic Rousseauian notion of going back to nature.

Perhaps Helge's own clumsiness with technology and modern devices contributed to his admiration for the "primitive." He was a master with an axe and hunting knife, and could shoot a rifle. But that was generally as advanced as he got. It was no wonder he admired those who created a viable way of life based solely on what nature could provide. Despite Helge's sincere respect and admiration for indigenous peoples, he was influenced and confined by early twentieth-century terminology and often used words and phrases that today would make us squirm.

The Land of Feast and Famine sold well in America and the book was translated into seven languages. But the English version of *East of the Great Glacier* was unfortunately a great disappointment. Helge's book *The Apache Indians: In Search of the Missing Tribe* also proved difficult to get published in English. Perhaps the linguistic peculiarities used to describe indigenous peoples, such as "wild," "domesticated," and "primitive" were one of the reasons. Another holdback was the outbreak of the Second World War shortly after the book was published in Norway, which delayed any offers to American publishers until the late 1940s. In the meantime, awareness of racial issues and Native American rights, and the use of politically correct terms began to emerge, and again some of Helge's word choices most likely grated strongly on a few publishers' ears.[37]

Helge was also, at the time, criticized by one person for denouncing "whites" in Arizona and glorifying the Indians.[38] But Helge refuted each of the assertions by providing detailed American sources and scientific references to support his claims. No damage was done to his reputation. On the contrary, he proved that his research was solidly based with thorough referencing and documentation. Far more favourable was a feature interview with him in the Norwegian newspaper *Dagbladet*:

> Helge Ingstad is a great figure … he is tall, of ideal character, a boy's dream of being a complete man. But sometimes one wonders how such a boy's dream really has it. The question is, do successful people think they are successful? … Ingstad doesn't appear to be; not dissatisfied with his lot, but all else than content … Ingstad has been utterly changed through the arduous years from when he gave up his legal robes and left for Canada: A quiet but vigorous disdain for civilization has become the backbone of his beliefs. And with that, a growing appeal towards the simple and genuine.[39]

This was an apt description. Helge's interest and respect for "primitive" people's way of life were entwined with a humble admiration of their ability to survive under difficult conditions and a conviction that they were still in possession of values and human qualities modern man was about to lose.

On his return to Norway, Helge greatly anticipated seeing his beloved dogs, Spot and Kazan, and hitching them to his sled and taking off across the Hardanger plateau. While in Arizona, Helge had received a letter from Norman Andersen, who was on his way home after spending the winter in Svalbard. He wrote that he didn't expect to return to Svalbard the following year so left Helge's dogs in the kennel at the governor's residence: "Your dogs are lying stretched out in front of their houses snoring. They don't want to leave. Spot is a nice dog, Kazan too, but Spot is smarter and more compliant. I like him very much."[40]

Not much later, Helge received a letter from Governor Marlow saying he decided to do away with his kennel and had sent the dogs south with one of the last boats to leave that summer. Because no vaccines were available on Svalbard, he had not been able to vaccinate the dogs against distemper. Helge immediately wrote to Kaare asking him to arrange for vaccinations: "Take no chances with Spot. If I do not find him well and fit when I get home it will be a hard blow."

Unfortunately, the regrettable did happen and both dogs contracted distemper and died shortly after arriving on the mainland. Upon returning to Norway, Helge wrote an obituary for them entitled "Two State Officials," which was published in the national newspaper *Dagbladet*. Helge took the loss very hard. He never again became so attached to a dog as he had been to Spot, the puppy from East Greenland who later saved his life on Svalbard.

An increasing number of young women hovered around Helge or sent letters. Perhaps the timing was ripe for the steadfast bachelor to relinquish some of his freedom. From Arizona, he wrote to his friend Odd: "It's good to be young and to have the whole world to yourself, but sometimes I also think I would like to have a wife. For I believe that, in the long run, it could be fairly good to have a woman around – even though at times it could be irritating."

He wrote something similar to his parents: "I am thoroughly tired of being a bachelor. I will now proceed home to Norway and find me a wife. This just isn't sufficient anymore."[41]

Helge eventually decided to resume contact with Anne Stine Moe, with whom he had corresponded, but never had pursued. That first beautiful portrait Anne Stine had sent to him in a fan letter four years earlier was forever on his mind. Here was a girl worth pursuing, as she absolutely captivated Helge's attention.

7 ANNE STINE

A once small town lay so beautifully on the sunny side of the north end of Lake Mjøsa. This was my town, my home, where I grew up. But everything is so different now – when a town grows large, people slip away from one another.[1]

Anne Stine knew the joy of growing up in a time and place that in many ways was unique, and she carried this feeling and awareness with her always. Lillehammer, with its surrounding mountains and valleys, stayed dear to her throughout her entire life. It was here that she kept returning, if not in person, then in mind.

Born 11 February 1918, Anne Stine was christened Anne Kirstine after one of her great grandmothers. Her father, Eilif Moe, an astute lawyer, and her mother, Louise (Lindeman), were both "immigrants" to the town, having moved there from Christiania (later renamed Oslo). Unless a person was born in the area, he or she was not considered a "local." Her parents settled in Lillehammer in 1915, newly married and, for her father, newly employed with the law firm Thallaug and Moe. Their marriage was a warm and trusting relationship. Eilif was tall and thin, had a glimmer in his eyes, and always seemed to be able to cite just the right poem or quote from his vast knowledge of classical literature. Often the centre of attention at parties, he was a smartly dressed gentleman with a hat and silver-handled walking cane that he would cheerfully swing as he strolled along. He was friendly, kind, and funny, yet commanded respect; when he was resting in the corner chair in the family library, everyone else would tiptoe around the house.

Anne Stine Moe, seventeen years old. She sent this photo along with her first fan letter to Helge.

Anne Stine's parents, Eilif and Louise, on the stairs outside their home in Lillehammer.

Louise, in her youth considered one of the most beautiful girls in Christiania, had a beauty which not only endured, but grew with the years. Every wrinkle made her only lovelier, perhaps because of her generous, radiating warmth and kindness. She was cheerful, considerate, and let out a resounding laugh in response to any good story – the perfect companion for someone like Eilif. She made friends wherever she went and never took a train ride to or from Oslo without at least one person confiding their life story to her. When Eilif died, too soon she thought, and her financial situation was tight, everyone helped her out in whatever way they could: a gardener helped without pay; a neighbour shovelled snow; and a taxi driver refused payment when he drove her to and from the train station.

When Anne Stine was born, her brother Tycho was then one-and-a-half years old. Poor Tycho, named after his great grandfather, used to say that "if I had known that I was being christened with that name, I would have hollered more loudly in protest in the church." But grandmother Moe was an overpowering lady and demanded that he be named after her father.

Anne Stine and Tycho were inseparable. She followed her big brother everywhere and adored him above all others. Tycho similarly watched over his little sister with the most tender of care. However, as big brothers do, he also teased Anne Stine at times. But if she gave any sign that she was upset Tycho would yield, then be so distressed that he would cry. Anne Stine, always picking up on any reckless mischievousness her brother got into, gradually developed what she considered to be a telepathic connection to him. She knew exactly whenever something painful happened to him, despite long distances between the two. Anne Stine had this connection to her brother throughout his entire life.

Tycho was a bright, spirited boy, always running from one thing to another. Today he might be diagnosed as hyperactive, but back then little was known about such conditions. Anne Stine never dared to say how scared she actually was sometimes when their play became rambunctious for fear he would not include her the next time.

Eilif was often very stern with Tycho to try to control his wild antics. He himself had grown up in a strict home and so adhered to "old school" child rearing. The willow whip, called "Master Erik," hung on a nail over the bathtub. Although seldom used, Tycho did feel its wrath several times. The boy, however, could sometimes gain the upper hand by beaming a most radiant smile at his father, making him forget to inflict all pending punishment. As he got older though, Tycho would just up and disappear, slamming the door behind him. He was a tough one.

Anne Stine said her father wielded the whip on her only once. When she was about eight years old, her parents organized a concert at their house for a visiting singer. Before the event, she overheard her parents lamenting about how awful the lady actually sang, but they felt obliged to open their house for the concert. After the woman sang, Anne Stine was asked to come forward and thank her for "the lovely song." The little girl felt this was so wrong that instead she chose to say "thank you for that awful song." On the way up the stairs to Master Erik, Anne Stine thought "I deserve this." But had she really? Throughout the years, she often mentioned this episode. I, in turn, have wondered if this lashing actually harmed her ability to stand up for herself and speak her mind.

Anne Stine with her two brothers, Ole Henrik (left) and Tycho.

Early one morning, when Anne Stine was two years old and Tycho almost four, Eilif came in to their bedroom and told them that he had been to the station to collect a little brother for them. Giving birth was not exactly an openly discussed topic back then. Their new baby brother, Ole Henrik, was named after his two grandfathers, and given the middle name Lindeman after his mother. It was now evident that Louise, whom Tycho and Anne Stine previously had all to themselves, was now more "occupied" with an additional child. Tycho and Anne Stine, feeling a little more separate from their mother, became even more dependent on each other. No doubt they were also somewhat jealous of their new little brother, especially Tycho.

Ole Henrik was a very different boy than Tycho. He was quiet, reserved, and watched his siblings' boisterous play with amazement. Much to his mother's great delight, Ole Henrik had inherited the Lindeman family's musical ability. He began playing the piano at the age of four, quickly became very adept, and soon exceeded the abilities of both Anne

Stine and Tycho, who had been playing for much longer. Both his older siblings felt a bit disgraced.

The Moe home was filled with Ole Henrik's piano playing, silent only during the hours the young boy was at school. Anne Stine did her homework literally "to the beat of the band" and learned how to concentrate with whatever sound or decibel level was in the house. It was different for Tycho. He needed quiet to concentrate on his lessons, and his desk was upstairs right above the piano. Anne Stine said sometimes when Ole Henrik played, Tycho would lie on his bed with his head buried in his pillow, screaming with rage. This created many conflicts, for which their parents were not totally blameless. Louise especially seemed to favour her musically gifted younger son, which made Tycho even more jealous.

Many years later, childhood friend Lise Forfang described the Moe family as having "two kinds of kids; boys who would grow up to be something and Anne Stine who would become a lady. She gracefully sat on the couch in a freshly-pressed dress. She was incredibly beautiful and from the age of five knew how to behave at a palace."[2] Perhaps an apt description, but not one totally aligned with Anne Stine's own sense of self: an active girl who loved the outdoors.

Country Charm

Eilif was one of the few in town who owned a car, an open Chevrolet sedan with a folding top. As he often had to travel around the district and valley to conduct landownership inspections, he had to have a car. There was little public transportation at the time and it was limited to the main roadways. Eilif worked on many lawsuits throughout the valley: people in conflict and upset over moved boundary stones and a constant number of inheritance cases. Eilif used to say, "I came to Gudbrandsdal valley charmed by the rural culture, but that all quickly changed."

Sometimes the children were allowed to go along on their father's inspection trips. The roads were miserable, usually narrow and dirt-packed, and slippery as soap when it rained. Eilif pulled up the folding top only when it poured rain, otherwise he left it down, even when it drizzled.

One of Eilif's clients, Guttorm Gjesling Sandbu, lived on a beautiful farm high above the village of Vågå overlooking the mountain range on the other side. Sandbu was a strong, tall man with neat white hair. Anne

Stine thought she had never seen anyone as wonderful as Sandbu. His family had lived on the farm for generations, since the Middle Ages, and were considered the most noble farming family in the country. They had a museum on the farm where they stored armour and weapons from the Middle Ages and from his own ancestors' days of glory.

In Lom, they met another client, Lars Sulheim. He too had a grand farm similar to that of the Sandbu family, with massive carved cabinetry at each end of the main room of his house. Reindeer horns, rifles, and reindeer skins hung along the walls of the magnificent staircase. All of this made a tremendous impression on Anne Stine and certainly made her a country romanticist for life.

Her father, on the other hand, became more and more disillusioned with life in the country. He turned to other types of legal cases and often spoke of his desire to move back to Oslo, but that never came to be. Eilif's interests then increasingly turned to intellectual property (copyright law). For years he had been the lawyer for the famous Norwegian writer Sigrid Undset. In 1928, Eilif even accompanied Undset to Stockholm to receive the Nobel Prize for her trilogy *Kristin Lavransdatter*, about a woman's life in Scandinavia in the Middle Ages. Eventually, many other authors also sought his legal advice and he played a significant role in establishing the Norwegian Association of Copyright Law.[3] He sat on the board of directors as well for Narvesen, a kiosk company, so his trips to Oslo became increasingly frequent.

In the end, Eilif chose to continue living in Lillehammer and travel to Oslo when needed. Much of his decision to stay was also heavily influenced by his interest in the local open-air museum there called Maihaugen, which had a growing collection of several antiquated buildings from old Norwegian farming culture. Following the model of what was called the Glass Friends at the Art Industry Museum in Oslo, he created a similar community of support for Maihaugen called the Sandvig Collection Friends.[4] Eilif was chairman of the Sandvig Collection Friends for several years before becoming chariman of the board at Maihaugen.

The children were happy not to have to move to Oslo. Though they never really felt as if they were living in the country since many worldly people came to their house seeking Eilif's help: translators, publishers, and authors. In the small town of Lillehammer, Eilif was able to establish a literary agency that helped protect authors' rights both domestically and abroad. Max Tau, a Jewish German writer, was one such author who often came to visit before the Second World War to collaborate with Eilif on publishing German literature in Norwegian. During the war, Anne Stine's family helped Tau to settle in Norway after his escape from Germany.

Maribuseter: The Family Mountain Cabin

As a child, Anne Stine and her family spent holidays both in the mountains and by the sea. They stayed part of the summer at Grandmother Berit's house in Åsgårdstrand, about 100 kilometres south of Oslo along the fjord. This was also where Anne Stine's mother Louise and her family spent some of their summers when she was younger.

One quite remarkable incident from Louise's childhood occurred when her family was visiting Åsgårdstrand. Louise, her sister Aagot, and a friend of theirs were about to cross over a bridge in the village. Suddenly they heard someone shout out to them, "Wait. Stand still, just there." They turned and there stood the famous Norwegian artist Edvard Munch, working on a painting. So the girls did stand still, a good long while. Whether this turned out to be the final work of one of Munch's well-known paintings, *Girls on the Bridge*, or just a sketch is unknown. But it certainly was a story for the girls to always remember and to tell their children and grandchildren about.

Louise, however, was especially fond of the mountains. In her own youth, she had spent time at a high mountain farm in the Vågå mountains, not far from the Jotenheimen mountains. It was her greatest wish that her own children could experience the same. She had heard of a mountain farm situated far in the valley of Gudbrandsdalen called Storhøliseter. It was known as the place where the Norwegian poet Theodor Caspari spent more than twenty summers and which he called the most beautiful mountain farm in Norway. It was here that the Moe family spent many of their summers until 1927. By then, Anne Stine was nine years old and had learned to milk and herd goats like a fully fledged milkmaid.

During the summer of 1924, the family took a different route to Storhøliseter over Espedals Lake. Going along in the boat, Eilif pointed up towards the mountain on the west side of the lake and said, "Up there children is our own mountain place and we'll go there one day." Way up on the mountainside they caught a quick glimpse of a small cluster of grey houses, then it all disappeared behind the tops of tall pine trees. Eilif had worked on a court case for the Bjørnstjerne Bjørnson[5] family, and when asked what he would accept as payment he answered, "You have an old seter up there in Espedalen, I would very much like that" – and so it was. The first few years, Eilif and friends only used it as a hunting cabin as it was much too ramshackle to stay in for very long. But then during the spring of 1927, Eilif received a visit from a previous client whom he had defended in court, "Quarreling Olsen." The man knew about the old seter and said, "Now I want to build a cabin for you there because I'm unemployed you see and a good carpenter." Eilif agreed it was a wonderful idea and by late summer the same year, the Moe family had a very nice new cabin.

It was a steep climb up to the place. But the pleasant trail followed a small river with trickling waterfalls and lovely pools to swim in. Because it was such a steep climb, the family rarely had visitors while they were there in the summers. However, one evening an unexpected guest appeared. One of the farmers from the valley knocked on the door, and strapped to his back was a beautiful old corner cupboard. "I carried it for a lady," he said. The lady showed up not long after huffing and puffing. It was Sigrid Undset. The whole family was so happy to see her, and the much-appreciated housewarming gift was placed in the corner by the sofa.

Trout fishing and swimming were big on the agenda at Maribuseter. Right from the start, Tycho began to wander the hills by himself with his fishing rod. He eventually got to know all the others at the surrounding mountain farms, who were there to either fish or herd cattle and horses. At first, Anne Stine missed Storhøliseter with all its animals and farm duties. But she eventually grew attached to Maribuseter with all its beautiful flowers and heather, birds, and wildlife – the same she knew so well from the other mountain farm.

Louise, who was convinced that her children were much too bright to spend as much time at school as the other kids, took them to the seter as soon as the ice disappeared and the path became manageable. Eilif came up and down as much as his work allowed.

Reading was also high on the agenda at Maribuseter and the place was full of books. Louise loved to read aloud, and a grey day was never dull when she plowed through *The Three Musketeers* or *The Count of Monte Christo*, not to mention the fifty-two volumes of the tales of Rocambole, the French fictional adventurer. These were so exciting that the children held their breath in suspense as they listened. Eilif was also good at reading aloud, as well as throwing in a bit of drama. Through Eilif, the Moe family became fond of many poets.

Eventually as the children grew older, they wanted a little more of their own space at their mountain home. Tycho came up with the solution. He sawed a hole in the kitchen ceiling and created a loft area. Soon the cabin was filled with young people coming to visit. He then thought of the idea of building another small cabin on the property. The Maribuseter plot included a fairly large parcel of woodland, and Tycho went to work in the summer of 1938 chopping down timber. Anne Stine helped by cutting off branches and stripping the trees of bark. Most of the summer of 1938 was spent working there in the woods. When the snow came, they were able to drag the timber up the slope. Tycho wanted to build a more traditional type of cabin, like a small copy of one of the houses at the Maihaugen museum. The following summer a couple of men from the valley came to set it up. Eilif advertised in the local paper for an old soapstone fireplace and was offered one almost immediately. Tycho carried the fireplace stones, one by one, on his back up the steep hill, the largest piece weighing nearly 100 kilograms. People throughout the district talked about this for a long time afterwards. The exterior framework of this cabin was finished by the fall, but the interior would take longer to complete. That winter, Tycho took pilot training and was later drafted to serve as a military guard at Kirkenes in northern Norway, where he served during the Winter War between Finland and Russia. When the Second World War broke out in Norway on 9 April 1940, Tycho was still in the far north of Norway. That fall he travelled all the way across Siberia and over Canada to reach the exiled Royal Norwegian Air Force training base near Toronto called Little Norway. He never came back.

8   A YOUNG ROMANTIC

Looking through the books lining the shelves at the family cabin, Maribu-seter, you can see that romance was very much on young Anne Stine's mind. Several "young lady novels" from the 1930s line the shelves alongside "priceless treasures" such as *The Sheik* and *The Sultan's Woman Slave*. It was highly unlikely that Ole Henrik or Tycho bought them.

Anne Stine most likely dreamt of being whisked away by a knight in shining armour, galloping off with him on a beautiful white horse. However, her fantasies eventually took on a more northerly flair. One Christmas, she and the Undset children went to see a film about a Sami girl named Laila. Anne Stine had never before been to the theatre or cinema, so it was an especially enjoyable experience for her. This was the time of silent movies, and the accompanying music was performed by the local dentist, Dr Olsen, who frequently performed on such occasions. The Swedish actress Mona Martenson played the role as the Sami girl Laila in the romantic melodrama about a young woman torn between two worlds, nomadic and settled. She was beautiful and impressive. "I identified completely with Laila. But it wasn't only that; all the life in the wilderness that I saw unfold upon the screen made an unforgettable impression on me. It was as if something opened up within me that I hadn't previously been aware of," she wrote in a draft of an autobiography.

Three years later, when she held in her hands a newly published book called *The Land of Feast and Famine*, she was determined to marry the man who wrote the book and join him on his adventures into the wilderness. "How strong a film can influence a child's mind – that it can determine one's life,"[1] Anne Stine wrote. Her friend Lise, years later, explained it differently: "Amundsen was long dead, Nansen had died in

The book *The Land of Feast and Famine* touched Anne Stine's heart.

the 1930s, so then it was only Helge Ingstad left – and he was incredibly handsome."[2]

"Why don't you write to him?" her friend, and Undset's niece, Charlotte said to her one day as they sat in the girl's hideaway that Eilif had made for her up in the attic of their house. On Valentine's Day 1935, Anne Stine wrote to Helge:

> Dear Helge Ingstad,
> Without ado, I will get to the matter. I turned 17 on February 11th and as a birthday present I was hoping to be able to write to you. So, I have thought affectionately of you for four years and now I think the least you could do for me is to send a photograph with a nice greeting (from yourself that is). That isn't too much is it? I know your book "The Land of Feast and Famine" by heart, and my mother and father are acquainted with you and your sister, so this isn't so impolite of me to ask.[3] Well now it is done and my name is Anne Stine Moe and I send you lots of greetings.
> PS – Don't laugh too much at me then. That would be quite cruel.
> A.S.

What would a thirty-five-year-old bachelor who had lived many of his adult years in the wilderness make of such a letter? At any rate, Helge took good care of these first letters his entire life. At the time, he was governor at Svalbard and most likely didn't receive the letter until the first boat delivered it later that spring. Unfortunately, his reply to Anne Stine is gone, burned along with all the others in her "letter fire" before she died. However, in Anne Stine's next letter to Helge dated 8 June 1935 she wrote:

> Dear Helge Ingstad,
> Oh how happy I am! I didn't know it was possible to be so happy. I am sitting here now with both a picture and a letter; I can hardly believe it's true! A simple thank you isn't enough I know, but what else can I say? Well, I extend my hand and say thank you very much.
> Your letter was so nice. And it was fun to hear about Spot and all your other lovely puppies and dogs. I too have a dog I am truly fond of. It is a grey elkhound. Remarkable that it is still so very

cold for you; but surely it will warm up soon in Longyearbyen. Yes, here it is lovely and warm and everything nice and green. In the garden, many alpine flowers are blooming that we have brought down from the mountains. Last year, we also had several flowers sent by airplane from Tyrol that are coming along very fine now.

Here is a picture of me which I am so glad that you asked for. Take good care of me then! I travel with a trembling heart.

Greet all the dogs and give them all a nice pat from me.

Yours sincerely,

Anne Stine

Touched by this very young admirer, Helge continued to correspond with her and received letters in exchange. On returning to the mainland, he did not dare ask her out alone, as she was so young. Eventually, he stopped by for a visit as he just "happened" to travel by Lillehammer on various assignments. This way, he became well acquainted with her family and in particular with Tycho, whom he got along with very well. Eilif was perhaps more skeptical. Someone courting his daughter who was only a few years younger than himself was not exactly what he had in mind for her. Louise, on the other hand, had met Helge at a social gathering in Christiania (Oslo) before she married and thought it was nice to see him again. The letters from Anne Stine suggest that the visits quickly evolved into something more than just a superficial acquaintance. There had even been talk of engagement, but Helge himself was a bit reserved concerning the large age difference of eighteen years. In the end, he sent her a letter and a telegram in which he made it clear that because of the age difference it was best if they didn't think about marriage.

Out into the World

When Anne Stine turned eighteen, the question arose, "What was she to be?" She herself dreamt of becoming an archaeologist after fervently reading about the discovery of Tutankhamen's tomb in Egypt. However, she also felt she had had enough of school and began to doubt this dream.

Everyone in the family had their opinion about this. Tycho definitely thought that she should finish her education, as did her cousin Boss. But

Eilif had old-fashioned ideas concerning women and would rather that she did not become a career woman. Louise agreed. But they did think it could be both useful and fun for her to travel to Paris and learn French. And so she did.

Anne Stine was accepted by a good language school near the Latin Quarter district in Paris. In a tiny little apartment, she was offered a closet-sized room with a view out to the narrow back alley full of rubbish bins. She gladly accepted, moved in, and got settled all in the course of one morning. Over her bed, she hung a photograph of Helge clad in his caribou parka.

She made friends with the other tenants of the apartment, four French architecture students, but still she grew horribly homesick and longed for the mountains. She lay in her bed imagining walking across frozen marshes across the plateaus near the family cabin. So she began taking long walks around Paris, riding the metro line all the way to the end station and then walking back. By doing this, she came across a beautiful church in between the houses and back streets where she often would stop and stay for mass. Eventually, she became captivated by the Catholic services, which gave her great comfort. This was the beginning of a development in Anne Stine that, later in life, led her to convert to Catholicism.

Helge and Anne Stine continued to exchange letters during her time in Paris, but only sporadically and then in more formal tones. On 6 January 1936, she wrote to him after receiving word that he would be hospitalized for major surgery. It was the tuberculosis in his kidney, which he clearly had not mentioned to her.

Dear Helge Ingstad,
Thank you very much for your letter! It was awfully nice to get it, but I was so sad when I learned that you would have to go into the hospital again. I truly hope that it isn't something serious! Was it when you somersaulted off that high snowdrift that you were injured? I read about the trip in the newspaper this summer. It sounded as if it had been very shocking. The part about the frozen sleeping bag and the cod liver oil from the lamp that you had to eat gave me the chills. I like so much to read about your trips and the life you lead in the wilderness, about the animal life, cabin

life and everything. Where did you like it the best, in Canada, Greenland or Svalbard? I wonder who lives in Heimen [back in Greenland] now? It sounded nice there … I haven't begun to use lipstick or eye shadow, and I won't either. That is such muck! Do you think it is pretty? If you do, maybe I'll start to use it, even though of course you don't see me. I'll be here until the middle of June. Then it will be wonderful to come home and go up to the mountains; in all honesty, I long for green meadows, heather and mountains. How fun that you have been so fortunate with the book. You have all reason to be proud. Where I stayed at Christmas they had a large library and in it I found "The Land of Feast and Famine." The lady was in fact Norwegian. She too admires your books.

How are the dogs while you are in hospital? Do they come and visit? Say hello to all of them from me again, if you can. Now you must get well again soon! Hope it doesn't hurt. Anyway, a very good and speedy recovery and a happy new year.
Many warm greetings from your Anne Stine

Complicated Love

They didn't meet again until later that year in August. Anne Stine accompanied Eilif on one of his trips to Oslo and Helge grabbed that chance to invite her, of all things, on a plane ride! His friends Bernt Balchen and Chris Braaten, whom Helge knew from Canada, where they had operated flights for mining companies, had just returned to Norway with a new Chicory aircraft. In a letter to his father, Helge tells about the plane ride, but not a word about the young girl who accompanied him.

On 17 August, Anne Stine wrote to Helge from Maribuseter – and once again they were on a first-name basis:

Dear Helge,
Thank you so much for our last time together! It was incredibly wonderful to be with you. I am now in the mountains again, but unfortunately not for long since my brother's school begins again on the 20th. Wish that I was allowed to be left up here, but I doubt it. Have you been out flying again since Thursday? You have no

idea how thrilled I am about my first plane trip. I boasted about it to my mother and Ole Henrik the entire Friday.
Are you soon travelling to the mountains? Farewell.
Yours sincerely, Anne Stine

At some point, most likely in 1936, a German man by the name of Werner showed up in Anne Stine's life. Max Tau had brought him to Norway to talk to Eilif about publishing a book of Werner's life as a trapper in Labrador in 1931.[4] In other words, yet another fur trapper! The book was published in 1937 and dedicated to "Miss Anne Stine."

Werner liked Norway and stayed for quite a long time. He learned to speak Norwegian well and became good friends with Tycho. He also loved being at Maribuseter, where on his first visit he was given the suitable duty, according to Tycho, of emptying the outdoor toilet. Werner was only a few years older than Tycho, wonderful and handsome, and Anne Stine fell in love with him almost immediately. The feeling was mutual, and it didn't take long before they were engaged. But it never crossed Anne Stine's mind that she might have to live in Germany. Perhaps she had hoped to make a Norwegian out of him.

Werner wasn't just any "boy next door." He was Baron von Grünau and supposedly one of the direct descendants of Germany's last emperor. Eilif was thrilled as he had a weakness for titles and fine families, and Louise too had no reservations about the relationship. But Tycho was not happy. He did not want a German brother-in-law nor Anne Stine living far away. Tycho always had strong opinions about whom his sister was seeing. She actually thought it was quite nice how much he cared about her, but this time, at least in the beginning, she chose not to listen to him. To what extent Anne Stine actually wanted to marry Werner or was just driven by a desire to please her parents, especially her father, is uncertain. Eventually though, she clearly agonized over her choice between the two men – Werner, or Helge, whom she still had contact with. She was only twenty years old.

While travelling south on a train to Germany to spend the Christmas of 1938 with her prospective in-laws, Anne Stine wrote to Helge:

My own dearly beloved Helge,
First of all, I want to thank you for the lovely words you sent me from Hamar; oh you made me so happy with them, thank you. I

too send you the same – I love you, love you and always will. It was so wonderful to be together with you those two days, incredibly wonderful. I thought and thought for days afterwards, but I must travel [to Germany] for Christmas; but you must not lose faith in our tender love for I have not. I love you and you me, is that not true and there must be a way.

I feel though that I must do and give as much as before, and in a way that he does not sense the obligation. Otherwise it is quite unfair to him. I am terribly sorry and dismayed about this, but I ask you, dear Helge, to not lose faith … Take care, my Helge, I always think of you and I kiss you in my thoughts – and in the moonlight – my darling Helge. Merry Christmas and Happy New Year and happy birthday on the 30th.
Always yours, Anne Stine

On the train ride through Germany, Anne Stine stopped to visit Max Tau and his wife Renate in Berlin. When she arrived on 10 November 1938, only Renate met her at the station. Anne Stine then learned of the terrible things that had happened during the night. Driving through the streets she was horrified to see broken glass everywhere; stores and shops were destroyed and windows shattered. Later known as *Kristallnacht*, or the "Night of Broken Glass," Hitler's attack on the Jews had begun in earnest. Max was a nervous wreck and didn't dare go out. Before Anne Stine left, he decided to escape from Germany and asked her to take a large suitcase for him. As she was travelling, it occurred to her that carrying this suitcase was perhaps dangerous since she had no idea what was in it. Fortunately, all went well.

Spending Christmas at her prospective in-laws' estate in Upper Bavaria was a shocking experience for Anne Stine. Their house was huge and cold, in both degrees and emotions, influenced by a domineering prospective mother-in-law and German upper-class family rule. Anne Stine felt lost and homesick and began to wonder what in the world she had gotten herself into. It was then Tycho stepped in. He called Helge, who was spending the Christmas holidays at his parents in Bergen, and said, "Now you must hurry and propose to my sister for she is about to get married in Germany." Helge quickly called her on Christmas Eve, not once but twice, yet did not propose. However, Anne Stine quickly wrote a letter to him on 26 December 1939 explaining that "I travelled here because I was convinced that it was the right thing to do; I could never have had peace of mind if I had done otherwise. I did it with the intention of doing my very best to make Werner happy, and myself, and I must hold to that all I can."

She continued by saying that when she boarded the train to Germany, she wished so much that she instead could have travelled to Bergen and to him, and that she could not break up with Werner while she was a guest in his house nor when he "lavished his love upon her." Then she asked Helge not to contact her until she returned after New Year's. Helge, however, did not heed this request and instead sent a card with a picture of two huge, rearing black stallions challenging each other. Its symbolic message left little doubt. Only a few words were written on the card: "Nothing like Norway. Greetings, Helge."

Not much else was needed. Anne Stine boarded a train headed north as soon as she could. The card sat on the fireplace mantel for years afterwards.

Immediately upon returning from Germany on 23 January, Anne Stine wrote to Helge from Lillehammer:

My dear, dear Helge,
I have thought so much about you and how you are. It was painful for me to write that last letter to you, but as it was I had to because Werner was so distressed and he almost insisted on it. I have been so afraid that all this time you have been angry at me after I sent that letter. Are you Helge? Oh please don't be, I am just as in love with you now as before and always will be … it is again uncertain when I will marry. From 7 February, Werner will be drafted into military service and it could be seven months before we see each other again … I often think of you Helge, you are a part of everything I love so much in nature. Just today, I was at that cabin where we last sat together; I drank a glass of milk and then left. Our evening there was wonderful, I will never forget it. Do you remember the crystal-clear sky when we walked down? I will never forget all the wonderful words you said to me and I have often read the beautiful poem you gave me – I am so happy to have it.
Dear, dear Helge, I must soon receive a letter from you saying that you are not angry with me despite all the pain I have caused

you. I have always dreamt of making you happy and then I've done just the opposite. My feelings for you have never changed even though everything now must be different … Good bye my darling. The most affectionate greetings from your Anne Stine. PS – I may travel back to Paris in February.

Life had certainly become dramatic for her! Perhaps she imagined herself as a heroine in one of her romance novels on the bookshelves at Maribuseter. Or was it simply youthful infatuation and ignorance that caused her to become so wrapped up in such a tangle? It must have been quite an ordeal for Werner having a fiancée visiting for Christmas who was constantly receiving letters, calls, cards, and pictures from another suitor.

But whether it was the prospect of having his German rival away at the front lines for seven months that finally prodded "the trapper" to take action or not, we'll never know. However, in Helge's next letter to Anne Stine he proposes a rendezvous in Paris in connection with a trip he was going to take to Germany to talk to publishers. Her response[5] must have been a bit of a jolt. She tells him that she is still engaged to Werner and asks him, for everyone's sake, not to come.

The Proposal

In the fall of 1939, Anne Stine once again left for Paris. She had been accepted into the famous Sorbonne University for a course on French literature and art history. She felt it a great honour to study in those magnificent halls at one of the oldest universities in the world. When she returned to Norway that Christmas, there was no immediate reunion with Helge. Although she was delighted to be back in Norway again, Anne Stine was still in agony over which suitor to choose. She was now formally engaged to Werner and had already begun to make purchases in Paris for the wedding.

At the beginning of November 1940, Anne Stine again wrote to Helge. By now Norway was occupied by Germany, but it was obviously her dramatic love life that was more on her mind. In the letter, she thanks him for two letters which he obviously sent suggesting the possibility of visiting her:

It would be nice if you came to visit Helge, but there are a few things I need to explain to you before you decide to come. I should have told you in my first letter, but then I thought I just wanted you to come. But it is not right of me. You see, I am still engaged to Werner. I couldn't bear to get married last spring as I was too uncertain. But this summer showed me that three years [in a relationship] is not easy to dismiss, and then the war came and all that.

Dear Helge, I know this hurts you, and I understand that you are still in love with me, and it all makes me unbearably miserable for your sake. You are so often in my thoughts, but now I can think of you without feeling the pain I did before. But I will never forget you, as you have been such a very great part of me and my life and I see and meet you in all that I love in nature. I feel an incredible joy and happiness in that, as I did before ... I do not know if after this you will come to visit, and perhaps it is best if you didn't and that you try to forget me ... I cannot bear to continue this letter, it is so painful. Farewell. You know that I wish you all the best.

Love, Anne Stine

Whether she finally mustered up the courage to end the engagement with Werner or whether it just slowly faded as a result of the war is uncertain. However, as the war progressed, the prospect of having a German son-in-law clearly grew less and less attractive to Eilif and Louise. It certainly made it easier for Anne Stine, and soon her relationship with Werner ended. Because he spoke Norwegian, Werner was stationed in Norway during the war. But as an opponent to the Hitler regime, he found it very upsetting. He had contact with Louise only once during this time but otherwise kept himself away from those he knew.[6]

Contact between Helge and Anne Stine intensified. With Werner out of the picture, their relationship grew more serious. Helge knew he had to make a decision before another suitor for this beautiful young woman came along. It was now or never! One day as they were out to dinner at a restaurant, Helge said, "Now let's see about getting married" – and so they did.

9 WAR BREAKS OUT

The first signs of spring were beginning to appear around the lake and mountains of Sølensjøen, a few hours northeast of Lillehammer towards the Swedish border. It was early April 1940. Easter had just ended and the few holiday visitors who had been at the cabins there had now returned to the valley and cities. It was only Helge and old hermit Nygardsen who remained.

Helge liked the area and had been there several times. The first time was with the Widerøe brothers, who had begun flying in Easter guests already in 1934. After that, he had either taken the train to Koppang, hitched a ride to Rendalen, and then either skied or hiked across the mountains. The landscape reminded Helge of the tundra of Canada and that is what drew him here, as well as the hunting and fishing. In winter, stretches of white, open spaces reached all the way to the lake nestled in the valley. The mountains behind could easily have been the hills surrounding Great Slave Lake.

Old hermit Nygardsen was a kindred spirit who had much in common with the trappers Helge knew from Canada. A weather-beaten, smiling chap in his fifties, Nygardsen had chosen the wilderness over civilization and lived year-round in a small cabin at the lake. For Helge, Sølensjøen was his refuge when he longed the most for the wilderness. Here he found solace in those things he had appreciated in Canada: whitefish and trout in the lake, grouse on the hillsides, and every once in a while, fresh reindeer. They say he even went wolverine hunting with the locals from the valley.

Helge had been invited to spend Easter week at Sølensjøen with Sheriff Lombnæs. But when the holiday was over, Helge wasn't yet ready to leave the mountains and asked Nygardsen if he could stay a while

Tycho (right) and a fellow pilot after a raid.

longer, to which he agreed. During the days, the two men strapped on their skis and wandered the hills. In the evenings, they played cards and listened to the old wind-up gramophone. Nygardsen loved that gramophone and would play his favourite song for hours on end. He even connected his alarm clock to it so that when the alarm rang it would play his favourite tune.

Nygardsen, despite his hermit-like life, did not scorn women or drink and would sometimes journey down to the village to partake in both at the local dance hall. On 7 April 1940, he and Helge had gone down to the village on one such visit and stayed the evening. The day after, on 8 April, they heard on the radio that the British had laid out a minefield along Norway's west coast to help prevent a Nazi takeover of Scandinavia. The two men postponed their return to the mountains. The following day, 9 April, news came on the radio that the Germans were advancing into Oslo and Foreign Affairs Minister Koht mumbled a vague statement about mobilizing to defend.[1]

 Helge acted quickly. He borrowed a local telephone and called Anne Stine in Lillehammer. Had she heard the same? He reckoned that Eilif, a man of importance in the community, would have heard something. Yes, she could confirm the rumour. They had a brief conversation, but both were too shaken to carry on talking. For Helge, it was important to get to Oslo; maybe the fighting against the Germans had already started. Staying in the mountains was not an option for him and he immediately left for the city. Little did Helge know when he left the mountains of Østerdalen[2] that he left the very spot where some of the heaviest fighting would occur between Norwegians and German troops.

Helge hitched a ride with a policeman down the valley to the local train station. He had expected to find full mobilization orders posted there – but found nothing. People waited intently for the train to arrive, which didn't show up until 5:00 that evening. Orders came, but without any details; no mention of day, time, or place, and therefore were completely useless. Helge and others boarded the train headed south to Oslo. Everything seemed so strange. Several young men were headed to sign up at military units. But nobody knew where or to what extent there was fighting, or if the city had already been captured by the Germans, or where they should go to enlist. Rumours spread. Some of the people on the train recognized Helge and came to ask for his advice. As the southbound train to Oslo pulled into the station at Elverum, 50 kilometres from the city, a northbound train came rushing by the station. It was carrying the king, crown prince, and several government officials. Few on the train headed to Oslo recognized them, but Helge caught a brief glimpse of the familiar faces, "some of our most highly-regarded politicians, but not looking so very high then," he said later.

Not long after, as another northbound train slowly passed the southbound train, people shouted over for any news. "The Germans are invading Oslo!" they yelled back, which Helge assumed meant there was fighting in the capital city. But when his train rolled into the Oslo station in the middle of the night, no sign of any combat was seen or heard. Only two fully armed German soldiers wearing steel helmets stood there watching as the train came in. At three o'clock in the morning, Helge wandered up a main avenue of Oslo, Bygdøy allé, on his way to his apartment. The streets were utterly quiet and deserted; no cars, no taxis, just German soldiers everywhere. German guards stood outside the parliament building and at the royal palace, and had even bunked down inside the National Theatre – horrendous, Helge thought. Oslo had clearly been captured.

Over the course of the next few days, the city changed completely. German soldiers were scattered everywhere; some troops marched through the streets chanting, others stood playing cards in front of the parliament. At the harbour, German troop ships continually unloaded soldiers, tanks, jeeps, horses, and other equipment. Oslo citizens looked on nervously, confident that the British would come to their rescue.

As the days passed and no help arrived, it became evident that they would have to help themselves. But what could they do? The Norwegian fascist politician Vidkun Quisling had been appointed "president minister" and played on national feelings to persuade other Norwegians to his side. The people grew divided and the government was on the run with no clear leadership to form a resistance movement.

Norwegian troops gathered from valleys and communities all over Norway, and Otto Ruge, commanding general of the Norwegian Armed Forces, gave orders to fight. In Oslo, however, details of this fighting were scarce. Rumours flourished, and one day news spread that the whole city was going to be bombed. People evacuated into Nordmarka, the forest north of the city, some hiding there for several days before realizing there was no bomb threat. Helge stayed in the city. He wandered around in the abandoned streets wondering what to do and how to get out of the city

German soldiers and Norwegian civilians unsure of each other during the first days of the German occupation of Norway.

to join the Norwegians fighting on the front lines around the country. All roads out were blocked, but skiing through the woods was an escape, despite a rumour of someone who had tried and was shot. But Helge had his bag packed and skis ready.

While trying to figure out what to do, Helge happened upon the Red Cross office. He went in, introduced himself, and asked to speak to General Secretary Arnold Rørholt. By then, Helge was a well-known writer respected for his tough trips in the wilderness. Inside the office, the people paced about confused and anxious. The Red Cross had doctors, nurses, and supplies, but despite their best efforts they had not succeeded in getting in contact with the front line. The German guards kept stopping them at the road controls.

"How are you making out?" Helge asked.

"Badly," replied Rørholt. "We can't get anywhere. The city is closed off and we can't get out."

"Give me a car," Helge suggested, "with the Red Cross emblem and full authority, and I'll try to get past the guards to the front line."

Helge received his request, and on 13 April he was ready with a car, a driver by the name of Ferdinand Juell, some first aid equipment, and medical student Ivar Hauge, who was willing to stay on the front line if necessary. They took off, Helge wearing a cap cunningly resembling that of a German uniform hat. Driving quickly past the German guards as Helge pleasantly saluted, they got through and reached the front line. Most likely, it helped that Helge resembled a German officer. The Red Cross team were prepared for not being able to reach the Norwegian side of fighting, but hoped to help fellow countrymen on the occupied side.

For Helge, going to war on behalf of the Red Cross resolved his dilemma of not knowing whether to leave the city or not. Even though he was not a declared pacifist, he was greatly against taking the life of another, even an enemy, who in this case were to a large extent young boys ordered to go to war. But he also wanted to serve his country in the best possible way. He strongly felt, almost like a calling, that it was through the Red Cross that he could help. Helge also realized that there were civilians with serious illnesses who were dependent on certain drugs to survive. With no access into the city for insulin or other essential medicines, he took these with him to give to those who needed them.

About 20 kilometres west of Oslo, Helge and the two others in their Red Cross car saw the first signs of fighting. Just outside of Sandvika, overturned cars lined the side of the road and one was riddled with bullet holes. Three Norwegian youths on their way out of town had refused to stop when ordered and all were shot. Farther north at Sundvollen, Helge and his companions learned that Norwegians had fought on the other side of the bridge and had blown it up the day before. Large holes in the frozen fjord showed where two German cars had gone through the ice. One had been carrying loaves of bread that were now scattered everywhere. Juell took a chance and drove the Red Cross car across the ice and the men made it to the other side. A few kilometres farther they heard stories of fighting just the day before. About a hundred

Norwegians had hidden in the woods and attacked the Germans. No Norwegian soldiers had been killed, but the Germans were furious over the attack. They shot three civilians and looted the general store before moving on. The front line continued moving north.

The Red Cross car arrived at Hønefoss, about an hour northwest of Oslo, at around seven o'clock that evening. Double the number of guards stood on both sides of the bridge, but Helge saluted with his cap in his now much-rehearsed method and their car was quickly allowed through. The town was full of German soldiers who were irate because civilians shot at them when they entered the town. A notice was posted proclaiming that if a single German were killed, a hundred Norwegians would be executed in return. "Best not to stay the night here," thought Helge and so they returned to one of the farms near the bridge. The farmer was there, but the rest of his family had evacuated. Helge, Hauge, and Juell were welcome to roll out their sleeping bags and sleep on his floor.

Early the next morning they were awakened by machine gun fire. There was fighting in the village. Then they heard a shot just outside their window. Helge looked out and saw a civilian running by and a German about a hundred yards down the road shooting at him. Helge ran out to the front stairs to see if he could help the Norwegian, who then collapsed at his feet. He was an older fellow who had been hit in the thigh. He didn't make a sound, "like a wounded caribou." Helge waved with his arms and called out to the German who was running towards them with his rifle aimed and ready. He was just a young kid who seemed dazed and confused. Excitedly the soldier explained that he had repeatedly ordered the man to put his hands up, but when he ran off he had to shoot. Helge helped the wounded man into the house, where medical student Hauge bandaged him. Several other Germans appeared and the young soldier kept stuttering his explanation of what had happened. His older comrades listened, then quite smugly said to Helge, "This is the first man he's shot."

In the town of Hønefoss, surgeon Hartvig Norbye was frantically taking in the wounded at a small Catholic clinic, San Fransiscus Hospital. Soldiers wounded in heavy fighting just a short distance away farther north came flooding in, both German and Norwegian. There weren't enough surgeons or medicine to handle it all, but Helge was able to provide some of the latter with what he had brought from Oslo. While they were taking in the wounded, a young woman came rushing in, bare-headed, breathless, and frightened. She said there was a Norwegian close to the German line who had been shot and was bleeding, and if he were not helped immediately, he could die. Helge hurried to get there. Fighting was intense; all the houses were on fire and machine guns rattled non-stop. A pig, caught in the cross fire, lay dead in the snow. Helge passed a German soldier lying lifeless by the side of the road with his face smashed in.

With the farm buildings burning and the cattle frantically bellowing, Helge wished he could run to let the animals out. But people had to come first. He spotted the wounded Norwegian in a small hollow surrounded by his silent, frightened family. The man was shot in the stomach and lay on a bloody mattress. Helge tried to help him as best he could with limited first aid. Then an entire German battalion came marching by headed to reinforce their troops. Helge thought, "What the hell! I might as well take the bull by the horns." He went right up to them with the Red Cross emblem visible on his arm. "It was actually quite strange to look in their faces," he later recalled. "How they looked just as they were going off to fight and kill people – young boys. There was something hard, unhappy and rigid about them. I said to one: There's someone lying here bleeding, can you help me?" A German then ordered a paramedic to try to stop the bleeding, while Helge ran as fast as he could to the hospital to get help to carry the wounded man down. Helge never knew in the end what happened to this man.[3]

More wounded Norwegians and German soldiers came pouring in to the hospital, and soon there was no more room to place them. Outside in the square, the dead began to pile up and coffins were rushed in, though not nearly enough. Dr Nordbye and the Catholic sisters worked as frantically as they could. In one of the rooms, they put the most severely wounded whom they didn't expect to survive. A few, however, did survive. "They had incredible tenacity those Germans," Helge wrote.[4]

The need for more surgeons, and access to the front, was obvious. So Helge approached the German commander in Hønefoss and explained the need for medical help, not only for wounded Norwegians but also for the Germans. He added that he would have to make several trips back and forth from Oslo through the German stop point. Helge managed to succeed in gaining free passage for the Red Cross for a week, a small victory. He travelled to Oslo several times to collect medicine, equipment, and more doctors and nurses to bring to the front lines of battle.

Helge in the ruins of a bombed and burned-down house.

Back in Hønefoss, Dr Norbye explained that they needed someone to help administer the field hospitals as well as perform basic relief work, not just on the front line but in all the areas where there was fighting in Norway. Norbye believed that Helge was the man for the job and that the Administrative Council (Administrasjonsrådet),[5] the civil government body in Norway during the occupation, should appoint him to the position with full authority at the front lines. Helge at first balked at the thought of taking on such a colossal job. However, in a letter dated 16 April 1940, Dr Norbye wrote to the Administrative Council recommending Helge for the position and ended by saying, "Negotiating with the Germans by a man of such authority could mean saving human lives."[6]

The Council at first wanted to appoint Helge chief of police in Hønefoss, which he had no interest in. What he wanted to do was form integrated action for the Red Cross across the country – not only to help the wounded soldiers, but also to more extensively aid civilians who were caught in the midst of war and in danger of being killed. Besides bringing medicine and food to these people, he also wanted to help communities get back on their feet.

Almost the same day and with immediate effect, the Administrative Council appointed Helge as the head of relief work in districts within the occupied territories. He was regarded as a representative of the Council and his main task was to "seek to reassure, help and advise the populations in these districts."[7] He also was given the authority to coordinate all administrative and police issues necessary to carry out these functions. Helge wrote in his journal that he felt good about the Administrative Council and that they were a group of "honest Norwegians, without political sway, who earnestly took to their task."

Initially, Helge worked mostly on the frontline. With the Red Cross car, the emblem on his sleeve, and a good portion of fearlessness towards the Germans in command, he was able to get anywhere he needed. His main task was to help the wounded, transport them to the nearest hospital, and notify their next of kin. He also negotiated with the Germans on the release of prisoners and for the exchange of Norwegian wounded soldiers for German. But Helge's efforts with relief work were equally important: transporting food and supplies to towns where shops had been destroyed and burnt, and distributing seeds to the farmers for spring planting.

Fighting in the Hønefoss area was over by 16 April but carried on farther north. As Helge headed in this direction, he heard about a group of thirty-three civilians, farmers from a local village, who had been taken prisoner. No one was certain where. Some were old, others were just boys, and one was clearly mentally disabled; they were all crammed into a large garage. One of the German guards told Helge the group was going to be driven south to Brandbu, where the residing general would decide their fate.

At Helge's request, they released the younger boys and the mentally disabled man, but the rest of the men were lined up and marched into a bus. Instead of continuing north to the front line, Helge followed the bus south. After reasoning with the general, who "looked to be Prussian, but still with a sense of humanity," Helge managed to get the rest of the men released.

The War Comes to Lillehammer

Anne Stine and her family had also spent Easter of 1940 in the mountains at their cabin. While there, they received word that Tycho was in the hospital after his plane had crashed in Finnmark, northern Norway, where he was stationed to patrol the border of Finland. The crash wasn't an exceptionally heroic deed, but typical of Tycho, who, as always, was clowning around. He and his navigator had flown over a ski jump where a competition was taking place, and in his youthful invincibility, he flew the plane low over the hill and jumper. As they neared the bottom of the hill and were about to lift up again, Tycho's uniform caught on the lever and the plane flew straight into the ground. Fortunately, neither he nor the navigator were badly injured. But the family hurried down from the cabin and back to Lillehammer to find out more of what had happened to him.

On the morning of 9 April, Anne Stine and Eilif were sitting listening to the radio. They heard that Denmark had surrendered without a fight and that the Germans were now in Norway. Later that afternoon, Ole Henrik arrived home from Oslo. He had travelled back to Lillehammer with Sigrid Undset and told them that the train had been packed full of people evacuating from the city. Undset spent the entire journey collapsed onto a folding seat in the corridor of the train, sitting and muttering prayers and psalms.

In the days that followed, all sorts of rumours spread. They heard that the Germans were just south of the town and it would be only a matter of time before they were under seige. Ole Henrik continually went to the police station to report for military duty but each time was told that no mobilization orders had yet been received. The atmosphere in town became frantic and people no longer waited for mobilization orders, but began to take matters into their own hands. Women joined the Women's Defense League and the men disappeared from the town one by one to fight the Germans.

A few weeks after war broke out in Norway, Helge arrived in Lillehammer, close to where the Norwegians had just surrendered in a nearby valley. In town, everything was all too quiet, and it soon became evident that most of the municipal officials had fled. In accordance with his role in the Administrative Council, Helge appointed a city administrative staff of three people: Mrs Haslund, Eilif Moe, and the chief of police. As previous mayor from 1929 to 1931, Eilif knew the municipal issues well. Helge's task in Lillehammer was otherwise to visit wounded soldiers in the hospital and convey messages to their families that they were still alive. He of course also looked in on Anne Stine and her family.

After the surrender in the south, Helge continued his relief efforts in northern Norway. This now mostly entailed bringing supplies of necessary food and rebuilding the damaged communities. Everything was in short supply and prices exorbitant. In Bodø, north of the Arctic Circle, it was a dreadful sight; the town had been shot to pieces. Burnt, destroyed buildings lay in ruins everywhere; about six hundred of the town's eight hundred houses had been destroyed, displacing some five thousand people. Some had gone north to the non-occupied areas, while others fled to the cabins and farmhouses in the surrounding area. After talking with the few remaining members of Bodø's administration, Helge was informed that all business had completely stopped and no money was available to either rebuild or support the people. He asked the local bank manager how much was needed and he replied, "As much as possible."

Helge travelled back to Oslo and discussed the situation of Bodø with the Administrative Council, who in turn contacted Norges Bank, the central bank of Norway. Soon, Helge was back in the car headed north with a million Norwegian kroner in cash packed in two large sacks. Everything went well until he approached Lillehammer. The road narrowed and a column of German trucks came barrelling towards him. Helge pulled off to the side of the road as far as he could with his car halfway into a ditch. A German commander jumped out of one of the trucks and shouted for him to move his car even farther out of the way. Helge replied that it wasn't possible to move over any farther. Then the commander yelled at his soldiers to come and tip the car into the ditch. As the German trucks drove on, Helge's car lay there with its tires sticking up in the air and its bags of cash still hidden inside.

Soon after, another column of trucks full of German soldiers came rolling by. Helge stood in the road and stopped the first car. This time the commander who jumped out happened to be a much more pleasant fellow, "and even a lawyer." Helge explained that he had been pushed off the road by the first convoy of trucks and needed help to get his vehicle back on the road. The commander ordered a troop of soldiers out of the trucks, and soon Helge's car, and the money, were headed north again.

Late that evening, he arrived at the Moe family home in Lillehammer. He gave the money bags to Eilif, quipping, "They will be weighed in the morning," then went to bed and slept like a rock. Early the next day, Helge drove on and the money reached Bodø. It was handed over to a very happy bank manager.

When Norwegian forces officially surrendered to the German troops on 10 June 1940, Helge was in the town of Narvik, far north in Norway. Most of the town had been destroyed and some seven thousand residents evacuated. Again, no businesses were operating and the population was quite paralyzed by the state of events. Helge appointed a municipal council to help restore a sense of order to the town and initiate relief efforts. Over the next several months, until the end of October 1940, he did much the same for most of the other towns and communities of northern Norway. As winter crept in, so too did an eerie feeling: heating fuel was scarce, an increasing number of German troops occupied people's homes, and the situation on the border with Russia grew ever more tense.[8]

Helge continued from northern Norway into Finland searching for any possibilities for his country to buy timber, cement, nails, and other building supplies. When he reached Helsinki, he read in the newspaper that Quisling had been appointed president-minister. The politician's pro-Nazi government, dominated by members of the political party Nasjonal Samling that Quisling himself founded in 1933, was working with the occupying forces.

From Helsinki, Helge headed for Stockholm,[9] where he met up with his brother Kaare, who was working with the Norwegian legation. In Stockholm, he was also able to confirm the rumours that had been circulating in Norway for some time: the Norwegian government in London was in the process of building up a Norwegian army in England. They also were training Norwegian pilots in Canada and had ordered a large number of aircraft from the United States. "I do not like this," Helge commented. "Norway has done enough for the super powers. No sense in throwing even more young boys into the cauldron."

On his last day in Stockholm, Helge was at the Swedish Red Cross and met with Prince Carl, father of the Norwegian Crown Princess Märtha. "A very nice gentleman who is 75 years old and hard of hearing. He talked all the time and I couldn't get a word in edgewise."

Before leaving Stockholm, Helge managed to secure a pledge from the Swedish Red Cross for four hundred prefabricated houses and one hundred tons of food, a gift totalling two million Swedish krona. In addition, the Norwegian government in London said they would pay for an additional six hundred prefabricated houses but had to conceal this under the Swedish Red Cross name.

After completing his mission in Stockholm, Helge travelled back to Oslo about mid-October. It had been a long journey. By his estimates, he had covered nearly 50,000 kilometres over the last six months. His work for the Administrative Council was now finished; the initial fighting had ended and assisting the wounded was no longer required. But as his letters to his father indicated, he couldn't bear the thought of having to cooperate with any officials who were part of Quisling's fascist party, Nasjonal Samling. So Helge retreated to a mountain farm and worked on his novel *Klondyke Bill*. When it was later published in 1942, both critics and public gave it good reviews. One critic wrote: "Helge Ingstad perhaps would never have debuted in the fiction genre had it not been for conditions that forced him to refrain from travelling. A man with such wanderlust in his blood seldom has time to write novels while travelling. Let us therefore hope that he puts another novel on the stack before the world opens its borders to him once again."

The Wedding

During their courtship, Anne Stine had begun to suspect that Helge was not quite the romantic "Prince Charming" she had hoped. He had been a bachelor for a long time and was used to doing things as his freely chose. And wooing ladies was definitely not one of his strongest traits. She recalled that while they were courting and dining out, Helge would often take along his newspapers and hang over them reading during the meal while Anne Stine sat and watched. She should have taken this as a warning but was most likely too young and too in love to do anything else. For Helge, a forty-one-year-old bachelor who had spent several of his adult years in the wilderness, adapting to marriage and a normal family life was not such an easy task. On 25 April 1941 he wrote to his father: "The wedding will be held on one of the last days in May. Everything should occur as quietly as possible – so as few people as possible. Will be glad when all the ceremonies are over. It's horrible." Two weeks later, Helge sent a new letter saying, "Marriage jitters now almost feeling like a tidal wave soon to knock me over. I am fairly nervous."[10]

Actually, it was quite amazing that there had been any time at all to plan a wedding considering the frantic pace Helge kept up with all his relief efforts during that first year of the war. However, on 21 May 1941, Helge and Anne Stine were wed in the beautiful old Garmo stave church at Maihaugen and a simple reception was held in the garden at the Moe family home. Many were missing. Tycho had left, Kaare was in Sweden, Sigrid Undset had gone to the US, and several friends had either died or been taken prisoner by the Germans.

In his speech to the bride, Eilif said to Anne Stine: "As a young girl, he was your dream hero, who now as a mature woman, you have found your way back to." And to Helge he said, "Accept Anne Stine as she is. Flawless she isn't, but I can say she is a worthy person and is dearly and completely in love with you."[11]

The honeymoon was spent at Maribuseter, which they could only reach by going across precarious spring ice covering the lake. It was very important to Anne Stine that Helge be happy at the place that meant so much to her. Later, they went on an extended visit to Balestrand on the shores of Sognefjord, where they rented a house. The young bride was to be introduced to good friend Odd and his wife Edel, and Helge was going to spend time finishing the manuscript of his novel *Klondyke Bill*; taking a holiday was not for Helge. From Balestrand, Helge wrote a birthday letter to his father on 1 July 1941:

Dear Pappa,
In another package, I'll be sending you a "thingy"[12] that I hope will be delicious. All is well here. Anne Stine has become fat and tan. She has become good friends with Odd's wife Edel and they seem to have a nice time together. We often eat at Odd's and then we eat well. Sometimes we dine on salmon heads.

In addition to his fishery, Odd manages several doctors' offices. But first and foremost, he is a fisherman … The first cherries have begun to ripen. Soon we will be eating lots of those. We also have the hotel's vegetable garden just outside our house and can help ourselves to radishes and delicious turnips. Most often we eat at the hotel. We pay 5 kroner for the two of us for each dinner. That's the best way to do it. Not much point in Anne Stine staying indoors on nice sunny days cooking when we can get it so cheaply. But if we are able to get a fresh herring or mackerel, she makes dinner at home. She makes very good food.
Many greetings, Helge

Anne Stine wrote to her in-laws on 31 July:

We are having beautiful weather here and the fjord is lovely and warm. It is a delight to go swimming. Helge is working hard, I putter around and enjoy myself. In the evenings, we take a stroll just like an old couple and Helge is the kindest husband in the world.

Later that fall, the newlyweds were back in Lillehammer and looking for a place to live. Anne Stine mostly wanted to be close to family and friends. Helge could pretty much live anywhere, especially now that the Germans had taken over everything in Norway and his help with the Red Cross was no longer needed. His main focus now was to write, and it was the book on Svalbard he wanted to complete. The idea for *The Land with the Cold Coasts* had been heavily on his mind for quite a while, but it was now maturing into something more than just a narrative of his own experiences. He wanted to include a proper presentation of the history, geography, biology, and wildlife of the area, as well as climate conditions. While he thought it was important to emphasize the Norwegian connection to Svalbard, discussion of this also piqued his scientific interests. But Helge was thorough, and such an extensive focus on one's own experiences required much research, and time.

For the Moe family, the first years of the war were dramatic. Ole Henrik was arrested by the Germans in October 1942 after a Nazi Norwegian co-worker exposed him as an infiltrator in the company Norwegian Hydro. The case was very serious, and the family feared he would be given the death sentence. Helge went to the Gestapo and defended his case, which ended in Ole Henrik being sent to the Grini concentration camp on the outskirts of Oslo. Eilif too was arrested in connection with his son's case and sent to the prison in Oslo until February 1943. Ole Henrik was later transferred to Sachsenhausen in Germany, where he was detained until the end of the war. He returned to Norway on one of the Scandianvian "white buses"[13] sent to rescue countrymen from Nazi-controlled concentration camps after the war.

The Moe family had little news about Tycho. When he was dismissed from the hospital in Kirkenes in northern Norway, after his airplane crash at the ski jump, he briefly visited Lillehammer before travelling across the whole of Russia on the Trans-Siberian Railway all the way to Vladivostok on the border of China and North Korea. Japan was his next stop, where he wrote a long, cheerful letter home to his family about a visit to a geisha house. This was one of the few signs of life from him during those years. From Japan he travelled to Canada, where he joined the Little Norway pilot training camp on Lake Muskoka in Ontario. After becoming a fully trained war pilot, he was sent to England to fly Mosquito aircraft for the 139th Squadron.

Also at this time, Anne Stine and Helge wanted to find a place to live near Lillehammer. They advertised for a house in the newspaper and immediately received a telephone call from the chief of police, who offered to rent them the main house at a farm called Bårdsetbakken.[14] Anne Stine worried about how they were going to fill a huge manor house on a farm with the little they had, but they still agreed to go the next day to see the house. They took the train to Moelv, about 30 kilometres south of Lillehammer, and from there a taxi straight up the hill to where the farm was located. They continued driving upward until eventually the road deteriorated into a dirt path of tree roots and stones. They finally arrived at a gate, and high on top of the hill they could see a cluster of a few brown buildings: a small farm in a sunny clearing in the forest.

It was a breathtaking sight; far below they could see Norway's largest lake, the Mjøsa, sparkling in the autumn sun, and to the south rose the Skreia mountains. This was absolutely a place where they wanted to live! Never mind the big rat hole in the kitchen floor, the lack of running water, or the outdoor toilet behind the barn – they had found their paradise. The house was relatively isolated, except for a few other farms in the area and a former pastor, Henry, who lived in another building on the farm. But it was close to Lillehammer and Anne Stine could easily visit her parents.

Christmas that year, however, was not a happy holiday for Anne Stine and Louise. Helge had to go to Bergen to help his parents move from their family home as the Germans had expropriated it for their own use. With Tycho halfway across the world and both Ole Henrik and Eilif in prison, Anne Stine and Louise were the only two in the family left in Lillehammer. They spent most of Christmas Eve walking the deserted streets. Money and food were scarce, but one of Eilif's previous clients from the valley came with some meat he had hunted and a word of comfort: "I tell you Mrs. attorney Moe, that there are none of us farmers up in our valley who believe Mr. Eilif attorney has done any wrong."

Sometime during the late summer of 1942, Anne Stine became pregnant and the couple were thrilled. Helge wanted a son who could carry on the Ingstad name, while Anne Stine hoped for a daughter. Their grief

Summer of 1945 at Maribuseter. Helge with an early version of a backpack-style baby carrier.

was great when she miscarried after a three-month pregnancy, but not long after, she was pregnant again. When I was born, 19 October 1943, Helge had come to terms with me not being a boy and sent a telegram to his parents in Bergen saying: "A healthy girl, all well." Anne Stine, on the other hand, thought "thank goodness, I at least now have my girl." In a letter to his parents following the birth, Helge wrote: "Yes, there we have it, and strange to think this girl will actually experience the year 2000. Hopefully, she will have a more peaceful world than we have." That he too would live to experience the year 2000 was surely not something he ever considered.

In the Moe family, I was a welcome diversion from so many of the heavy thoughts and worries, especially for Louise. At the time, Tycho was in England and assumedly about to set off on bombing raids over Germany. Ole Henrik was still a prisoner in Sachsenhausen and Eilif had recently been released from the prison in Oslo in relatively poor condition. The churches were closed at the time as part of the pastors' protest against the German occupation, and so I was baptized by the local minister in an old pewter dish at home in the living room at Bårdsetbakken. Helge's parents Olaf and Olga came from Oslo and stayed for a time. Helge had tried to persuade them to buy a house in Lillehammer since the Germans had now taken over their house in Bergen. They instead ended up living in Oslo, close to their daughter Gunvor.

The years at Bårdsetbakken were a pleasant and good time for Anne Stine despite the war and were some of the best years she had in her marriage. Helge, mostly, remained at home and family life was as she longed for. At the same time, she was close enough to Lillehammer to visit her parents and friends as often as she liked. Anne Stine and Helge wanted to buy Bårdsetbakken after the war, but it was not for sale. Had the family stayed there, life would have been so different.

Tycho Dies

Anne Stine naturally worried about Tycho. But she comforted herself with the fact that he had often figured his way out of dangerous situations as a child, so this was also probably the case now. She dreamt about him every night, even though she was actually more worried about Ole Henrik in Sachsenhausen. One night in February 1943, she suddenly awoke screaming from a nightmare. She dreamt that a plane had crashed, and then she had that same intuitive feeling she always had as a child when something was wrong with Tycho. In her dream, she rushed over to where the plane had crashed and there on the ground lay someone covered with a Norwegian flag. She did not have to lift the flag to see who it was – she knew. After that night, Tycho never appeared in her dreams again; "the invisible bond that had always existed between us was broken forever."[15] At the time, she didn't tell anyone about this dream.

Not long after, Eilif received a message that his son's plane had been shot down on 26 February 1943 and that he was reported as "missing in action." Eilif consulted with Helge and they agreed not to tell the women in the family, so as not to worry them. Anne Stine was pregnant with me and Louise was bedridden from anxiety about her two sons. Later, it emerged that she had a heart condition. Eilif thought it was wise to wait until the war ended to see if Tycho had managed to bail out and was sitting in a German war prison. Helge and Eilif managed to keep this difficult secret for an entire two years.

Once, however, Anne Stine nearly found out. She and Helge were attending a large party at a farm in Brumundal during Christmas 1944 when a man came over to her and said, "my condolences about your brother." She replied, "Oh, but he isn't dead." Assuming it was a misunderstanding, she still deep in her heart feared it was true.

10 LIBERATION AND PEACE

On 8 May 1945, the entire country burst into euphoric celebration. The Germans had finally surrendered. Helge quickly drove to Oslo while Anne Stine stayed behind in Lillehammer with me, for the time being. He had driven the route numerous times during the war and, as he headed down over the last hill he was always used to seeing the city crouched in a dull darkness. But this time it was different. He arrived late in the evening and was astonished to see the city bathed in light. Oslo was alive again! Adults and children cheered and sang in the streets. People walked around waving the Norwegian flag and everyone was bursting with joy.

On 10 May, Helge bumped into his old journalist friend Henning Sinding-Larsen, who asked him if he wanted to join him and a Swedish journalist to witness the relinquishing of the royal residence outside of Oslo at Skaugum. The place was still officially in German hands, so upon arrival they were met by the guards of Josef Terboven, the German Reichskommissar for Norway who had taken over the crown prince's residence in 1940. After being mistaken for an Allied commission, Helge and the two journalists were let into the house. A few Norwegian police officers milled about, but no other authorities had yet arrived. Helge and the journalists inquired about Terboven. One of the Norwegians showed them a flat rock containing a piece of flesh and tattered clothing. It was all that was left of the man after he blew himself up in a bunker at the royal residence compound using 50 kilograms of dynamite. "It fulfilled its purpose to the utmost," Helge thought.

Two buses came driving up the entrance road to the royal residence. One was filled with Norwegian police and the other with Home Guard soldiers. The German troops, Terboven's guards, marched down the same road, stopped, and faced the Norwegians. "Ich uberliefe Skaugum in Name der Deutschen Kommandantur" (I deliver Skaugum in the name of the German Commander), said the German captain. He saluted, but without a "Heil Hitler." Then he turned to his men and commanded, "Right face. March." The green-uniformed Germans marched down the street. The royal residence of Skaugum was once again in Norwegian hands.

Afterwards, Helge and the other two men headed back to Oslo. "A wonderful feeling in the city," wrote Helge in his journal. "People smiling and everyone seems to know everyone. The streetcars are packed and people just hang on the back; no one says anything about it, or the illegal smoking ... There's been less shooting during the night, [but] a few of the Home Guard have been killed. Otherwise, everything else is remarkably calm, yes, quite incredibly restrained and cordial. The Home Guard are everywhere in the city; numbers of them. They wander around in blue uniforms, rifles and machine guns slung over their shoulders; hearty fellows. Prisoners from the Grini concentration camp (on the outskirts of Oslo) strut around in their numbered prison suits and caps. Incredible stories both from the prison and sabotage attempts spread like wildfire."

While Helge took in all these emotions and feelings of freedom, a group of boys came chanting up the street: "Victory is ours, Quisling's behind bars!" Hearing this news, Helge thought about all the Norwegians whom the Germans had been ordered to shoot and who could have, and should have, been saved by Quisling.[1] Helge felt a strong need to talk to Quisling and find out why he didn't stop these executions. Quisling, along with several other leaders, was being detained in a prison in Oslo. It was easy for Helge to gain access into the prison, first because the line of command was not yet organized, and second, because he knew one of the guards. Helge was let in. There he sat and talked to Quisling:

English planes flying overhead. People out on the streets waving flags and smiling, celebrating peace. Spring with all its green and newly budding birch. Dark, shadowy rooms. To the right, the hallway to the prison cells. Out in the corridor are Norwegians in uniform. Everyone is armed. On the platform out towards the courtyard are several members of the National Unity party[2] awaiting to be processed as prisoners. More people being continuously brought in.

I'll begin with Quisling who I just finished talking with. I have to hurry and write before my initial impressions vanish. First, I looked through the peephole in the door. He sat on the bunk, restless and kept scratching his head. He no longer wore his collar insignia and his face and entire demeanour showed great signs of utter despair. I went in and told him who I was and explained that I wanted to write about Norway's history at this time. He was forthcoming but very upset. First he asked about his wife, then he said that it was completely unreasonable that he, Norway's commanding officer for the past five years, be treated like this. "I," he said, "who have done for Norway what no other Norwegian has ever done deserves national recognition."[3]

He went on to explain to Helge that it was the Germans who forced them to execute the Norwegians. And if they hadn't, the Germans would have killed a number of police officers instead. "We had no choice," he told Helge. Then he repeated: "No other Norwegian has done more for Norway than I and then to be treated like a common criminal. I have toiled like a slave for Norway's concern for five years. It has been martyrdom."

When Helge left Quisling's cell,

he gave me a friendly smile and stretched out his hand to me. I answered that I couldn't accept it. It was scathingly cruel to say that to a man who was about to die ... What is right and wrong in life? It depends somewhat on a person's inner self. I do not doubt that Quisling is an idealist. He has aspects, but the aspects of a semi-insane man. There is not a doubt in his soul that he thought he had saved Norway. The doctor apparently thinks that he isn't quite normal.[4]

Quisling claimed that he had an especially good relation with Hitler and that this was what made it possible for him to help his country like no other – if only the Norwegians had co-operated. The man held enormously one-sided opinions; not for a moment did he perceive that others might have a point. He continued to repeat that if the Norwegian Home Guard and others had joined him, rather than go against him, "we would have had the strength against the Germans."[5]

Helge met with Quisling a couple more times, thinking that their meetings might provide material for a book or an article. But Helge felt increasingly uncomfortable exploiting the need of a prisoner who wanted contact, especially one who most surely would face a death sentence soon. In questioning what to do in such matters, Helge generally talked with his father. But Olav was such a rational man he might have instead emphasized the unique opportunity of material for a new book. Helge's mother, on the other hand, was more sensitive and advised Helge to follow his conscience. Which he did. As Quisling's trial proceeded, Helge did not visit him anymore, even though he felt he could have gotten more information out of him. Helge opposed the idea of a death sentence, even for someone like Quisling, which he had no doubt would be the final verdict.[6]

A New Life

The war left much deeper marks in Anne Stine's life than in Helge's. The most dramatic incident for the Ingstad family was that Olaf and Olga's home in Bergen was seized by the Germans. Helge's parents initially moved to Oslo temporarily, but by the end of the war they decided not to return to Bergen. Shortly after the war, Olga began having heart problems, and on 11 October 1946 she passed away. I was carried into to her to say goodbye. She lay in a large bed, a small lady with white hair. I had seen so little of her that she was almost a stranger to me, but for Olav and "the children," a mainstay in their lives was now gone.

Helge's closest friends, like himself, were well over forty at the outbreak of the war and most likely too old to have registered as "one of the boys from the woods," or the Norwegian Home Front. At least they all made it through the war with their lives and health intact – with the exception of Gunnar Eilifsen, a friend from Levanger who was executed by the Gestapo.

For Anne Stine, however, the war turned much of her life upside down. The loss of her brother Tycho was by far the worst. When Tycho's fellow pilots returned, the Moe family finally learned what had happened to him. He and his navigator were part of a squadron of Mosquito planes who had just completed their first raid on a German factory in Rennes, France. On their return, the squadron encountered combat with a fleet of German planes. Tycho's plane lay farthest back, but nobody registered it being hit. Not until the squadron landed in England did they notice his plane was missing. It was assumed it must have crashed into the sea. The loss of Tycho was devastating to his family in many ways. Anne Stine wrote about it in a draft of an unfinished autobiography: "Tycho who was always so full of life, joy and fun, and so caring and protective of me – how am I to live without him? I had looked so forward to him becoming more acquainted with Helge – those were his last words to me, that I should marry him, and that I did. Those two would have understood one another, I am sure. Could my life ever be whole without my brother ever coming home again?"

The family created a memorial for him on a big boulder up the hill from the family cabin Maribuseter. Tycho had used to say "that rock there, that's me" and would lay on its slanted surface shooting at targets out in the marsh. His family engraved his name on it along with the inscription "Fallen in battle for Norway." A large crowd gathered there for his memorial, including several men from the Norwegian Home Front who stood as honorary guards at the stone.

With the death of Tycho, Anne Stine felt that she had lost a part of herself. Her grief was especially prolonged after strongly feeling something had happened to him, but never knowing for sure. And because his body was never found, there was little closure. Having little brother Ole Henrik return from Sachsenhausen after the war was a great joy, but he came home to a family grieving the death of their eldest son Tycho.

But not only Tycho was gone. At the outbreak of war, the Moe children and cousins were at the right age to be recruited as both pilots and resistance fighters. Many close friends, and friends' children, also never came back. Anne Stine mourned as well for her favourite cousin, Boss, who died in a climbing accident. Had he died fighting in the war, at least he could have been grieved as a hero.

Due to circumstances, our family had earlier left the farmhouse at Bårdsetbakken and were now living in Lillehammer. Anne Stine and I stayed with her parents; she slept in the boys' old room and I slept in a green trundle bed next to my grandparents. Helge rented a room at the neighbour's across the street. I often wondered about this arrangement, for a relatively newly married couple. According to Helge, there "wasn't room for more than one chief in that house." Even though Eilif and Helge got along well, they also respected each other's territory.

However, there were lifelong consequences of this living arrangement. Because Anne Stine was once again living with her mother and father, her ties to her childhood home became even more ingrained and strained any thoughts of leaving. It was not good for the marriage and the idyllic feelings of living together as a family at Bårdsetbakken began to crumble. One day, Anne Stine came crying to her father and said, "I'm so unhappy," to which Eilif replied, "Who the hell told you that you'd be happy? Do your damn duty." And so she did, for the rest of her life.

In that little green bed next to my grandparents, I experienced warmth and love. Every night, as I crawled up to their bed while they said their evening prayers together, it was the safest and best place I knew. Anne Stine once commented that she felt her mother took me from her then, which perhaps was correct; Louise's love was strong.

Regaining a Foothold after the War

After the war, all "good Norwegians" who were lawyers were expected to serve during the trials of Nazi collaborators and sympathizers. Since we were still living in Lillehammer and because he didn't have a routine job that required his time, Helge was naturally asked to work on the trials in the area. For escape, Helge would sometimes go off to his friend's place in Skjåk to hunt and fish or work on his Svalbard book. Eventually, though, he became fully involved in the questioning of some of the worst Nazis in the Lillehammer area, including August Stuckmann, chief of the Gestapo of the headquarters there.

Helge agreed to this work out of a sense of duty, but he did not care for it, for several reasons. First, it was unpleasant to hear about the worst Nazi atrocities committed in Norway. Second, Helge was aware that several of those that he questioned would receive the death penalty,[7] something he was deeply opposed to, even for the worst of criminals. "I thought the death penalty was an abomination. On the whole, killing people was disgraceful."[8]

In particular, Helge was so deeply affected by the case of the young Arne Braa Saatvedt that he talked about it several times later in life. Saatvedt was only twenty-three years old when he was executed by a firing squad at Akershus Fortress on 20 October 1945. Convicted of murder, which could very well have been the result of an accidental shot,[9] and torture of a prisoner in the Hamar jail, he lost his appeal by a vote of four to one. Saatvedt was genuinely remorseful about his "naivety, excited fanaticism and obstinacy. Consequences of which were: disillusionment, punishment, death."[10] He wrote to the mother of the person he had killed asking for forgiveness, but neither that effort nor his young age changed the verdict: death by execution.

Helge said that "he was such a determined young boy who had been so sadly misled. It was unfortunate that he received such a fate … I was up at the police station and there he sat in handcuffs ready to be transported to Oslo. He had tried to commit suicide, but hadn't succeeded. He seemed to be quite sympathetic, but they claimed that he wasn't any better than the Germans. I talked with him a bit. 'What good is it to talk about it anymore?' he muttered."[11] Saatvedt was unlucky that his case was one of the first and was therefore convicted more harshly. Later, others who had committed similar deeds were also convicted, but received milder punishments.[12]

Building the Family Home Brattalid

Our family was still without our own home, and the question of whether we should find a place in Lillehammer or in Oslo stood unresolved between Anne Stine and Helge. All those close to her lived in Lillehammer and all those close to him now lived in Oslo. Helge also wanted to be in the capital to be near the artistic community, the writers in the Authors' Union, and close to Theatre Café where they often met. But he also thought the atmosphere at Lillehammer was too confining and that Anne Stine's connection to her parents was too stifling. Deciding where to live was a sore point between them until, in a way, it determined itself.

The decisive factor was the scarcity and rationing of building materials immediately following the war, and the great housing shortage. In Lillehammer, there was a plan to tear down the barracks abandoned by the Germans, and Helge and Anne Stine tried, unsuccessfully, to buy the timber. When that did not work, Helge contacted the office for "enemy property" in Oslo and learned that Terboven's large log house outside of Oslo at Høvik was going to be sold fully furnished. He acted quickly and bought the house, which included a large garage, and all its possessions. Unconcerned about property rights at the time, Terboven

Louise, Benedicte, Anne Stine, and Eilif in front of Brattalid.

had built his house on land owned by another who now wanted it removed – immediately.

While the house had stood empty, a Norwegian officer returning from London had moved in without permission.[13] When Helge, with papers in hand, finally succeeded in getting the man ousted, the officer left taking everything in the house and on the property. It was probably just as well – it was all basically stolen anyway. Helge and Anne Stine then had to go in search of another plot of land. Helge imagined a place on the outskirts of Oslo, as far away from people as possible. Anne Stine still wanted to live in Lillehammer so was only semi-interested in the project.

One day in the upper north part of the city, Helge came upon a small road that led up into the woods along the west side of the hill called Vettakollen. It was a pleasant little road with two tracks and grass growing in the middle. At the very end of the track was a small cottage, surrounded by forest. Helge liked it very much.

He checked into who owned that area of the forest and discovered it was part of the Grimelund farm at Vindern, a few kilometres down the road. One evening, he called the owner Yngvar Huseby, introduced himself, and made his request. "That's strange," Huseby said. "I'm sitting here now reading 'The Land of Feast and Famine' to my children. How many acres do you want?" Helge explained how he thought of situating the house, and Huseby arranged to sell him a 12-acre plot. Later, the Grimelund forest area was sold to the municipality and became part of the preserved forest boundary of the city. That is how even today our home has maintained its peaceful location.

After the summer, work consisted of dismantling the house and garage from down by the Oslo fjord and moving it all up to the new plot of land. The garage was reassembled almost identically, whereas large changes were made to the house. The floorplan was changed and an additional floor was added. In this way, it became our house, not Terboven's, making it less likely for him to haunt the place. That they called the house Brattalid, after Eirik the Red's farm on Greenland, was an early sign of a commitment that would come to influence both their lives.

Trip to America

Eventually, the Svalbard book, *The Land with the Cold Coasts*, was finished. It was released on 16 December 1948 and received rave reviews. It had taken a long time to write as it evolved into a very thorough and methodical piece of work. Helge's own experiences were intertwined with perspectives on history, geography, and wildlife. It was a book marked by historical precision and depth, which later became his trademark.

After the manuscript was sent to the publishers, my parents decided that we should all travel to America to visit Kaare, who was now the Norwegian consul general in Los Angeles. Brattalid, recently completed on its new plot, was rented out. The plan was to be away for six months. In his bags, Helge packed his books *The Apache Indians* and *The Land with the Cold Coasts*, as well as his play titled *The Last Boat*, in hopes of finding an American publisher. He also hoped to hold lectures at Norwegian organizations along the way. In addition, Norway's national newspaper *Aftenposten* paid him 4,500 Norwegian kroner to write articles about the journey.

Our voyage was on a new ship, the *Tudor*, owned by the Norwegian shipping company Wilhelmsen. In exchange for Helge giving a few lectures on board, we were provided accommodation in the shipowner's cabin. Once out in open sea, however, an incredible storm broke loose, hurricane-like, and everything had to be tied down. The storm continued for most of the passage, which left us rather worn out by the time we arrived in New York at the end of February 1949.

First on our agenda was to buy a car and make sure that Anne Stine got her driver's licence. She had never before sat behind the wheel of a car, yet after only a few hours of lessons she took her driving test in the middle of New York City – and passed with flying colours! Not long after, we headed west, first to Arizona. Anne Stine and I were to meet Helge's old friends on the Apache reservation.

It was a long drive before we finally pulled up in front of several small white houses at the mission station at Whiteriver. We were graciously greeted by Reverend Edgar Guenther, his wife Emily, and their nine children. We stayed for two weeks and also ended up taking a short trip to visit the Uplegger family in San Carlos, where Helge had lived briefly before trying his hand at being a cowboy. Out of all the elderly Apaches that Helge had met during his first visit, the only one still surviving was Taipa (A100) – now a small, rumpled old man with long, tangled hair and parched, wrinkled skin who sat in front of his cabin. He seemed quite frightening to a six-year-old Norwegian girl who had never seen a real Apache warrior before. It was much more fun to spend time with the Apache girls at Mrs Guenther's school. They quickly made the new blonde girl the centre of attention in their play. For years afterwards, these children sent me letters and drawings.

From Whiteriver we headed north to the Navajo and Pueblo Reservations and on to the Grand Canyon, an amazing sight then as now, but with far fewer tourists. The Navajo still lived in their "hogans" (sod huts) with herds of sheep wandering around in the arid landscape. The women sat outside their huts weaving the most beautiful rugs. The Pueblo still lived in dwellings carved into the sides of canyon walls and mesas. Little had been done to develop health care facilities and schools for the Native Americans in these areas, and when we stopped our car, people came rushing to us asking for medicines.

In California, our family rented an apartment next to Kaare's in Long Beach and we enjoyed quiet, sunny days together. I got a kitten and my first real doll, a plastic black doll called Amosandra that could be fed and bathed. I really loved that doll. Everything was perfect until our neighbour knocked on our door and complained: "White girls should not play with 'nigger' dolls."

Officially, this was a family trip, and the plan was to stay for six months then travel back to Norway together. However, later revealed in his saved letters, Helge had other plans in mind, plans that he had not shared with Anne Stine. Lying quietly on the beach for months was not for him. He had earlier toyed with the idea of going back to the Northwest Territories. But months before their America trip, October 1948, Helge sent a letter to Norwegian-born Bernt Balchen,[14] now Commander of the 10th Rescue Squadron of the US Air Force located in southern Alaska. He inquired if Balchen could arrange a trip for him to Alaska with the US Air Force "as the US government's guest. It's a bit rude, but sometimes you have to be a bit rude."[15] Balchen replied that it was a slim chance but that he would contact the Department of Interior in Alaska.

Anne Stine, of course, knew Helge dreamt of going to Alaska. However, she assumed it would be only a short side-trip before they would again travel home to Norway together. Besides, the main reason for their trip to America was first and foremost a family visit with brother Kaare. She was, however, completely mistaken. Helge once again yearned for adventure, intensely. Letters to his father show that even after a few days upon their arrival in the United States, Helge had visited the State Department in Washington. Here he met a nice government official in charge of Alaskan affairs who promised him free transportation by military plane to and around Alaska.

A few years earlier, Helge had received a private research grant of 15,000 Norwegian kroner for his planned expedition to Siberia. These funds had remained untouched in a bank account while he waited to get the sought-after travel visa. He now requested to have the money reallocated for a trip to Alaska in order "to gain better insight into the rapid development that had recently taken place in Alaska, both economically and otherwise."[16] By studying how this development was taking place, he wanted to form a comparative analysis for other minority groups in Arctic regions. That was at least the official reason.

Then one day, as we sat enjoying life on the sunny coast of California, Helge imparted the heavy news. He was going north to Alaska, and

Anne Stine and I, for the time being, would be left behind with Kaare. If we did not hear from Helge within a certain time frame, we were to drive back to the east coast and board the ship *Stavangerfjord* that would set sail for Norway from New York on 21 July. The car would be sent by freighter a few days later.

Anne Stine was furious. She had married a trapper hoping to follow him into the wilderness. But Helge was not prepared to take along a wife and child to such conditions. Kaare was equally furious and thought it totally irresponsible to send my mother and I across the summer desert on our own. Years later, Anne Stine said she had never seen the two brothers so angry with each other as she did then. I too remember a fierce argument between my parents in a cabin deep in the San Bernardino Mountains, where we had gone to celebrate their seventh anniversary. But Helge didn't budge, and proceeded with his plans to travel north.

After he left, back in California my mother and I first received several cards and letters. Then nothing came but silence. It was evident he had gone deep into the wilderness, exactly where we didn't know. By June, Anne Stine realized if she were to make the drive across the desert, it would have to be now before the heat grew even more intense.

On 23 June at eight o'clock in the morning my mother and I headed off. She could not have chosen a worse time. It was a scorching hot day, and even before the sun was up the heat was almost unbearable. The car had a very simple type of air conditioner fastened on the inside of the window. Water was filtered through sawdust, and every once in a while, it splashed out a few cold drops that I tried to catch in my mouth. Anne Stine's great fear was that the car would break down in the middle of the desert, which would have meant certain death for both of us in that heat.

After two days of almost continuous driving, we arrived at Phoenix. It felt lovely and cool as we headed up through the pine forests towards Whiteriver. We rested a few days at the Guenther family's home before heading out again across the long remaining stretch to the east coast. Two other women Anne Stine had become acquainted with joined us. The Guenthers wanted us to stay much longer, but Anne Stine thought Helge would be home for Christmas and wanted to get Brattalid in order after having rented it out.

We arrived in New York a few days before the ship was scheduled to leave and stayed at the Seamen's Mission, where I was lavished with candy from men who missed their own children back home. Our ship set sail, and after about a week at sea we were back in Norway. Louise, Eilif, and Hans, Sigrid Undset's son, were all waiting on the quay on a sunny day when *Stavangerfjord* came gliding into the dock. After a celebratory dinner at a restaurant, we took off straight away to Maribuseter, the place Anne Stine longed to be. As she sat in the heather looking out across the mountains, she wrote to Helge:

> What are you doing now? We talk so much about you. I have heard nothing since I left New York, but you are presumably far away! I dreamt of Arizona last night; my words are nothing but praise for Arizona and I know I will long to go there again. Thank you, thank you for everything you've let me experience. I am so unspeakably grateful. I feel that I have expanded in soul and not least in independence. It has done me good to be in charge and on my own. It wasn't always easy, but it feels so good in my soul afterwards to know that I did it. I hope you are satisfied with me.[17]

What the tone of this letter doesn't reveal is how Anne Stine never quite forgave Helge for leaving her to drive across the desert alone with a small child. He himself admitted, years later, "that was quite terrible, that was."

11 NUNAMIUT

The question was: where exactly was Helge? Travelling from Los Angeles on 30 May 1949, he first headed to Seattle, then to the Alaskan capital of Juneau. From there he journeyed on to the small community of Petersburg, mostly inhabited by immigrant fishermen from northern Norway. Helge continued on to Anchorage, which at the time was the closest thing Alaska had to a large city, with a population of about thirty thousand people, a few traffic lights, some tall buildings, and construction going on everywhere. There was a time when the rich salmon fishing drew many to the area. In a letter to his father on 25 June, Helge wrote: "The Indians here are somewhat more civilized. It should be better farther north."

Next stop was Fairbanks. Here he got to know people at the university and became involved in work to establish a student and lecturer exchange between the University of Oslo and the University of Alaska. He wrote home to his father in August that he was also interested in getting involved in improving management of the domesticated reindeer that were brought over from Norway to Alaska in the 1890s. However, these first attempts of Helge's at searching for a foothold in Alaska were put aside as other adventures began to unfold.

He moved on to the village of Kotzebue, situated at the tip of a peninsula facing the Bering Sea. Among the people he met there was an old mistress of Norwegian explorer Roald Amundsen (during his 1903–06 conquest of the Northwest Passage) and a trader well known for flying with a live polar bear in his plane. From Kotzebue he travelled to Deering, another small village along the coasts of the Bering Sea with

Aguk, one of the elders of the Nunamiut group.

large expanses of tundra stretching beyond. "Good-natured and friendly people," he wrote in his journal on 25 August. It was here he met the Danish archaeologist Helge Larsen, who had just come from excavating at Point Hope, the most westerly village in Alaska that points straight out into the Bering Sea. Larsen had been digging on a site that revealed a two-thousand-year-old Inuit culture and had found evidence linking the Inuit to Asia.[1] The excavations also showed that the early people of Point Hope differed from other Inuit cultures in that they used hearths for heat rather than whale oil lamps.

Nome, the town founded during the 1898 gold rush and, at its peak, boasting nearly twenty thousand inhabitants, was Helge's next stop. It looked almost like a ghost town now. Several old, derelict houses lined Front Street, and huge, forgotten gold-digging machines littered the outskirts of town like skeletons of a bygone era. Helge didn't care much for Nome and left as soon as he could catch a flight out. He had no detailed plan for his trip, other than to travel around and become familiar with Alaska. "Perhaps something interesting would show up along the way," he thought. If not, he could always write something about his experiences of travelling around the state.

In Fairbanks, Helge met Sig Wien, a bush pilot who flew supplies into all the small communities that otherwise were isolated from the outside world. Wien and his three brothers, who happened to be of Norwegian descent, established and ran the company Wien Alaska Airways. Wien and Helge quickly became good friends and through him Helge heard about a small group of Inuit who lived in the middle of the Brooks Range Mountains in northern Alaska. The Brooks Range stretches east to west from Canada to Alaska, and much of the landscape lies above the treeline. Wien occasionally flew in to the area with mail and supplies and was allegedly these people's only contact with the outside world. They lived like their ancestors before them, primarily hunting caribou that migrated from the tundra to the forests across the wide Anaktuvuk Pass every spring and fall. A small group who waited for these large herds to migrate every season called themselves the Nunamiut, the inland people.

Helge listened to Wien's story with growing interest. Inuit who lived inland were quite unique. Other Inuit cultures in the Arctic region were more closely connected to resources from the sea: fish, walrus, seal, and whale. The fact that these inland Inuit were caribou hunters made it that much more interesting to Helge. They reminded him of the Caribou

Eaters whom he had lived with around Great Slave Lake in Canada. Helge made a decision – he wanted to go to where the Nunamiut were.

To what extent Helge was aware of, or willing to realize, the scope of the Nunamiuts' previous contact with what he called "civilization" is uncertain. In his letters home, he at least made a big deal out of this little group of inland Inuit who lived a "primitive" life, much like they had done for generations and who were relatively untouched by modern life and technology. This resonated with Helge's appreciation of living in harmony with nature and was in line with ethnographical research at the time that was heavily focused on documenting so-called "primitive" cultures before they disappeared.

In a way, Helge was right about the "untouched life" he saw and experienced in Anaktuvuk Pass. At the time, the Nunamiut had few sources of income other than the sums they earned by hunting: $50 per wolf, as well as profits from wolf and wolverine hides that were primarily exchanged for whale oil with the Inuit along the coast. Arctic fox were rare. With little money, there was not much they could buy; they made their footwear, snowshoes, clothing, tents, and simple tools using traditional techniques.

Anne Stine and I had long since returned home to Norway. Eventually we received a letter telling us where he was headed and that he would not be back for Christmas. Not any big surprise! We made do as best we could, and Anne Stine began taking piano lessons at the Robert Rieflings Music Academy to pass the time.

Into the Wilderness Again

On 5 September, Helge took off in a little two-engine plane with Wien at the controls. Far below them in the dense forests, the lakes looked like islands in all that green. Here and there they caught sight of a huge Alaskan moose and once spotted a grizzly bear catching a salmon in a river. As they crossed the Yukon River, the forests gradually became sparser and they could faintly see the outline of the Brooks Range Mountains to the far north. They flew deeper into the narrow valleys flanked on either side by steep mountains. "Look there," shouted Wien. "Wild sheep." And sure enough, running up over the steepest mountainside ran a flock of white animals. Surprised by the sound of aircraft, they stopped, curiously looked up into the sky, then sped up the hill again. Helge could make out only the familiar curved horns of the ram that ran in front of the flock. The valley widened as they approached Anaktuvuk Pass. It lay like an open gap in the mountain mass with pyramid-shaped peaks on both sides, almost as if someone had taken a knife and cut out a chunk of the mountains. A small river flowed through the valley that ended in a pool of water called Tulugak Lake, or Raven Lake.

The plane landed on the water, and when Helge and Wien stepped out, a small group of people walked towards them. The women, hesitantly standing towards the back of the group, were dressed in seasonal long caribou parkas: colourful cotton material on the outside, fur-lined on the inside. Their hoods were fringed with wolverine fur, and peering out from under these were many small baby faces. Some larger children hid behind their mothers' legs and glanced curiously over at the men. They had not seen many white men before in their young lives. The Inuit men wore short caribou parkas with grey textile coverings.

The man standing in front of the group reached out his hand, gave Helge a good handshake and a friendly smile, "I am Simon Paneak." Helge greeted him in return and then told him he would like to stay for awhile. "That's fine, you are welcome," replied Paneak, and with that they began to unload the plane. Helge was allocated a place close to the round, hide tent of Paneak and his wife Umealaq (also called Susie)[2] and their four children (sons Wirâq/Robert, Kanigjak/Raymond, Kanayok/Roosevelt, and daughter Sikiarjuk/Mabel).[3] There Helge pitched his thin canvas tent that would be his home for the next nine months.

Wien soon took off in his plane, and with it disappeared Helge's last link to the outside world. During the period Helge spent with the Nunamiut, Wien would sometimes fly in with mail and essential supplies, but otherwise these people were on their own. They did, however, have a radio, and important messages could be sent by telegram from Norway to a program called "Tundra Topics."

In decades past, the Nunamiut population had been greater. But in 1949, the year Helge was there, only a small group of them still lived as nomads in the Brooks Range Mountains. Their principal livelihood was hunting caribou, which provided food for both people and dogs, hides for clothing, shoes, and lodging, sinew to sew with, and, not least, content for their stories and legends. The caribou also provided them with a sense of self and an identity as *inland people*, which set them apart from their neighbours to the north, the coastal Inuit who provided for themselves primarily through hunting sea mammals. Coastal Inuit were the groups that experts from all over the world at the time used as the only example of the culture. Encountering other Inuit who lived inland, and almost entirely off caribou, was practically an academic sensation. No wonder Helge felt like he won the luck of the draw!

The Nunamiut, however, had not always exclusively lived in the mountains. Around the turn of the century, the people were struck by several tragedies that led to a gradual decline in population. When they travelled to the coastal tribes in the north to trade for seal and whale blubber, and modern goods such as tobacco and flour, they succumbed to illnesses such as the measles and flu, against which they had no immunity. Later, caribou populations continued to decline several years in a row, partly due to over-exploitation by whalers and gold diggers. A famine between 1905 and 1907 claimed many victims among the inland people. The remaining Nunamiut decided to leave the Brooks Range for either the tundra north of the mountains or for the coast. Except for a few scattered families, the Brooks Range was practically abandoned (around 1920). During these years, the Nunamiut provided for themselves in various ways, primarily as trappers along the coast and on the tundra north of the Brooks Range.[4] But then profitability of fur trading dropped dramatically around 1930, the same year Helge left his life as a trapper in Canada.[5]

During Paneak's childhood and youth,[6] his family had to migrate to various parts of the country: inland to the Old Crow area in the Yukon Territory of Canada, to Humphrey Point on the coast where they built a mud hut, and inland again to Arctic Village and Fort Yukon.[7] This was how he, and a few other Nunamiut men whom Helge met, had learned to speak English. The entire time young Paneak's family had to live elsewhere, they still considered the Brooks Range Mountains their home area, and they still considered themselves Nunamiut, inland people. They continued with their group's traditional skills and passed on their stories and legends to the young seated around the evening campfires in the big tent.

When the caribou population showed signs of increasing around 1938, Paneak's father and other Nunamiut men decided to take their families back to the Brooks Range Mountains.[8] Such a decision also meant that they essentially returned to their old nomadic life. There were no trading posts in the Brooks Range, nor schools nor health services.

The Nunamiut had to provide for themselves. When they returned to the mountains, they took back rifles and a little ammunition which they had traded for. Later, bullets were often cut from the animals they hunted and used several times over. Old hunting methods were once again used such as catching caribou by chasing them into the water or into traps built on land. Initially, several Nunamiut families lived and hunted throughout the mountains. But in 1949, a short time before Helge arrived, the last two family groups joined the others at Tulugak Lake in Anaktuvuk Pass. A total of sixty-five people were part of the community when Helge stepped out of the plane.

Simon Paneak and Helge were the same age, and soon a close friendship developed between the two. Helge could not have had a better teacher and mentor. Paneak himself was deeply interested in Nunamiut traditions and had taken it upon himself to talk with the elders to gain as much knowledge as possible.[9] Helge and Paneak shared a common interest in writing down this knowledge. Eventually, Helge had a tape recorder flown in, and he recorded songs and stories. Before long, Paneak also noticed that this newcomer was no novice hunter, and therefore could join in hunting. However, Helge had much to learn about the Nunamiut's way of living.

Hunting

"We will call you Ikâksaq," smiled Paneak's father-in-law, Elijah Kakinnaq, "because your face is almost like his." Ikâksaq was a famous hunter of this group who died a long time ago. They emphasized that he was a very able fellow with a long face and white skin. Helge felt honoured to be named after this man and to continue his tradition.

Only three days after his arrival, Helge went hunting with three of the men: Frank, Elijah, and Hugo as well as Elijah's son. Most likely, they wanted to see if he lived up to his new name.

They first came upon a small herd of caribou on the other side of the valley. Helge's inclination was to walk upwind, but the Nunamiut's method was apparently to wait and watch the animals' movement. Eventually, the herd moved closer to them and the men fired a few shots, but the animals were much too far away and then disappeared completely. Not long after, they saw another herd. This time they decided to use another tactic. The men spread out in a graduated V-shape walking

Elijah Kakinnâq and son-in-law Simon Paneak.

towards a small lake. The animals were driven into the water and then shot or speared. They were able to slay a total of ten animals, a fair supplement to their food supplies for the people and two hundred hungry dogs. They lit a fire and cut out the delicacies: fat, kidneys, liver, and marrowbones.

Helge noticed that the caribou here seemed smaller than those he was familiar with in northern Canada. He thought it must be because of cross-breeding with domesticated reindeer. In fact, one of the animals they shot was tagged on the ear, which indicated that it must have been brought over from Norway.[10]

It was the middle of summer when Helge arrived at Anaktuvuk Pass. One morning during about his second month there, he awoke to find a thin layer of snow covering the ground and the puddles frozen. The kids skated across the smooth ice and thought it was great; they were never short of anything to amuse themselves. A sled pulled by ten beautiful dogs raced off at full speed in through the valley. The dogs were delighted to finally pull a sled again and returned a couple of hours later with a full load of willow twigs. Wood was scarce and the little that was available was quickly used up at the various campsites. Helge had to insist that the women accept his help with finding twigs, something men generally didn't do. Most of the firewood was found in small clusters along the riverbeds, but sometimes it was difficult to find even the least amount.

Helge was soon in great need of some proper winter clothing: preferably two caribou parkas, one lined with fur and one with the fur on the outside, fur mittens, and mukluks. Paneak took him to see an unmarried woman renowned for her sewing skills. She took a quick glance at Helge and then went about busying herself with other things. "I guess she'll have me return later for measurements," he thought, but nothing happened.

During the days that followed, however, he noticed that the woman was continually looking over at him. It was so noticeable that the other men began teasing him about it, and even Helge began feeling quite smug that he had aroused her attention. Then one day he was told to go to her tent. When he arrived, hanging inside were his specially made clothes – completely finished! She had sewn them entirely based on visual measurements, and they fit perfectly! His male vanity might have taken a jolt, but at least now he had two of the most beautiful, warm parkas anyone could ever have wished for. He was well prepared for the winter.

Then it was time to move to a new site on the other side of the river. This was an effective way of disposing of biodegradable waste and conserving firewood throughout the area. But ice hadn't completely formed on the river, and it was a strenuous passage across in the freezing water. Two dogs drowned while trying to swim with the sled.

The new site was called Emerenik. Helge again pitched his tent close to Paneak and his family. It was as if he had become a part of their group. His thin canvas tent looked a bit flimsy compared to the solid lodges made of curved branches and caribou skin covers, grizzly bear flaps, and willow branch floors covered with caribou hides. If he were to have such a lodge, he would have had to have his own dogsled and wife. Transporting and constructing these tents were too much for one person alone. Besides, it was the woman's job to gather the willow for the floors.

Whether Anne Stine could have filled the role as a Nunamiut wife was debatable, but not completely out of the question as she was quite hearty at the time.

For the most part, Helge was able to keep his tent warm. But when it became much too cold he was welcomed into Paneak's family lodge, where it was cozy and snug. The high-spirited kids also helped ease Helge's feelings of missing his own daughter. As for the children, they learned quickly where Helge hid his goody bag and thought up all sorts of ways to get hold of it.

Everyone anticipated the caribou. The group's fresh meat supplies had eventually run out, leaving only a little dried meat. Now and again, they were able to catch a stray animal, but the vital autumn migration with the fat bulls had not yet arrived. On 12 October, they moved to a new site called Kangomavik, the gathering place. Helge was told that in the olden days, Dene people from the south met here with the Nunamiut, sometimes for a friendly exchange, other times for a life and death combat. For ages, Nunamiut have been skeptical of "forest people" whose language they could not understand. A small mound in the middle of the valley was apparently an ancient burial site of Dene warriors.

Helge often went hunting into the mountains on his own. He was growing physically stronger and woke in the morning feeling healthy and fit. He also noticed that he was slowly sliding into the same mindset as the Nunamiut: "I feel my thoughts aligning with theirs, conforming to the simple ideas which are of importance here. And I hardly miss a thing, for their world is full of brightness; indeed, I am among people who feel a joy in life denied to those who are condemned to wear out shoe leather in a city street."[11]

One day, Helge and Paneak went hunting for Dall sheep to help remedy the diminishing meat supply. Sheep were only an occasional target, but herds of over a hundred of the animals had been spotted farther south. Hunting with Paneak was a very special experience. He knew the landscape and was a great storyteller. Small incidents along the way could trigger lengthy stories, sometimes about nature, animal behaviour, and tracks or other hunting-related topics. Other times there were long accounts about his ancestors' hunting experiences, or myths and legends associated with the hunt.

It was a strenuous hike to where the sheep were. Helge wore a Telemark-like ski boot with a slippery, stiff sole. Paneak was much better equipped with his soft leather footwear that hugged the terrain. In the beginning, walking along the valley floor where it was nice and dry was fine. But when they began to climb the steep mountainsides covered with ice, Helge slid backwards as much as he climbed forward and struggled to keep up with Paneak, who kept going at a good, steady pace.

Helge looked everywhere, but saw no sign of any animals. "There are four," Paneak blurted. Only then did Helge catch sight of the sheep up on a steep slope. How on earth could they get within shooting range? The animals caught wind of them and scurried farther up the slope. The only possible way was to drive them farther down over the side of a steep ravine where there were large stones the men could hide behind. But how? Then all of a sudden, without warning, Paneak lay down for a nap in the heather. He was soon softly snoring away. Helge sat there quite perplexed, and then started picking lingonberries.

Suddenly the sheep began moving towards them and over the ravine to the desired spot. Paneak jumped up as if he had been watching them in his sleep. He grabbed his gun, fired off a few rounds, and brought down a ram. "It is nine years old," he said after counting the rings on the horns. First, he carved out the fat glands between the hooves and up the middle of the neck, both which were considered delicacies.

Such animals could weigh up to 100 kilos, and it was a struggle hauling it back to camp. The dogs, tied up farther down the hillside, were given the hooves full of meat, and the hunters each carried a load as heavy as a man could manage. On the way back, the men saw fresh tracks of a grizzly bear that had not yet hibernated. It was too late in the day though to follow after it.

The men arrived back at the camp after the sun had set, and the northern lights began their dance across the sky. "The air people are now playing ball with human heads," said Paneak referring to an old tale familiar to most Arctic people.

Rumour of the catch spread quickly across the camp, and when delightful smells wafted from Umealaq's cooking pot, one after the other came streaming in to get a taste of that fine, greasy mutton. Craving for fat was a familiar phenomenon for people who lived almost entirely on a meat diet. This was another reason why the Nunamiut traded with the peoples of Point Barrow and Kotzebue – to get hold of seal and whale blubber.

Illness and Death

One of the biggest challenges for the Nunamiut was acute illness. They knew the benefits modern medicine could provide, but distances and poor radio contact made access to it nearly impossible.

One day, the most beautiful girl, Kimmak, became sick. She initially had an infected tooth, which they tried to surgically remove with a hunting knife. This later developed into, in all probability, blood poisoning. Her face swelled, a fever rose, and she was clearly in danger of losing her life. The people in camp grew deeply concerned and were unsure of what to do. There was talk of transporting her out, but no one took the initiative to do so.

In the end, Helge suggested sending a few men south to Bettles to request help, and they agreed. The next morning, four men stood ready to go, each with a dogsled. The journey would take several days and they feared there might be deep snow on the south side of the mountains. The dogs were so thin for lack of food and it was uncertain whether they could even make it.

Helge wrote a letter to his pilot friend Bernt Balchen, stationed in Anchorage, to send along with the Nunamiut men going for help that read: "An Eskimo girl very sick. Hope 10 Rescue will send a plane for her right away. The reason may be a rotten tooth. She seems to be infected. Her face very swollen, her pulse high and it appears to be getting worse. Three kids died here during last few months. Cannot take chances. Take along tooth extractor."[12] A few days later, the Nunamiut messengers returned with exhausted dogs and many tales from the land farther south.

It was two weeks before the Nunamiut camp heard the murmur of plane engines in the distance. Kimmak was still alive, but only just. They carefully hauled her down by dogsled to the landing strip on the ice. When the plane took off, no one knew if they would ever see the girl alive again. She was flown to Fairbanks, where she was given medical treatment, and soon recovered. In the spring, she returned to Anaktuvuk Pass full of stories of all that she experienced in the south.[13]

However, it didn't always turn out so well when someone fell ill. One day, word spread that Tullaq, the little three-year-old son of Elijah Kakinnâq, was seriously ill. Helge had spent time with this charming, lively little boy and felt they had a special friendship. So he went to the family's tent to see if there was anything he could do. The place was full of people, mostly women and young girls.

Sitting on a caribou skin with the child in her lap, Kakinnâq's wife held the boy close to her chest. He was burning with fever, his jaws were clenched, and his little body shook every now and again with convulsions. You could see fear in the mother's eyes, but she still managed to remain calm and composed. The father sat and stroked the boy's head every time he went into a convulsion. "There was pain in that strong face," Helge wrote in his journal, and found it heartbreaking. "Tetanus," he thought, knowing there was little anyone could do so far from a hospital.

Off in a far corner of the tent lay a few other kids sleeping. The night wore on and some of the young women slept where they sat; the others followed the young boy's last struggles. It seemed evident that he wasn't going to survive. Outside the northern lights flickered over the mountains in the west and the dozens of dogs in camp occasionally filled the night air with their sombre howling.

Over the door hung a large, brown bear skin, and Umealaq, Paneak's compassionate wife, every so often lifted it and peeked in to see if anything was needed. It helped to have a little coffee and a piece of dried meat. Otherwise, everyone in the tent spoke softly with each each other and often smiled. "It wasn't the same sombre feeling of death as with white people. Not because it affected the Eskimos differently, but because they had the ability to experience death in a stronger way," Helge wrote in his journal on 9 September.

Dawn came and the sun slowly rose over the snow-covered mountains. The sky was a deep, autumn blue. Little Tullaq was still struggling, but grew weaker and weaker and was clearly reaching the end. Kakinnâq felt his son's legs under the caribou skin and then turned towards the others and said, "His legs are beginning to grow cold. Soon I shall have no son."[14] At six o'clock in the morning, little Tullaq died. His mother closed his eyes, Kakinnâq caressed the boy's face. That was it; no crying or expression of pain, every emotion suppressed. Helge and the others walked out of the tent into the blinding sun shining across the tundra and mountains. The dogs were curled up and asleep.

The next morning Helge awoke to the sound of hammer pounding coming from Kakinnâq's tent. They were building a small coffin for Tullaq. Later, a worship service was held in their tent during which they read from the Bible and sang psalms in their own language. With his beautiful, deep voice, Paneak read from the Psalm of David, after which they carried the small coffin out onto the tundra for burial. Helge began making his way back to his tent, not wanting to intrude, but Paneak insisted that he join them and that he take pictures. "There will be fun and games," he said, "we do this so it isn't so bleak for the family."

The others had already gone ahead, and when Helge and Paneak arrived they were all sitting on the ground, smiling and laughing. Half a caribou and several bags of dried meat had been laid out, a campfire was lit, and the women gathered more dry willow twigs. A hefty pot of boiling caribou hung over the fire. Only a few metres away, a man had already begun digging through the permafrost, and they took turns as it was heavy work. Kakinnâq sat strong and confident by the grave giving instructions.

Suddenly, someone sighted a herd of caribou on other side of the valley. One of the men took off and soon they heard a series of shots. He came back and said that he had managed to shoot seven of the animals. Life went on. The caribou meant everything to the Nunamiut. Even a funeral couldn't deter hunting.

The young children played a boisterous game. The grave was finished and the coffin lowered onto a bed of twigs, then covered with another layer of twigs before dirt was thrown over. Lastly, a small wooden cross with Tullaq's name was placed at the grave. Next to his lay the graves of two small girls who died of dysentery earlier that year.[15]

For such a small group of people, the deaths of several of their children and young in such a short span of time was quite dramatic, especially when there was little they could do to prevent it. Growing contact with the outside world led to changes in diseases and epidemics. Even during the January Helge was there, contact with the people on a plane that stopped at Anaktuvuk Pass spread whooping cough and influenza among the group, and two more infants died.

Helge noticed that the Nunamiut didn't make use of healing herbs to the same extent as the Caribou Eaters in northern Canada. It may well have had to do with the vegetation available in the area. However, Paneak did know a technique of massaging an ill person's stomach to make them well. Helge gave it a try on a feverish boy and measured with his thermometer that his temperature sank a half-degree after the treatment.

Umealaq (Susie) with her youngest child Wiraq on her back.

Helge was a bit astonished by what he perceived as the Nunamiut's lack of any clear leadership structure. Paneak was without a doubt an informal leadership figure, but the rule of collective applied here as it did with other Inuit cultures. Helge, however, experienced that in situations such as when Kimmak was sick, it could result in a type of a paralysis of action. Various hunting situations, he thought, could also have benefited from a greater degree of leadership and collaboration. But the Nunamiut preferred to hunt on their own or in pairs from the same household. The strength of the collective principle was that whoever had been the luckiest in hunting would share with those who had been less lucky. In this way, security was ensured by their numbers – as long as there was enough to share.

In reading Helge's journal, it is evident that his admiration for the Nunamiut grew steadily stronger. Not just for their ability to survive in nature, but also for the non-materialistic aspects of their culture: trad-itions, ways of thinking, caring for each other, and their light sense of humour even in difficult situations. He was also fascinated by their myths and legends, which showed the close interaction between the Nunamiut and nature. That is why Helge asked Sig Wien to bring a tape recorder with him the next time he came – to help preserve some of the Nunamiut culture for future generations.

Christmas with the Nunamiut

Christmas was approaching and Helge was very uncertain as to what he should do. He had promised Anne Stine that he would be home for Christmas, but he also believed that what he was experiencing in Anaktuvuk Pass was so valuable and important that it would have been terrible to leave too early. Like so many other times in his life, advice from his father was crucial for his decision. Olav's letter, dated 5 December 1949 read:

> As much as we would enjoy seeing you soon, we don't expect to see you until late spring. When you first have had the rare opportunity to meet a culture that still retains its primitive quality and continuity of its past, it would be completely wrong not to use this chance to experience this and explore it to its depths … only living longer with the tribe will you be able to attain knowledge of the most valuable aspects.[16]

Also included in the pre-Christmas post was a letter from Helge's lawyer, who said that the Norwegian Scientific Research Council had allocated 15,000 Norwegian kroner for his Alaskan expedition and an additional 15,000 kroner had been redistributed from his Siberian grant. This was good news because the family account was quite depleted. Helge decided to continue his stay in Anaktuvuk Pass.

The caribou had not yet migrated, and Helge, based on his experience with the Caribou Eaters in Canada, knew the lack and hunger that could result. He worried. The Nunamiut, on the other hand, showed no signs of concern, even though they were not able to hunt the fat bulls at the first autumn migration. Without enough fat in their diet, they would soon experience its deprivation in the form of fatigue and apathy – catastrophic for people who need to go out and hunt every day. Helge himself had experienced this when he lived with the Caribou Eaters in the Northwest Territories. And now, once again, he was craving fat.

The week before Christmas, they were at a camp called Qalutaq, a windy spot in between the mountains. There was little daylight now, only a greyish twilight during midday. The dome-shaped tents lay between sparse willow shrubs, which provided plenty of fuel. Those who were more fortunate with the hunting shared with the others, but most who went out returned with nothing.

A little earlier, the small group had divided; those called the Kitlikmiut[17] had left and gone their way while Helge stayed with the Raven people. Dividing into smaller groups was a traditional way of increasing chances for finding caribou and decreasing the need to have to feed so many people and dogs when someone was fortunate enough to shoot something. Behind the stove in Helge's tent he kept a lean, frozen knuckle of meat. In Paneak's tent, food was almost as sparse. The group decided to break up into even small clusters; this time Paneak's family and Helge were going to try it on their own. One icy cold morning they dismantled their tent, loaded their sleds, and harnessed the dogs. They headed into the dark with Umealaq and the kids on the sled and Paneak and Helge following on snowshoes and skis respectively.

After a considerable time mushing, they came upon some fresh tracks that led to a Kitlikmiut camp. It was a cheerful reunion and all were invited into the tents for raw and cooked caribou meat. But here too food was sparse. After a short rest, Paneak felt they needed to move on. The Kitlikmiut stood outside their tents watching them as they left – a cluster of people clad in caribou parkas beautifully lined with wolverine fur[18] and trimmed with wolf fur. A beautiful young girl by the name of Aqarwik helped Helge to untangle the dog harnesses. "We will meet for Christmas," she smiled. Helge was aware the Nunamiut knew a little of the white people's Christmas, but he chose not to ask as he wanted his presence there to have as little impact as possible. But now that it was mentioned, the feelings of Christmas came over him. He thought about us back home and felt a little sorry for himself. But those feelings quickly passed.

The group carried on through the cold, grey light to a camp called Oquluk – meaning the protected spot. They set up camp in a thicket of willows. Early every morning Helge and Paneak left across the mountains to hunt. It was tricky hunting in that half-dark, especially when it came to judging distances. Helge didn't particularly have much luck. The first day he saw a pack of fourteen wolves only to have them disappear in a flash across the valley. Paneak had a bit more luck. He found a caribou carcass that the wolves had only begun to chew; it at least provided a little food for the hungry people and dogs. In the evenings, they sat in Paneak's family tent. Umealaq sat and sewed, cooked food, or tanned hides while Paneak told stories. They grew even closer when it was just the few of them.

On Christmas Eve, Paneak caught sight of a large herd of wild sheep way up on the hillside. But this posed a dilemma. If the men went after the sheep, they would not make it back to celebrate Christmas. They chose Christmas celebrations and set course for the camp at Qualutaq, where the Kitlikmiut also planned to gather. It was a wonderful trip in the icy cold air. Helge, Paneak, and Umealaq each mushed a sled. The three oldest children sat on top of their mother's sled, and the youngest lay warm and cozy inside his mother's parka with his little head sticking out of her hood. Along the way, they saw grouse in the willow thickets and stray caribou off in the distance. But for once there was something more important to them than hunting.

When they pulled up to the tents at Qualutaq, the kids came running towards them. Everyone was to gather in the lodge of Elijah Kakinnâq. Helge wondered how sixty-five people could all possibly fit into one tent. "It will hold them all," said Paneak. "We have an old proverb, *tupiq qâlaitsug* (a tent never bursts)."[19] And he was right. The beds were moved out of the way and there was space enough for everyone in between the caribou walls. Of course they sat like sardines packed in a can, but the atmosphere was wonderful.

Mikiâna, who had visited the coast and had learned a few things there, held a short service. Then they sang a few hymns in their own language including a familiar tune Helge recognized as "Silent Night." Afterwards, it was time for festivities. None of the families had much food and so Helge didn't expect much of a Christmas meal other than dried meat and some boiled marrow bones. But then Kakinnâq stood, casually brought out a bag, and emptied its contents onto the caribou-hide floor. They could hardly believe their eyes: a little pile of small pieces of caribou fat, a coveted delicacy! Helge counted the pieces and saw there was just enough for everyone. Once again, Kakinnâq confirmed his reputation as a great hunter. But the women too had a few surprises in store. From underneath the heap of hides along the walls, one of them pulled out a bag of flour and a little yeast, then baked a loaf of bread to everyone's delight.

Agmaliq then passed around gifts from a small leather bag. Helge also had gifts for each of the children: barrettes, balls, pocket mirrors, shiny rings, and other equally exciting objects. The adults cheerfully, giddily exchanged gifts: a fox fur, a little tobacco or some matches neatly wound with sinew. Helge also received gifts, so thoughtfully given he was truly touched; Maptirâq had carved a small box from an old mammoth tusk and Ayaunik had sewn beautiful mittens and caribou boots for his daughter back home. They knew me from my picture Helge kept in his tent next to his sleeping bag.

It was warm as they all sat close together on the willow-lined floor. Outside it was biting cold, quiet and full of moonlight. The bear-skin flap door was tied open and frosty mist lay white along its edges. Sitting by the door were two young girls, Tatkawinna and Sisualik, with their arms around each other. Behind them, an incredibly large moon shone like a yellowish-red wall. It was almost as if they leaned up against it. Soon the drums began beating and everyone joined in on the traditional songs and dances.[20]

The days leading up to the new year passed quietly and peacefully. A heavy snowfall made it impossible to hunt. The only notable incident that occurred was when Kakinnâq came upon some wolverine tracks, which he followed until he tracked the animal down. Wolverine fur was a highly coveted lining for parka hoods since frost did not cling to it in the cold.

Then an important day for Helge approached. On 30 December, he wrote in his journal:

I am 50 years old today. Went hunting towards the west. Not a sign of life. The sky was remarkable, red from the sun behind light clouds. Have been horribly missing those dearest to me this past week, but it will pass. When I returned from hunting, the kids piled into the tent – my good friends. They sang Eskimo songs. So I sang a few Norwegian folk tunes, one of them they almost know by now. Then I brought out a piece of bread sprinkled with sugar and tea with sugar. They dug into the sugar box and I pretended not to see. Out walking today, it was almost as if I felt mamma there. My dear mamma.

The same day he wrote a letter to us at home:

My dearest two,
So I am now 50 years old ... I have longed for both of you lately. Just horribly. I said to myself, I should leave the first chance I get; leave the tent, storms and darkness. But it would be no good. It would be running from half-finished work. This melancholy I'm sure is caused by the darkness. It will quickly pass, but not my longing for you and our home.[21]

At Brattalid, Anne Stine held a large fiftieth birthday party attended by family and friends – but with the birthday honouree far, far away.

"What does a city look like?"

"What does a city look like?"[22] Kakinnâq asked one evening as they sat on the caribou furs in the large tent and talked. The others looked up interested. Helge began to explain, trying to draw comparisons with things they were familiar with. He told them of New York City's skyscrapers that were as tall as some of the high mountains west of Anaktuvuk and of the streets that were like the valley floors. He described cars rushing down the street and the people who hurried about, in and out of all the tall buildings. When he finished, it was quiet for a while. The hunters sat and stared into space thinking.

"How many people can be in such a city?" asked one young hunter.

"Many more than there are caribou in the mountains," Helge answered. This caused quite a response, since the caribou, when they were at their greatest number, could cover the land as far as the eye could see.

"But all these people, why must they constantly have to hurry around like you said?" Paneak asked.

"When they are in a hurry it's because they want to get rich, that is what is important to them," said Helge.

Paneak thought a while and then continued: "If they just took it a little more easy, it would do no harm. Often when we are out hunting, we have the best luck when we don't try so hard, but instead use our eyes well."

Another young hunter chipped in: "All the whites are rich and have a lot of things."

"There are many who are poor, so poor that they have nothing to live on," Helge replied.

"But then are they not helped by others?"

"No."

"But don't they do as we do and share with each other when someone is having a hard time?"

"No."

They looked at him blankly, and then a perplexed Paneak asked, "When they're always so busy down there in the cities, how can they have time to feel good, sit together and sing like we do or play with the children?"

"Oh, they do have some fun," Helge answered, "but often they are quite tired after work."

"And they live in such a city the whole time?"

"Pretty much the whole time."

"But if the houses are so tall and there are so many of them, how are they able to see the mountains?"

"They cannot see the mountains from there."

There was a long pause. Anyone who didn't know Paneak might have thought he was finished discussing the topic. But he always paused to ponder. Eventually he slowly said, "I have never seen a city, but after what you said, it must be quite hard to be happy there."

Then they began talking about the wolf hunt. Kakinnâq had just that day shot two large beasts and talked lively about it. Their evening conversations in the tent were the regular news service which most of the hunters participated in. Afterwards, traditional songs filled the night air. Happy kids tumbled in after playing outside in minus 40°C. It was bedtime and soon everyone went to their own tents. The wind died down and the northern lights flickered reds and purples across the valley.

Standing in front of the tent, Helge reflected: "I think of these people who only know the wilderness as their home and who have such a rich sense of humanity it would put many a white man to shame."

Caribou!

The new year came and still no sign of the great migration of caribou. Every once in a while a stray animal was shot, but far from enough to feed both people and dogs. Almost every thought was about food: fine fat caribou! "Just wait," Kakinnâq said, "til the moon grows small and lies like a basket in the sky, for then it will be filled with caribou. When it tips down towards the mountains, the beasts will pour out upon the country. You will see."[23]

And finally, the caribou arrived. On 26 January, Helge described what it was like:

It is a chilly, blustery day. I am sitting in the frost-covered tent, smoking my pipe, and pondering. Behind the oven lies a frozen knuckle of meat, so at least there is a little food in the house. I just have to resolve the issue of whether to cook it or eat it raw. Outside on the rack, I also have a small piece of caribou stomach if the knuckle proves to be too little. Today is saved. As for my food for tomorrow, well that is still walking around on all fours ... Suddenly, the flap of caribou skin covering my tent door is pulled open and little Ayaqiujak in his white sheepskin anorak comes bouncing in breathless and wide-eyed and says, "Tuttuwagjuits' (lots of caribou) ... And hanging low in the sky over the mountains is a crescent-shaped moon. "There you see," said Elijah, "It was full of caribou just like I said."[24]

First there were just a few scattered herds, and then more and more came until they poured in like a grey river over the pass. They were everywhere in all directions as far as the eye could see! The Nunamiut were cautious and careful. They did not rush out after them for fear the herd would be frightened and change direction. Only when there was a steady flow of animals did the hunters go out after them, each heading in his own direction. At first, the herd was restless and easily spooked. But eventually they calmed and settled into the valley for awhile, grazing calmly as if they were on a mountain farm. With the intense need for food lessened, the days grew lighter and brighter in many ways.

On 3 February, the sun finally reached high enough over the mountains to shed its first rays across the camp and valley. Now everything was somehow easier. People started to recover from the whooping cough and flu that arrived along with the plane that landed there a month earlier. The caribou continued to graze in the valley and the hunters went out every morning to shoot what was needed. The women busily skinned the animals, cut the meat into strips, hung it to dry, tanned the leather, and carried out many other hunt-related tasks. Sometimes, they also had to mush out a dogsled to load and transport the catch home. The children enjoyed the brighter days and playing outside. They slid down the slopes on small sleds or swung a willow-shafted disk at a log, similar to a game Helge himself played as a boy growing up in Bergen. However, it was the skiing that thrilled Helge; the snow was now perfect and packed. He soared down the slopes, at times right through a terrified herd of caribou that leapt out of his way. The kids also had a go on his skis, and a couple of the boys were especially quick to learn the technique, actually becoming quite good.

The light, long days brought life everywhere. The young girls took evening walks arm in arm out across the melting snow and the young men drove off in their dogsleds competing to see who was the best musher. People began returning from other camps; there were happy reunions, as well as sorrowful ones because of those who had passed away. Two infants who had died from the whooping cough epidemic lay in separate coffins waiting to be buried as soon as the snow melted, as was the custom.

For Helge, it was a melancholy time. On the morning of 2 May, it was the first time he woke to no ice on the bucket of water. Squawking V formations of grey geese flew overhead. It was time to think about returning to Norway: "My thoughts are turned abruptly to the world where I belong. It has become remote and unreal. A faint picture of streets filled with hurrying swarms of people, noises and tired faces comes to mind. I think how few really happy people I know there."[25] The Nunamiut had gained a very special place in his heart. He had been taken in with openness and trust and had experienced friendships that would have an effect on him for the rest of his life.

The thought of returning home also made him a little nervous. It had been so long since he and Anne Stine had seen each other. Would their reunion go well? Would there still be fierce arguments with frightening outbursts of her temper? Could he trust the authenticity of the loving tone of her letters he had received, or were they just pleasant words? As early as January, he wrote in a letter to Anne Stine:

> You write such nice letters. But when you sometimes think of me, and perhaps anticipate my return, you must not forget my many weaknesses so that, as women often do, you are not disappointed by the stark reality. I remind you of my following great faults:
>
> 1 Snore at night. Sleep quite unattractively with open mouth. Toss and turn making the bed creak.
> 2 Grumpy in the morning
> 3 Sloppy clothes and not very meticulous in other ways
> 4 Unmusical
> 5 Can speak harshly to wife about work. Also would like her to help with weeding in the garden, etc.

When the time came for him to leave, he became even more concerned about what his homecoming would be like and expressed this in another letter on 19 April:

> It will be strange to come back to Brattalid. Such a great pleasure that I am a little afraid. Yes, a little. Such is life ... I have no photo of you as you never sent one to me. I try to see your face and your beautiful eyes. I wonder how you will be when I see you? And to think that I will see Benedicte again, my goodness ...

The evening before Helge was to leave Anaktuvuk Pass, he sat in Paneak's family tent talking about the journey home. Then Paneak suddenly said, "We will give you the mountain which stands at the beginning of the 'Giants' Valley.' It shall bear your name and we will remember you." And then he added in a matter-of-fact way that "our people remember such things for many generations."[26] Helge was very touched by this gift. The mountain was one he knew well and would remember fondly for its nice slopes reaching down to the valley. Many times on his way back from hunting he looked forward to skiing down those fine inclines. "The man who raced down the slopes on his skis" was how the Nunamiut still remembered him years later.

It was highly unlikely that Helge would ever see the Nunamiut again. If he did, he knew it would be a different Anaktuvuk Pass than the one he experienced.

On 14 May he recorded in his journal: "Arrived in Fairbanks to so-called civilization." On 6 June he was in Seattle where "civilization" hit him full force with street traffic and busy people everywhere. He longed to return to the valley between those mighty mountains and to the people who had time enough to enjoy the simple things. But for him, that way of life ended here. He was on his way home to those who waited for him.

Changes at Anaktuvuk Pass

For the second time in his life, Helge had been incredibly lucky. He was able to experience a place where people lived their lives very much as they had for generations. Living in northern Canada from 1926 to 1930 as a trapper and his year with the Caribou Eaters had been his first such experience of traditional living. But the modern age soon seeped into both these places not long after Helge left.

Finding different ways to earn income became increasingly more important for the Nunamiut. The Anaktuvuk Pass archives at the University of Alaska[27] contain a number of letters written by Paneak to various scholars. He, and some of the other Nunamiut men, earned a small income by helping these researchers with various tasks throughout the years: catching and collecting birds,[28] taking temperature measurements, collecting larvae from caribou, recording stories, and, in collaboration with John Martin Campbell, recording Paneak's own life story.[29] Paneak's sons once caught seventeen wolf pups, which they sold to the Arctic Research Station in Point Barrow. The women started to make caribou-hide souvenirs for people living outside Anaktuvuk Pass.

Helge also sent packages of clothing and shoes to Paneak and the others which were followed by requests for more. Traditional clothing and footwear made from hides were no longer considered adequate enough. An obvious change that became apparent in Helge's correspondence with them is that the people in Anaktuvuk Pass gradually began to feel that they were *poor*. They compared themselves with people elsewhere and became more and more dependent on goods that had to be purchased, such as tobacco, coffee, tea, sugar, manufactured clothing and shoes, and so on. "We have no money left," Paneak wrote in a letter.

Perhaps the Nunamiut themselves wanted the changes that increased contact with the outside world offered. Helge, however, cautioned them. In a Christmas letter to Paneak in December 1951, he wrote:

My dear friend Paneak,
I wish you a happy Christmas and New Year with plenty of caribou. And I also wish happiness for you in other ways. No sickness. Don't think for a minute that I have forgotten at all about you people even though time has passed. I think about you very often and remember you as a kind and good people who treated a stranger from far away as a friend ... I hope that my book somehow will be a help for you ... at the same time, I do hope that you people are not too eager for civilization, that you continue with the life in the mountains. A man can earn money in civilization and buy a few things. But there is one thing he cannot buy and that is freedom. The free hunting life is a fine thing, nothing will make you more happy.

Helge continued the letter by saying that he had sent twelve pairs of children's skis, boots, bindings, and poles. Also, he sent a package with clothes, toys, and chocolate for the children which he left up to Paneak to divide fairly among them. It took a long time for the package to reach Anaktuvuk Pass, but the following Christmas, Paneak wrote and thanked him for it. He reported that in 1952 many people died of measles followed by pneumonia: "because we have no medicines, they died." The knowledge of health care options farther away had now created a feeling of isolation which had never existed before, even when they had been more cut off from the rest of the world. In this way, their desire for access to modern health services gradually became one of the greatest driving forces for change.

After a few attempts of seasonal schooling for Anaktuvuk Pass children, full-time teaching began in 1960.[30] With this, the last of the nomadic families moved to Anaktuvuk Pass for good. The same summer a private plane company built a landing strip. With regular departures and arrivals, eventually daily, it grew increasingly easier for health care personnel, educators, and other officials to visit Anaktuvuk Pass. Building materials and other equipment were also more readily brought in. Gradually, the traditional hide tents and sod huts became a thing of the past and prefabricated houses and modern school buildings emerged. With established residences, firewood became even more limited and so oil or coal burning furnaces were installed in the houses. This too required money, and the lack of available sources of income was perceived a major problem.

Step by step, this same modernization process repeated itself not only in Anaktuvuk Pass, but also in all the other small local societies in the Arctic. The only difference was that this process came later in Anaktuvuk Pass than it did in other places. The changes were inevitable, despite Helge's wishes that the Nunamiut be "saved" from the influences of civilization.

12 STILL TOGETHER, DESPITE IT ALL

As she struggled her way across the American desert on her own, there was one thing that Anne Stine clearly came to understand. She wanted an education to become more independent and to rely less on Helge.

Ever since she was a child and read about the excavation of Tutankhamen's grave, she wanted to be an archaeologist. She had begun compulsory classes in Latin at the university before we left for the States, but now she wanted to further her studies. When Helge finally did come home from Alaska, he was met with a surprisingly determined wife, something he wasn't initially thrilled about.

I myself do not remember a thing about Helge's homecoming on 7 July 1950. A bit odd, considering I was nearly seven years old and hadn't seen my father for an entire year. As an adult, I read a yellowed newspaper clipping and was quite astonished at the choice of words:

> Nonchalantly, somehow quite casually, Helge Ingstad sat with his
> beautiful young wife and little daughter Benedicte this afternoon
> as if he had never been abroad; nor least of all having lived an
> entire year with the Eskimos in the very heart of Alaska. He sat
> there enjoying himself smoking his cigar. Calm and unaffected.
> And quite civilized.[1]

However, what I do remember well, and even to this day find painful, is that the mood in our home suddenly changed. After I went to bed, loud voices rose from the living room in heated discussions. That is to say, Anne Stine clamoured away and Helge eventually withdrew into his office and closed the door. He was stubborn, harsh, and sulky. She was rash and temperamental, but could quickly let it go.

Anne Stine's studies were one of the problems. Helge appreciated that she had interests, and especially that they complemented his own. However, in his world a woman was to respect the man in the house, stay at home, care for both husband and children, and be gentle and lovable – just as his mother had been. Anne Stine grew up much the same way, confirmed by a few lines her mother Louise wrote to Helge in Alaska:

> Anne Stine is wonderfully sweet and good with her (Benedicte).
> She has matured and now lives only for you and her. She is enjoy-
> ing making your home nice and pleasant for when you return
> home. Yes, we are in all ways satisfied with her, she finds great joy
> in living for her husband and child.

Anne Stine indeed had much to rebel against if she were to realize her dreams. However, she was never able to do so without feeling a sense of guilt or failure. Had she been born a generation later, the situation would have been quite different.

Despite her initial challenges, Anne Stine followed through with her plans and took introductory philosophy and three semesters of Latin in one year. She then took core subjects in History of Religion, Ethnography, and graduate-level courses in Nordic Archaeology during the spring of 1960. Her father, Eilif, never saw her graduate as an archaeologist, but in 1954 as he lay dying, he asked for her forgiveness for not understanding that she too should have an education.

Another issue between Anne Stine and Helge was that they both desired more children, which did not happen. It was important for Helge to have a son to carry on the Ingstad family name. Whether they had a boy or a girl didn't matter to Anne Stine, as long as it was a healthy child. One miscarriage after another made her increasingly more depressed. After an operation that still did not help, they basically gave up. Anne Stine wanted to adopt a child like a friend of hers had done, but Helge flatly refused. For him, if the child was not his own biological son it would not be the same. Perhaps this was for the best as it was questionable whether the stoic Ingstad feelings of kin could embrace a child born outside this family structure. Anne Stine from the beginning was well received into the Ingstad family, but the family's domineering male attitude made her feel as if she had not fulfilled their expectations.

A Sunday family dinner at Brattalid proceeded something like this: first Anne Stine made dinner and set the table; after dinner, Anne Stine and Helge's sister, Gunvor, did the dishes while the men went out to "walk the borders" of the plot, that is, to see where the boundary markers stood. Because there was no male heir, I too was graciously allowed to join them. What this ritual clearly did was emphasize both gender differences and connection to the property. When members of the Ingstad family spoke or wrote letters about Brattalid, it was always "Helge's house," not both theirs. No wonder Anne Stine felt excluded and longed for her family in Lillehammer.

As life in Oslo went on, their age difference also grew more distinct in various ways. One of Helge's main reasons for moving to Oslo was to have contact with other writers and artists through the Authors' Union, which at the time was a relatively small group of people who knew each other well. He became especially good friends with Arthur Omre, who in the past had been a convicted smuggler but who later turned to writing. Helge was drawn to the adventurous.

The Authors' Union meetings often ended with late evenings at the Theatre Café, from which Helge would come home a little the worse for wear. Anne Stine did not approve. However, her training in "domestic studies" and her stay in France made her the perfect hostess when famous Norwegian authors such as Aksel Sandemose, Sigurd Hoel, Arnulf Øverland, and others were invited home for dinner. Beyond this, though, she wasn't included within that circle. She sat at home tending to their child. But Anne Stine was still young and she too wanted to go out and have fun. The gradual realization that she would not be able to bear any more children made her even more certain that she needed to create her own profession.

Several of Anne Stine's old friends had moved to Oslo, but they were mostly fifteen to twenty years younger than Helge. My parents' age difference determined whom they socialized with for many years until it no longer mattered. Only when she started to study at the university did Anne Stine make her own friends in Oslo and begin to go out on her own. At first, Helge was not pleased but eventually accepted it.

Worse than the lonely evenings for Anne Stine were the long periods when Helge was away. After he returned from Alaska, he quickly fell into the same routine as he had before they were married: travelling around giving lectures. We had to have some kind of income, and for a self-proclaimed freelancer it was a necessity. Besides, he loved the feeling of freedom of having no one hanging over him telling him what he should do – or having anyone *he* needed to tell what to do. He liked meeting people of all kinds and felt a kinship with the travelling salesmen he often chatted with in the evenings at the hotels: "They sell shoes and I sell lectures, it's pretty much the same." His lectures often drew large crowds but his schedule was demanding, a tiring marathon across all of Norway. At times, he had up to two lectures a day, including film and slides, seven days a week followed by long journeys by bus, boat, or train.

When he was writing, he was not at home much either. When he reached the final stages of a book manuscript, he left for months at a time. He found a place to stay up in some valley or at some farm where they were willing to house him. Then he sat and wrote intensively until the book was finished. And so it continued: lecture trips, book writing, and new expeditions in a never-ending cycle.

Anne Stine eventually had to accept that the main responsibility for both home and family, which she thought was only temporary while Helge was in Alaska, was to be, more or less and periodically, permanent. As for me, I missed my father and thought it sad every time he left to travel. But the joy of having my grandmother Louise, then widowed, show up at Brattalid almost as quickly as he left and stay until he returned made up for missing him.

The material from the *Nunamiut* book became the source of our livelihood for many years. In a newspaper interview, he was asked whether it was going to become a doctoral study.[2] Helge answered, "First let it be popular reading and then we'll see." The manuscript for *Nunamiut* was written while Helge stayed up in the mountain area of Skjåk with his friend Jo Storbråten, a mountain man who had great regard for Helge. Published the following year, 1951, the book was well received by both critics and readers.

The more scholarly part of the material, such as the tape recordings of songs and legends, was especially fitting for further research. Specialist of Inuit language Professor Einar Bergsland worked on the song texts and legends while Evind Groven, a composer, transcribed the music.[3] Helge never did pursue a doctoral degree, and much valuable ethnographic material still lies unprocessed in the archives.

Humour and History

One of the things that kept the marriage together, despite the problems, was Anne Stine's sense of humour. She could break into such infectious laughter that one almost laughed at the laughing more than at the actual episode. She could see the humour in most things – especially things Helge said or did. My father too had a sense of humour, but not as round and developed as hers and without her sense of self-irony. But he dutifully laughed after the funny espisode was explained to him.

Once on a train journey to Lillehammer, they sat in the same compartment as a young, darker-skinned man. He was clearly from southern parts of the world. Helge, who always liked to get to know people from other countries, leaned forward and asked with a hint of nationalism, "Have you ever seen mountains before?" The man looked a bit puzzled and then answered, "Oh yes, I am born in the Himalaya." Anne Stine burst out laughing, but Helge couldn't understand what he had said that was so funny. It turned out that the man was an exchange student from India studying at the University of Oslo. During the journey to Lillehammer, they all became good friends and later he often visited our family at Brattalid.

Another time while watching the Norwegian Independence Day parade on 17 May in Oslo, Helge began chatting with a Norwegian American. In his broadest, jovial trapper English Helge asked, "Are you faaa ... rming ower there?" It was perhaps the only thing that he could think that a Norwegian immigrant would do in America. "Oh no," the man replied, "I am a professor at a university." Anne Stine again laughed hysterically and often referred to the episode as "typical Helge."

History was their great common interest. They especially enjoyed driving up the valleys reading old names of places and farms from the road atlas and then discussing the origins of these. In many ways, this was a precursor to Helge's later discourse on the origin of the word "vin" in Vinland. Eventually, as Anne Stine progressed in her studies and her knowledge of her subject grew, alongside Helge's growing interest for the Sagas and the Vinland mystery, meal times at Brattalid became full-fledged history lectures followed by academic discussion.

Perhaps the most important elements that kept the marriage intact were family expectations and the raising of a child. Divorce was non-existent in either the Ingstad or Moe family, so strong forces kept them together.

In the middle of this mildly turbulent family situation, magazine journalists turned up regularly at the door to write about the romantic story of the young girl who wrote fan letters, got her Arctic explorer, and lived happily ever after. And of course, they also wanted family pictures to go along with the story. Looking at an old photo and the angry expression on my face as a child, I was reminded how much I hated this type of performance, which I experienced as being incredibly false.

Almost Rich

In some ways, Helge was frugal, almost bordering on penny-pinching. Food had to be eaten regardless of how mouldy or foul-smelling it had become; nothing was to be thrown out. The monthly household money given to Anne Stine, her "allowance," was carefully counted and handed over with a ceremonious air as if he were presenting a great gift. It's strange that she put up with this ritual. However, she continued to take her "allowance" even after she started earning her own money, which she adamantly kept as her own private funds, not to be used to pay any bills or cover any everyday expenses.

Some of the reason for Helge's frugalness was his fear of not having anything to fall back on as he grew older or if he became ill. He was very much dependent on earnings from his books and lectures and did not qualify for the Norwegian national accrued social pension. Concerning larger expenses, however, he could be quite generous and when he saw fit show up with large gifts or contribute to an exciting trip. Then you had to be careful to clearly show your appreciation and thank him many times over, otherwise he would later say: "Were you pleased with the gift, or not?" As the years progressed, he also had little understanding of the inflation of things. He would grandly present his grandson Eirik with a 10 kroner coin as payment for a job thinking it quite a sum – just as his own grandmother did when she presented him with 2 kroner when he first arrived as a young student in Kristiania.

Helge never truly became a wealthy man, nor was it ever his intention. But the dream of a big win still at times enticed him, as it does for most of us. Once, he almost did become rich. As mentioned previously, Helge bought a mineral claim in Pine Point, Canada, in 1929 for what he considered a tremendous sum of $50. The day after his purchase, he regretted it horribly and sold it back to the man who talked him into it. Years later, sometime in the 1960s, Helge was invited to a formal dinner in Oslo and was seated next a Canadian geologist. Well into the dinner, Helge made the comment, "I had a claim in Canada once, at a place called Pine Point in the Northwest Territories, but I suppose nothing ever came out of it?" The geologist looked at him wide-eyed and said, "Pine Point? That holds the largest lead and zinc deposits in all of North America. If you had kept that claim, you would have been a multi-millionaire today!" Helge hurried to the phone and called home to Anne Stine, who had a good laugh. Afterwards, they both agreed that a person isn't necessarily happier with so much money. He was glad it turned out the way it did.

Throughout Helge's entire life, however, he dreamt of finding a small-business concept, one that wouldn't necessarily make him rich but could at least be fun to manage on the side and be profitable – or, at the very least, break even. It also had to be original, something not yet done by others and preferably connected to nature or the Arctic areas. He thought of many things: importing border collies from Scotland for herding Norwegian sheep; importing Shetland ponies; raising reindeer in the southern mountains of Norway; breeding muskoxen for their wool; and several other more or less wild ideas that never transpired beyond an exchange of a few letters. He was definitely not cut out to be a businessman.

Later in life, though, he did serve on the board of directors for a business called Norwegian Polar Navigation, of which his good friend Einar Pedersen, chief navigator of SAS Airlines, was a founding member. The company planned to explore for oil on Svalbard and had also acquired certain exploration rights near Prudoe Bay in northern Alaska. Helge's willingness to get involved, and to be a shareholder, was most likely due more to friendship and an interest in Svalbard than any hopes of becoming wealthy. Investing in the stock market was also not quite his forte as he was much too financially cautious.

Norwegian Polar Navigation, however, did experience a brief, and for Helge, surprising upswing in the markets when the Americans discovered large deposits of oil in Prudoe Bay, not far from where Norwegian Polar Navigation had their claim. It was satisfying enough for Helge to sell half his shares and build an office extension onto the house. After that, the shares fell and the company eventually faded away.

Lacking any real skills in entrepreneurship, Helge continued to support our family with revenues from his books and many lecture tours. During the decade before television, it was still possible to earn a reasonable income this way.

As I grew older, I learned how to handle some of the film projection equipment and often accompanied Helge on these lectures during weekends and school holidays as a "technician." This way, the two of us had many very nice trips together. I particularly remember a summer trip to Finnmark in northern Norway during the middle of the 1950s. Helge held a presentation about the Nunamiut for a group of soldiers, after which one of the officers promised to take us night fishing to a lake out on the tundra. It was one of those rare summers when the Finnmark plateau was as warm as the hottest spots in Europe. We drove across the tundra in a military jeep, and every now and again we passed a small Sami family dwelling, which I found very exciting. The midnight sun was shining, it was warm, still, and beautiful. Arriving at the lake, however, we faced our greatest challenge: mosquitoes! Nothing to worry about, though, as Helge had such incredible mosquito appeal that they didn't bother me. He stood there shrouded in a black cloud all night long but took it stoically – for there were trout to be caught!

13 EXPEDITION TO SOUTHWEST GREENLAND

Exactly when in Helge's life he first thought about searching for Vinland is hard to pinpoint. His interest in the Norse Sagas and the stories they told about the Vinland voyages started when he was perhaps thirty years old, at least from the time he was living in East Greenland. His idea of taking a journey west to follow the path of the Vikings, however, most likely emerged gradually. At the same time, Helge began to lose interest in studying "primitive" communities in the north as he felt they were soon to be "corrupted by civilization."

Helge's full focus was now directed towards the mystery of Vinland and where it might lay. He extensively studied all that was written about the Vinland voyages, and I remember the piles of books, the Sagas and other sources, stacked high on his desk. The first step of his plan in search of Vinland was to take an expedition to southwest Greenland in the summer of 1953 and to follow the Vikings' footsteps to the areas the Sagas called Østerbygd (Eastern Settlement) and Vesterbygd (Western Settlement). It was here that migrating people came sailing in to Greenland from Iceland around the years 985 or 986.[1] Twenty-four boats in all[2] embarked from Iceland with men, women, children, and all necessary animals and equipment to establish a new life for themselves. But only fourteen ships made it to Greenland; the others were either lost at sea or forced to return to port. It was a dangerous sea voyage with open boats in ice-filled waters.

The bold leader of this journey was Eirik the Red, who was born in the coastal area of southwest Norway in about the year 950. Eirik was forced to leave his native country for Iceland when his father, Thorvald, was exiled for manslaughter. In Iceland, most of the good land was

Viking Voyages

already taken, and so the family settled on the remote, barren northwest coast and built a farm called Drang. Thorvald died and Eirik married the strong-willed Thjodhild, who was of Norwegian royal blood and had powerful relatives in Iceland. They moved south to Hvamsfjorden, the innermost part of Breidafjord, where her family lived, and here they built the farm Eirikstad. But in Iceland, Eirik was banished from the country for three years for committing a killing.

Eirik had heard of sailors who had seen an unfamiliar land to the west of Iceland and went in search of it. What he found was Greenland, a beautiful land of glaciers and high mountains, and seasonal green, fertile areas farther inland. After exploring the land for three years, Eirik decided to return to Iceland to persuade others to come and live here. To make it more alluring, he called the place Greenland.

People came and settled in two southern parts of Greenland: the Eastern Settlement, which, despite its name, lay farthest south on the island, from today's Cape Farewell to the areas around Ivittuut (formerly Ivigtût); and the Western Settlement, at the head of what is now called Nuup Kangerlua Fjord near the country's capital of Nuuk. In the Eastern Settlement, ruins of five hundred farms have been found and in the Western Settlement about ninety-five.[3] Those coming from Iceland were farmers with cattle and sheep as their most important livestock, so the grazing land attracted them. Fishing and hunting of both sea mammals and reindeer, however, were also important. The Sagas tell of how these Greenland settlers travelled farther north to hunt at a place called Nordseta, which researchers think must have been in Disko Bay. Signs of Norse people, including a runestone, have been found as far north on Greenland as the areas around Upernavik on the western coast. These findings indicate that the Norse also had contact with the Inuit people. Carved wooden figures clearly showing Norse characteristics and headgear have been discovered among Inuit artifacts.

Eirik the Red claimed land in the Eastern Settlement. He chose an area at the farthest end of Eiriksfjord (Tunulliarfik), where he built a grand farm he called Brattahlid, meaning slope or steep hill. Here he settled with his wife Thjodhild, their sons Leif, Thorvald, and Thorstein, as well as Freydis, his illegitimate daughter. Thjodhild had converted to Christianity in Iceland and strongly desired her husband to follow suit. When he refused, she threatened to not share her bed with him until he became a Christian; "Eirik was not pleased,"[4] the Sagas say. To appease her, Eirik built a small church close to the farm. A reconstruction of this church now stands near the original site.[5]

The Norse settlers lived in Greenland for about five hundred years and then disappeared without a trace. What happened to them? Where did they go? Various theories have been suggested: Did a colder climate lead to dwindling cod fishing, hunting, and pastureland and cause the end of them? Or did the outbreak of the plague sever connections to Norway and therefore important supplies? Was it because walrus tusks, the main commodity of trade for Greenlanders, were no longer in demand after the plague in Europe severely diminished the interest in such luxury items? Or were tusks from the north replaced by ivory, now available from colonies in Africa? Did the Norse settlers die in battle with the Inuit, who gradually migrated south along the Greenland coast, or did they integrate with them? Did they die from plagues and diseases or because of degeneration due to so much intermarrying?[6] Were they killed or abducted by pirates? Did they emigrate, and if so, where? Helge believed that several of these conditions and events could have played a role, but the most important question to him was: Where was the Vinland of the Sagas? And it was this question to which he devoted the rest of his life.

The first thing he wanted to do in this search was to see and explore the land where the Norse had settled in Greenland. He explained: "How did the Norse Greenlanders live? What happened in the end? My intention of the expedition [to Greenland] was primarily to acquire a first-hand assessment, and a larger perspective – from the western part of the land where the Norse people lived and worked."[7]

In the summer of 1953, Anne Stine and Helge headed for West Greenland, the initial step in their search to locate Vinland. On 12 June, they sailed from the Norwegian western coastal town of Ålesund onboard the ship *North Frost*. Joining them was their specially selected expedition skipper Harald Botten, a local from the rugged coastal area of Sunnmøre. Helge was convinced that men from this area of Norway were the only ones capable of such a rugged job sailing around Greenland.

Hoisted up onto the *North Frost*, and leaning on deck, was their little expedition boat dubbed *Benedicte*. A small 28-foot dory, its past included perilous journeys between Norway and the Shetland Islands during the Second World War.[8] I was along in name only, as I had been happily placed in the care of my grandmother Louise and grandfather Eilif in the mountains at Maribuseter.

North Frost took off from Ålesund in a thick fog that didn't lift until the Faroe Islands appeared in the distance. The ship headed in that direction and in through an inlet surrounded by low, grassy islands. The landscape was amazingly green on top of sheer cliffs that dropped to the sea; swarms of birds were everywhere. The ship sailed into the dock at Thorshavn just as rays of sunlight pierced through the fog for the first time on their voyage. Anne Stine and Helge went ashore at what looked like a fairytale village shrouded in a haze: small, old houses with turf roofs and fishermen's cottages all in a row along the harbour. Their visit to the Faroe Islands was short, but they were able to see some old houses still in use and get an impression of how the Norse settlements on Greenland might have been today if they had still been standing.

On the fourth day at sea, they caught sight of the Greenland coast and the ice-filled waters surrounding it. At Færingehavn, many Norwegian and Faroe Island fishermen anxiously awaited the ship, which was also carrying letters from home. For many years, Færinghavn was the only harbour along the western coast of Greenland where the Danes allowed foreign vessels to moor to refuel and refresh their water supplies. Den Kongelige Grønlandske Handel, established by Denmark in 1774, had had a monopoly on all the trade in Greenland up until 1950. This imposed trade arrangement was one of the contentious issues in the East Greenland issue and Helge certainly must have had a thought or two about it when he went ashore.

The *Benedicte* was lowered into the water at Ivittuut, north of Eiriksfjord (Tunulliarfik).[9] Helge, Anne Stine, and Harald hauled all their things onto the smaller boat and thought how nice it was to be on their own deck. The boat, however, was so small that when Helge slept on a bench by the table he had to lie with his legs sticking out the cabin door. He didn't mind; they were in Greenland and adventure lay ahead.

In their little boat *Benedicte*, they set sail for Eiriksfjord. The first thing they saw were high, steep mountains that dropped to the sea, but then the fjord widened and revealed a more hospitable landscape. Farthest in at this deep fjord they spotted it: Brattahlid (Qassiarsuk)! This was the very place Helge and Anne Stine had named their own home after. Sheep and Icelandic horses peacefully grazed on the surrounding green meadows and hills. The little expedition team stood on deck and looked out across the land. They all thought it was absolutely breathtaking. Large chunks of drift ice on one side of the fjord forced them to anchor on the opposite side, by the ruins of another Norse farm, Stokkanes. They then rowed their dinghy over to Brattahlid. Greenlanders, kids, and dogs all came rushing down to the beach to greet them and had a good laugh at Helge's wobbly rowing technique in the little skiff.

Helge and Anne Stine walked across the meadow surrounded by a horde of children. They thought about the Vikings who once galloped on their horses along here. This was where Thjodhild, Freydis, and the other women fetched water from the river and where Leif Eiriksson's ship lay moored before embarking for Vinland. A short distance up the shore lay distinct remains of a large building situated on a natural terraced slope. Centuries ago in that hall, people sat gathered around the burning evening fire to tell and listen to stories about travels to distant lands. Close to the ruins of this building, and not far from a small, newly reconstructed church, lay the ruins of the church that Eirik had built to appease Thjodhild. The current Greenlanders now raised cattle and sheep in the area around the ruins and vegetables in the great hall. Otherwise, the landscape, the beautiful view across the fjord, and the ice- and snow-covered mountains were all the same as when the Norse lived here.

Later in the evening after Helge and Anne Stine had returned to their boat, they heard a sudden splash in the water. "Salmon," Helge thought and threw out his line. He immediately got a bite. However, it wasn't salmon he caught, but a huge cod. The waters around them were teeming with fish. Helge knew cod swam into the deep waters of the fjord and that the Norse Greenlanders had had food right outside their front door, literally.

From Eiriksfjord, the trio travelled on to Narsaq and then onto Hvalsey Church, one of the best-preserved Norse ruins in Greenland and the place known for the last written record of the Greenlandic Norse. Old writings state that a wedding took place here in September 1408 between an Icelandic man and woman from one of the Greenland settlements. Not long after this, a ship travelled back to Iceland with all the wedding guests. The recorded account of this wedding at Hvalsey gives no indication that life was going poorly for the Norse people in Greenland. However, sometime after this occasion they all disappeared. No other written record from these Norse communities has ever since been discovered.

Helge, happy to be on an expedition again.

From Hvalsey, the little boat *Benedicte* sailed onward down Einars-fjord, as the Sagas called it, where the land appeared less wild than in Ei-riksfjord. When the Norse lived here, their farms spread across the land on both sides of this fjord. The expedition team anchored the *Benedicte* in a bay the Sagas called Thorvaldsvik and the next day continued down the fjord to the most important destination of their journey: the old epis-copal seat of Gardar (Igaliku). They arrived just as the sun was slowly sinking behind the mountains.

The next morning they went ashore and were met by Grethe Egede, a Greenlandic woman. She was most likely a descendant of the Norwe-gian bishop Hans Egede who settled in Greenland in 1721. Egede came to Greenland to preach to the Norse settlers, but when he arrived, they were no longer there. He instead established a mission among the Inuit and founded the colony at Godthåp, today known as Nuuk, the capital of Greenland.

Gardar plays a significant role in the stories of the Sagas. It was the place where Einar, one of the first Norse settlers, went ashore and was so delighted with all the surrounding green areas that he built his farm here.

His son Thorvard married Eirik the Red's daughter Freydis. But most importantly, Gardar became the established episcopal see of Greenland from 1125. A number of churches were built, as well as a monastery and a convent. In total, there are remains of over forty building sites spread across a large area.

The most important archaeological find at Gardar has been the discovery of a skeleton of a sizable middle-aged man. He wore a ring with missing stones (most likely removed at his funeral) on his right hand and a bishop's staff was placed across his body. The remains were first thought to be the Bishop Jon Smyrill, King Sverre's foster father who died in 1209. However, carbon dating of the skeleton later indicated this to be wrong and that the skeleton most likely was from a period between 1262 and 1393.[10] Examinations of other skeletons in the cemetery showed that the Norse who had lived here were a healthy and hearty people without signs of physical decline or illness.

Helge used a good deal of his time at the Gardar ruins. He walked around and thought of the many stories from the Sagas that took place here. In one area, he came across an old irrigation system, previously undiscovered. In another, he found a piece of iron that may have come from the old church bell that no doubt could have been heard all the way to the end of Einarsfjord. As an avid chess player himself, he especially ruminated over the chess pieces that had been found in the Gardar ruins. Since presumably this was also the seat of rule, people came to Gardar from afar to meet for both worldly and spiritual purposes.

From Gardar, the little boat *Benedicte* carried on down the fjord again, this time with a compromised motor and a rope twisted around its propeller. But Harald lived up to Helge's expectations of sailors from Sunnmøre with their seafaring abilities and fixed it all. They continued down the fjord passing Sydproven (Alluitsup Paa) on Vatnaverfi Peninsula's southern tip, a windy little place on smoothly eroded rocky cliffs. They soon approached Uunartoq, a place called "the warming island." "To shore!" Helge commanded. Anne Stine, however, made it quite clear she was not about to go into those pools of water. After much persuasion, she gave in. As she stood there standing in the wind without a stitch, she thought it was absolutely horrible. Then she jumped in and to her amazement the crystal clear water was beautiful and warm, nearly 40°C. For two hours she lay in a pool hollowed out in the heated sand with bubbles rising from the centre of the earth. The fog lifted and she

Anne Stine enjoying the hot springs at Uunartoq.

could suddenly see great icebergs out in the fjord just beyond, floating by on their way to the Labrador Current. Getting up out of the water was much worse than getting in.

Their trip to Greenland was a good period for Anne Stine. Finally, she was able to join Helge on one of his expeditions, and as an archaeologist she was in her element with the Norse ruins. Eventually, though, she grew restless at being away. She longed for home, for the mountains at Maribuseter, and for me. But perhaps what was most on her mind was her father. He had been operated on for stomach cancer the year before and his health had begun to decline before she left for Greenland. There was reason to believe that this could be his last summer at the cabin. In the end, she returned home after two months in Greenland. Helge stayed on, and he and Harald continued their journey to what the Saga called the Western Settlement, the most northern Norse settlement in the Nuuk fjord. On the way, they passed the mountain Pisissarfik (archer's mountain), a large pinnacle that sticks straight out of the water. The place is associated with one of the few Inuit legends that tells of an encounter with the Norse people. The legend says that a Norse man and an Inuit went up on the mountain to shoot at a target with bows and arrows. At the foot of the mountain, they placed a white leather hide and the man who missed the target was to throw himself off the mountain. According to the legend, the Inuit won and the Norse man ended his life at the foot of that mountain.

The farm ruins at the Western Settlement, like in the Eastern Settlement, lay farthest in the fjord where it was warmer and greener beneath the mountains. The pastures were not nearly as big as those in the Eastern Settlement and the steeper mountains cut more drastically into the sea. Cod also found their way far down this fjord, and Helge was told that during spawning season the small community of Kapisillit turned into a very busy fishing village.

It was also here, in a smaller arm of the Nuuk fjord, that the Norwegian polar explorer Fridtjof Nansen and his companions came down Austmanna Valley after making the first crossing of the interior ice cap of Greenland in 1888. They made a boat of branches, covered it with canvas, and managed to sail to Godthåp (Nuuk). But by the time they arrived, the last ship of the season had already sailed south so they had to spend the winter there. Helge walked up Austmanna Valley and noticed that there were many Norse ruins all the way up to where the inland ice began. This meant that the first Norwegians who crossed the inland ice of Greenland came down a valley where people of their own kin had lived centuries earlier.

Helge and Harald continually searched for ruins around the Western Settlement and did indeed find several. A few appeared to be previously undiscovered, but others were already recorded and excavated by Danish archaeologists. One of the greatest of these was a large farm called Sandnes, beautifully situated on a headland surrounded by fireweed and bluebells. It is said that Eirik the Red's son, Thorstein, had lived here with his beautiful wife Gudrid. Thorstein died in an epidemic and later Gudrid remarried Vinland voyager Thorfinn Karlsefni. The Sagas say he stayed here at the farm on his journeys both to and from Vinland. Discovered in the ruins at Sandnes have been both a flint arrowhead of Native American origin and a lump of anthracite coal believed to come from North America.[11]

Danish archaeologists have made many important discoveries here that explain how the Norse people lived.[12] In the barn, they found a variety of household articles which could possibly mean the farm was abandoned in haste. They must have buried certain belongings they couldn't take with them and which they didn't want to end up in the hands of others. At the cemetery, an entire family was found buried in the same grave; a man, woman, and two small children. The bodies were generally well preserved and showed no signs of physical impairment. In the age-old rubbish heap, bones of domesticated farm animals were discovered, the same as at the Eastern Settlement: small cows, goats, horses, sheep, pigs, and dogs. They have also found bones of seal, walrus, whale, polar bear, grouse, hare, and swan, which shows that, just as in the Eastern Settlement, hunting was an important part of the people's existence.[13] A *primstav*, or an ancient Norse calendar stick, was also found, revealing that they kept track of time. The ruins of a large church have also been discovered, supposedly dating from a time after the farm.

Helge's expedition was nearing an end and autumn was upon them, which meant that caribou hunting inland had begun. It would have been very unlike Helge to leave Greenland without taking the opportunity to go hunting. As they headed out to hunt, Helge and Harald passed a few reindeer herders whom they asked to join them. The hunting party shot a caribou and the Greenlanders began to quarter the animal. Helge watched their technique with fascination as it was virtually the same as he had seen with the Caribou Eaters in Canada. The Greenlanders cut out the stomach and excitedly helped themselves to its contents, which were a favourite delicacy. The hunters packed the meat onto their backs and carried the heavy load back to their camp, where smiling faces came running to greet them. In the evening, they all sat around the campfire and Helge got to hear the stories of yet another group of people for whom caribou played a vital role. It was a meaningful ending to an adventurous journey.

On his return to Norway, Helge's schedule included a new round of lecture tours all across the country. The goal was to earn enough money so that he could take the time to finish the book about the Greenland trip. His lectures still attracted crowds, but not always. On 27 October 1954, he wrote home to his father: "All is well with me. I enjoy the car trips and meeting various people ... strangely enough, hordes of people come to my lectures. Almost always a full house." But on the southern coast of Norway in the small town of Flekkefjord it was not quite as successful: "It is said to be the worst town in these parts by my travelling business friends. The hotel is quite primitive and the host hasn't smiled since he got married."[14]

The book Helge wrote about Greenland, *The Land under the Pole Star*, took longer to write than his previous books. Much material had to be processed. It was published in 1959, was nearly six hundred pages, and differed from his earlier books in that it focused more on historical, scholarly aspects, rather than primarily being a descriptive narrative of the journey. The book was based on thorough research and gave a comprehensive account of all that was then known of the Norse settlements on Greenland and the Vinland voyages that embarked from there. Helge raised two vitally important questions: what happened to the Norse Greenlanders (the mystery of their exodus) and where was the Vinland of the Sagas?

As for the disappearance of the Norse, Helge's main conclusion was that it must have occurred gradually and was due to several concurrent factors, with deterioration of the climate being the most significant. He believed that if they had all died at about the same time, such as from an epidemic, then a number of skeletons would have been found in several of the houses. This was not the case.

Helge, like Fridtjof Nansen, also believed that the Norse could not have been completely obliterated in battle with the Inuit, or *skræling* as the Saga calls any indigenous peoples. Ivar Bårdsson, who was ordered to the Western Settlement by the bishop in Bjørgvin in 1364, found the villages empty of people but with domesticated animals grazing wild in the fields. A hunting people like the Inuit would have killed the animals too if they had killed the people. A more likely cause of their disappearance, thought Helge, was that the Norse had emigrated. In that case, they would have been able to transport only a small number of the livestock on the boats. The only question was, emigrated to where? Helge believed that the route southward, to Vinland, was the most likely.[15]

The Western Settlement is estimated to have been abandoned about 1347. At the Eastern Settlement, it is believed that people remained there until the middle of the 1400s. No sources have been found that tell of any arrivals of ships from Norway at this time, but Helge held the idea that English and German ships may have been driven off course by storms and then ended up in the southernmost parts of Greenland. Moreover, the Norse Greenlanders still had goods that interested European traders:

During Helge's visit to West Greenland, kayaks were still in use by hunters there.

dried fish, down, leather, furs, and whale blubber, for example. Despite the decline in trade of walrus tusks, Greenland had plenty of other commodities to trade.

Another possible factor in the disappearance of the Norse, he believed, had to do with pirates. Several sources in Europe testify that pirate raids did occur along the Norwegian coast, the Faroe Islands, and Iceland during the 1400s and 1500s. Native tales tell of similar devastation; when the pirates came, the natives fled farther down the fjord with some of the Norse women and children and helped save them from being taken captive or killed.[16] Their stories say that when they later returned to the farms, they were horrified to find everything taken and the houses burnt. In the Eastern Settlement ruins, there are signs that churches and some of the farms were destroyed by fire.

Pirate raids, falling prices for dried fish, and the end of shipping to and from Norway are the main reasons Helge thought that the Norse people at the Eastern Settlement eventually emigrated. Some may have gone to the British Isles, where there were significant Norse settlements. However, Helge felt that at one time there also must have been a Norse settlement in what the Sagas referred to as Vinland and that those from the Eastern Settlement may have joined their compatriots from the Western Settlement who might already have emigrated there. The route was known from earlier journeys described in the Sagas as well as trips to gather wood to a place they called Markland, meaning Forest Land. The travelling distance to Vinland was also described as being shorter than that to England or Norway.

Helge's father, Olav, never lived to see the publication of *Land under the Pole Star*, which was dedicated to him in memory. Olav died peacefully in his chair on 22 May 1958, ninety-one years old, and of sound mind to the last. This was a great blow to Helge, even though he was relatively prepared for his passing. He had lost his most important adviser and supporter – a role model he always looked up to, respected, and aspired to become. However, just as with other events in his life, Helge took it stoically and calmly, and carried on seemingly unaffected. He bore his grief alone, never sharing it with anyone.

Anne Stine catches small flounder in a tidal pool, using a method also described in *The Saga of the Greenlanders*.

(*above*) The ruins of Hvalsey Church in Greenland. (*below*) Epaves Bay at sunset.
(*opposite, above*) L'Anse aux Meadows seen from the south. The discovery site
with the village in the background. Farthest back to the right is the mountain
Round Head, which resembles the keel of a boat. (*opposite, below*) The *Halten*
sailing by an iceberg in the Strait of Belle Isle.

(*above*) The first summer's excavations. Notice the beach terrace across from where the ruins lay. (*below*) House F from the inside. The picture shows that the columns of the temporary protective structure stood outside of the actual ruins. (*opposite*) Helge's tent near L'Anse aux Meadows.

One of the Colbourne boys inspecting Anne Stine's digging methods.

The Vinland expedition required great efforts, but Helge and Anne Stine were also able to experience proud moments and recognition during the years that followed.

Helge on the Great Wall of China, 93 years old. Photo by Arvid Bryne.

14 WE FIND VINLAND

Beginnings

Returning from the expedition to West Greenland, my father spent the next few years not only completing his book about the journey, but also preparing for an upcoming expedition in search of Vinland. One of his more unique attempts in looking for clues was his effort to find the famed Hønen Runestone, lost in Norway. First found shortly before 1817 on a farm in Ringerrike in the southern part of the country, the runestone was subsequently lost again between 1825 and 1838. The importance of this metre-long stone was its runic inscription, believed to be from the years A.D. 1010 to 1050, which may have contained the Old Norse name Vínlandi. Fortunately, before it was lost again, antiquarian L.D. Klüwer measured the stone and copied down the inscription. It was then later translated into Norwegian by two men, first by Norwegian historian Sophus Bugge in 1902 and then by Magnus Olsen, professor of Old Norse and Icelandic languages and literature, in 1951. According to Bugge, the part of the inscription that read "Vínlandi á isa" meant "from Vinland over ice."[1] This interpretation was of particular interest to Helge because, according to Bugge, it was the oldest known source in Europe with mention of North America. Olsen, however, had a less encouraging interpretation of the same sequence of words. He translated "vindkalda á isa" as "over the wind-cold ice."[2]

Which was correct? There was only one way to determine this and that was to find the Hønen Runestone. So Helge went to work looking for it. He applied to the Fridtjof Nansen Fund for Scientific Research and received 5,000 Norwegian kroner in support of his search for the elusive stone. Then he went to see a local psychic known to be an expert in helping to find missing objects. Helge searched the various spots this man suggested, but found nothing. Then he consulted another "medicine man," who told him that the stone had been moved and was now part of the foundation of a house in the town about an hour from Oslo. So Helge went to the location, knocked on the door of the house in question, now owned by a seventy-three-year-old widow, and asked to dig in its foundations. He was granted permission and dug there for weeks. Unfortunately, he came up with nothing but dirt in his hair. His funding for "scientific research," however, helped pay for a nice new cement foundation for the widow for which she was very grateful. For a long time after, my father intermittently received letters from others in that area who were sure they had the runestone in their foundations and wondered if Helge wanted to come and dig there too.

That Helge, an otherwise grounded person, would think of using psychics to help him search must be understood within the context that his own father, Olav, was able to locate water by dowsing. This made the Ingstad family believers that there had to be more between heaven and earth than what people could rationally explain.

Other attempts to look for clues about Vinland included an infrequent family vacation in 1952, when we travelled to Normandy, France, then over to England, Scotland, and the Orkney and Shetland Islands, returning to Bergen by ferry. With my father's meticulous attention to detail, we scoured England and Scotland for every Viking ruin, every monastery the Vikings might have raided, any place the Sagas mentioned, and any other site that might have contained clues. After this vacation, I was thoroughly put off anything to do with history or the Vikings for several years after.

Family Crises

In 1957, my father became quite ill as tuberculosis once again flared up in his body. This time it was in his lung, which his doctor wanted to surgically remove. Helge said "no way." He was lucky. Not long before this diagnosis, a new and promising medicine was introduced in Norway and it was decided that he would try it. Once again, Helge was able to fight off the tuberculosis bacteria.

Also during this period, my mother was nearing the end of her archaeology degree and began wondering what she would do when she finished.

There were many excavation sites she could work on, but few that offered full-time positions. That her education would later be useful in Helge's work was not something that crossed her mind before she began her studies. She had mostly been interested in Stone Age archaeology.

At this time Anne Stine learned of a curatorial position at the Norwegian Forest Museum in Elverum about 140 kilometres north of Oslo. It was advertised as initially a one-year contract, but with an option of continuing in a full-time position. My mother applied and got the job. In the spring semester of 1960 she finished her master's degree in archaeology at the University of Oslo and shortly after planned to start work at the museum in Eleverum.

Back home, her news dropped like a lead ballon, and she was offered little support or understanding. Helge refused to move, even though he was able to, and I refused to change schools. Grandma Louise, to put it mildly, was stunned by her daughter's news.

In the end, it was decided that Anne Stine would commute, find a place to live in Elverum, and come down to Oslo on the weekends as often as she could. Meanwhile, my grandmother moved in at Brattalid to care for Helge and me. She thought she had to, in order to make up for what she considered her daughter's own shortcomings as both a wife and mother. Helge acted as if he had been wronged, and I gave clear signs of feeling neglected. It was quite hard on Anne Stine.

However, she loved working at the Norwegian Forest Museum. For the first time, she was able to combine her interests in Norwegian romanticism, hunting, and wildlife with long road trips up through the local valleys. She especially liked talking with elderly locals about their early experiences in timber use and hunting and fishing. Anne Stine was well suited for creating exhibits and displays in a museum as she had a genuine love of old things, had a good aesthetic eye and artistic flair.

During her time working at the museum, Anne Stine was enthusiastic, committed to her work, and managed to have several old buildings re-erected as well as an annual review published. She ended up not coming home that often; whether it had to do with lack of time or desire was unclear. Most likely, it was her attempt at trying to detach from Helge and to start a new life on her own.

Then, at the end of June 1960, the unexpected happened. I was seventeen years old and staying with my grandmother up at the family cabin Maribuseter. We were expecting my mother to arrive from Elverum on a Friday afternoon. But Friday came and went and no Anne Stine. Then on Sunday, a man from the local town came with a message: my mother had been admitted to the hospital in Lillehammer.

Anne Stine had locked herself inside her parents' home in Lillehammer and had taken an overdose of sleeping tablets. She happened to be found on Saturday by someone who had stopped by to water Louise's plants. The dosage must not have been extreme as she was able to sleep it off after a couple of days and was awake when I arrived at the hospital on Sunday evening. It was likely a call for help.

My father was in Canada at the time and the pre-arranged plan was for me to meet him there. After leaving the hospital, Anne Stine first went to the mountains with her mother and then back to work at the museum. I travelled to Canada to join Helge as originally planned. Not a word was mentioned by anyone about the overdose, nor did Anne Stine receive any offers of help. Life supposedly returned to normal – until it happened again.

At the end of September that same year, I again received news: my mother had been admitted to Elverum hospital. When she had not shown up for work on Monday, or answered the telephone, her door was forced down and she was found unconscious. This time the situation was much more serious. "I can't take any more," Grandma Louise said to me. "You go." Helge was away at some place or another on a lecture tour. So I, a seventeen-year-old, was sent on my own to deal with this critical situation, unreasonable as this was. It was several, intense days before anyone knew if my mother would survive.

A few days later Helge showed up and Anne Stine eventually awoke. Not long after, she returned to her job at the museum. Her suicide attempts were nearly never mentioned in our family, but the fear and anxiety of it happening again forever hung over Helge and I.

What was the reason for, as we called it in the family, "Anne Stine's nervous breakdown"? Most probably, one of the main reasons was that she wasn't able to escape from family or cultural expectations and obligations. Living independently in a new place was a radical break from all she was ever raised to believe in or felt restricted by. The belief that she actually had a *right* to live a fulfilled life, in whatever way she felt most compelled to do so, deeply conflicted with her ingrained traditional beliefs and developed into feelings of a life not worth living.

It would be unfair to lay all the blame for my mother's crisis on my father (or on me for that matter). Without a doubt, she had a tendency towards depression, something she struggled with her entire life, and which was compounded by the difficulties between her and Helge. Anne Stine was also affected by unresolved grief over losing someone whom she perhaps cared for more than anybody: her brother Tycho.

It is also fair to say that Helge must have been almost totally devoid of any psychological insight. That anyone would want to commit suicide was beyond his understanding. Throughout his entire upbringing, he was surrounded by harmonious people who barely raised their voices to each other. When confronted with Anne Stine's mighty outbursts, he was rendered nearly helpless. It was not easy for either one of them.

The spring of 1961, Anne Stine resigned from the Norwegian Forest Museum. The reason given was that she was to accompany her husband on an expedition to Canada. Whether it was her own decision or not I do not know, but I very much doubt that at the time my mother was in any position to be able to choose freely for herself.

Searching for Vinland

It appears that Helge originally planned to travel to Canada in 1958 or 1959; however, it was not until the spring of 1960 that he finally did. Some friends of the family talked of joining him, but in the end I was his sole travel companion. Shortly after Anne Stine's first "nervous breakdown," I travelled as originally planned and she stayed in Norway and returned to her work at the museum. I was eager to fly across the Atlantic Ocean to Canada for the first time and it was always exciting to travel with my father.

Having completed his exploration of West Greenland, with close scrutiny of the Norse ruins and land from which the Vinland voyagers departed, Helge was now ready to begin a serious search for Vinland of the Icelandic Sagas. More importantly, he was eager to look for traces of possible Norse settlements. It perhaps seemed like looking for a "needle in a haystack," but Helge had certain clues to go by. Most significant were the actual stories from the old Sagas which described travel routes, distances, and wind directions. Helge believed that seafaring people like the Norse would have accurately conveyed such information to later generations. The stories may have been embellished and changed throughout the years, due to the nature of oral storytelling before their written form, but information about directions and discovery of new land, that would have been specific. But what exactly do the Sagas tell of Vinland?

The Saga Tales

The stories about the first discovery of Vinland are found primarily in two Icelandic sagas: *The Saga of Eirik the Red* (*Saga Eiríks Rauða*) and *The Saga of the Greenlanders* (*Grænlendingasaga*). The latter is considered the oldest record, written around A.D. 1200, nearly two hundred years after the actual events it describes took place. *The Saga of Eirik the Red* was written in the fifteenth-century manuscript called the *Skalholtsbók*[3] (but is thought to have been originally scribed in the thirteenth century).[4] Both Sagas are based on old oral traditions and should be read with that in mind.

The Saga of the Greenlanders[5] tells about the journey of Bjarni Herjolfsson, who on returning to Iceland from a trading voyage to Norway, found that his father, Herjolf Bårdsson, had gone off to live in Greenland. Bjarni arrived in Iceland the summer of the same year that Herjulf had left for Greenland in the spring. Bjarni decided to go in search of his father despite protests from his crew that it was a senseless trip in unfamiliar waters.

Nonetheless, they set sail and journeyed for three days until they were blown off course by northerly winds and fog. After several days, the fog finally lifted and Bjarni and his crew were able to renavigate their course using the stars. After then sailing for another day they spotted land, but could not see any mountains, only low, wooded hills. They sailed close but did not go ashore as Bjarni did not think it could be Greenland since there were no large fields of ice.

They sailed north for two more days before they sighted land a second time. But once again, Bjarni wouldn't go ashore since he didn't think the landscape fit the description of Greenland; it was flat, covered by forests, and without any glaciers. They turned their ship around and headed back out to sea, southwesterly winds filling their sails for three days until they again spotted land. This time, the land had high mountains and glaciers, but looked barren and fallow. Bjarni took the boat closer to shore but yet again did not embark as he thought this land was of "little use." The Norse set sail towards the east and sailed for four days before they saw land for the fourth time, and this time Bjarni believed it to be Greenland. He sailed south along this coast until he found his father's farm at Herjolfsnes in the Eastern Settlement at the farthest southern tip of Greenland. There Bjarni lived for the rest of his life.

As we have seen, the story of Bjarni's journey in *The Saga of the Greenlanders* gives a relatively detailed account of distances and wind and sail directions. Bjarni also went to Brattahlid, to Eirik the Red's home and family, and told them himself about his journey. *The Saga of the Greenlanders* relays that there was much talk in the Eastern Settlement about Bjarni and his travels and that people could not understand why he didn't go ashore and explore the land he had seen.

Leif, son of Eirik the Red, decided to return and explore those lands Bjarni had seen, so he bought his ship. The Sagas describe Leif as a big, strong man who was also wise and of striking good looks. He managed to enlist thirty-five men to accompany him on the trip and then sailed out to sea following Bjarni's route in reverse. First, they found the land that Bjarni had seen last. Here there were high mountains and glaciers further inland, but from the edge of these glaciers down to the sea there were only large slabs of stones everywhere. They thought the land looked of little worth, but they went ashore and Leif called it Helluland (meaning Land of Flat Stones).

They boarded their ship and sailed south and found the second land; they dropped anchor and rowed a smaller boat ashore. Here the land was flat, covered by forests, and had a shallow, white sandy beach as far as they could see which they called Furðustrandir, or Wonder Beaches. Leif named the land for its distinct characteristics and called it Markland (meaning Wood Land).[6]

They then sailed farther south driven by northeasterly winds and were at sea for two days before they saw land. Here they went ashore on a small island north of the land and mentioned that there was dew on the grass sweeter than they had ever tasted before. They boarded their ship again and sailed into a strait between the island and a cape of land that jutted north, then headed westward from this cape. But here it was very shallow at low tide and their ship went aground far from land. They were so eager to get ashore that rather than wait for high tide, they ran ashore at a place where a river flowed from a lake. When the tide came in, they sailed their ship up the river and from there farther up to the lake. They decided to spend the winter here and built large houses. In the river, the salmon were larger than they had ever seen back home in the Eastern Settlement. There was such good grazing fields that no winter fodder might have been needed for the cattle.

The Sagas also tell of a fellow voyager who in the spring suddenly went missing. He was a southerner named Tyrkir, well known from Brattahlid and therefore a concern for Leif when he disappeared. They went in search of the man and soon found him. Tyrkir showed clear signs of being intoxicated: he spoke incomprehensible German, darted his eyes here and there, grinned, and laughed. He told them that he found vines and grapes and this was something he knew about since he came from a country where there was much of the same. They then filled their ships with the vines and grapes and returned to Greenland. It is said that Leif named the land according to this fruit and called it Vinland, all of which happened around the year A.D. 1000.

According to the Saga, there was much talk about Vinland at Brattahlid that winter, and Thorvald, Leif's brother, thought they should have explored this further. So it was agreed that he would borrow Leif's ships and the houses they built in Vinland. Thorvald and his crew set sail and reached Leifsbudir, "Leif's Camp," in the autumn. There they fished for what they needed and quietly spent the winter. The next summer, Thorvald sailed towards the east and north to explore the land. Not far from a cape, they ran into heavy weather and were driven in towards shore where the keel of their boat broke. They called this cape Kjalarnes (Keel Point), which also had a landmark that resembled an overturned keel of a boat. They then sailed eastward and into a fjord, where they went ashore into a heavily forested area. Thorvald liked it and said that he would like to build a farm here. But then they caught sight of three hide boats pulled up onto the beach with three men in each boat. The Norsemen killed all of them except for one who got away. Not long after, several other hide boats appeared in the fjord, which led to a battle, wounding and killing Thorvald. His people remained in Vinland that winter, later gathered grapes and vines, and then returned to Greenland.

The third of Eirik's sons, Thorstein, was intent on voyaging to Vinland to retrieve his brother's body to be buried in Greenland. He equipped the same ship with a crew of twenty-five men and Gudrid, his wife. However, he sailed off course and ended up in Lysefjorden in the Western Settlement of Greenland, where at the time an epidemic had broken out and Thorstein died. Gudrid returned to Brattahlid and settled there with Leif, who was now master of the household after Eirik had died.

Eirik's illegitimate daughter, Freydis, also eventually sailed to Vinland and stayed at Leifsbudir. She journeyed with two Icelandic brothers, Helgi and Finnbogi, who had another boat of their own, and with five other women. Conflict arose between Freydis and the Icelandic brothers and she managed to persuade her husband and crew to kill all the men. When they refused to kill the women, she killed them herself. They then filled up the two boats and returned to Greenland.

The biggest difference between the *Saga of the Greenlanders* and the *Saga of Eirik the Red* concerning the Vikings' discovery of Vinland is that the latter does not say anything about Bjarni Herjolfsson's journey. The *Saga of Eirik the Red* briefly mentions that Leif was in Norway with King Olav Haraldsson, who asked him to return to Greenland to convert the people there to Christianity. On his way, he was driven off course and discovered a land of grapevines and self-sown wheat fields. The name of the land was never given.

In Eirik's saga, we meet the Icelandic trader Thorfinn Karlsefni,[7] who is said to be of good lineage and wealth. One summer he travelled to Greenland and was invited by Eirik the Red to stay the winter at Brattahlid. Karlsefni then asked to marry Gudrid, widow of Thorstein Eiriksson, who was known to be both wise and beautiful. There was a large wedding and great joy at Brattahlid that winter. Karlsefni heard about the voyages to Vinland. He decided to journey there himself and made arrangements for several ships with a total of 160 men, most of them from Greenland.

They sailed for two days with northerly winds and arrived at Helluland (Land of Flat Stones), where they found an abundance of arctic fox and slabs of stone so large that two men could lie stretched across them, foot sole to foot sole. They sailed a further two days again driven by northerly winds and found a land with great forests and many animals, and called the place Markland (Wood Land). After two more of days of sailing, they arrived at a cape with land to their starboard. They rounded this tip and saw long sandy beaches. On the cape, they found the keel of a ship and called the area Kjalarnes.

Onboard the ship were two Scottish runners, a man by the name of Haki and his wife Hekja, rumoured to be able to run faster than any animal. Karlsefni sent these two ashore and told them to run southward to explore the land while the ship lay anchored. After three days, the runners returned carrying grapes and wild wheat, which convinced Karlsefni this was good land. They sailed onward, and at the mouth of a fjord they came upon an island surrounded by a strong current. This island was so full of birds that the Norsemen could hardly step foot in between the eggs. They called the island Straumsey and the fjord Straumsfjord. They carried on into the fjord, then went ashore along with their load and livestock. It was a beautiful area with mountains and much grass and they decided to stay for the winter. It was a hard winter with little food or winter fodder for the animals, but they managed to survive.

In the spring, Karlsefni sailed south a fair distance until he came to the mouth of a small river that originated from an inland lake that then flowed out to sea. It was possible to sail up this small river but only at high tide. They called the place Hóp. Here they found fields of wild wheat all along the valley floors and vines covering the slopes everywhere. Every stream was full of fish, and if they dug out pits in the sand, these would fill with halibut when the tides ran out. The surrounding woods were filled with animals of many kinds.

Karlsefni and his people stayed there a month and loved the land. But then, early one morning, they spotted nine hide boats with men swinging clubs. Karlsefni thought perhaps it could be a sign of peace and walked towards them carrying a white shield. The strangers were described as dark, unpleasant fellows with big eyes and wide faces. After staring at one another, the two peoples then rowed back each to their own side.

Karlsefni and his people stayed the winter in huts they built. Snow never fell and the cattle could graze throughout the season. But when spring arrived, the strangers, whom they called skræling, again appeared, but this time including several others. They first came to trade; the skræling exchanged hides for clothing, but when they wanted to trade for swords and spears, Karlsefni said no. Three weeks passed and the strangers came again, this time in even greater numbers. Karlsefni then marched towards them carrying a red shield and the fighting began. The skræling outnumbered the Norse and Karlsefni's men showed signs of wanting to flee. But then Freydis, daughter of Eirik the Red, emerged from the hut. She mocked the men for their cowardliness, grabbed a sword lying beside a dead man, bared her breast, and held the sword as if to cut it off. The skræling were so terrified that they ran to the boats and rowed away. The Sagas say that Karlsefni and his people now realized that even though this was a good land, they would never be at peace with the people who were there before them and they decided therefore to return to their own land.

Gudrid, wife of Thorstein Eiriksson and then later Karlsefni, bore a son, named Snorre, in Vinland,[8] most likely the first European born on the American continent. Later, after Karlsefni died, Snorre returned to Iceland with his mother, who later became a nun.

Where Did Vinland Lie?

The great mystery for several Saga scholars, historians, archaeologists, and geographers throughout the years has been: where exactly did Vinland lie? This has also been of great interest to Americans of Norwegian and Icelandic descendants, whether as a question of identity or acknowledgment of the fact that their ancestors reached the shores of America five hundred years before Columbus. The second Monday in October has long been a public holiday in the United States celebrating Columbus Day, while Leif Erikson Day on 9 October[9] is declared as only a "day of observance."[10]

Helge, however, was not the first to follow the route to Vinland described in the Sagas. Years earlier two other men – historian William A. Munn from Newfoundland and geographer Väinö Tanner from Finland – separately traced the route with relatively accurate assessments of a possible location.

Because Munn was from the area, he knew the coast of Labrador and northern Newfoundland well and after reading the Sagas was convinced that Helluland, Markland, and Vinland must be somewhere along these coasts. In 1914, he published a series of articles in the *St John's Daily Telegram* newspaper explaining his theories. Munn assessed Helluland to be located around Hamilton Inlet and Markland along the long beaches on both sides of Cape Porcupine. About Vinland, he wrote:

> They went ashore at Lancey Meadows, which they are called today, where there is much grass ... they boarded their ships again and sailed into a sound between a headland and north-lying island and then journeyed west of this headland. This brought them right into the shallow Pistolet Bay where the ship went aground on one of the large banks there ... they continued further into the bay

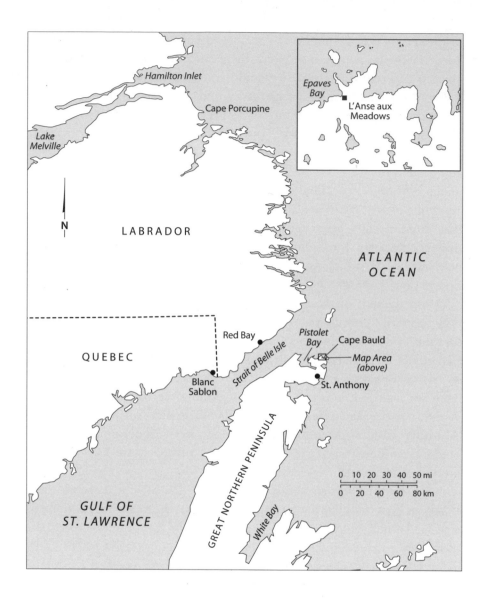

where there was a river at the opening of Milan Arm ... the lake
is about three miles long and one mile wide, they cast anchor and
Leif built his houses there and stayed the winter.[11]

It is interesting to note that Munn particularly mentioned L'Anse aux
Meadows, the place where Helge discovered the ruins years later. According to Munn, Leif and his people went ashore here before sailing off

towards the direction of Milan Arm, on the southeast stretch of Pistolet Bay.[12] Helge said he had not known about Munn and his work until 1961, the year after Helge had discovered the ruins.

Tanner was a professor of geography at the University in Helsinki, Finland. During the years 1937 and 1939, he travelled extensively along the North American coast, from northern Labrador to the state of New York. He too wanted to decipher where the Norse Helluland, Markland, and Vinland were situated according to the Sagas. A principal point made by Tanner was that the Sagas' stories must have had a certain amount of truth but that throughout the years these had become more like "captains' stories, assumingly one or two centuries after the narrative events occurred and elaborated upon from the original stories."[13] He believed that the stories about grapes and wild-sown wheat must have been "captains' stories."

Tanner focused on the origin of the prefix *vin* in Vinland. Like Söderberg, the Swedish linguist, he claimed that *vín* must have originated from the old Norse word also found in place names such as Bjørgvin and Hovin and which can be translated as grazing pasture or meadow and not *vin* meaning vine or wild grapes. This distinction dissuaded Tanner from searching in southern areas where grapes grow wild. Tanner assumed that it was quite unlikely Icelanders, and certainly not Greenlanders of that era, had knowledge of wine, and even less about how it was made. In addition, he pointed out that in the *Saga of the Greenlanders* they filled their ships with grapevines before they departed in the *spring*, which is botanically impossible.[14]

Tanner's theory was that Helluland must have been "north of Hudson Strait ... in much the same geographical position as communities on the southwestern coast of Greenland."[15] He mapped the corresponding area to be the southern tip of Baffin Island, around Frobisher Bay. As for the location of Markland, Tanner, as well as Munn, pointed towards the long white beaches south of Hamilton Inlet, which he thought had to obviously be Furdurstrendir, with Cape Porcupine as Kjalarnes. He believed Markland had to be the area to the north and south, namely the forested sections of Labrador's Atlantic coast.

Tanner, like many others, perceived the location of Vinland to be the core of the Saga tales. He believed, based on the Sagas' detailed descriptions of distances, that Straumsfjord must have been the Strait of Belle Isle and that Belle Isle must have been Strausmey of the Sagas. As for

Vinland, he concluded that it "stretched towards the north to the Strait of Belle Isle and that Leif's camp would have been somewhere in the area of Pistolet Bay on Newfoundland's narrow northern peninsula."[16] That was where the land with the good meadows could be found.

In other words, Tanner's conclusions were almost identical to those of Munn's twenty years earlier. In the small booklet in which he presented these theories, Tanner explained that he had never heard of Munn until they met in St John's in 1939 when Tanner was on his way home from his Labrador expedition. By then, he had already written a draft of an article in which these theories were to be presented. It was no doubt an interesting meeting.

Like Munn and Tanner, Helge too wanted to explore the landscape described in the Sagas. His dream was of course to find Leifsbudir – Leif Eiriksson's own settlement in Vinland. Another important source Helge had to go by was the sixteenth-century Skálholt map, which places Helluland, Markland, and Vinland (written as Winlandia) almost exactly where Munn and Tanner also indicated, and marked an area Helge felt compelled to explore.

We Find Ruins

Helge and I planned to meet in St John's, the capital of Newfoundland, at the end of June 1960. I left Norway after the school year finished, but Helge travelled ahead and began his journey farther south. Almost feeling obliged to investigate the wild grape theories, he started his search farther down the American coast at Rhode Island but did not expect to find anything of great interest. In the small fishing town of Newport, there was a large old edifice in the middle of town called the Newport Tower. A few scholars believed it to be of Norse origin from around the fifteenth century, and effects of this idea were evident around town, including a "Viking Hotel" with huge paintings of Viking ships and bearded Vikings swinging their bloody axes in battle.

While in Newport, Helge went to investigate this eight-metre-high tower. It did look unusual, but nothing typically Norse in his opinion. Excavations taken in later years concluded it was a stone chimney from around the 1700s – mystery clarified. Of much greater interest to Helge was the closed-down coal mine in Willow Lane, six miles out of town.

He found the place and picked up a lump of meta-anthracite coal, which he carefully studied. A similar chunk had been found on the Sandnes Farm in the Western Settlement on Greenland, the place Vinland voyager Torfinn Karlsefni had been given through his marriage to Gudrid, widow of Thorstein Eiriksson. Could that piece of coal found in Greenland possibly have come from here? Helge searched the area to find a river and a lake that resembled the Saga description of the place called Hóp,[17] but did not find anything. However, he did find wild grapes.

From Rhode Island, he travelled to the Cape Cod area and from there farther along the coast to Boston, New Hampshire, and Maine. He explored these areas as thoroughly as he could given that many other scholars believe Vinland to be situated farther south. Helge never disputed the theory that the Norse could have possibly reached this far south, at one time or another. But he had little belief that they could have travelled the far distance from Greenland to that area in one long stretch. In that case, they would have needed a more northerly headquarters.[18] Therefore, it was farther north that Helge wanted to focus his search.

Making his way north along the North American coast, Helge next stopped at Nova Scotia. In the early nineteenth century, a stone assumed to contain a runic inscription was discovered in the small coastal town of Yarmouth at the southern tip of the province. There is dissension among the experts, however, whether they are actual runes.

On the northern tip of Nova Scotia is Cape Breton Island, a place some scholars[19] presumed to be Kjalarnes, believing that the long beaches and Vinland were possibly south of here. Helge explored the area, but did not find any significant beaches that fit the description of the distinct landmark that the Norse seafarers called Furdurstrendir (Wonder Beaches). He did, however, wonder about Cape North, the most northernly point of this island. If the Vikings had come sailing south from the Strait of Belle Isle, they could not have missed sighting this peninsula.

Just south of Cape North is a small fishing village by the name of Dingwall. A strange coincidence. Scottish emigrants had settled here and brought with them a name from their homeland, Tingvall – an old Norse name literally meaning "assembly place" (and precursor of the modern concept of "parliament"). Helge continued his explorations down the eastern coast and eventually came to the town of Sydney. He had now explored most of the places that other scholars believed relevant to the

Vinland Sagas without finding anything he considered of any particular interest. It was now time to explore Newfoundland, an area he was much more optimistic about.

Newfoundland is an appealing island, a little larger than Iceland, that juts out into the sea as the most easterly point of the North American continent. It looks like a clenched fist with its thumb sticking up towards the left; the coastal areas around both sides of this "thumb" were of particular interest to Helge. With its marine climate, Newfoundland has weather that is milder than that of areas at the same latitude such as Labrador to the west. The indigenous peoples of Newfoundland were the Beothuk tribe, whose numbers began dwindling when, among other things, the first Europeans either killed them or brought various illnesses which these people had no immunity against. In 1829, the last surviving Beothuk woman died of tuberculosis, making the entire tribe extinct.[20] But much further back in time, people from the Palaeo-Eskimo Dorset culture also lived along these coasts from approximately 500 B.C. until around A.D. 1000.[21]

Out at sea, east of the island, is a group of underwater plateaus called the Grand Banks, once an incredibly rich fishing ground. However, intensive large-scale fishing has depleted the fish stocks and commercial fishing is now banned. The fishing boats are gone, but large icebergs, much like the one that hit the *Titanic* in 1912, continue to float by, carried down with the Labrador Current from Greenland.

While waiting for me to arrive, my father went to explore parts of the long eastern coastline of Newfoundland. Deep fjords cut far into the land, creating many bays that could have enticed the Norse seafarers. At one place, Helge met a fisherman who wondered why he was making such a fuss about old ruins and asked suspiciously,

"What is it you want with such old stuff?"

"To dig it out,' Helge replied.

"You don't fool me," the fisherman retorted, "we'll find the buried treasure in these parts ourselves."

Eventually, Helge and I met up in St John's. We were given a warm welcome by the people at Memorial University of Newfoundland, who listened attentively to Helge's accounts of his theories and plans. After a few days, we boarded one of the local coastal boats, the *Baccalieu*, which stopped at just about every fishing village of any size up the coast to St Anthony on the northern tip of the Great Northern Peninsula. Many of these communities were isolated, so it was quite an occasion when the boat came in. Few families lived at each of these places and mostly in simple, square, and often unpainted houses along the shores. It seemed that each house also came with its own rickety-style dog kennel, whose mangy pooches were winter's transportation. Otherwise, their only other transportation was the small fishing boats lining the beaches and moored at the wharf.

We went ashore at the communities where the coastal boat made its stops. We asked people if they knew of any ruins in the area and took a look around the landscape. Helge noticed that there were several distinct landmarks similar to those described in the Sagas: a *hóp* (an inlet), a fjord with a strong current and a nearby island, a peninsula which could possibly be Kjalarnes, and an extensively long beach. Helge believed that the land described with the flat slabs of stones, Helluland, was farther north, where he hadn't planned to go at the time. The coastal boat continued its northern route up the eastern coast of the Great Northern Peninsula and we disembarked at St Anthony on the northern tip. This was a slightly larger community than the previous others, but with similar simple houses and kennels along the shores. Here also were a few larger buildings such as a church, hospital, school, and even a small hotel, St Anthony Inn.

Grenfell Mission, an organization founded at the end of the 1800s by British physician and missionary Sir Wilfred Grenfell,[22] had its headquarters in St Anthony. The Grenfell Mission that we experienced in 1960 was an efficient organization that provided health care to the entire northern tip of Newfoundland and all along the Labrador coast up to Nain. The organization was in many ways ahead of its time[23] with health stations led by nurses in smaller communities, clinics with a doctor in larger communities, and a modern hospital at St Anthony, where the more serious cases were transported and treated. They also had an outreach program with a boat and seaplane that delivered service along the entire northern peninsula of Newfoundland and up the Labrador coast, and a radio network that ensured quick response for help. There were no roads at the time.

The head of Grenfell Mission when we were there was Dr Gordon Thomas, a nice fellow in his forties who amazingly resembled Dr Kildare, aka Richard Chamberlain, in the 1960s American television series.

As a teenager, I undeniably went weak in the knees when he came out in his sea-green scrubs and wished us welcome. He was a multi-specialist and could have undoubtedly amassed a fortune in more southerly locations. However, like Dr Grenfell, he idealistically chose to dedicate his life to helping the less fortunate along these windswept cold coasts. Dr Thomas and his wife became good friends of the family and was an invaluable support during the expedition years that followed.

After a few days in St Anthony, we were graciously granted further travel with the Grenfell Mission's 44-foot-long boat *Albert T. Gould*, with Captain Norman Small at the helm. The boat's mission was to carry nurse Pamela Sweet westward around the northern peninsula to vaccinate small children. This was the area Helge was most optimistic about and it was the location he knew Tanner had marked Vinland on the map. Munn had also indicated the same spot, but Helge was unaware of Munn and his theories at the time.

As we sailed around the northern tip and past L'Anse aux Meadows, it struck Helge that the flat, green areas he spotted farther inland were worth exploring at a later time. We arrived at the large inlet of Pistolet Bay and went ashore in Raleigh, a very nice little fishing village situated farthest in the bay. Dwarfed spruce, grass, and grazing cattle dotted the terrain, but no one knew of any ruins or signs of old dwellings here or around the Pistolet Bay area.

Together with two local boys, Horvey and Abel, Helge wandered up and down the shores of the eastern side of the bay, searching but finding nothing of relevant interest. He was just about ready to give up looking around Pistolet Bay and was quite disappointed as he had been very optimistic about the area. Then as Helge was walking along, he coincidentally ran into a man by the name of Harvey Taylor. Once again, as he had done so many times before, Helge stopped and asked the same question, "Are there any ruins here?" The man replied, "Yes. I have heard of something like that over at L'Anse aux Meadows, but you need to talk to George Decker."

Helge grew hopeful and enthused; not only was this the place that Taylor mentioned on the northern tip of the peninsula, but it was also the site of those alluring, flat, green open meadows that originally drew Helge's attention when we had first sailed by. Our first stop after leaving Pistolet Bay was at Ship Cove on the west side of the inlet of Sacred Bay. Here we met an old woman by the name of Berthe Decker who, despite

George Decker – "Big Chief."

being ninety-four years old and blind, had an impeccable memory. She also said that she knew of some ruins at L'Anse aux Meadows and told us that they had been there even before the first white settlers came to these areas, "but nobody knows where they come from," she added.

We were provided transportation back to L'Anse aux Meadows with a Norwegian vessel owned by Karl Karlsen Shipping company, which operated in Canadian and Arctic waters. The ship docked farthest out on the peninsula where a few houses stood scattered about on land. We went ashore, wandered along in the sunshine towards the great green meadows in front of us, and saw a man approaching us. He was a relatively small, sturdy fellow in his late fifties with dark hair peppered with gray and a pipe hanging out of his mouth. He introduced himself as George Decker and it appeared that he was thrilled to have a chat. Few strangers visited this hamlet.

Helge eventually asked Decker the same clichéd question about any old ruins. This time, however, the man did not reply by shaking his head no. Instead, he enthusiastically said that there was something like that over by Black Duck Brook, not far from where we were standing. Moreover, the suspicious contours were on his land. He had a few cows and sheep that grazed in the meadow and had posted a wooden sign saying "Private Property, No Trespassing. By order of George Decker & Sons."

We walked a little farther and came to a large brook, and there on a crescent-shaped terrace not far from the shore we could clearly see some raised, rectangular shapes in the green grass. It was a beautiful place. Below the marine terrace was a shallow beach, just as the Sagas described. The grass was unusually high and lush, and the brook meandered idyllically through the green and out to sea. To the north, the mountain called Round Head had the remarkable shape of the keel of a ship. Everything about the place had a "Saga" feeling to it.

"Has anyone dug here?" Helge asked. "No strangers have ever seen them [the raised contours] and no one sets foot here unless I know about it," quipped Decker. He was clearly a man with authority. Decker explained that nobody knew who made the ridges and that they had been there long before any white person came to the place. It looked more and more promising. Helge told me that he had a strong feeling that this was a land that the Norse seafarers would have liked. Perhaps this was Leifsbudir – Leif's camp?

There was little more that could be done just then and the *Gould* was waiting to pick us up on its way back to St Anthony. Helge promised Decker that he would return the following summer and take a closer look at the possible ruins, and left it at that: the ruins remained in peace and no one else was told about them.

After this, we still had more to explore along the coast. A single-engine plane from the Grenfell Mission flew a crew north across to Labrador and we were given the opportunity to join them. In addition to this, the government also provided us with a plane for several more days, which enabled us to fly low over the landscape and scout for ruins. At places where people have lived, the grass is clearly greener due to the organic waste littered on the site. From the air, it's possible to see contours of ruins that are not so readily visible when standing in the midst of them. We saw several ruins that appeared like bright green circles of green in the terrain; most were from indigenous people. When conditions permitted, they landed the plane on a lake so we could take a closer look. However, nothing appeared to be especially promising from a Norse perspective. My father was primarily looking for possible places to further explore the following year when he intended to return and travel by boat.

Once during this scouting trip, while high in the air, we felt the plane's engine sputter and stop. Suddenly and unexpectedly, everything went completely silent as the propeller stood motionless in front of us. We glided slowly downward, the hissing of the wind against the fuselage the only sound as I frantically looked for the closest lake. The pilot, also frantic, pushed and pulled a few knobs and after a few spits the propeller started up again. He had "only" forgotten to switch to the reserve fuel tank.

We then flew over some long beaches, which stretched out below us like a white ribbon all along the coast, interrupted only by Cape Porcupine, which stuck out to the east. Was this Furðustrandir of the Sagas, the actual Wonder Beaches? Munn, Tanner, Helge, and the Danish archaeologist Jørgen Meldgaard all believed it was, and a more obvious landmark is difficult to imagine. According to the Sagas, the beaches could only be seen from far out at sea. The forests grew all the way to the edge of the sand, and as we flew close to the ground we could see a black bear come wandering out of the woods. It glanced up at us, wondered what kind of a strange bird we were, then disappeared back into the woods.

Just north of these beaches lies a deep fjord called Hamilton Inlet that stretches 140 kilometres inland. Beyond its narrow opening, it expands into a larger body of water called Lake Melville. About halfway across the lake, on the north side, was a small community called North West River. On one side of the river was a Catholic missionary station with a church, school, store, and a few houses for the missionaries and teachers. Grenfell Mission also had a clinic at this place with one doctor, Dr Paddon, as director. He had been in these areas for years and provided us with much good information.

One day we rowed over to the other side of the river, where a tribe of Montagnais had their camp, mostly tents. Canoes made of hide were pulled up along the shores, and large, fat trout hung everywhere to dry. The children came running up to welcome us, but the adults were much more reserved. It helped some when Helge began talking about hunting and fishing with one of the older men.

After a few days, we flew with the Mission plane farther to Nain, the northernmost settlement on the Labrador coast. Drift ice hugged the shore and required delicate manoeuvring from the pilot to find a spot on the water to land. The Inuit at Nain were far less reserved than the Montagnais at North West River and crowded around us, chatting, laughing, and clearly seeming to enjoy having visitors. Of all the places that we visited during this first trip to Canada, it was North West River and Nain that I remember the best. Perhaps it was because this was my first encounter with indigenous people. After a couple of days in Nain, we flew back to St Anthony together with two patients on their way to the hospital. For my father and I, this marked the end of our summer and our wilderness adventure. It was time to head home to Norway.

Halten Expedition 1961

The finding of the ruins at L'Anse aux Meadows remained a great secret throughout that fall and winter. I was given strict instructions not to say a word about it to any living soul. The promise wasn't difficult to keep as I was so completely focused on school and living life as a teenager that I hardly gave the heaps of turf any thought at all.

Helge hectically went to work looking for funding for the upcoming year's expedition, which was planned to be a much bigger affair. He used his well-proven method of going from shipowner to shipowner and from business to business with his hat in his hand. He succeeded in securing the funding he needed. What Anne Stine thought about all this I cannot say. She was still at Elverum but had agreed to give up her beloved job to join the expedition.

We had to have our own boat if we were to sail along the coast and visit every bay and inlet like Helge wanted. The idea was not only to travel to L'Anse aux Meadows but also to explore the entire southern coast of Labrador and northward all the way up to Hamilton Inlet – perhaps farther if time permitted. Of course, Helge also wanted to carefully explore the areas on both sides of the northern tip of Newfoundland.

We were offered a reasonable price for a 48-foot Colin Archer[24] rescue boat called the *Halten*. It had two masts and was built like a standard rescue boat but had been used most recently as a pleasure boat for a Norwegian shipowner in the Mediterranean. So it had been refurbished with a deck cabin that also included a bar, couch, and large windows. This soon proved to have ruined the boat's stability and it rolled horribly in heavy waters.

A boat must have a crew, so Helge proceeded to recruit a skipper from the western coastal county of Sunnmøre. He was still completely convinced that no other skipper in the world would do other than one from Sunnmøre, and no one could persuade him otherwise. His hard efforts to find one paid off, and Paul Sørnes, a very pleasant fellow who played the banjo, was hired as skipper. Next, a photographer was needed; Erling Brunborg, who had sailed around the world in a similar boat, fit the bill. He was a humorous fellow who spent more time filming on top of the mast than he did on deck. His only regret was that the *Halten* had a motor so sailing at all times was out of the question. Just as well since the "cocktail house" ruined the boat's ability to sail anyway.

Helge's old childhood friend and fellow Hardanger plateau explorer, Odd Martens, was also to be a part of the expedition. The two of them had for years talked of finding something fun to do together and now was their chance. Odd was a doctor but became the expedition's delegated cook. As it happened, he wasn't especially thrilled to have to deal with sick people. Whenever we stopped anywhere and mentioned to the locals that we had a doctor aboard, he was not very pleased. And once when Helge fell out of his bed during a storm and broke two ribs, Odd just said, "It will probably get worse." However, he loved to fish, and together with Sørnes, an old fishing boat skipper, they stood glued to the sonar screen in the wheelhouse scouting for schools of cod. Anne Stine was of course to be the archaeologist in charge and I, who was given time off from school, was to help Odd in the galley, which he seldom let me do except to wash dishes.

Both Erling and I asked my father why he hadn't chosen to sail the Viking route from Greenland, but he only laughed. He was intent on starting serious exploring straightaway and did not want to waste time on other things, even if it meant good PR.

On the docks of Norway at the end of April 1961, the *Halten* was loaded on board the ship *Byklefjord*, which then headed for Canada. "Skipper," as we now called Paul, and Erling accompanied the *Halten* across the sea and the rest of us followed by plane. We all met up in Montreal, where the *Halten* was unloaded and docked, looking like a small, white egg shell compared to all the other huge boats surrounding it. Passersby gave it a good hard stare. Anne Stine and I sat on deck soaking up the warm spring sunshine, Erling was running around getting the boat ready and teaching me a few sailor knots, while Helge and Odd were on land getting the necessary equipment loaded on board. The Norwegian Consulate had arranged for a press conference on the dock, so our departure began with a bit of hoopla.

Finally, on 10 May we set out. In glorious spring sunshine, we sailed down the St Lawrence River headed for the unknown. Above us flew a flock of geese as if sounding the way. We spotted Quebec City off in the distance to our north, but soon all the big cities and towns disappeared behind us. The unknown and unexplored awaited.

My mother and father spent much of their time studying maps and discussing the landscape in relation to the Sagas' descriptions. Our earlier endless dinner conversations about Vinland were now set within a completely new context. There was a slight chance that the Gulf of St Lawrence, where the river widens and flows into the sea, could possibly be the Straumsfjord that was described in the Sagas. But Helge was not convinced. He believed that Straumsfjord was farther north, between the northern tip of Newfoundland and Belle Isle. However, he never wanted to leave a stone unturned, so the coast was to be explored as thoroughly as possible.

As we did the summer before, we searched for characteristic landmarks described in the Sagas: long, white beaches; a fjord with a heavy current and nearby island; and an estuary, or *hóp*. There were an amazing number of estuaries along that coast and I think we must have visited them all. We stomped around in the underbrush and thickets of spruce, sometimes so dense that we had to follow tunnels in the undergrowth made by black bears, all the while hoping we wouldn't meet one around the next corner. As we scouted for ruins we asked people we met the same old question: "Are there any ruins here?" Sometimes we did find ruins, but they appeared to be circular, suggesting that indigenous people had lived there. At other times, test digging quickly uncovered pieces of porcelain or other more modern artifacts.

We quickly slipped into a comfortable routine and were quite content on board. Anne Stine and I slept in the "cocktail house," Helge and Odd in the bunks down below, which turned into sofas and a table during the day. Skipper Sørnes slept on a small cot in the machine room and Erling in the forward cabin. In the evenings, Skipper would play his banjo while Erling belted out sailor tunes.

We had a good amount of food with us from Norway, especially bars of Norwegian chocolate from one of our sponsors (Freia), which were carefully rationed out on special occasions. In addition, we fished. Sometimes the shoals were so plentiful and thick that we only had to dip our lines in and draw the fish up by the dorsal fin. Neither Skipper nor Odd could stop fishing, until the deck was so full that the boat almost tilted. Then came the dilemma of knowing what to do with all the fish. Some were hung to dry on the rigging and along the railings, to the point that our boat resembled a Christmas tree, much to Erling's disgust. A Colin Archer, he thought, ought to look proper.

The fish we weren't able to eat were taken to the local town, where, in the end, we almost had to force the people to take them. Food should never be wasted, Helge believed. There were even more fish in the rivers; large, Arctic trout grabbed at the hook as soon as we threw it in. There was definitely no lack of food on our end.

Once when we had gone ashore, we bought a big barrel of live lobsters. At first we didn't understand why they were so cheap, until later when we learned that the lobsters had long outlived their season. Happily ignorant, we ate the lobsters for dinner several days in a row. Each day, the creatures grew more sluggish, and Erling thought that perhaps exercising them on deck would help. Several of them just disappeared behind crates and coils of rope and we had to struggle to get them back into the barrel again. We had lobster for every meal until the last died a natural death. It was a long time before any of us desired a bite of lobster again.

We had just gotten far enough away from "civilization," as Helge used to call it, and from any nearby shipping repair yard when the motor of our boat seized. Skipper spent an entire day tinkering with the motor while large billows of exhaust rose from it like signals coming from an old tribal campfire until finally the motor coughed and started again. In the middle of his struggle, he cried out to Odd, "Do you think the Devil has a Union motor in hell?" whereupon Odd dryly replied, "Oh you know, he probably has an old banged-up one he keeps on using."

Our joy over the repair, however, was short lived. As we approached a small town called Sept-Îles (Seven Islands) in eastern Quebec, a spring in the motor broke and it was impossible to go any farther until we had a new one sent from Norway. So we had a long wait moored at the dock there. Sept-Îles was a large enough place that it had all things that were important for us just then: stores, a laundromat, and a movie house! My mother and I went to see a cowboy film. Besides us, the only other audience were a few indigenous locals. They booed at the cowboys and cheered for the movie "natives," perhaps not exactly what the producer had in mind. A few teenagers sat at the back of the theatre with rifles, and when it was toughest for those on the screen, they shot a few rounds into the ceiling to help their fellow kinsmen.

Our waiting period in Sept-Îles gave us time to take the dingy out on a few short excursions around the area. One day, Anne Stine, Erling, and I went out to one of the seven islands that lay about nine nautical miles from land. There we found the remains of a small spruce forest where grey-tinged, needle-less trunks that obviously had burnt were scattered about. Incredibly, on top of nearly every one of these bare trees was a cormorant nest, where long black necks and outspread wings stuck out, almost like a star on top of a Christmas tree. Erling climbed around in the thicket and up the slopes to take pictures of them. At first, the birds reacted surprised and flew dutifully up but then returned and settled again into the same position with wings stretched out and without the slightest bit of interest in us.

When we went to start the outboard engine on the dingy to return, we too got a bit of a surprise – it was completely dead. Earlier that day when we set out, the weather had been nice and calm, but now it began to blow and rain, and as we had no rain gear we soon were soaked to the skin. We gathered some driftwood and lit a huge bonfire but couldn't do much else other than wait to be rescued. Time passed and it started to get dark. Suddenly, off in the distance we heard a familiar chugging sound. Never had we ever been so happy to hear the sound of that old Union motor. It was the *Halten*; the motor part had arrived from Norway and we could sail on.

After Sept-Îles, we followed the coast of Quebec and stopped at many small and, at that time, remote places with no roads such as Mingan and Havre St Pierre where people made their living by fishing as well as hunting and trapping. At one place, we saw an eagle's nest at the top of a tree and Erling climbed like a goat up an adjacent cliff to take pictures of the fledglings in the nest. However, the mother eagle didn't like this a bit and Erling barely made it down again unscathed.

Then one day it began to blow. "Gale," announced Skipper. I lay on the bunk in the "cocktail house," not because I was seasick but because I found it impossible to stand. Anne Stine and Odd each lay on a bunk below feeling very unwell, while Helge sat quite unaffected tapping away on his typewriter. Erling sat at the top of the mast and filmed the huge waves as they washed over the deck. He had his camera in one hand and a firm grip on the ladder with the other and had a marvellous time. Every now and again, he clambered down below deck to tell us excitedly that the wind was picking up. The storm lasted an entire day and night and Skipper never left the helm. When it was over, he didn't take a well-earned rest, but instead played his banjo for several hours. We were busy putting everything back in its place, as there was not a single thing, inside or out, that stood where it had before the storm.

Eventually, we approached the Strait of Belle Isle, which Helge (and Tanner) believed could possibly have been Straumsfjord of the Sagas. Quebec was behind us, Labrador to our port. To our starboard lay the northernmost tip of Newfoundland with L'Anse aux Meadows as our most anticipated destination. We passed huge icebergs drifting southward with the Labrador Current. They were enormous things with towering pillars and spires, looking almost like floating ice cathedrals. The *Halten* was tiny in comparison, and both Anne Stine and I were a bit nervous if one were to calve and pull our boat below with its undertow. But all went well. Skipper had experience sailing in the Arctic Ocean and knew how to manoeuvre. Erling, as usual, was at the top of the mast filming.

From Red Bay, an old Basque whaling station, we headed across to L'Anse aux Meadows. The green open meadows looked beautiful and inviting. Just like the Norse people, we were too eager to wait for high tide to sail in farther. We anchored the *Halten* farther out and rowed as close to the shore as possible, then waded in the last few metres.

Helge was of course very eager to see what Anne Stine would say about the ruins – she too was just as enthusiastic to see them for the first time. In particular, there was great curiosity over the raised contours that looked like the shape of a house. They were not round like indigenous people's dwellings and they looked too old to be from whalers or other more recent European settlers. And the landscape amazingly fit the description of Leifsbudir in the *Saga of the Greenlanders*: a long shallow bay, a small river that flows into the sea, a headland to the north in the

Anne Stine and Benedicte on the *Halten*.

shape of a keel, a relatively narrow ocean inlet with a heavy current that could easily have been mistaken as a fjord, and a nearby island.

Later, the river also proved to be full of salmon just as described in the Sagas, and we were able to catch small flounder in tidal pools along the beach after the tide receded. The summers were relatively mild and cows peacefully grazed in tall green grass. Clearly, it was land that would have enticed people who came sailing southward about this time of the year. And not far from the shores were great, dense forests full of timber, an invaluable resource for people from treeless Greenland. Needed not only for firewood, but also to repair and build ships, trees otherwise had to be transported much longer distances from Norway.

George Decker, chipper as the sunshine, came down to meet us. He had assumed the position of chief caretaker, and so Helge gave him the nickname Big Chief, which actually quite pleased Decker. One of his duties, he believed, was to get rid of the ghosts that he thought haunted the place. His was an unconditional friendship right from the start and the feeling was mutual. We came to care very much for both him and his wife Mae.

We pitched our tents in a semicircle around the brook, and early every morning Big Chief came walking by with his dog Traveller and a bundle of kids following behind. "Tent ahoy," was his usual greeting, at which point we had to get up whether we wanted to or not. Sometimes we slept on land and sometimes on the boat, depending on the weather conditions. Skipper, however, never set foot on land except for once, and then hurried back to the boat as fast as he could. He would sit out on the boat deck with his binoculars watching each and every one of our moves. In the evening he might have said, for example, to Odd, "What were you sitting on that stone over there for?" Needless to say, we were under surveillance.

And so our excavations began – first on what was later called House A, a rectangular outline closest to the river. Not all the sides were equally visible, but Anne Stine was quite hopeful that there could be a foundation. The main thing was first to find out what type of people had built it, or rather to exclude that it could have been built by either indigenous people or whalers from around the 1400s.

To help us out, we hired a few local people: Job Andersson, Carson Blake, the oldest Colbourne sons, Big Chief's son Lloyd, and eventually several others. The turf, in between what Anne Stine presumed were the walls, was cut into long strips that were pulled up and peeled back from the ground. Then the workers began carefully scraping with their trowels. The local boys no doubt wondered why anyone would use such an impractical tool to dig, but once it was explained to them, they understood why and even became real experts at it after a while.

Anne Stine had expected the walls in the house to be made of stone, but discovered to her amazement that they were made of turf. After we had carefully scraped down to the so-called "cultural layer," a layer of darker earth which had been the floor of the house, the exciting work really began. It was here that discoveries could be made! The cultural layer was carefully and meticulously scraped with the trowel, and the dirt sifted so that we did not miss anything man-made. The most important thing at this point was whether we would find large traces from indigenous peoples, which would rule out anything Norse. So far we hadn't.

This was how we spent the days: up early, then scraping with a trowel and brushing the entire day. I have to admit that as a seventeen-year-old, this wasn't exactly my ideal way of spending a summer. It perhaps also played a decisive role in my not choosing a career in archaeology but rather a degree in social anthropology studying living people. However, our days of digging had a few bright sides. The weather was nice, quite pleasant most of the time, and the little river with the quaint name Black Duck Brook enticed us to an occasional dip in the water. It flowed through the terraced meadow in gentle falls and pools, creating delightful small swimming holes, despite the cold water.

Soon wild blue iris began to bloom all across the green fields, one of L'Anse aux Meadows most spectacular sights. On the marshes behind the ruins, little white cloudberry flowers appeared, and yes, it was all very beautiful. Out in the strait, a sound like a cannon shot rang out every time one of the great icebergs calved a wall of ice. Sometimes, an enormous berg would also go aground in the shallow Epaves Bay, where for days we would watch it slowly melt and then disappear.

One of the nicest things to do was to go on a photo shoot with Erling along the shores. He was a storehouse of tales and always in a good mood, plus he had an eye for finding unique beauty in nature. We found bird nests, shells, and rare tree stubs, and he taught me the best angles from which to take photographs.

The local community of L'Anse aux Meadows was a story in itself. The houses were small and simple, some unpainted and most with two floors. Every house had a long pier that stuck out and a kennel beside, similar to those we saw at the other communities. At the time, the place had no roads and no regular ferry schedule, other than the sporadic visits from the Grenfell Mission boat, the *Gould*. There was no post office, but rather a simple type of telegraph office, with connections only to the Grenfell Mission in St Anthony. Mail had to be collected from the neighbouring port of Straitsview.

The children went to school in a neighbouring settlement a good distance away and had to go back and forth in all types of weather. But at times it must have been a fairly irregular schooling since even the youngest was indispensable during the fishing season when the cod was cleaned and hung to dry. Overall, life in this little fishing hamlet was primarily based on a subsistence economy and family co-operation. If people became ill, or had other important errands in St Anthony, they had to travel in small, open boats. It could be a strenuous and dangerous trip around the northern peninsula with the sea and icebergs flowing down from the north.

At the time, thirteen families lived at L'Anse aux Meadows. Big Chief's grandfather was the first to settle the area around the beginning of the 1880s. Soon thereafter, the Andersson family arrived. They were descendants of a Norwegian immigrant from Ådal who settled in Makkovik on the Labrador coast, married an Inuit woman, and had many children. Job Andersson looked more like his mother, but his mindset was more like a farmer from Ådal. He hated fishing and the fisherman's way of life. Instead, he preferred to try his hand at raising cattle and growing potatoes, which was only somewhat successful. So he was exceptionally delighted when new job opportunities besides fishing presented themselves such as helping to dig on the ruins. We quickly became acquainted with him and the others and had no problem in finding any assistance we needed.

The Colbourne family was the last to settle in the community after a violent storm destroyed their house and pier farther south. When we were there in 1961, the Colbournes had eleven relatively young children. Their second-eldest son, Clayton, was a teenager about the same age as me.[25]

At the beginning, it was difficult to understand what the locals were saying. They spoke a very special dialect, similar to a British cockney accent, with many *oy* sounds and *h*'s before vowels, or missing in the most remarkable places. Anne Stine especially, who was already a bit hard of hearing, found it very difficult. It wasn't easy to understand that *haice* meant *ice* and *oice* meant *house*, but eventually we figured it out.

Another aspect of social life we eventually became accustomed to was their ways of stopping by to visit. The people were keen on paying visits

Job Andersson.

to each other, so their doors were never locked. They went about it by coming quietly into the kitchen, which was the main room on the first floor of the houses, and sitting down on a chair by the wall. Without speaking a word, they would sit and observe while the family continued with their usual chores. They did the same when they visited us in our tents. Several would come at a time, set themselves down, and then just sit there a good while without speaking a word.

For my mother, this was quite nerve-racking as she felt she had to be a good Norwegian hostess – offer them something or find something to talk about – but never seemed to receive any mutual response. We eventually got used to this and understood that it was just their usual custom. I'm sure there were also strange things for them to observe about us: such as types of food they had never seen, technical wonders like gas camping stoves, cameras, and filming equipment. We represented a world that was very different from the one they were accustomed to, and now they got a chance to catch a glimpse of ours. Little did we know that our presence at L'Anse aux Meadows that year would later affect their lives so dramatically.

After conducting sample excavations in four of the raised contoured areas that looked to be houses of various sizes, we decided to travel northward to explore the Labrador coast. Skipper was starting to get impatient; we all needed a break and I needed to travel back to Norway soon to begin a new school year. We hoisted the anchor and chugged away out of Epaves Bay. It was exciting to be at sea again. We headed north towards Belle Isle and came upon even larger icebergs than before. The island seemed to be surrounded by steep cliffs, and since it was blowing fiercely, we decided not to go ashore. Could this possibly have been Straum Island (Straumsey) described in the Sagas? Was it here that the Sagas tell of the dew that the Norse tasted and thought sweeter than anything they had tasted before? At the very least, it was clearly a distinct landmark for the people sailing down from the north.

We crossed over to the Labrador coast by Chateau Bay, where we set anchor. The approach was narrow but widened into a large, sheltered bay. This had been one of the most important ports during the earlier whaling period. We were still scouting for grassy fields, an estuary, and ruins but didn't find anything that looked promising. At one spot, however, we unforgettably cast our fishing lines into a small river and pulled out several huge trout. When we gutted them we discovered their stomachs were full of mice. I quickly lost my appetite while the others eagerly gobbled up the fish.

Along the outer coast of Labrador lies a small archipelago called the Gannet Islands. We heard that there were incredible numbers of birds there and we headed to take a look. The Sagas had also mentioned an island full of birds.

It was a nice, quiet sunny day with only gentle swells on the sea, so we were very optimistic about going ashore. But as we approached, the island was much the same as Belle Isle, with steep cliffs straight down to the sea and no sight of any bay to enter. "We'll try with the dinghy," Erling said, not being one to give up so easily. We boarded the little dinghy and circled the islands. The small swells that looked so innocent out at sea came crashing onto the cliffs and it all looked very hopeless for going ashore.

Just when we were about to give up, we caught sight of a small opening. "Let's try that," said Erling, and riding atop a wave we sailed the dingy in through a narrow passage and into the world's finest small lagoon. There was a white sandy beach and bright green short grass growing along the banks. Puffins and razorbill seabirds flew around characteristically flapping their wings, and their screeching was almost the only audible sound. Anne Stine chose to remain lying in the meadow staring at the sky and the birds while the rest of us climbed up to take pictures of the flat, green fields at the top of the island.

While many had sailed by and seen the razorbills on the cliffs, few perhaps had seen the green open fields on top of the island, home to thousands of puffins. We took photos by the hundreds and couldn't tear ourselves away until the sun began to go down and it was time to get back to the *Halten*. We slid down the hill in a small ravine back to Anne Stine and then waited for the right wave to carry us out through that narrow opening. The lagoon lay behind us: an incredible hidden utopia.[26]

We chugged farther north along the coast. At one place, we came across a huge radar station that was part of the North American Air Defense Command, a network of control towers designed to protect against any air attacks from the Soviet Union during the Cold War. Quite a contrast to the surrounding nature! We were invited into the station, welcomed by a pleasant commander, given a tour, and shown the control room where the men sat and stared at enormous screens waiting for the "enemy." The commander told us that he passed his time in remote nature by listening to his extensive record collection of classical music. "Then you must play something for my wife," said Helge, who thought it would delight Anne Stine. The commander tried to politely decline but Helge insisted, so Anne Stine and the commander went to his quarters, where he played a Beethoven symphony on the record player. The two sat there on the edge of the bed listening, he clearly uncomfortable with it all until Anne Stine realized that women were probably not allowed in their rooms.

The soldiers lived in large bunkers partly built into the side of the mountain. Here they lived surrounded by the wild, beautiful nature of Labrador drinking Coca-Cola, eating hamburgers, and watching western films. One of them said he had not been outside the bunkers since he had arrived as they were all connected with heated tunnels. When we left, they wished us well on our continued journey but looked at us quite strangely as we splashed our way along in our little eggshell of a boat.

Travelling up the coast of Labrador, we had intended to go ashore on the remarkable long beaches, very likely Furðustrandir of the Sagas, but it was too shallow and windy. Skipper refused to cast anchor. So we sailed by and hoped for better weather on the return trip. An endless stripe of white to our port, these beaches clearly must have been a very obvious landmark for those sailing along these coasts. Halfway up the coastline, a small cape stuck out, Cape Porcupine, which some believe to be Kjalarnes (Keel Point) from the Sagas.

We then sailed into the estuary at Hamilton Inlet, where the tide flowed as fast as four to five knots. This could very well have been Straumsfjord, so we decided to explore the surrounding area more closely. We came to the mouth of English River, which also had a fast current but not so strong that we couldn't take the dinghy a good distance upriver.

Trying to go ashore, we now understood what true virgin territory actually meant. Dead and living spruce trees hung like a tangled mess across the banks of the river. The undergrowth was as dense as a wall and we could not find a single place to set foot along the banks. The only possibility for going ashore was to follow the tunnels hollowed out by the black bear who used them to get to water and fish. None of us felt especially tempted to do this. We ended up going back to the *Halten*, but we at least were able to get a feeling for what Helge and other scholars believed must have been Markland of the Sagas: a place of incredibly dense forest and virgin territory.

Cape Porcupine, Labrador. On the Wonder Beaches (*Furdurstrendir*), as described in the Viking Sagas. Odd, Anne Stine, and Erling.

We carried on into Lake Melville, where the Hamilton Inlet widens, and sailed in towards North West River, where Helge and I had been the year before. Farther inland, the wind died down, and in the glorious sunshine, Anne Stine and I went ashore to a sandy beach on an island. Suddenly a fighter plane came flying by, incredibly low and right over the top of us. Then another flew by and another. They came in low and circled around. It was then we realized naked women sunbathing was probably not a common sight in remote parts of Labrador and we were probably more visible from the air than we knew. At the end of Lake Melville was Goose Bay, an American air force base. Rumours most likely had spread among the pilots about the two women sunning themselves on an island beach in Hamilton Inlet.

Goose Bay was not only a military base, but also a runway for a few commercial flights and the place where I caught a flight to head home for school. I flew to New York and boarded the Norwegian American Line ship *Bergensfjord* sailing to Norway. The cruise company had sponsored the expedition by providing return first-class travel. Today, those who quickly cross the Atlantic in just a few hours and in crowded, cramped planes don't know what they're missing. Travelling on the *Bergensfjord* allowed for a peaceful, slow journey that provided time to catch up with one's soul; and of course, for a seventeen-year-old, it was incredibly fun.

The others on the *Halten* continued their own journey, first out of Lake Melville and Hamilton Inlet and then south to the long beaches. They were finally able to go ashore and explore the part of the beach north of Cape Porcupine. But Skipper refused to go close to land in that difficult, shallow water, and getting ashore in the dinghy took a long, cold, and wet effort. As they rowed in, the sea glistened with small capelin fish chased by bigger cod hoping to get a mouthful as the waves crashed against the beach. When the *Halten* crew finally did reach shore, they gathered some kindling and started a huge campfire, almost burning themselves trying to get dry. Out on the headland, Anne Stine found an old moss-covered cairn. There was a hollow space inside, very similar to those found in many places in Norway. Whether this was from Leif Eiriksson and his people she could not say, but it was an exciting thought.

Leaving those long beaches behind, the *Halten* headed towards Cartwright along the southern coast of Labrador and near the entrance to Sandwich Bay. Grenfell Mission had a clinic here run by a young, idealistic nurse by the name of Louise Greenfield, who helped Anne Stine catch a flight back to St Anthony. While the men spent time sailing farther up the Labrador coast to Nain, Anne Stine returned to L'Anse aux Meadows to continue the excavations.

However, back then it wasn't easy to get from St Anthony to L'Anse aux Meadows. Anne Stine first hitched a ride with an ambulance on the short stretch of road to Pistolet Bay. Then she travelled by open fishing boat in full storm. When she finally arrived back in L'Anse aux Meadows, old and familiar faces greeted her and she felt like she was coming home. Despite Big Chief's great concern, she chose to stay in her tent by herself. This led to him patrolling the place with his old muzzleloader every night. It was ghosts, not people, that worried him the most.

About a month later, the *Halten* showed up back in L'Anse aux Meadows. The Colbourne kids came running down and eagerly announced they had seen the boat north of Round Head. It was a warm reunion, and Anne Stine was excited to show Helge what she had accomplished while they had been away. Overall, the summer had yielded promising results. Six dwellings had been found and excavation samples taken from each. Anne Stine had not yet found any artifacts that were clearly Norse, but the shapes of the houses, hearths, cooking pits, and ember chambers that kept coals hot during the nights spoke for themselves. Everything was similar to types found in Greenland and Iceland. In addition, she had found two iron rivets which revealed that the people who had lived and built these houses must have known how to find and make iron. That excluded indigenous people.

When the expedition team left L'Anse aux Meadows for the season and headed to Halifax, everyone on board the *Halten* was cheery and optimistic. They had in all likelihood succeeded in their goal of finding the first Norse settlement in America. Helge also believed, when taking into account the Saga's descriptions of travel distances and characteristic landmarks, there was very good chance that what they found was Leifsbudir – the houses Leif Eiriksson built in the place the Sagas called Vinland.

But yet another challenge remained for this little expedition. As they approached Nova Scotia, their motor began giving them serious problems. Skipper diagnosed the problem, a broken cylinder. They had no other choice but to chug along with only one cylinder. There was, however, also a very strange feeling at sea. At first it was dead calm, only long rolling waves. After a few hours, those waves became a high, choppy sea washing across the deck from all directions, and yet, not a breath of wind. The radio on deck was not working so they could not hear any weather report, nor were any other ships in sight. The waves continued to grow ever more choppy, making it almost impossible to stand. Then the spanker gaff snapped and fell to the deck with a loud crash, the wood stove tipped, throwing soot everywhere, and the toilet broke, spewing a sludgy mess over the floor. They had no chance of cleaning it up since it was all they could do to hold on in the storm.

Finally, at midnight on 22 September, with only one working cylinder, the little *Halten* chugged into the Halifax harbour. The place was chock full of boats all moored and secured with heavy, crisscrossing ropes. Tie them down well, they were told, because Hurricane Esther was approaching. The *Halten* was the last boat to sail in, two days after all the others. But no matter. The summer's expedition was completed and a Norse settlement had been discovered.[27] Rather than being concerned over the incoming hurricane, the *Halten* crew instead were happy and thrilled at the prospects of what the following year's excavations might bring.

15 ENVY, INTRIGUE, AND FURTHER EXPEDITIONS

The Dispute with the Danes

Discovery of the Norse settlement at L'Anse aux Meadows was made public at an Oslo press conference held at the end of October 1961. Helge had just returned from the *Halten* expedition after a brief stop in New York, where he also talked with journalists at a meeting in honour of Fridtjof Nansen. A week later, on 9 November, the headlines of the Danish newspaper *Berlingske Tidende* read:

DANES DISCOVERED VINLAND
We hid the discovery and now others are digging it out. Norwegian amateur archeologist's excavations have triggered this statement from curator Dr. Aage Roussell.[1]
Five years ago, a Danish researcher secretly identified the location where the old Norsemen most likely went ashore in America around the year A.D. 1000. However, now Denmark is too late to be a part of the first excavations there, despite planned major collaboration between the Canadian and Danish National Museums.
This summer without much notice, a private Norwegian amateur archaeologist, Helge Ingstad, excavated several finds at just the place where researchers believe was the greatest chance.[2]

These Danish newspaper headlines, and the subsequent articles, triggered a conflict about the discovery of the Norse settlement in America that affected Helge and Anne Stine for the rest of their lives. The professor

The Oslo press conference in 1961 when the L'Anse aux Meadows discovery was publicly announced.

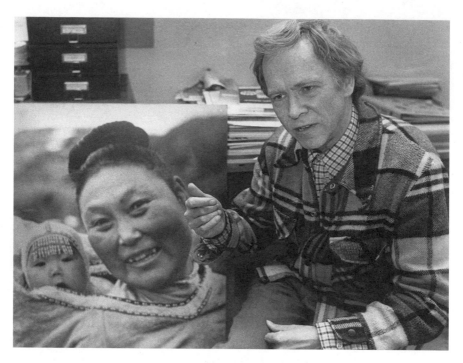

Jørgen Meldgaard, photographed by Bjørn Fjørtoft for the Norwegian newspaper
Aftenposten.

that Roussell referred to in the interview was the Danish archaeologist
Jørgen Meldgaard, whom Helge had met at the National Museum in
Copenhagen in 1953. Based on Helge's notes, that appeared to be their
first meeting. Apparently, they talked about the Norse discoveries and
excavations in West Greenland which the Danes had been working on
the past several years. Meldgaard had been a key figure in these excavations, along with Aage Roussell and Christen Leif Vebæk whom Helge
also met at this initial meeting.

For Helge, this initial discussion with Meldgaard was all part of his
research for his own planned expedition to the Norse settlements on
Greenland that would later help in his search for Vinland in Canada,
something he was quite open about. Most likely, though, Helge was also
unsure of how they would react to him concerning his ties to the 1930s
East Greenland occupation. For many years after, Greenland was almost
completely off limits for non-Danish scientists, so Helge was pleasantly
surprised at the reception he received.

At the end of July 1954, Helge wrote to Meldgaard and thanked him for his help. He informed him that his journey to West Greenland had been successful and that he discovered three previously unknown ruins at the Western Settlement. Helge knew that Meldgaard was also planning to take part in excavations at an Igloolik area near the southern coast of Baffin Island that summer and said, "I am very excited about the (coming) results of your America trip and studies there."

Meldgaard's first response to Helge's letter was not until 19 February 1955:

> Many thanks for your previous letter with information from your trip to the Western Settlement and the newly discovered Norse farms [there] … Yes, it has also been a successful summer, not only in providing a fine chronology of the oldest Eskimo cultures, but also, for the first time, of houses and graves of the Dorset culture.[3] I had actually thought of just spending half the season up there and thereafter give the Vinland voyages the other half, but the Eskimos kept me engaged. The Vinland trip was otherwise scheduled in segments, and then with assistance from the Government of Canada, flying reconnaissance with RCAF, etc. But that had to wait. Possibly, I will get there this summer in collaboration with a couple of American archeologists. Otherwise, here at the National Museum, we are planning an expedition in 1956 in collaboration with Canada and Norway, perhaps also Iceland. Apart from that, Eskimo and Native American archeology on paper, and presumably also in practice, will take priority.

With this, Helge was informed in writing about Meldgaard's plans. It came as no big surprise, as their shared interest in finding Vinland had already been confirmed in their earlier encounter. At the same time, Meldgaard clearly stated that archaeology of indigenous peoples was of equal interest to him as the Norse.

On 1 March 1955, Helge answered:

> I see that you, as well as the [Copenhagen] National Museum, are organizing exploration plans concerning the Vinland voyages. Greatly interesting. If information from the Norwegian press[4] is

republished in Denmark, you will perhaps know that I too for quite a while now have been preparing for an expedition aimed at exploring Vinland in collaboration with scholarly institutions and archeologists. It pleases me to hear that you have similar plans. The more who search the better, it concerns a very vast territory ... Otherwise, I would like to say that the valuable information you provided me before my departure (to West Greenland) was very useful. It is very seldom one receives such an open reception as you showed me then.

Best regards, Helge Ingstad.

It does not appear that Meldgaard responded to this letter, but Helge wrote again asking him for a few references on West Greenland that he could use in the book he was writing (*The Land under the Pole Star*). On 8 August 1955, Helge received a reply:

My summer was spent this year searching after Vikings and Stone Age people within the Danish borders, a welcome change from the Arctic at least. And the Vinland trip was never taken this summer as you understand. Funds were received too late, but they came. Next June the boat will depart from St. Johns. How is it going with your America plans? Your book about the Norse in Greenland is surely well in progress. I very much look forward to reading it. Sincerely yours, Jørgen Meldgaard.

Helge replied with a handwritten letter from Edinburgh on 25 August 1955 when we were on our previously mentioned family holiday.

Dear Jørgen Meldgaard,
... My sincere congratulations on your receiving financial funding in regards to your Vinland journey and that you can now start in 1956. When my journey will be is still unclear. Most likely, it will be later than yours. But it does not matter. Between the two of us there is, of course, no competition. It only concerns finding traces of the Norse, something that can be difficult enough in such a vast area. I wish you all good luck. You have better prospects than most in succeeding in this endeavor.

I hope to come to Copenhagen sometime this fall. Are you available to meet then?

Cordially, Helge Ingstad[5]

However, Helge never did make that fall trip to Copenhagen due to his last bout of tuberculosis, and it wasn't until June 1958 that he was able to go. He was then in the process of finalizing his Greenland book *The Land under the Pole Star* while also making plans for a trip in search of Vinland. This was two years *after* Meldgaard had conducted his trip in search of Vinland. For some unknown reason, Meldgaard's expedition was not the big international collaboration he had first indicated in his letter to Helge dated 9 February 1955. Instead, in 1956 Meldgaard journeyed up the Labrador coast and around northern Newfoundland on his own.[6] Nothing had yet been published about this trip either. In Helge's detailed notes from his meeting in Copenhagen in 1958 under the title "Meldgaard on Vinland" he wrote:

> Labrador, only possible place for Norse is Hamilton Inlet. Conditions for raising animals more favourable than on Greenland. He also flew partly over Newfoundland from Belle Isle to White Bay southwards on the east side down the long peninsula. Also here more favourable conditions than Greenland. Saw something that he will later try excavating. Got a plane from the mission station.

If this "something" Meldgaard wanted to excavate was presumed to be Norse, he would hardly have waited five years (1956–1961) before making it known, especially when he knew that Helge was planning a similar expedition in the near future. It is important to remember that Meldgaard not only researched the Norse, but also worked with palaeo-Eskimo cultures (Saqqaq, Independence, Dorset, and Thule) so that what he may have wanted to investigate could have been ruins from these indigenous peoples, which perhaps then were not as urgent to excavate. In any case, Helge obviously didn't know any more about Meldgaard's trip other than what was stated in his notes.

In late autumn of 1960, Helge was again in Copenhagen in connection with the launch of the Danish version of his book *The Land under the*

Pole Star. The Arctic Institute held a reception in which Meldgaard, who had written a positive review of the book, was also present. A newspaper journalist interviewed Meldgaard and asked him when he intended to further pursue his earlier expedition. Meldgaard replied that he was planning a trip soon, perhaps in the coming year. Helge, who had found the ruins at L'Anse aux Meadows just that summer, said nothing. Even though he intuitively felt that these ruins were Norse, archaeological analyses were still needed before he could announce the discovery.[7]

In an article printed in December 1961 (published two months after Helge had announced his findings at a press conference and more than a year after we had discovered the ruins), Meldgaard stated that the most probable area of a Norse settlement was the northern tip of Newfoundland. He also indicated that he did not find any concrete evidence of a settlement during his journey (earlier that year) and that the primary goal of the trip was to identify the geographic location of Vinland.[8]

And herein lies the crux between Helge's discovery and Meldgaard's claim: discerning the difference between Vinland as a *territory*, including obvious landmarks such as Furdurstrendir (the "Wonder Beaches" along the Labrador coast), and Vinland as a real discovery in the form of *house-sites* and *artifacts* of distinct Norse origin. The first could not be conclusive before the second.

Helge and Meldgaard had both, but separately, determined that the landmarks mentioned in the Sagas, as well as Vinland and Leifsbudir, should be searched for along the Labrador coast and northern tip of Newfoundland. Helge had even published this theory in 1959 in *The Land under the Pole Star*. It seems, however, that neither of these two men were aware, at least initially, that Munn had drawn the same conclusion. They of course knew about Tanner's work. Meldgaard had quite rightly set foot in the assumed Vinland territory before Helge, as had Tanner and Munn even before him, yet never found any artifacts or evidence. Later we also learned that, in the wake of Munn's article, several Newfoundland locals had for years searched for ruins in the area around Pistolet Bay in vain and never claimed to have "found Vinland."

Reactions to the controversy came from near and far. One professor wrote an article about the Icelandic man Sigurdur Stèfanson, who in about 1590 first presented the theory that Vinland was most likely located on Newfoundland, and referred to the Skálholt map which showed this. Several English-language newspapers and press bureaus covered the story; some referred to the Danish perspective and others to Helge's, but most presented a confused, incorrect report regardless of either perspective. Even the Chinese threw themselves into the discussion and said *they* had discovered America before Columbus or the Vikings.[9]

Not long after, the Norwegian television channel NRK interviewed Helge and Meldgaard. The interview began with Meldgaard explaining how he perceived the situation:

> I do not want to discuss this issue about the discovery of Vinland, but I would like to say a little about my work in trying to locate this area. For years, people have tried to locate Vinland in a number of places and stretches along the east coast of America. In 1956, I took a journey along the Labrador coast and around northern Newfoundland where the Finnish Professor Tanner emphasized that the Vinland ruins should be searched for. I travelled partly by aircraft and partly by small boat and naturally used the Saga descriptions of the land and landmarks ... Around the northern tip of Newfoundland I sailed around the many small inhabited places, Raleigh and St. Anthony, and I realized that this area needed further exploration. *But I can only repeat that I did not see the ruins that Ingstad excavated.*[10]

The essential purpose of Roussell's statement that was so misconstrued in the newspaper, Meldgaard explained, was to provide awareness that Danish researchers were also working on the Vinland question and that in 1956 they had determined that Newfoundland was where the ruins must lie. He then added:

> Helge Ingstad, on the other hand, did find the ruins and the discovery of these ruins will be absolutely substantial. It is very possible that Helge Ingstad has been so lucky as to have found Leif's houses and when decisive evidence from the excavations is presented, then Ingstad will, and should, stand as the true discoverer of the fabled Vinland of the Sagas. I wish Helge Ingstad all best if he has found the ruins and I for my part have nothing else or more to say in this ongoing discussion about Vinland.[11]

Helge then added that the entire episode was regrettable because Roussell's words to the press had gone out across the world and could easily overshadow the truly important work of the expedition. Even worse was that the expedition's archaeologist was being "harassed" and questioned before any of the scientific findings were even prepared or submitted, which violated a basic ethical principle against criticizing scientific work before it was ever published.

Helge ended by saying that he appreciated Meldgaard's honesty, especially because it must have been disappointing to explore the same geographic area and not find the ruins, and that it also must have been difficult to have been the man who museum curator Roussell pushed to the front line of the issue.

This debate continued like a broken record, with Meldgaard always confirming that he had never been to L'Anse aux Meadows, only in and around the surrounding areas. Then the newspapers would again ask, "Who made the real discovery?" to which Helge responded, "*What* has Meldgaard discovered?" Roussell's original attempt to affirm Danish research and the search for Vinland became ever more entangled until eventually the National Museum of Canada issued an official statement: they had not heard anything about finds of Norse settlements in Newfoundland until quite recently in connection with the announcement of Helge Ingstad's discovery. They also denied any agreement made between Danish and Canadian scholars and institutions to keep a 1956 discovery a secret or any other agreements to collaborate on an excavation.[12]

One could easily understand that the Danes were disappointed that their scholars from the National Museum had not made the discovery, particularly since Meldgaard had been so close to the site on his expedition. But it was a huge leap from disappointment to Roussell's statement about a secret discovery that triggered this entire debate. Roussell could have chosen to regret the mistake and the commotion it caused. However, he didn't. Instead, he blamed the Ritzaus Bureau, an independent Danish news agency, for misquoting him as saying that Meldgaard had discovered the *ruins* and not the *area* of Vinland.

But even early in the discussion with the press, Roussell referred to Helge as an "amateur archeologist," possibly not yet aware that Anne Stine, the expedition's archaeologist, was fully qualified in her field. One professor quoted in a Danish newspaper gave Anne Stine his full support and added that "Mrs. Ingstad is of course a fully educated archeologist so it is misleading to think that there wasn't a qualified specialist along."[13] This of course pleased Anne Stine, but at the same time she was disappointed that so few of her Norwegian colleagues publicly supported her. Most remained neutral, finding it easier to side with the Danes.

In radio and newspaper interviews, Helge stated that he considered Roussell's statements a "highly offensive denial of the Norwegian archeologist who had led the excavations, namely my post-graduate educated wife Anne Stine Ingstad." But not even as a fellow archaeologist could Roussell find it in himself to apologize for his statements. On the contrary, he repeatedly stated in several interviews that the Danes were the leading authority of Norse ruins and that if the "real" experts were not included in the excavations, there could be a risk that "these [houses of Leif] in Newfoundland will be presented in future history books as the [presumed] location of Vinland: Accepted by some, denied by others and questioned by most, and whether it was Leif's house they actually excavated in 1961–1962."[14]

Had it not been for Roussell's statements that instigated this debate, correctly or incorrectly reported in the papers, Helge most likely would have invited Meldgaard to join the following year's expedition. Helge knew that future work on the Vinland site would require numerous specialists from various countries. Meldgaard was one of the undisputed experts on Norse ruins in Greenland, but after the subsequent media storm, Helge had had enough of Danish archaeologists. Thus, one can say that Roussell's fumbled attempt to champion the Danes ruined Meldgaard's, and other Danish scholars', opportunity to be invited to excavate the Vinland site.

Helge grew strong in the face of adversity, but for Anne Stine it was quite the opposite. He was concerned about her mental health after the debate and afraid she might have another "nervous breakdown." She took Roussell's comments about her qualifications quite personally, and the lack of support from some of her scientific peers did not help; nor did the positive statements from those who expounded on her expertise and qualifications. She had relinquished her position at the museum in Elverum to join Helge and now the joy of the discovery at L'Anse aux Meadows had turned to despair because of these conflicts and accusations.

Feeling degraded as a woman also played a part in her gloom. Would Roussell have attacked a male archaeologist in the same way? Hardly. Helge tried to support her as best he could. When one considers his previous attitudes towards women's education and careers, it was actually quite admirable how he changed his views. In his future work with Anne Stine he praised and acknowledged her part whenever he had an opportunity to do so. But then, of course, it was also quite useful for him that she coincidentally chose to become an archaeologist.

The debate with the Danes eventually died down, but neither Helge nor Anne Stine ever got over it. Helge felt that his integrity had been unjustly questioned and that an attempt had been made to disgrace his name. Anne Stine never forgot that her expertise was unjustifiably slighted. To maintain peace at home, "Danes" was a word rarely mentioned in the family.[15]

1962 Expedition and the Icelanders

Not long after his return to Norway from the first summer's excavation in 1961, Helge began planning the next year's expedition. He of course had already obtained a research permit. It was clear to Helge that he would need to have international participation, but inviting any Danish archaeologists was out of the question. Icelanders, however, were a positive option since they had as much knowledge about Viking ruins as the Danes. Helge also wanted to involve experts of indigenous cultures from American and Canadian museums and universities to help in differentiating possible ruins from these cultural groups. A Norwegian pollen analyst, Kari Henningsmoen, was already recruited. She was going to take samples of the soil at varying depths to examine the vegetation and how it had changed over time.

Anne Stine was not especially motivated for this excavation. She was depressed after the ensuing debate with the Danes and most likely would have preferred spending the summer at Maribuseter with Louise and me. However, she did not feel she had much of a choice; she needed to finish what she had started.

Helge would soon find out, as he suspected, that the conflict presented by Roussell would indeed affect his future work. On 29 November 1961, an American photographer by the name of David Linton stationed at the US research station in Antarctica wrote a letter to the premier of

Newfoundland, Joseph R. Smallwood.[16] It almost seemed that he and Smallwood were familiar with each other beforehand:

Dear Sir

I am writing to you from the South Pole where I am temporarily photographing scientific work. News has reached me about the contradictions between Helge Ingstad and the archeologists at the Danish National Museum concerning the discovery of what could be Norse settlements at L'Anse aux Meadows. I am writing to you because I know something about the background of this case and because I feel that it is of great importance to achieve a successful solution.

I have followed [the work of] Jørgen Meldgaard from the Danish National Museum for several years. Later, I have also followed Helge Ingstad's project. I have spoken with both of these men and interviewed Ingstad on his way home from Newfoundland just a few weeks ago.

I am convinced that Ingstad's findings were based on information given to him by Meldgaard. Long before Ingstad announced any discovery, I knew Meldgaard had told him where to look. It seems clear that Ingstad did not waste time searching other areas, otherwise he could not possibly have spent so much time at L'Anse aux Meadows as he did ...

Mr. Ingstad has said that he intends to come back next summer to further excavate the ruins at L'Anse aux Meadows. When Danish researchers, who are widely known to be the leading authorities of the Viking Age, suggested that he ask them for assistance from [their] qualified scientists, Ingstad replied with a temperamental snub on Norwegian radio.[17]

Linton continued by saying that it was important that the discovery site be protected against "exploitation by private individuals for their own gain and against unqualified diggers" and that there are many examples of important findings being ruined by inexperienced diggers even when they have had the best intentions. He also pointed out that modern archaeology reaches far beyond digging and that different tools must be used by trained specialists from several disciplines. The essence of scientific research, in his opinion, was full openness, not only about results, but also about methods and material in order for other researchers to verify and possibly improve upon the work. And he continued:

> Mr. Ingstad has proven to be elusive concerning the details of his work and secretive in regards to artifacts and photographs from his work. He has previously given conflicting information about funding and organization of his expeditions. The Danes, however, I am convinced told him all they found in their unfinished research. These studies would have been completed and published if they had had funds and workers available. One should also note that the Danes reported their findings to the Canadian National Museum. I would not be so concerned if I did not believe that the findings were important. There is, I believe, a great chance that this is actually the first European settlement in America. The chance is so great that no risks should be taken that could result in destruction of artifacts.[18]

Linton concludes his letter to the premier with a plea to take action immediately and to "put all excavations at the site under the control of qualified researchers." He proposes the creation of an international committee to oversee and coordinate all explorations at L'Anse aux Meadows. He then lists possible participants such as representatives from the Danish National Museum, National Museums of Canada, Newfoundland National Museum, and Mr Ingstad. Other scientific institutions such as Islands National Museum and the American Museum of Natural History could also be asked. Only in this way could Newfoundland, according to David Linton, ensure that the discovery be rightly recognized by the scientific community.

This letter was written only a few weeks after the *Halten* expedition had returned home and long before it was ever possible for Helge and Anne Stine to present any scientific results. It clearly shows how tales and intrigue can spin from a scientific environment where both funding and fame are generally scarce.

However, the significant concern of this letter entailed two questions: Who influenced Linton, a seemingly unknown American photographer, to write to the premier of Newfoundland to give advice on the matter? And, did Helge know Linton or, in particular, anything about this letter?

One can only speculate. Linton could possibly have decided to write to the premier himself after reading the newspaper articles, which had been reprinted in several English-language papers, albeit with incorrect information. But it seems more likely that Linton was acting as a spokesperson for the Danes. As was presented earlier, Jørgen Meldgaard wanted to put the issue to rest after he clearly stated to the press that he had never set foot in L'Anse aux Meadows. One could conclude, then, that only one other person could have spurred Linton to his actions: Aage Roussell. This, of course, may never be proven.[19]

Whether Helge knew of Linton or his letter is quite doubtful. If he had, it would have created such a stir in the family that I would have heard about it at the time. There is no trace in his records of any correspondence between these two. Despite being unaware of this letter, Helge still felt the full effect of it anyway.

After having received Linton's letter, Premier Smallwood naturally grew uneasy. The case was brought before the Cabinet and presented to Dr Raymond Gushue, the president of Memorial University of Newfoundland. Gushue in turn contacted Ian Whitaker, professor of sociology at the university, and asked him to investigate the issue. Whitaker was British, had a large network outside of Newfoundland, and suggested consulting with neutral specialists from England or America.[20] He scripted a standardized letter portraying Helge as "a Norwegian archeologist whose credentials are unknown" and Meldgaard as having "impeccable" qualifications and sent it to a number of institutions. Whitaker's letter also stated that Meldgaard's participation in the dispute required greater emphasis to be placed on the discovery than perhaps otherwise required. Not a word was mentioned about Anne Stine's qualifications. Furthermore, he wrote: "It is said that Ingstad wants to excavate the ruins this first coming summer, which of course is very undesirable."

Given how the issue was now being presented, much was needed to turn the tide of favour towards Helge and Anne Stine. Instead, Sir Mortimer Wheeler, secretary of the British Academy, responded predictably by saying: "According to the circumstances, it is my opinion that Dr. Meldgaard should be given authority to conduct a limited excavation at the site, no more than two seasons, with clear instructions to present (to Newfoundland) the artifacts that are found and to have a report ready within two years of commencement."[21]

Dr William Wyse, professor of archaeology at the University of Cambridge, similarly wrote in a letter: "We have had experience with Dr. Meldgaard at this Institute and hold him in high regard. I do not know which is right or wrong in this discussion, but anyone who knows Dr. Meldgaard will readily accept his word."

Helge and Anne Stine, however, also received some support. A man by the name of R.A. MacKay from Carleton University in Ottawa wrote: "I have known Ingstad for four years and regard him highly ... he is not an archeologist, but belongs to that tradition of the imaginative and persistent amateur ... His wife is an educated and experienced archeologist and I can remember that Professor Hougen had very much good to say about her work. It is my understanding that it is she who will be responsible for the excavation."[22]

Completely unaware of the new storm brewing around him, Helge travelled to Newfoundland at the end of February 1962 to organize equipment for an entire excavation season at L'Anse aux Meadows. Upon arriving at St John's, he was faced with a shocking surprise. The research permit that he had received the year before had suddenly been revoked, without explanation. Instead, Canadian government officials had decided that an international committee was to be appointed and responsible for further excavations. A letter written by Premier Smallwood dated 15 February 1962, but not yet received by Helge as he had already travelled, stated:

> In view of the fact that the eventual findings in this area may have great significance, the Government is of the opinion, with which I am sure you will agree, that all future exploratory work should be entrusted to a body of an international character, that all activities should be carried out under permit from the Government and that independent efforts should not be allowed. Accordingly, the Memorial University of Newfoundland has been requested to proceed with the formation of such a body comprising of representatives of various museums and other organizations throughout the world which might be interested in the L'Anse aux Meadows work, and this matter is now receiving attention. I have no doubt that you will be invited to serve on this body.[23]

Being denied any further possibility of leading the explorations of the discovery that he himself had made, and then "graciously" invited to become a member of a group of specialists, was not something Helge wanted any part of. He had used years of his life and great sums of his own money to achieve this goal, and was now being pushed aside!

Helge immediately began contacting anyone and everyone he could: authorities, influential people, academicians, as well as the Norwegian government back home and the Norwegian foreign ministry in Canada. In the end, concerted efforts helped and he was finally granted a research permit again as well as control over the excavations. Helge never did find out what was really behind this conflict – but he had his suspicions. It was not until many years later, and after both Helge and Linton had died, that I found the actual letter from David Linton in the archives at Memorial University in St John's, Newfoundland.

The third expedition to L'Anse aux Meadows began in mid-June 1962. But because of the ice conditions, it took longer than usual to reach the excavation site. At this time there were still no roads in the area and access was either by plane or by coastal boat to St Anthony then a hitched ride from there with a fishing or mission boat around the northern coast. They were able to make it to St Anthony, but no farther. The ice conditions around Cape Bauld made it impossible to travel, so all they could do was to sit tight and wait. It took several days before the ice began to break up.

While the previous summer had been sunny and a little breezy, they now faced a summer of biting winds and heavy rain. That happy, optimistic mood at the end of the *Halten* expedition had all but evaporated. The Danish controversy hung over them like a dark cloud and Helge fervently wanted to prove that the ruins they had discovered were definitely Norse. Anne Stine mostly longed for home and wrote to her mother: "I have little to tell of life here. It is only cold, gray and horrible. We keep it going with our little stove as best we can, but otherwise Kari and I have moved over to the Decker's house at night – we awoke with our tent under water one morning."[24] She further wrote that she had too much work being the head archaeologist as well as doing the cooking and cleaning for the men. Employing fourteen-year-old Mildred as the cook eventually helped the situation.

In addition to Helge as expedition leader and Anne Stine as head archaeologist, others who were along this season included pollen analyst Kari Henningsmoen and photographer Hans Hvide Bang. Shorter visits were made by archaeologists Dr Rolf Petré from Sweden, Dr William Taylor from the National Museum in Ottawa, and Dr Ian Whitaker from Memorial University of Newfoundland as well as three others from Iceland and one from Sweden.

Earlier that year in February, Helge and Anne Stine had travelled to Iceland and had met with the director of the National Museum at Reykjavik, archaeologist Kristiàn Eldjàrn.[25] Anne Stine had been especially anxious to meet Eldjàrn, who had studied archaeology in Copenhagen. She was unsure of his standpoint concerning the conflict with the Danes. But his welcome at Reykjavik was genuine and the rapport between them was good, so they felt reassured – so far. Eldjàrn agreed to come to L'Anse aux Meadows but wanted to bring along two colleagues, history professor Tórhallur Vilmundarson and archaeologist Gísli Geston. They were not, however, able to come until the end of the season.

It was not until 17 July that the Icelanders came to L'Anse aux Meadows together with Rolf Petré from Sweden. According to Eldjàrn's journal,[26] they were met by Helge and Anne Stine, who were very glad to see them. William Taylor had already left, which was very disappointing for Eldjàrn, and Henningsmoen had also departed after taking the samples that she needed. But Helge conveyed that Taylor had enthusiastically surmised that these ruins did not originate from any tribes of indigenous people.[27]

Before Eldjàrn arrived, Anne Stine and her assistants had conducted test digs on dwellings A, B, C, D, and E.[28] Work on House F had only just begun. None of the excavations were completed, but enough had been revealed to get an impression. The most significant discovery was that the dwellings had the shape of longhouses similar to those excavated in Iceland and Greenland. Nearly as important, they clearly differed from known indigenous peoples' settlements in other parts of northern Canada.

Inside the houses, the small excavation team found hearths, cooking pits, a piece of red jasper, iron rivets, and other iron fragments, all of which were uncovered in the relatively thin cultural layers (visible in cross-sections as streaks of dark soil). The definitive artifact was yet to be found, but both Helge and Anne Stine believed that the shape of the houses and iron rivets were enough to draw the conclusion that these findings were of Norse origin.

Eldjàrn, if one is to judge from his journal, believed himself to be a sort of unofficial inspector of the excavations and was obviously skeptical

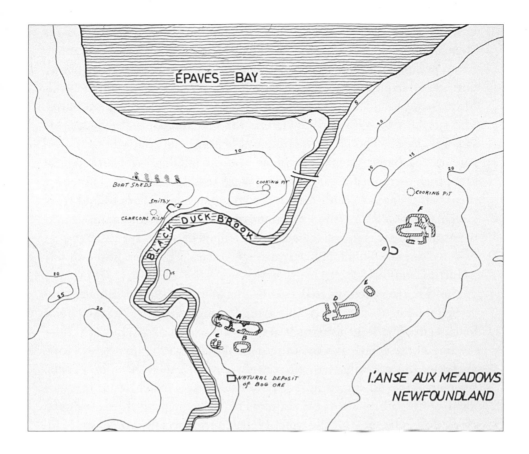

ÉPAVES BAY

BOAT SHEDS

COOKING PIT

SMITHY

CHARCOAL KILN

BLACK DUCK BROOK

COOKING PIT

F

A

C

B

NATURAL DEPOSIT
of BOG ORE

L'ANSE AUX MEADOWS
NEWFOUNDLAND

even before setting foot on Newfoundland soil. He was provoked by Helge's apparent confidence and suspiciously afraid of being used as a "dupe" in Helge's presentation of the findings in international media.

It soon turned out that Helge and Eldjàrn had very different personalities and did not easily understand each other. Helge had expected more zest and enthusiasm from his Icelandic counterpart, but got just the opposite. Eldjàrn was quite reserved and careful not to mention anything that he was not completely sure of or had yet proven. Helge was openly enthusiastic, if perhaps a little too eager.

During the conflict with the Danes, Helge had made quite a declaration when he claimed to have found Leifsbudir (Leif Eiriksson's houses). Perhaps it was this that irritated Eldjàrn. How could anyone say with certainty something like that without first finding a runestone etched with the name, or something of that nature?

However, Helge had good reason to be enthusiastic. Much that was already found indicated that the site was indeed a Norse settlement. Seven preliminary radiocarbon dating samples taken the year before all pointed to around A.D. 1000.[29] The discovery site corresponded with Munn's and Tanner's calculations of where Leifsbudir would be situated. The site also correlated with Helge's interpretations of the Sagas. He saw this to be a good land, comparable to Greenland, where the resources the Norse people would have been familiar with and sought after, such as timber, game, and fish, were readily abundant. Therefore, there was no need to settle farther south where the journey to and from Greenland would have been much more difficult.[30] Helge's main objective at the time was to create as much excitement about the discovery as possible to ensure funding from various sources. Therefore, it didn't pay to be too cautious.

The first issue that created tension between Helge and Eldjàrn concerned lodging during the excavations. Icelanders were given the choice to stay either with the fishermen in the village or in a tent. Eldjàrn chose lodging in the village and the other two decided to stay in a tent. However, they did not choose to pitch their tent with the others, in a social semicircle around the campfire, but instead at a place some distance away on the other side of the brook. There they kept to themselves and spoke Icelandic most of the time. Helge, and especially Anne Stine, interpreted this as the Icelanders not wanting anything to do with the Norwegians and siding with the Danes.

Anne Stine took this all very hard. She felt that there had recently been so much struggle with the Vinland excavations that she could not take it anymore and decided to return home earlier than planned. A few days later, on 23 July, she left for Norway. In his journal, Eldjàrn reacted strongly to her sudden departure. He argued, with some justification, that it was a breach of contract in that he was there as a guest but was now placed in responsibility of further excavations. It did not seem that he mentioned any of these feelings to Helge or Anne Stine.

Concerning Helge, Eldjàrn wrote that "he is gray in the face and looks old. It is clear that Anne Stine's departure has affected him deeply. He is also probably worried that it could create repercussions for him with the government since, of course, he had received permission on the condition that she was the head archaeologist."[31] But Helge was loyal, saying only that "Anne Stine has taken ill."

The Icelanders' camp by Black Duck Brook. The smithy is on the hill to the left.

The only thing in Eldjàrn's journal that clearly indicates any interest in the conflict with the Danes is found in the first paragraphs of his notes:

On 27 July 1962, George Decker in L'Anse aux Meadows told Thórhallur Vilmundarson how Ingstad found the ruins.[32] Carson Blake who also heard what was said promises that the story was correctly told. The story goes like this:

A few years ago [i.e., 1956], Meldgaard was on a trip to Pistolet Bay and met Harvey Taylor, my brother-in-law, in Raleigh. Harvey Taylor joined Meldgaard in searching for ruins around Pistolet Bay. The next time I met my brother-in-law, I asked what they had been doing. He told me that they had been searching for Viking ruins. I said to Harvey that he should have talked with me because

I could have shown him ruins that I thought were from the Viking age, although people have called it Native Camp. I took Harvey to Black Duck Brook and showed him the ruins and he said, "You have something there." When Mr. Ingstad came here the first time [i.e., 1960] he went to Pistolet Bay and met Harvey Taylor, but he sent him further to me to see the ruins which I had shown him. Ingstad told me that he would be back next year with his wife to look more closely at these ruins.[33]

The main details of this story are identical to how Helge described his discovery of the ruins in his book *Westward to Vinland* and how I myself experienced it travelling with him. It is also important here that George Decker says that he took his brother-in-law from Raleigh to the ruins *after Meldgaard had left* (in 1956).

When the Icelanders first arrived at the site the summer of 1962, Anne Stine had asked them if they could possibly complete excavations on House A that had begun the first year. Initially they did, but according to Eldjàrn's journal, they eventually thought this quite boring and had little belief that there was anything to left to find. Helge was optimistic about a visible depression in the grassy slope on the other side of the brook and asked if they wanted to dig there. Big Chief said that when he was young he used to take girls to this hollowed-out spot on dates and so they nicknamed it "Decker's Love Nest."

This depression proved to be the most important find that year. Right beneath the turf emerged large amounts of charcoal, bog iron and a medium-sized stone with a flat surface. It looked as if it were broken in the middle and was half of something bigger. Most likely what they uncovered was a smithy with a stone anvil. Helge was thrilled.[34] The Norse people on Greenland knew how to extract bog iron, but Greenland was so dry and had so few marshes that there was no bog iron to exploit.[35] Finding a land where bog iron was abundant would have been in itself a great discovery for the Norse. Later samples of the marshes behind the ruins showed that the bog iron hung in large clusters under the turf, almost like grapes on vines.

During the course of the 1962 expedition, the government of Newfoundland declared the L'Anse aux Meadows discovery a historical monument. On Helge's recommendation, George Decker was employed as caretaker, a job he took pride in and was earnest about.

Also during the summer, it became evident that the exposed ground was now more vulnerable to wind, rain, snow, and especially Black Duck Brook, which regularly flooded onto and into the excavation sites. Helge sent a letter to the government suggesting that buildings be built to protect the ruins. They agreed that this was a good idea and the work was completed before the snow came. The government of Newfoundland was beginning to realize the significance of the discovery and that it could possibly turn into a very large tourist attraction.

Anne Stine Takes Ill

"Anne Stine is nervous," Helge told me. In reality, she was very depressed and there was every reason to be concerned. She was admitted to the "nervous ward" at the hospital in November 1962, where she remained until the spring the following year.

The therapist assigned to her was a famous Freudian who dug into her childhood and her relationship to her deceased brother, much to Anne Stine's indignation. He probably did uncover something there, but had it been a few decades later, family therapy would probably have been the more appropriate and productive option. Only once were Helge and I called in for a family dialogue, and little came of it. She eventually felt that she was becoming addicted to both sleeping pills and valium. With all her might, she decided to break free from both the therapist and the pills, and succeeded. When she really wanted to, Anne Stine could be strong. She was discharged from the hospital in time to join us on the next year's expedition to Newfoundland. Whether she really wanted to go I do not know.

1963 Expedition

As usual, preparations for the coming year's expedition began almost immediately upon the return home to Norway. There was much that needed to be ordered and shipped and arrangements made with researchers for the following year. Samples needed to be sent to the appropriate institutes, and, most importantly, reports had to be written for the government of Newfoundland. In addition to all this, Helge needed to write articles for the newspapers and hold lectures at various venues. Unlike most other participating researchers who had salaries from their institutions while in the field, Helge and family were dependent on what he earned from these other functions.

Funding also had to be arranged and there wasn't a wealthy person, organization, or fund manager in Norway who did not receive a letter or visit from Helge asking for financial support during these years. Had it not been for that energy, enthusiasm, and belief in the project that had irritated Eldjàrn as a scientist, the expeditions could never have been financially supported.

As the years passed and the discoveries eventually became known internationally, the government of Newfoundland also partially contributed to the project. Helge and Anne Stine, however, never received salaries, other than being paid for contractual projects such as writing brochures and other material.

Early in June 1963, they left for the fourth expedition. That year's team consisted not only of Helge and Anne Stine but also the photographer from the year before, Hans Hvide Bang, and his assistant Nicolay Eckhoff. I flew in to join them during the middle of June, after my high school graduation.

During the summer, the excavations received visits from a number of prominent people. Dr Henry Collins from the Smithsonian Institute in Washington, DC, came at the request of the National Geographic Society. On 5 July, he enthusiastically wrote in a report to Premier Smallwood that "it is highly likely they are actually Viking ruins." This was obviously very encouraging for Helge and Anne Stine. He also pointed out that they now had the results from twelve radiocarbon datings from the sites which dated the samples to be around A.D. 1000.[36]

Dr Junius Bird, curator of archaeology at the American Museum of Natural History in New York, also visited, along with the president of the Early Sites Foundation. In his report of the visit, Dr Bird wrote: "The L'Anse aux Meadows dwelling sites in northern Newfoundland ... are undoubtedly of pre-Columbian Norse origin. Whether it is Leif Eiriksson's house is still debatable, but there is reason to believe that this is the case. Mr. and Mrs. Ingstad deserve great recognition, not only for the discovery of the site, but also for the excellent and careful excavation ... the location of L'Anse aux Meadows meets the Saga descriptions so perfectly that the possibility of giving a foolproof description of the route from Greenland is obvious."[37] Dr William Taylor, head of the archaeology department at the National Museum of Canada, also visited and voiced a positive statement. Wonderful support such as this was greatly appreciated by Helge and Anne Stine.

Later, however, these comments were used against Helge and Anne Stine because these archaeologists were not experts on the Viking age but on American indigenous peoples. It was crucially significant to determine that the L'Anse aux Meadows ruins did not originate from such indigenous peoples. The Dorset lamp and few fragments of flint that were found in the upper layers of soil were interpreted by other experts, as well as by Helge, as proving that indigenous people had used the ruins for shorter periods of time, after they had been abandoned by the Norse.

Helge's request the year before suggesting the government build houses to protect the most important and vulnerable ruins resulted in huge, quite unappealing, temporary structures while the excavating continued. Big Chief was quite proud of them and now felt like a proper caretaker over significant buildings and walked around with a rattling ring of keys. No one was going to be allowed into the ruins without his permission.

The expedition work this year largely revolved around cleaning up after the construction period and further protecting the ruins. Another objective was to complete the excavations in the houses that had already begun. There were now a total of eight contours of houses that had been found. Inside one of them, they found a new hearth and outside two of the other houses they found an iron rivet and iron fragment. Otherwise, test trenches were dug in between the houses and other places on the same marine terrace. Close to the smithy, on the other side of the brook, they found a deep depression with stones at the bottom which clearly must have been human-made. It could have been a kiln where coal was made for melting bog iron.

I left L'Anse aux Meadows at the end of July and headed to Arizona. I had gotten a job at the Trading Post on the White Mountain Apache reservation, the same spot where Helge had lived as a cowboy when he was younger, and I stayed there for three months. I managed to persuade Helge to meet me there on his way home so that we could travel together back to Norway across the Pacific Ocean stopping at a few exciting places along the way. Anne Stine was already home in Norway and flying her back to America for this trip would have been very expensive.

Helge met me in Phoenix at the beginning of November. From there we flew to Hong Kong, where Helge's brother Kaare was living with his

There were good moments too.

family and working as the Norwegian consul general and whom we had not seen in three years. On the flight over, we managed layovers in both Hawaii and Japan. After our visit in Hong Kong, we then flew to New Delhi, where we stayed at the Norwegian ambassador's residence. Here we met the Maharaja of Bikaner, Karni Singh, and were invited to spend a week at his palace. Quite a contrast from the wilderness of Canada and wild west of America where we had just been living a month earlier.

By then, Christmas was approaching and Helge and I were faced with a difficult dilemma. Should we hurry home to Anne Stine, something we both felt obligated to do, or should we take the opportunity of being in this part of the world and travel to Nepal to see the mountains? The spirit of adventure got the better of us, and with a very bad conscience we sent the following telegram back home: "Travelling to Himalaya, Merry Christmas." It took a long time before Anne Stine ever forgave us. Not because we didn't come home for Christmas, but because she wasn't there with us.

More Intrigue

When we got back to Norway, the Vinland dispute returned in full. We had had such a good time on our trip, and for the first time in many years Helge had talked about things other than just Vikings and Vinland. But now, everything was back to how it was before we left.

After the 1962 expedition, Helge assumed that most everything was in order with the government of Newfoundland. However, opposition continued to smoulder. Professor Ian Whitaker visited L'Anse aux Meadows briefly in July 1962, on behalf of Memorial University of Newfoundland, while the Icelanders were there. He had been given responsibility from the university's director to monitor the excavations, despite the fact that he was not an archaeologist but a sociologist.

Helge and Whitaker had, Helge thought, a nice chat late one evening after a few beers. Eldjàrn however, who had gone to bed earlier that evening, wrote in his journal the next day, "Helge doesn't understand that it is he [Whitaker] who is the dangerous one,"[38] which turned out to be true. Possibly spurred on by the Icelanders' skepticism of the discoveries, Whitaker travelled back to St John's also a skeptic and remained so even after leaving Newfoundland. During the fall of 1964, Whitaker was appointed a professor of sociology at the University of South Wales, England. However, he seems to have continued as an informal adviser for Memorial University concerning L'Anse aux Meadows.

Whitaker proved to be a major source of the government of Newfoundland's suspicion toward Helge and Anne Stine,[39] probably without Helge's full awareness of the situation. In February 1963, Helge received a letter from Whitaker thanking him for sending the results of the radiocarbon dating analysis, which he goes on to describe as particularly satisfying: "I really must congratulate you on this most satisfactory finding. This now convinces me that the L'Anse aux Meadows site is in fact a Viking one."[40] And with that comment, Helge assumed that Whitaker had no further issues concerning authenticity or qualifications. However, that was not the case.

In June 1964, over a year later, Dr Whitaker wrote to Raymond Gushue, president of Memorial University of Newfoundland in St John's. Whitaker had earlier received a copy of Helge's report about the excavations from the previous year. He claimed that Helge had not been "entirely truthful" and that the 1963 expedition had been small and understaffed. He argued that Anne Stine, as well as Dr Collins and Dr Bird, had only been there for a short time, and that this reflected Anne Stine's professional commitment. He once again brought up the issue of establishing an international committee of experts who could provide the Newfoundland government advice regarding L'Anse aux Meadows. In other words, he wanted Anne Stine and Helge out of the way.[41]

On 2 June 1964, Whitaker wrote a letter to Eldjàrn asking him if the Icelanders had taken any pieces of charcoal home to Iceland from L'Anse aux Meadows. Eldjàrn replied yes, but that "unfortunately these charcoal samples were not sealed nor witnessed to be from the ruins."[42] Whitaker's aim was to discreetly send new samples of charcoal to another lab to get a "second opinion" about the radiocarbon datings. He reasoned that "the whole question of the province of the samples is most important." But in reality he insinuated that either Helge or Anne Stine had consciously tried to trick people about the pieces of charcoal and their radiocarbon analysis, or that the laboratory results from the Norwegian University of Science and Technology (NTNU) were not to be trusted. Both alternatives represented deep mistrust. NTNU's laboratory was considered one of the best in the world for such tests at the time. Eldjàrn responded in a long letter stating that he "took … a souvenir (just in case)," but that he didn't want to go behind the backs of Helge and Anne Stine, which he didn't think was "currently necessary."[43] That was a loyal answer (if we ignore the word "currently"), and thus nothing more was done.

About the same time that Whitaker sent the letter to Eldjàrn, Premier Smallwood sent a letter to Helge that undoubtedly was also inspired by Whitaker. Having re-established his interest in the excavations and their possible Norse origins, he wrote: "As far as I can determine from reviewing your reports, we have not yet received conclusive evidence concerning the authenticity of these ruins."[44] It was only after scientific confirmation that the Newfoundland government could officially declare that the discovery was authentic. If we read between the lines, the letter conveyed that no financial support could be expected until the ruins were officially declared as Norse.

The letter closes with an instruction: to submit an immediate final report including all test results and analyses accompanied by certified documents from the institutions that had conducted them. In addition, a written statement was required from each expert who had had anything to do with the expedition and who had an [educated] opinion of the findings. This was expected "at the earliest possible date as a complete report."

The request was quite an impossible task. The 1964 expedition had not yet begun and the number of remaining expeditions was still undetermined. A perusal of the nearly three-hundred-page final report,[45] including numerous diagrams and references, shows that the task could not have been completed in a hurry. It was a job that would take several years after all the expeditions were completed.

Helge does not expound on this in his one-page reply to the premier other than to say he will ask all contributing researchers to submit their reports as soon as possible. He then directs the premier's attention to an article he had written that was about to be published in the *National Geographic* magazine. It is a bit unfortunate, Helge says, that they have not yet found any more tangible evidence from the Viking age but "that is the nature of archaeology, you have to work with what is available."[46] Tangible evidence, however, was about to emerge; they just didn't know that at the time.

Another element at play in this pressure to provide concrete evidence was in Eldjàrn's reply to Whitaker about the bits of coal; he also expressed concern that Helge was about to write a "mainstream" book about the discovery. Whitaker sent the letter to Raymond Gushue at Memorial University saying he too was similarly concerned about the lack of substantial enough reports.[47] Gushue then immediately wrote to Helge and said that Whitaker had received a confidential letter from one of the members of the L'Anse aux Meadows team a while ago. The letter continued: "I can say as much that he is concerned to hear that a mainstream book about the discovery will soon be published in Norway. He says that in his opinion, this goes against the verbal guarantee given by each participant; specifically that a scientific report was to be given first priority and come before a general mainstream presentation of the findings."[48]

It was not very difficult for Anne Stine and Helge to imagine who the anonymous person was: Eldjàrn. The letter from Gushue goes on by quoting Whitaker as saying, "The academic archaeologists in the UK are not satisfied with National Geographic as being the [correct] type of publication and feel that this form will be repeated in the manuscript about to be published in Norway."

Helge responded to Gushue refuting the allegations about missing reports by referring to the lengthy report about the excavations that had been sent the year before (18 November 1963) and significant reports from both Dr Henry Collins from the Smithsonian Institute in Washington, DC, and Dr Junius Bird from the American Museum of Natural History in New York. He reiterated the very positive radiocarbon dating results and argued that these provided more than sufficient evidence to currently and quite confidently confirm that these had to do with Norse ruins.

The final report will be voluminous and detailed, wrote Helge, and will need considerable time to collect all the test results and reports from the various scientists who will be collaborating on the final conclusions. And the final report cannot be completed until the last expedition ends.

Gushue then sent Whitaker copies of this letter, and *all* other earlier correspondence between him and Helge, including the report from 1963.[49] Whitaker replied 6 December 1964 by thanking him for the letters and report and then gave a lengthy discourse on his issues with Helge and Anne Stine: the experts (excluding Eldjàrn) who had been invited had been there too briefly and did not have specialized expertise on the Vikings; he thought it was unfortunate that Danish archaeologists had not been invited to participate; he doubted the accuracy of the radiocarbon dating which had been tested in Norway; and regretted the lack of any artifacts that could solidly confirm Viking origin.

One thing neither one of these men took into consideration when they accused Helge of publishing his "popular science" book before completion of the final report was the fact that Helge had a family of three to support and that they could only live so long on royalties of long-past published work. Helge was dependent on creating more income if he was to continue the excavations at L'Anse aux Meadows. Up until this period (1964), the actual funding[50] of the expeditions and excavations had been financed by more than seventy different Norwegian sponsors, something that required considerable effort to procure. The government of Newfoundland was still sitting on the fence, partly due to Whitaker and his correspondence with the tentative Eldjàrn.

But Helge proceeded with his book and *Westward to Vinland* came out the following year, in 1965.[51] The main emphasis of the book was the discovery of the ruins in 1960 and a description of the journey on the *Halten* and the trip to the Nascapi people in Labrador. It also included a summary of the Vinland Sagas and a discussion of where Vinland could possibly lie.

Quite naturally, the accusations of doubt affected our family. As before, Helge grew stronger in adversity whereas Anne Stine grew more weary. She had managed to recover from her first episode of depression, to an extent, but was still quite vulnerable. Her condition was in the back of Helge's mind the entire time, and everything that he wrote to the government of Newfoundland reflected this concern.

The 1964 Expedition and Discovery of the Spindle Whorl

Another accusation was yet to come, this time from a totally unexpected source. During the 1963 expedition, Helge and Anne Stine had a brief visit from a Canadian author by the name of Farley Mowat, who arrived completely unannounced. He was there to gather information for a book he was working on, later titled *Westviking: The Ancient Norse in Greenland and North America*,[52] and wanted to see for himself whether the ruins were Norse or not. He was welcomed and shown around as was the custom for other visitors.

Sometime later, Helge received a letter from Mowat in which he quite arrogantly demanded access to all the research results from the expeditions so he could use this as background material for the book he was writing. He mentioned that as a Canadian citizen, he believed he was entitled to this information. Helge replied that this was, of course, impossible. For one thing, he was under obligation to the government of Newfoundland as well as to the other researchers who had been part of the excavations. In addition, the material was still being compiled and had not yet been scientifically published.

However, in the end, Mowat managed to persuade the government to give him a copy of the site drawings. These had been made in collaboration with Helge with the expressed agreement that they would not be available to others until the final report was completed. Helge was furious.

One day in early 1964, Helge received a newspaper clipping from a Newfoundland newspaper with a message from Mowat saying that others were questioning the authenticity of the ruins at L'Anse aux Meadows. An article written by a Mr Harold Horwood under the heading "Inside Information: The L'Anse aux Meadows Mystery,"[53] presented a number of allegations that were so far-fetched that they were not even worth commenting on if it had not been for the last and most absurd. He accused Helge and Anne Stine of tucking away a clay pot that they had found during the excavations – evidence that disproved their own theories. The author of the article also mentioned an anonymous outsider who had visited the ruins and had taken some wood and iron material that was later analyzed. The iron, he said, was "proven" to come from modern processes.

For the record, Helge wrote a letter to James Channing, clerk of the Executive Council of the Government of Newfoundland in which he said that he considered the allegations so unreasonable that he could not find it worth the trouble to go to the newspaper to debate the issues. Eventually Whitaker convinced Helge to respond and a crushing counter-argument to Horwood's allegations was published in the newspaper. Dr Junius Bird from the American Museum of Natural History in New York also did the same. When Helge later heard that Farley Mowat and Harold Horwood were good friends, pieces of the puzzle fell into place.

Sometime later, Whitaker wrote to Helge to confide that the story about the confiscated clay pot could have stemmed from himself. George Decker had told him that Ingstad had found a pot with a treasure of gold that they had taken with them and Whitaker had relayed the story to Mowat. Big Chief had a lively imagination which included ghosts and tall tales. As a professor of sociology, Whitaker should have included this when he relayed the information to Mowat.

It was not until the beginning of August that the 1964 expedition to L'Anse aux Meadows finally departed. Helge stayed behind in Norway to finish writing his book *Westward to Vinland*. The year's expedition was fully funded by the National Geographic Society under the expressed condition that Helge would write an article for their magazine and that they would be the first to publish news about any discoveries made that year.

In addition to Anne Stine, and a few locals to help dig, this expedition included a young Swedish student by the name of Birgitta Wallace, who had written and asked if she could participate. Anne Stine was a bit concerned that Birgitta was still too young and inexperienced to assume any serious archaeological responsibility, as the visiting Icelanders had for the excavation of the smithy. But Anne Stine kindly agreed to take her on to help out. Dr Junius Bird from the American Museum of Natural History in New York also came for a shorter visit along with his wife Peggy and a younger fellow by the name of Tony Beardsley.

It was a sad occasion for Anne Stine to return to L'Anse aux Meadows as Big Chief had died the previous October. He had suddenly and unexpectedly collapsed while inspecting the ruins. His life ended in the very place he had helped make world-famous. Never again would Anne Stine and her team be awakened by "tent ahoy" or encouraged by his amusing, playful comments and warm smile.

Anne Stine made a wreath of beautiful blue iris from the meadow and laid it on his grave. His wife Mae was of course still grieving, but was very happy when Anne Stine decided to stay with her. The Deckers' son, Lloyd, had taken over his father's duties as caretaker, a position paid by the government of Newfoundland.

It was late in the summer season when the expedition team arrived at L'Anse aux Meadows. Their main task this year was to finish cleaning up after the construction of the protective buildings as well as combing through the already excavated houses. The government had plans to build a road to the fishing hamlet, which would bring even more tourists to the area. Everything had to look nice and ready to be viewed.

One day as they sat digging, Anne Stine suddenly heard a shout from the ruins where Birgitta and Tony were digging. Tony had found something strange in the ground and Birgitta, who leaned over to take a look, saw at once what it was – a spindle whorl.[54] Anne Stine came running, saw what they found, then they threw their arms around each other laughing and crying.

The whorl lay there, round and fine with a hole like a donut. It was made of soapstone and had a little soot along one side which showed that the material could have possibly come from a broken kettle. After carefully cleaning the dirt away with a brush and taking the necessary photographs from every possible angle, Anne Stine carefully lifted it out of the earth. She was completely breathless as she stood there with the whorl in her hands. There was no doubt that it was of Norse origin. Similar whorls had been found in recognized Norse areas, while nothing like it existed in local indigenous cultures, who were hunter-gatherers.

Photos that show the similarities between the spindle whorls found in Greenland and in L'Anse aux Meadows.

Whorls were associated with raising sheep and spinning wool. Here it was, the definitive proof they had longed for! Now nobody could dispute the fact that the settlement was Norse.

As she stood there holding the whorl, Anne Stine began thinking that the whorl not only proved that the Norsemen had lived at L'Anse aux Meadows, but also that they had brought women along just as the Sagas had said. Who though? Was it Thorfinn Karlsefni's beautiful wife Gudrid? She who had given birth to her son Snorre in Vinland and then later became a nun in Iceland? And what kind of thoughts and dreams passed through her mind as she sat against the sunny wall spinning on the spindle when suddenly the whorl fell off and went missing in the grass? No one will ever know for sure, but we can only imagine. Anne

Stine hurried to send a telegram to Helge with the good news: "Whorl of Norse type found."

The news of the spindle whorl exploded in the press. Helge had barely managed to send a message to the government officials in Newfoundland and to National Geographic Society, the expedition's sponsor, before the news appeared in almost every newspaper in Europe, the US, and Canada.

A few days later, Anne Stine received a telegram from the National Geographic Society requesting that she come right away to their headquarters in Washington with the spindle whorl. She didn't feel, however, she could leave that quickly for two main reasons: first, she was not yet finished with what she had planned to complete at the excavations that year; second, and what bothered her the most, was that she had not taken along any nice clothes on the expedition and had nothing to wear. She had flown directly to Gander in Newfoundland from Norway and had every intention of travelling back that same way. Besides her boots and digging pants, she had only a crumpled blue and white summer dress at the bottom of her bag – not exactly appropriate attire for a trip to Washington, DC.

She tried delaying the trip by sending a telegram saying that she first had to finish that season's excavations. However, that excuse didn't work and she received a new telegram saying that the Society was waiting for her to come to DC *immediately*. She consoled herself by thinking that everyone knew that coastal travel in northern Newfoundland could be unpredictable. So she sent word again that she would take the Grenfell Mission boat, the *Gould*, to St Anthony the following week. That at least gave her a few days to finish things and pack.

In the end, there was no escape. The *Gould* arrived and she had to board. During the few days she had to wait at St Anthony Inn, she was able to wash and iron her summer dress, which she then felt much better about. With the spindle whorl in a small box in her handbag, which she clung onto as if it contained a precious jewel, she left for Washington.

When she finally arrived after several transfers, she was astounded by the huge turnout of journalists waiting in the arrival hall at the airport. At first, she thought it was arranged by the National Geographic Society in their excitement about the spindle whorl. But she was relieved to find out that all the commotion was about a first-class passenger on the flight: Robert F. Kennedy. She was able to sneak by and out to the street to get a taxi that drove her to the Society's magnificent marble building. A large assembly of experts were all anxiously awaiting her and ready to inspect the spindle whorl. In the next room, several small round tables were set and decorated with beautiful flower arrangements. She could see that an elegant lunch was planned and she again began to feel uneasy in her old summer dress.

During the meal, she was asked to take out the spindle whorl. It was passed around from table to table before she put it safely back into her bag. When comments such as "This changes the history of America" began to spread, she wished that Helge were there to share this incredible moment with her. They were finally being rewarded for all those years of struggling in the rain and cold.

The National Geographic Society had booked her a room at the Jefferson Hotel. She knew nothing about the hotel, but it turned out to be one of the oldest and most elegant in town. She was shown to a suite that almost made her faint. It had the most lavish rococo sitting room that she had ever seen and vases bulging with flowers everywhere. There was a large bedroom with an elegant bed and an en suite marble bathroom. There was a bar with drinks of all kinds and a refrigerator filled with mineral water and sodas. Outside was a shady balcony with deep reclining chairs. Yes, this suite was perfect for an archaeologist who was used to sleeping in a tent and sleeping bag. She regretted very much that she had requested a ticket home the following day but decided to enjoy the luxury to the fullest and did not leave the suite during her entire stay in Washington.

Upon her return to Norway, an excited Helge and a press conference were there to meet her. Everyone was happy and all was splendid – for a while at least. The discovery of the spindle whorl was made just in time to be included in Helge's book and in the article for *National Geographic* magazine which came out in November 1964. Between Christmas and New Year's Eve, Helge turned sixty-five years old and Anne Stine arranged a large party at our home, Brattalid. It was truly marvellous, a party only Anne Stine could have prepared so wonderfully.

Acclaim and Further Expeditions

The announcement of the discovery of the spindle whorl led to a remarkable outpouring of recognition and tribute from around the world.

Even the Canadian and Newfoundland government authorities now dared to finally believe in the discovery of a Norse settlement at L'Anse aux Meadows. J.D. Herbert, director of Chief Historic Sites Division for Newfoundland, sent congratulations and a cheque for the $250 that had been held back from their contract pending final proof of Norse authenticity. "There no longer seems to be any doubt that you have been right," he said.[55]

Ian Whitaker sent congratulations from England, but still couldn't stop himself from hounding them once again to submit a final report as soon as possible, which Helge ignored. The report was to be a thorough job, and therefore would take time.

At the end of January 1965, Helge held a lecture at the University of Oslo on behalf of the Norwegian Geographic Society. The title of his talk was "Westward to Vinland: The Discovery and Excavations of Norse Pre-Columbian Sites in North America." Seated in the over-crowded auditorium was King Olav of Norway. This grand event was followed by lecture after lecture around the country and media coverage in all the newspapers.

In the spring of the same year, a surprising new issue emerged that would create even more publicity about the Viking discovery of America. Yale University Press launched a book about a well-hidden secret, namely an assumed pre-Columbian map indicating Vinland on it. Besides showing Africa, Asia, and Europe, it also showed land areas southwest of Greenland with "Vinland" clearly marked.

Good marketing and a book tour including representatives from both the publisher and Nordic faculty, resulted in much focus on the map. Helge, like many others, was hesitant about the authenticity of the map, which was later correctly debunked by historian Kirsten Seaver.[56] However, publicity about Yale's published map didn't draw any attention away from Helge and Anne Stine's work. On the contrary, it seemed to reinforce and increase public interest in Vinland, especially in America.

A colossal amount of mail began streaming in from everywhere. Ladies from Minnesota wrote to say they had a strange stone in their garden and wondered if Helge had anything to say about it or, better yet, could come and take a look. Young students working on projects asked for pictures, notes, and autographs. Knowledgeable people from around Norway said they too had been studying history and offered good advice or new ideas.

Helge never had a personal secretary, either before or after the media press about the discovery. He was too obstinate to manage another person like that, and besides his personal finances did not allow for one, other than for the occasional editing of manuscripts. But also, throughout his entire life, he had a fixed idea that *all* letters should be answered personally. A school student, for example, would receive a two-page letter from him with a long answer to a question for a project. This of course led to an enormous amount of extra work for Helge. During this period, he also took the time to write an article for the Norwegian newspaper *Aftenposten* about another matter important to him: the protection of polar bears.

In August, Helge wrote to Lloyd Decker asking him how the winter had impacted the ruins and if many tourists had been to the site. He also explained that he had not yet been able to get to L'Anse aux Meadows but had hoped to come before the end of the season. However, he never did make it there that year as more and more acclaim for his work came pouring in that entailed more and more travel to accept these honours.

Finally, Helge and Anne Stine began receiving recognition for their hard efforts. First, they travelled to Washington, DC, to receive the annual Franklin Burr Award presented by the National Geographic Society's scientific community. It was awarded to both of them and was particularly welcome since it also meant $1,500 to share. Second, Helge was presented with the Fridtjof Nansen Award from the Norwegian Academy of Science and Letters, which included a medal and 10,000 Norwegian kroner. Then St Olaf College in Minnesota contacted them saying the university wanted to award Helge an honorary doctorate degree in November. At the same time, Helge learned that they had been given a Norwegian government grant, initially for three years. Helge also received word that he would be awarded Commander of the Royal Norwegian Order of St Olav, one of the nation's highest accolades.[57] Helge received this honour in 1965; Anne Stine in 1979.

Despite Helge's constant and consistent emphasis on Anne Stine's important role in the discovery, it was hard to ignore that almost all the focus was on him, and sometimes only him. Invitations for the awards ceremonies, not only from St Olaf College in the United States but also from the University of Oslo, stated: "We also hope that your wife can attend." A nice gesture, but one that conveyed a lack of acknowledgment of Anne Stine's contributions. He was the one who received most of the honours.

Anne Stine didn't always mind this, as she was shy about publicity and everything associated with it. However, she very much would have liked more recognition for the work that she actually did. She found it especially irritating when letters continually came addressed to *Mr. Archeologist Helge Ingstad and Wife*. She was the one who was the archaeologist!

The following July 1966, they arrived again at L'Anse aux Meadows. Most of the summer was spent completing the already excavated houses. However, new finds also emerged, including a door between two of the rooms in House D, a doorway on House B, and a new, thick cultural layer when they lifted some flat stones that had probably been on the roof of House C. In addition, test trenches were dug in all directions outside and between the houses. It was important to ensure that there were no further houses, waste piles, graves or the like which were not visible above ground. After they returned home, they received a letter from Lloyd Decker, who said that the governor general of Canada and Premier Smallwood had visited L'Anse aux Meadows that fall. They arrived by naval ship and together with several naval officers in full uniform came ashore to view the site.

In the spring of 1967, both Helge and Anne Stine were invited to give lectures at Yale University, where interest in the Vinland mystery had increased since the publication of the book about the assumed "Vinland Map." In June, Jørgen Meldgaard invited them to the opening of a Nordic exhibition in Copenhagen. This invitation was a positive gesture and to a certain degree helped to heal old wounds.

Helge and Anne Stine did not leave for L'Anse aux Meadows until September of that year. It was the first time they could drive on the newly constructed road that extended from St Anthony all the way to the village. The road was intentionally not built all the way to the ruins so that a certain control could be kept over who went there. It was sunny and warm, a perfect day to inaugurate the drive.

The first thing they saw as they arrived was Lloyd's new car. Lloyd was now married and had built a new house near his parents' old one. As the only one in the village with a steady salary and car, he was quite the VIP. Lloyd's mother Mae had passed away the year before, which Anne

Stine was especially sad about. She had had a close relationship with her and often found solace in her cozy kitchen after spending hours outside in the freezing cold.

The equipment Helge had arranged to be delivered for the season had not yet arrived, so he had to return to Gander to get it. Meanwhile, Anne Stine continued to comb through the ruins and dig test trenches in the terrain like the year before. This time, however, she was continually interrupted by tourists who had driven to the site expecting a guided tour. The weather began to worsen and the temperature sank to below zero during the middle of the night. Anne Stine, who was still waiting for her sleeping bag, had only a few borrowed blankets to use and was bitterly cold most of the night. She was staying in a little unheated hut that the government had built when they were working on the structures to protect the ruins. Eventually, Helge showed up with the equipment and circumstances improved. Outside it rained and blew quite a gale, but inside the small hut it was now nice and cozy as they settled in and shared a bottle of red wine Helge brought along.

The weather improved and work on the site could continue. Local kids often showed up with bucketloads of hand-picked cloudberries and raspberries and sometimes a halibut or cod. It had been a catastrophically bad year for fishing in the area, a sign of the problems ahead. Capelin fishing had never been worse, which in turn had affected the cod fishing. Mrs Colbourne baked bread for them as she always did and they were able to buy eggs from a girl in the neighbouring village. They lacked for nothing.

Visitors began to arrive. First, Junius Bird, who of course had been there before, came to take a closer look at the moss-covered cairns he had found on the hill south of the brook. The locals believed they had been used to catch wild fowl, but Bird concluded that they could very well have been Norse.

Then Professor Bjørn Hougen, Anne Stine's old archaeology mentor, together with Professor Mårten Stenberger of Uppsala, Sweden, arrived. They had been invited by the government of Newfoundland to examine the findings and give an account. Anne Stine and Helge looked forward to showing them around. On a stormy day in September, they arrived by seaplane and managed to land in the bay. They were shown around the site in pouring rain and ended their tour in the newly scrubbed and decorated hut where they were served stew and beer. They returned to St

Local children bringing cloudberries and other gifts.

Anthony for the evening, stayed the night at the magistrate's house, then drove back to the site the next morning in an ambulance from the Grenfell Mission. The statement they issued after their visit was very positive and without reservation: they proclaimed the ruins to be pre-Columbian and without a doubt the first known European settlement in America.

Anne Stine and Helge then left L'Anse aux Meadows together with Hougen and Stenberger since they could catch a ride with the government plane from St Anthony. After a round of good-byes in the village, which Anne Stine remarked in her journal became more and more difficult each year, they also said their farewells in St Anthony before leaving for Norway.

Helge and Anne Stine never knew who would still be there when they returned. Many of their old friends were gone and much would change for the younger ones now that the road had been built. Anne Stine realized a new era was approaching and they had to accept their share of the "blame" for that. Both she and Helge were afraid that their friends in the village could be compromised in the process. She liked the way it had been and wished it could stay that way, but also realized that change was inevitable. She and Helge just happened to quicken the process.

After leaving L'Anse aux Meadows, Anne Stine, Helge, and I then travelled to Buenos Aires for an International Congress of Americanists conference together with Yvonne and Thor Heyerdahl. This was the first time Helge and Anne Stine presented their material from L'Anse aux Meadows to a wider audience of scholars. They were a bit anxious to see how some would respond to their findings, but it went well and they received a very positive response.

When they arrived back in Norway, some good news was waiting. Radiocarbon dating of a whalebone Mårten Stenberger had found in one of the house sites had come back with a register of about A.D. 1025 (with the obligatory plus and minus 100). The news could not have been better.

Every single spring for several years, both Anne Stine and Helge claimed that "this would be the last expedition." However, new features and artifacts continued to be found that made it important for them to travel there "just one more time." The season of 1967 was no exception. They had found two new rooms that had to be more closely examined and there were also indications that there was more to House A than originally realized. In addition to this, they had long been aware of some elevated areas in the turf on the terrace farther down from the houses that they suspected could be boat sheds. Therefore, another expedition was planned in 1968, but this time it truly was to be the last.

This last expedition consisted of a more balanced male–female ratio of Norwegian experts than before. In addition to Anne Stine and Helge, there was also the pollen analyst Kari Henningsmoen again, archaeologists Sigrid Hillern Hansen and Arne Emil Christensen, and, later in the season, Birgitta Wallace. Christensen was an expert on boats and boat sheds from the Viking era and was assigned the task of excavating the suspicious elevations down by the beach. His conclusion was that these were man-made and in total consisted of four boat sheds.

Anne Stine had long suspected that House A, situated closest to the brook, could have been something more than what was earlier believed. The first time it was excavated was in 1961, and it was I who primarily sat there and dug. Only a thin layer covered by much gravel was first discovered – no real signs of any cultural layers. The second time it was excavated, the Icelanders dug a test trench and found signs of a deeper cultural layer.

Anne Stine now decided to give it another try to see what secrets lay hidden there. She followed the Icelanders' trench and soon found that, sure enough, there was a deeper cultural level. The originally excavated upper layer must have been disturbed from regular flooding of Black Duck Brook. The new cultural layer looked promising. It proved to be a large longhouse that included four rooms in total. Parts of the walls had been washed away from the flooding, but in other places they were very visible. Excavations revealed two doorways, several large cooking pits with partially burnt stones, and more hearths, iron rivets, and a type of jasper. The house was clearly a longhouse of the same kind as the houses found in Iceland and Greenland.

Then one rainy day in early fall, while everyone lay scraping away in their assigned areas, Sigrid Hillern Hansen suddenly said:

"Anne Stine, I have [a piece of] bronze here."

"No," replied Anne Stine, "that isn't possible, it must be that green stone that has fooled me so many times over the years."

"No Anne Stine, it's bronze," insisted Hillern.

Anne Stine ran to get a brush and together they leaned over the piece of bronze.

"You dig."

"No, you."

Neither one of them dared, it was all too exciting.

Sigrid made a careful stroke and more of the green appeared. Both the women let out a squeal. Sigrid brushed again and even more green appeared. There was now about eight centimetres visible of something that must have been a pin. They squealed again and held their breath. Both were very aware of its historical importance. Sigrid made the last few brush strokes, which completely tipped the balance. They howled, screamed, hugged each other, and fell over like they had gone mad. In between them lay the most beautiful little ring-headed pin anyone could have wished for. Then they put a bucket over the pin and waited for the others to get there, which Anne Stine thought took an eternity.[58] Hearing the women's screaming and commotion, the others had come running. When Anne Stine lifted the bucket, they all stood there absolutely speechless.

The bronze ring-headed pin as it was found.

The rest of the day was spent photographing the ring-headed pin from all angles and sides. Not daring to pick it up out of the dirt, they cut out a square of earth including the pin and made a special box for it. A few days later, Helge wrote in his journal: "It is September 2nd, the 50th anniversary of my school graduation. My peers are gathered in Oslo to celebrate, but I am enjoying it more here with the [discovery of the] ring-headed pin."[59]

The discovery of the house sites and the spindle whorl were already enough evidence that proved the ruins were Norse. However, the ring-headed pin was a pleasant, definitive "crowning glory" of proof. Tourists flocked to L'Anse aux Meadows that summer. They came by helicopter and seaplane, by car all the way from New York and with huge buses from Minnesota. It seemed clear that this was about to become a very popular tourist attraction.

Anne Stine and Helge now considered their work at L'Anse aux Meadows finished. They had found and excavated eight Norse-type houses, one of them a smithy, in addition to four boat sheds. They found a spindle whorl, a ring-headed pin, and remains of a Norse-type sewing needle of bone, various rivets, jasper, as well as various artifacts from the Dorset culture and other aboriginal peoples. Several radiocarbon dating tests placed the majority of the results to be around the year A.D. 1000.

The original walls and floors of the ruins, including hearths, cooking pits, and ember pit were covered with turf and restored to their original state to help preserve them. Anne Stine believed that it was important to leave them in this condition so that future archaeologists could have the possibility of looking at them with a fresh perspective and new methods. Besides, it was most important for the original ruins to be showcased to the public. Helge and Anne Stine explained their reasoning to the governmental officials of Newfoundland when they ended their excavations.

Later that fall, Anne Stine and Helge were in Iceland to present a lecture. There they met Eldjàrn, who was now the president of Iceland, and were invited to dinner at the presidential residence Bessastadir. They presented their latest findings and analysis results, and Eldjàrn stated that he was now finally convinced that the ruins at L'Anse aux Meadows were Norse.

To Helluland

Anne Stine considered herself finished with the cold excavations at Newfoundland and looked forward to relaxing summers at Maribuseter. For Helge, however, one thing still remained unfinished. He was convinced that he had found Leifsbudir, the houses of Leif Eiriksson, as well as Vinland. He was almost certain that Markland had to be the Labrador coast south of Hamilton Inlet and that Kjalarnes was Cape Porcupine with those long beaches on both sides of the headland and that dense pine forest that reached all the way to the beach. But he had not yet found a landscape that resembled Helluland, Land of the Flat Stones, of the Sagas. If he could establish with reasonable certainty that this was Baffin Island, then all the travel distances, directions, and other such information would fall into place.

At the end of June 1970, he took off again on another expedition. He had just turned seventy. Anne Stine refused to let him go exploring in northern Canada on his own, so he took along two young assistants, Bjørn Økern and Nicolay Eckhoff. They first flew to Montreal, where they rented a suite at the Sheraton Hotel and spread aerial photos of Baffin Island, borrowed from the Canadian Air Force, across the floor. They laid on their stomachs for a week staring at the stereoscopic photos, a type of 3-D imaging taken by two cameras angled towards each other. Wearing the necessary glasses, the three men scoured the entire coastline in three dimensions. They looked for cairns, house sites, or any other traces of Norse, but found nothing. Helge didn't actually think they would find anything like this, as the Sagas said that Helluland was a barren and disagreeable land that sent the Norsemen sailing farther south. However, the distance from Baffin Island to the settlements at Greenland was relatively short. Helge thought that perhaps the Norse could have erected cairns and simple dwellings which could have provided shelter for the night. Their main lead was *The Saga of the Greenlanders*, which described Helluland as Bjarni Herjulfsson had seen it: "There was no grass. The inward land had large glaciers, but from the sea and to the glaciers the land was like a giant flat stone."[60] Could they find this landscape?

From Montreal, they flew to Frobisher Bay and landed at Iqaluit. To a large degree, the community confirmed Helge's own judgments of the damage "civilization" can cause when it clashes with the indigenous way of life in the Arctic. After a few days here, they then flew across Cumberland Sound stopping briefly in another small village called Pangnirtung, a hamlet of about six hundred Inuit residents. According to Helge, these people were doing somewhat better than those in Frobisher Bay. Modern times had not yet fully affected the people, for whom hunting was still very much a way of life.

Continuing their journey north and following the eastern coastline of Baffin Island, they then landed on Broughton Island at Qikiqtarjuaq. From here they planned to explore by boat, but were held up for several days due to an unusual amount of drift ice. Eventually the ice dissipated enough for Inuit Thomasee Kooneloosie and his nephew Peter to take them in his 20-foot wooden boat south towards Cape Dyer. It was a strenuous trip with many near episodes of getting stuck in the drift ice. Once when they did get stuck, Helge and the others hopped out onto a thick sheet of ice to push it away. Unluckily, Helge slipped and broke a few ribs as he smashed onto the ice and fell into the water. He was hauled in quickly, shivered horribly, and was sent down into the boat to dry off. But they continued sailing south and explored the beaches along the way. They found a few old Inuit ruins here and there, but no signs of the Norse. At Cape Dyer, they turned around and headed north back to Broughton Island.

They were then able to catch a ride on a small plane headed north to Clyde River. As they flew over the wild landscape, they could see high mountains and white glaciers farther inland to the west. They also spotted a strange peninsula that jutted out into the sea: Cape Aston, the area they wanted to reach once they landed at Clyde River. They hired a guide named Kidlaq, a pleasant fellow who knew the coastline well, and a younger kid, Julio, as interpreter. They took off in two canoes with outboard motors. The ice conditions here in the north were fortunately a little more favourable than they had been in the south.

As they travelled up the outer edge of the Cape Aston peninsula, they stopped midway and pulled the canoes ashore. The coast here was so flat that it looked like it had been measured with a ruler and cut clean. All along the coast stretched a broad white beach that turned directly into a land of flat stones. It was a barren area, but farther inland rose incredible mountains glistening with white glaciers.

Helge walked a good distance inland and got a strong impression of how remarkably flat this land was, all the way up to the foot of the mountains. Yes, this must be it! This must be Helluland, Land of the Flat Stones. It was exactly as described in the story of when Bjarni Herjulfsson and Leif Eiriksson came upon land in the *Saga of the Greenlanders*. Only 80 nautical miles to the east was Disko Island, the Norse people's old hunting grounds. It was inevitable that over the years these seafaring people had come to exactly the spot where Helge now stood, not only in the quest for new lands, but also on hunting expeditions.

Helge was now at the end of his journey following the trail of Leif Eiriksson. He strongly believed that he had found Leifsbudir in Vinland, had walked the long beaches in what had to be Markland, and now finally stood in Helluland. It was time to go home. Now the only thing that remained was to "just" write a book.

16 NEW STORMS

The dispute over the discoveries eventually quieted down. But was it too good to last? A sign of impending problems arrived in a letter to Helge in 1969 from Dave Webber, director of the History Department at the Ministry of Provincial Affairs in Newfoundland. He explained that after realizing the great importance of the finds at L'Anse aux Meadows, responsibility for them would be transferred to the National Historic Sites Services, administered by Parks Canada, which oversaw all important historical sites in the country. Parks Canada would manage all practical aspects of the site. An International Research Advisory would also be formed to help formulate a plan for further development of the area and "the [site] would be given priority over all other similar places in Canada."[1]

So far so good. Later, however, Anne Stine and Helge received a message, more like an order, that all notes, drawings, photographs, and the like were to be sent immediately so that the new International Research Advisory could be in possession of all information. The committee wanted the findings to be assessed from a pooled collection of all material – of "written records and archeological finds ... all efforts are to be made to ensure a correct interpretation."[2]

Helge sent a clear message in return: neither he nor the other researchers could understandably send the material before they were finished processing it. And how would they ensure that no such material would not fall into the wrong hands before Helge and his team had published? He referred to the situation with Farley Mowat and the layout drawings which, against Helge's wishes, were released by the same authority that was now ordering him to relinquish all data. He also said that he considered such a "control committee" to be an insult to himself and his scientific colleagues. He ended the letter by saying:

It is of course up to the Government of Newfoundland to decide how they will best manage L'Anse aux Meadows, but if such an international committee is desired, then we will withdraw from everything that involves the planning and preservation of the findings ... I will add that I and members of the international expedition team did not expect such a letter after eight years of procuring for the Newfoundland Government the first known Viking settlement on the continent, and one of the most important tourist attractions in North America.[3]

This was strong ammunition. Every researched site includes journal notes and photographs that are the researcher's own, and no government can claim ownership. In addition, most of the notes in this case were written in a language that the committee could not understand, unless they were Scandinavian. This is what Helge feared might happen: that the Danish researchers who had been so against him would now come in and gain final control over the findings.

Helge wrote to Junius Bird about the situation and mentioned that he was also a little hurt that he had never received any official thanks from the government authorities of Newfoundland for what he had done for them. With relatively little financial support from them,[4] he and Anne Stine had devoted a combined total of sixteen years of work to L'Anse aux Meadows. They had to acquire money from other sources to pay for virtually every expense. This important tourist attraction had so far cost Newfoundland very little in terms of funding or effort.

"A crisis is brewing"

In 1970, when the government of Newfoundland decided to transfer responsibility of the management of L'Anse aux Meadows to the federal government, it was a rather reluctant decision. A few Newfoundland authorities were concerned about this move due to dissatisfaction with Parks Canada's work on other protected sites in the province. The reason for the transfer, however, was that the Viking ruins were of *national* importance.

A national park was established covering a relatively large area that also included the local community of L'Anse aux Meadows and the surrounding small islands. Helge and Anne Stine were concerned about the consequences that this would have on the local population's use of the area and its natural resources. The Decker family's burial plot and the outermost headland also fell within the proposed park area. Because of this, Helge and Anne Stine emphasized in a letter to the government how important it was that the local community be able to preserve both its freedom and unique character. In addition, they stipulated that they would continue their work only if the Colbourne family who lived on the headland were not forced to move or restricted from bringing fish ashore. This condition was accepted.

In 1969, Helge and Anne Stine once again departed for St John's, Newfoundland. This time, the purpose of the journey was for Helge to receive an honorary doctorate degree from Memorial University of Newfoundland.

In 1970, Parks Canada, with its newly assumed responsibility for L'Anse aux Meadows National Historic Site, had agreed that development would continue and be prioritized on a national level. In 1972, an International Research and Development Committee was established to oversee development of the site as a tourist attraction and for future study and research. Helge conceded to this, but was able to influence the selection of an "amiable" Danish Viking expert, Ole Crumlin Pedersen from the Roskilde Museum, as representative of Denmark. Anne Stine and Helge were asked to sit on the committee as representatives of Norway, along with Professor Sverre Marstrander.[5]

In March 1972, Peter H. Bennett, assistant director of the National Historic Sites Services, also asked Helge and Anne Stine to be paid consultants for further development of the site as a tourist attraction. They accepted, on the condition that they be consulted prior to any work and that they would be assured their advice would be taken into account. Helge further clarified that these conditions pertained to "the archeological work connected with the stabilization and restoration of the sites." It was also expected they would continue as members of the international committee while they also served as scholarly consultants.[6] Moreover, Helge clearly expressed that no work was to be conducted in the area around the brook as they themselves had set this area aside and hoped to excavate it at a later date.

No written confirmation from Bennett accepting these conditions has been found in the archives. Helge and Anne Stine interpreted his silence as consent when they continued as members of the International Research and Development Committee. At the time, there was no evidence of any official plan for further excavations by Parks Canada alone.

The committee held its first meeting in St John's in May 1972, followed by a trip to L'Anse aux Meadows. According to the official notes from the meeting, there was agreement to protect the original excavated sites; the turf walls were not to be tampered with and were to remain in the original state they were found as much as possible and covered with earth for protection. This was in line with my parents' wishes. Another important point was to protect the ruins from the annual flooding of Black Duck Brook. They agreed to tear down the protective shelters that had been constructed, as they seemed to be causing more harm than good. Anne Stine and Helge conveyed their concern about having engineers without any archaeological expertise wandering around the ruins and strongly emphasized that all such operations had to involve them.

A letter dated 4 August 1972 from J.H. Gordon to Ed Roberts[7] implies that Parks Canada already had other plans for the site and seemed intent on pushing Anne Stine and Helge out of the picture. The letter discussed planned excavations the following summer as well as the search for a competent archaeologist who could live onsite during the summers for a two- to three-year project. Parks Canada planned to use $2 million on the project over the course of a five-year period. Swedish archaeologist Bengt Schönbäck was selected as chief archaeologist and was later assisted by Birgitta Wallace.

In June of 1975, Anne Stine and Helge were on a quick trip to L'Anse aux Meadows as part of a guided tour for the Canadian prime minister, Pierre Elliott Trudeau. The two noticed that plastic lines were strung across the ground in House F, as was the norm when marking archaeological test trenches. Anne Stine was taken aback and asked Schönbäck about the markers. He told her that they were set up as markers for the engineers who were to tear down the temporary shelter.[8] At the International Research Advisory Committee meeting held in January 1975, Anne Stine had raised the question of further excavations. The official minutes from the meeting state: "Mrs. Ingstad raised the issue of conservation of the original foundations (sod walls) and reiterated her earlier point that all the original evidence must remain untouched and not removed during future archeological work."[9]

The minutes of this committee meeting also state that, after a lengthy discussion, agreement was reached: first, the original turf walls in principle should be preserved as they were, and second, if there were important issues concerning this, Schönbäck was to consult with Anne Stine. However, it was added that Schönbäck should have "a certain degree of freedom during examination of the site to allow for effective daily work."[10]

A clear understanding, thought Anne Stine. However, it was not as clear as she thought. In August 1975, she agreed with Schönbäck and Wallace that, before the following committee meeting, she would travel to L'Anse aux Meadows to finalize House F, which Anne Stine thought would involve scraping away loose gravel before covering the house site with turf. This had been discussed, and agreed upon, by Schönbäck, Professor Marstrander, Helge, and Anne Stine at a meeting in Oslo in April.[11]

House F was one of the largest houses with a total of six rooms, where Anne Stine had spent many hours over the last several years carefully scraping to expose contours of walls, hearths, cooking pits, and much more. However, when she arrived in August, she was shocked at what she saw. Huge trenches were dug across the site. Large parts of the floor and the delicate contours of the turf walls were gone, as was an original hearth. Terribly shaken, she asked Schönbäck, while in the presence of Wallace, what the purpose of the digging was. She was told that he had wanted to find out if there could be an older house under the original floor. This was an issue that Anne Stine had ruled out long ago, and he could have easily contacted her, as was the agreement.

This disloyal and unethical conduct from a colleague shook Anne Stine; she felt it showed a complete disregard for her own and others' work. Schönbäck's reply was that when the trenches were filled in again and turf placed on top, everything would be restored. He also argued that "nothing should remain when you are finished with an excavation." This issue represented two fundamentally different and competing views of archaeology: a total excavation, when an historical ruin has to be removed (for example with road construction), and a strategic research excavation, which aims to protect the most important elements of a site. Anne Stine's response was that throughout the entire excavation, she had focused on retaining the authentic features, both to preserve the original Norse settlement and to save something for later generations of archaeologists to research. The possibility of attaining either of these objectives was forever gone for this house. In addition, she was never consulted, as was agreed at the committee meeting the previous January.

She also eventually learned from the locals in L'Anse aux Meadows that during the previous year, several other houses, now covered with turf, had also been dug out and "rebuilt" in the same manner. On top of the turf that covered House B, a "copy of a hearth" was set up, but not in keeping with the original find. Incredibly, the ruin had been scraped away and covered with new sod.

After Anne Stine had seen what she strongly believed was the destruction of House F, she sent a telegram to Helge in Norway and told him that she wanted to return home immediately and that she would not attend the upcoming committee meeting. But he managed to persuade her to stay and then flew to Newfoundland a few days later to see the state of the site for himself.

The committee meeting this time was held at L'Anse aux Meadows. Schönbäck argued that all the house walls should be scraped away and a reconstruction be built in their place. Anne Stine and Helge insisted, once again, that the walls and as many of the original Norse features as possible be retained. If these requests were not respected, they would withdraw from the committee.

My parents returned home and thought very hard about what to do. They discussed the situation with Professor Marstrander, who supported them fully. Helge wrote a letter to Pat Thomson, Parks Canada regional director of the Atlantic region, providing an account of their views on the matter: "This letter is to inform Parks Canada that we consider certain aspects of Dr. Schönbäck's activities in connection with the L'Anse aux Meadows project to be so appalling that we find it impossible to continue to cooperate with him."[12] Helge goes on to say that if Schönbäck were allowed to continue with his position for Parks Canada, or as a member of the International Advisory Committee, both he and Anne Stine would resign from the committee. This stand was also being taken by the third Norwegian member of the committee, Professor Sverre Marstrander, director of the Museum of Cultural History at the University of Oslo. Helge concluded the letter by stating:

> Since the discoveries are now so famous around the world, it
> will be inevitable that the press will require an explanation as to
> why so many have withdrawn from working with Parks Canada.
> We would of course like to avoid giving such an explanation,
> but if it is in the interest of all our scientific colleagues to

do so, we will try to do our best to minimize the damage to Parks Canada.[13]

Perhaps this was a drastic measure, but not completely out of the question. Thomson must have needed time to consider the options and consult with his colleagues at Parks Canada as he didn't respond for three months. He said he regretted that Helge and Anne Stine had not addressed the issue at a committee meeting so that it could have been resolved in person and pointed out that a public conflict between committee members would only reduce the significance of the discovery of the site in the eyes of the national and international community.

He further stated: "It must be pointed out that L'Anse aux Meadows is now a 'National Historic Site' which means that certain information is now required that was not previously needed. We must, for example, have more details about the circumference of those parts of the buildings that you intentionally did not excavate since such information was not necessary for your purposes."[14] This, he argued, was the main reason why they set up an archaeological program. He claimed that Anne Stine and Helge were reasonably forewarned and given time to respond.

Thomson also said that most of what Anne Stine interpreted as destruction of House F was due to the demolition of the protection shelters. He added that "my colleagues and I have studied the accusations but have concluded that not a single finding (hearth, postholes, ember chamber) has been destroyed or removed during the course of Parks Canada excavations."[15] He concluded that Parks Canada's experts find Dr Schönbäck's work at L'Anse aux Meadows to be fully acceptable and gave him their full support. Thomson also stated that Schönbäck offered to resign due to the criticism, but Parks Canada did not accept his resignation because they believed that he had worked within the guidelines provided by the International Committee.

Helge and Anne Stine's grievances could not have been more clearly marginalized. They felt that Parks Canada had a completely different sense of the situation. Their friend Bill Taylor from the museum in Ottawa also wrote a letter to Helge and Anne Stine supporting Parks Canada's position, which was especially upsetting.

Through the years, Anne Stine had left contact with the Newfoundland government authorities and Parks Canada to Helge, but now she felt compelled to write a letter to Parks Canada Regional Director

Thomson.[16] In her message, she emphasized that House F could not have been destroyed by the deconstruction of the protective sheds as Parks Canada, and Schönbäck and later Wallace, claimed. This is because all the posts had stood in the walls of the ruins and not in the middle of the house (see picture of House F in colour section) Therefore, such work could not have affected the central parts of the house site as Schönbäck's trenches did. She ends the letter by saying:

> I feel Schönbäck's conduct to be incredibly impertinent. It includes demeaning the work I have conducted throughout the years on L'Anse aux Meadows as head archeologist. However, it does not affect just Helge and I, but also all the experts from the various countries who have participated in our expeditions and who have completed their excavations with the utmost care. I would never have behaved so disloyally towards either Schönbäck or any other archeologist ... Since I have been exposed to such disrespect I can no longer continue working with Parks Canada as long as Schönbäck is affiliated with the L'Anse aux Meadows project.[17]

At the same time, Helge wrote a letter to James Channing, the clerk of the Executive Council of the Government of Newfoundland, outlining what he described as "Dr. Schönbäck's regrettable activities at the Viking site."[18] He further stated that he had considered contacting the Secretary of State in Ottawa but had decided against it because "[bad] press about the conflict would damage the Viking Settlement as a tourist attraction and Newfoundland's interests."[19]

The letter from Helge spurred Channing to write a letter stamped "confidential" to Frank D. Moores, the premier of Newfoundland, which stated:

> There is absolutely no doubt that Newfoundland is completely indebted to Dr. Ingstad and his wife, and that their views on the development of the site cannot be ignored ... The transfer of responsibility of the site from Newfoundland to the central government of Canada was not an easy decision and was made with considerable reservation. The reason for the uncertainty was due to previous significant dissatisfaction with Parks Canada in this province.[20]

He further expressed concern that both Newfoundland, and Canada as a nation, would be damaged if the nature of the conflict were to be made known. That is why Premier Moores wrote back to Channing saying that "a crisis is brewing."[21]

Discussions around the issue eventually calmed, to an extent. Helge and Anne Stine were reluctantly persuaded to join the International Advisory Committee again, but their relationship with Parks Canada forever remained strained and full of mistrust. Committee meetings began to wane and then ended all together.

It seems that 1976 was the last year Parks Canada excavated at L'Anse aux Meadows, when the visitor centre opened with its exhibits. Schönbäck also apparently ended his contract with Parks Canada at the same time, but Wallace remained with the organization as the L'Anse aux Meadows resident expert and spokeswoman.

During the dispute with Schönbäck, Wallace had supported her superior while she simultaneously stepped forward as an "expert," highlighting her participation in the initial excavations at L'Anse aux Meadows. She secured a position as archaeologist with Parks Canada with special responsibility for L'Anse aux Meadows, which allowed her to participate in the excavations with Schönbäck.[22] Anne Stine found it especially hard that Wallace, the young student whom she had taken under her wing, could turn against her during the conflict.

Parks Canada was a powerful organization supported by acts of Parliament and federal funding. However, they seemed to have a similar reputation for managing other such sites around Canada as they did at L'Anse aux Meadows. At the time, plans were to focus much of the agency's attention towards L'Anse aux Meadows for a five-year period and make it into one of the country's most important tourist attractions. Perhaps an aging Norwegian "discoverer" and his archaeologist wife were considered more of a hitch in the plan than a resource. That the "discoverer" did not let go so easily and instead threatened to withdraw his involvement, resulting in a potential public scandal, made him a thorn in their side.

When Parks Canada employed its own archaeologists for the L'Anse aux Meadows site, it was a clear sign that the agency wanted to conduct its own excavations, make its own discoveries, and publish its own scientific reports. However, the removal of the original turf walls led to meagre results: a single glass pearl. The surrounding terrain unearthed more: a plank that appeared to be a floorboard of a Viking ship, some twine made of twigs, and two butternuts that have never been dated. In Parks Canada's reports of their own excavations, it was stated all too clearly that extensive re-excavation had been completed on all the houses. This meant the removal of most of the elements of the houses: walls, hearths, postholes, cultural layers, and more. In addition, long trenches were dug across a relatively large area of the ruins and the sections that Anne Stine had chosen to set aside for "future archeologists with new methods" was completely dug up. The boat sheds which Arne Emil Christensen had so carefully excavated, and which he was always convinced were man-made,[23] were "defined" by Parks Canada as nothing more than natural turf ridges and therefore removed. Christensen's layout diagrams and charts of this section are not to be found in the visitor centre or on maps of the site.

Doctoral Degree, Recognition, and More Illness

The pressure to complete the final L'Anse aux Meadows scientific publication was relentless. There was some relief when, in 1970, Anne Stine published an article in the prominent archaeological journal *Acta Arkeologica*.[24] However, she still had to finish the enormous cross-compiled manuscript. In addition to her own research, which was a central part of the manuscript, layout charts of the site needed to be drawn and the other scholars' research and analyses had to be collected and included.

Despite the challenges, things were not all bad all of the time. In August 1974, P.V. Glob, the director of Cultural Heritage in Copenhagen, invited Anne Stine to travel to the Eastern Settlement in Greenland with a group of experts from Nordic museums who were going to inspect the ruins and plan the coming year's work. This invitation warmed my mother's heart and proved that even Danish colleagues were acknowledging both her and Helge for their work. However, she became sick before the trip and could not go, so Professor Sverre Marstrander travelled in her place.

While waiting for her co-workers to submit their final reports on L'Anse aux Meadows, Anne Stine, quite unexpectedly, became inspired to write a narrative account about her experiences during the excavations. She felt that there was so much to tell about the people and land, about funny and difficult episodes – everything a scientific report could never contain. Her book, *The New Land with the Green Meadows*, was published in 1975 and was well received by the public.[25]

In October 1976, Anne Stine wrote a letter to Eldjàrn concerning some edits in his section of the report. At the end of this letter, she wrote: "I myself am so tired of the book and will dread when it comes out. But no matter what kind of criticism I may get, I'll be very glad to be done with it. It has been one long nightmare; so much pain and difficulty has been involved with it."

The report, a large book titled *The Discovery of a Norse Settlement in America*, was completed in the spring of 1977 as volume 1. Volume 2, Helge's historical account, was published later in 1985. About the same time, Anne Stine submitted her work as part of a dissertation for a doctoral degree at the University of Oslo. She hesitated doing so for a long while but was persuaded by Helge and her colleagues. A doctoral degree awarded on the basis of the material would be a professional stamp of credibility, a convincing piece of evidence that would be good to have should there be future controversy. My father had also considered pursuing a doctoral degree with his historical research, but decided not to.

Shortly after she completed all this demanding work, and while the conflict with Parks Canada still raged, Anne Stine had a small stroke that led to partial paralysis of her left side. Knowing that mental health can affect physical health, it is not inconceivable that the stress and pressure she was under contributed to her stroke. Luckily, my mother was treated quickly and she suffered only minor repercussions in the form of a weakness in one leg.

Anne Stine's doctoral dissertation was accepted, and in November 1978, only half a year after her stroke, she was scheduled to defend her dissertation. The night before the big event, she received a telephone call from the Norwegian Royal Palace. Crown Princess Sonja wanted to attend Anne Stine's dissertation defence. Would she mind? This could easily have rattled any doctoral candidate, but Anne Stine took it quite calmly. Of course she wouldn't mind.

The following day, Anne Stine stood in the beautiful old banquet hall of the University of Oslo with the Crown Princess of Norway seated in the front row. The dissertation committee praised her work and had little to criticize. I think that was the only time in her life, except for

Archaeological work can be intricate. Here Anne Stine patiently brushes away the dirt. Notice ring-headed pin in the earth, lower right corner.

when she found the spindle whorl and ring-headed pin at the excavation site, that she was truly happy about her Vinland work.

Afterwards, peers from around the world showered Anne Stine with praise and recognition for her successful doctoral achievement. And those who were considered experts of the Viking and medieval ages seemed to have dampened their skepticism and criticism. The status of the discovery at L'Anse aux Meadows as being a Norse settlement seemed now to be generally accepted.

The government of Newfoundland also finally understood the full potential of the discovery. In 1979, Anne Stine was awarded an honorary doctorate from Memorial University of Newfoundland in St John's (Helge had received the same in 1969) and a building on the campus was named in honour of both Helge and Anne Stine. Both my mother and father appreciated these honours as well as the public support and acknowledgment from Newfoundland for what they had done for the province.

The "Last Straw" of Conflict

Soon after Anne Stine had finished her doctoral dissertation, more conflict arose. This time it came from a Canadian archaeologist, Thomas E. Lee, who was considered controversial in certain academic circles. Years earlier, Lee had failed his doctoral examination at the University of Michigan and afterward made himself quite unpopular in certain academic circles by sending complaints to a number of prominent archaeologists. He later declined to take the exam again, but still continued to lead several expeditions and was unofficially recognized as an archaeologist.[26] Lee was also the self-appointed editor of the *Anthropological Journal of Canada*, which meant that he had access to a public forum and control over what was published.

Back in January 1966, my parents were informed about possible discoveries on Pamioq Island in Ungava Bay in northern Quebec, Canada. Jacques Rousseau, director of research at the Northern Studies Centre of Laval University, announced that the ruins were of Norse-type longhouses. The excavations were led by Lee, and later assisted by his son, Robert. Helge thought it was very interesting news and immediately inquired about travelling to see the ruins the following summer. He was coolly declined.

Some scholars were skeptical of this discovery, and experts on the Dorset culture claimed to have found similar Dorset ruins in several other places in Arctic Canada.[27] Lee, now older, reacted negatively to his life's work being clouded in doubt and reacted even more so when Helge announced his discovery as "the first confirmed Norse site in America"[28]

When Anne Stine wrote her doctoral thesis, she mentioned Lee's findings in Ungava Bay and pointed out interesting parallels with Norse ruins. However, she presented good reasons to dispute his final assumption. But she still positively summarized his work by saying, "I agree with Thomas Lee when he says that the Norse Greenlanders must be considered, but to use this material beyond its capacity harms any objective assessment ... this material includes so many interesting problems, that we can only hope that further excavations can shed light upon them."[29]

Apparently, this was not to Lee's liking. After Anne Stine's book was published in 1977, he seemed intent on crushing her professional reputation. In 1982, Lee, his son Robert, and a few other scholars selected to support Lee's arguments, wrote a series of articles in the *Anthropological Journal of Canada* about how the ruins at L'Anse aux Meadows could not be Norse.[30] They made strong accusations: for example, that the government and public were being "hoaxed," that there was "a manipulative and deliberate cover up of conflicting facts," that the work was "incompetently carried out," and that the spindle whorl (presumably also the ring-headed pin) "were brought from Norway and planted."

The articles written by Lee senior and junior also had a very condescending tone, especially when they referred to Anne Stine as "Annie," a nickname she had never used. All other researchers were referred to by their last names. The tone was even more severe in the Lee's correspondence with Edward Roberts, Canadian politician and previous lieutenant-governor of Newfoundland and Labrador, in which it appeared that Lee was bent on revenge for not receiving either the funding or the recognition that L'Anse aux Meadows did.[31] The correspondence also revealed that Farley Mowat[32] and Harald Horwood were close acquaintances of Lee and often talked with him on the telephone. Lee also tried to get an article published claiming that the proof of L'Anse aux Meadows was fraudulent, but no newspaper accepted it for publication.

Not much later, an article in a Newfoundland newspaper allegedly mentioned that Anne Stine had brought the spindle whorl and ring-headed pin from Norway and planted these artifacts in the ruins at

L'Anse aux Meadows.[33] Who was behind this article? Was it Lee, Mowat, Horwood? Or perhaps a couple of them? Whoever it was, the situation affected Anne Stine deeply.

Likewise, at a Viking conference in Denmark, Sigrid Hillern Hansen was seated beside an American professor. The man, who did not know that Sigrid had been a part of the team at the L'Anse aux Meadows excavations, made a passing comment about how regrettable it was that Mr and Mrs Ingstad had planted the ring-headed pin at the ruins. To this, Sigrid replied, "If anyone had planted the pin, it would have had to have been me since I am the one who found it!" The professor suddenly grew uneasy and didn't say a word. Infuriated, Sigrid got up and left.[34]

Sigrid later related the incident to Anne Stine, who of course took it very hard. To be accused of being deceitful and fraudulent was the "last straw" for Anne Stine, and after that she wanted nothing more to do with the Vinland discovery.

17 LIFE AFTER VINLAND

Throughout all the years of the Vinland expeditions and the subsequent commotion, life back home in Norway never stood still, even though at times it felt like it did. Both happy and sad events occurred in our family during those years. One of the sad ones was the death of my grand-mother Louise in 1967. Her heart finally gave out. She was convinced that it had been the war and the anxieties it created for her, worry over her husband and sons, and, in the end, Tycho's death. My grandmother represented sound stability in an otherwise turbulent family situation. I doubt I would have landed on my feet as an adult if it had not been for her. For Anne Stine, her mother had been a source of support, but also of guilt and expectations – someone to whom Anne Stine was deeply connected, but still had the need to tear herself away from (but never managed to). For Helge, Louise had helped him more than he was ever aware. If she hadn't been there at Brattalid during the times he was away on expeditions, lecture tours, or writing sojourns and when Anne Stine was away excavating, family life would not have functioned.

During my schooling at university, I met medical student Edwin Sandberg and eventually married him in 1968. Without living with him beforehand (unthinkable at the time) and knowing relatively little about marriage, I must say that I was lucky. Edwin was what my mother called "the salve" in our family: kind and easygoing with always a quick, witty response to things. Edwin came from the southwestern coastal town of Stavanger and hadn't skied much before coming to Oslo. However, he transitioned well and became not only a keen skier but also eventually a dog musher – in other words, the perfect son-in-law for my father too. Most importantly, he was able to handle becoming part of a well-known family while maintaining his own identity and self-esteem.

I tried to distance myself from my parents and everything connected with the turbulence around Vinland when I got married, but did not get very far since my husband and I built a house only 40 metres away from Brattalid. After a while, Helge and Anne Stine's grandchildren came one by one: little Helge, Ingunn, Kristin, and then Eirik, Anne, and, the youngest, Marit. Growing up as an only child, I knew that I wanted to have several children as an adult. Anne Stine enjoyed being a grandmother, even though it did not always suit her busy schedule. She especially focused her attentions on little Helge, who we soon discovered was severely disabled and therefore needed much care. He was her special grandson. Helge also appreciated being a grandfather, but when most of his grandchildren were young he was much too busy with his own life to take the job very seriously.

For all the years that Anne Stine worked on the Vinland project, she did so mostly as an unpaid scholar. But in 1977, she was given a Norwegian lifelong government grant. Finally she was earning her own salary, although it initially consisted of only 42,000 Norwegian kroner a year. The disadvantage of this was that colleagues thought they could unload some of their workload onto her since she now had a government salary. Her greatest joy during this time was working with the Oseberg textiles (found in a queen's grave chamber of the Oseberg Viking ship). She had promised Professor Bjørn Hougen before he died that she would finish this work, something she herself barely managed to do just before she died. She was in her element with this work. She was able to revive her old weaving skills, was given an office in the Viking ship museum, and enjoyed a work environment that was all her own and had nothing to do with Vinland.

Helge as Activist

It was both surprising and predictable when my father got involved in the 1970s debate over Norway joining the European Common Market. Surprising because, despite his general interest in society, he had never before gotten involved in party politics, which this debate was about. Predictable because this issue hit a patriotic nerve in Helge related to several events: Norway's independence from Sweden in 1905, the German occupation of Norway during the Second World War, and, not least, the loss of Norwegian territory in East Greenland, which also meant the loss of hunting rights. The slogan "Sovereignty of Our Country" was what primarily inspired him to get involved. He began by holding a speech in front of the City Hall during a large demonstration opposing Norway's membership into the Common Market:

> We are now facing one of the most important decisions in our country's history. The question is: Should we continue to rule over our own country or should we essentially relinquish control of the legacy of our past generations? ... In key areas our sovereignty would be slashed, yes common [market] rules would even come before our own constitution. We would increasingly be subject to a distant governance from the enormous Brussels bureaucracy without the safety that lies in [our own] parliamentary control.[1]

It was also typical of my father that when he first got involved in something, he was very thorough about it. This time was no different, and he travelled extensively talking with experts in economics, politics, fisheries, oil production, and much more. He wrote articles for the newspaper and read piles of books on the subject. He did not want anyone to try to stump him about any facts.

He gave two years of his life to supporting the opposition movement and almost continually wrote, spoke, and debated against Norway's joining the Common Market. Years later, Arne Haugestad, a Norwegian Supreme Court lawyer and leader of the People's Movement against Joining the EEC, wrote a eulogy for Helge describing their first meeting:

> Had I there and then drawn a living phantom image of what we most wanted, it just walked through the door ... tall and with piercing blue eyes, who neither turned away from the power of authorities or feared standing alone. Everyone knew that his life was unquestionable evidence of the importance of sometimes having to resist and persist to finally win ... against capital destruction of society, nature and certain ways of life ... If we are ever forced to do it again, we will need, perhaps more than ever, people like Helge Ingstad.[2]

When the results of the September 1972 public vote came in and presented a clear opposition majority, there was an outburst of joy and celebration at Brattalid. The next round of the European Union debate took place in 1994, but by then Helge was an old man and didn't have the energy to get involved in the same way as before. But he followed the debate closely and his point of view remained the same.

However, the old fighter wasn't yet ready to stop getting involved. This time, in the late 1970s, the battle was about a proposed hydroelectric power plant in the Alta River in northern Norway, an area populated by Norway's indigenous people, the Sami. It started with a parliamentary resolution to develop the Alta-Kautokeino watercourse, which among other things meant that areas of the beautiful Finnmark plateau and the small Sami village of Masi would be flooded. After meeting a good deal of political resistance, the plan was later modified to a less extensive plan that at least saved the town of Masi. However, they still planned to dam up the Alta River, which meant destroying a beautiful natural area and devastating the wild salmon fishing there. But a vitally important point in the whole case was that these development plans were never discussed with the Sami population: the people were never told about these plans, and those who were especially dependent on the natural resources for fishing and reindeer herding seemed to have no rights or say at all.

A people's movement was formed to help fight against the development of this Alta-Kautokeino watercourse and protests quickly grew. The opposition group advocated "passive resistance" and began planning actions to stop the machines at the construction site. In October 1979, a group of Sami held what was labelled an "illegal demonstration" when they erected a *lavvo*, a traditional tent resembling a Native American tipi, in front of the parliament in Oslo and then started a hunger strike. Helge showed up to support the demonstrators and said to journalists, "I am astounded that our politicians agree to cause irreparable damage to nature [there] and to the Sami people. The demand for Parliament to re-evaluate the Alta development is a demand of the people."[3] Helge showed up with the demonstrators several times and did his best to support them with both words and actions. In a full-page newspaper interview, he was pictured with the protesting Sami and quoted as saying that if he had been any younger, he too might have joined the hunger strike.[4]

My father then went to Alta, in northern Norway, and held a lecture on the Nunamiut and then asked for support for the Sami demonstrators. From Alta, he was going to be driven to Stilla where construction on the dam was to begin and where several demonstrators were camped trying to stop the work. He was eighty years old at the time and not very sturdy on his legs. Nonetheless, after the police stopped the car Helge was in, he got out and walked a fair distance to the demonstrators' camp.

My father stayed in the camp at Stilla for several days. I have often wondered what went through his mind as he sat there with all those demonstrators. Certainly he must have thought of his indigenous friends from Alaska, Arizona, and Canada. But perhaps he also thought of his grandmother Eilertine, who he said was a very small, religious woman from northern Norway. It is quite likely that she was a coastal Sami herself, making Helge a quarter Sami.[5] Perhaps that is why he always felt so good being together with indigenous Arctic people.

The Alta conflict escalated with massive popular protest actions in both Stilla and Oslo, and on 14 January 1980 Helge addressed one thousand people in front of the parliament building. The next day in the newspaper was a picture of a Sami woman in full traditional clothing being carried away from Stilla by four policemen. On the same page, Helge was quoted as saying these images would be sent around the world: "The police action in Stilla is a disgrace to our people. We Norwegians believe we are so openhearted and good at taking care of indigenous people. This reputation will be quite heavily tarnished out in the world after this."[6]

Helge continued to write articles on what he called the "Alta scandal" in order to support the demonstrators and the Sami cause. He also held several appeals and spoke at a large public meeting in Oslo and to the ruling Labour Party, who were then the principle opponent to the Sami cause.

The case became a prestigious battle for the government, and, as we know today, the people's movement and the Sami people lost. The Alta River Dam stands now like a monster in nature. To top it off, Gro Harlem Brundtland, prime minister at the time, admitted in 1989 that the development had been unnecessary. But out of this issue grew an increased awareness of the Sami population's identity and rights and eventually the establishment of a separate Sami parliament. The environment movement's core issues also came to light due to the Alta conflict.

At Helge's funeral, the Sami parliament placed a beautiful wreath of flowers by his coffin. To this day, it is nice to have the name Ingstad whenever I am in Sámiland.

World Heritage Site and the Opening of the Museum at L'Anse aux Meadows

After having been heavily involved in two of the most emotionally charged debates facing Norway since the war, it was now Vinland and the discovery at L'Anse aux Meadows that came to occupy most of my father's time and thought.

After the publication of Anne Stine's mainstream book in 1975, then her doctoral dissertation in 1977, followed by Helge's publication of his historical work in English, publicity about the discovery grew both in Norway and internationally. They were given awards and honorary medals, and finally Anne Stine began to receive due acknowledgment when the honours were eventually presented to both of them, a shared recognition. But invitations would arrive from the Norwegian royal palace or other institutions of high regard still addressed to "Archeologist Helge Ingstad and Mrs. Anne Stine Ingstad" or "Professor Dr. Helge Ingstad and Mrs. Ingstad." Whenever Helge was called archaeologist, Anne Stine snorted indignantly; the rest she could take.

Anne Stine loved to go to such lavish parties. She liked getting dressed up and looking beautiful and feminine. She was now making up for all that fun she missed out on while Helge was off on expeditions or lecture tours. Helge also looked nice in his tuxedo, but felt quite uncomfortable in such trappings. Anne Stine's huge fear was his table manners – or lack thereof. There was no doubt that his "fur trapper habits" didn't always suit fancy dinners. For example, he never could figure out how to handle a knife and fork, especially when there was more than one of each kind. It was even worse with finer table settings such as the embassy dinners that featured a small finger bowl at each place setting. Anne Stine, who sat across the table from Helge, once looked up and discovered to her dismay that he was about to drink from the bowl. HELGE! she whispered loudly across the table and stopped him just in time from causing what she thought would be quite an embarrassment. My father was completely unperturbed about such things but could have a good laugh afterwards when he was made aware of it.

Contact between my parents and Parks Canada had now dwindled to the point of not even existing. In 1980, Professor Sverre Marstrander wrote to Parks Canada telling them that he had not heard anything from them since September 1978. He asked if he was still considered a member of the International Advisory Committee,[7] but a reply never seems to have been made.

In 1978, UNESCO began work on establishing L'Anse aux Meadows as a World Heritage Site along with the pyramids of Egypt, Machu Picchu in Peru, and many other famous places. The formalities had taken time, but in 1980 this new UNESCO status was going to be celebrated with a ceremony at L'Anse aux Meadows including the premier and many other prominent people attending. Helge and Anne Stine received a formal invitation for the event from Parks Canada that explicitly said it could not pay for their travel or accommodation. Anne Stine refused to go, but Helge thought he should and asked the Norwegian Foreign Ministry if they could cover the costs of travel, which they did. My father travelled there together with his friend and journalist Arvid Bryne.

While at L'Anse aux Meadows, Helge later regretted not staying home. All the prominent people from UNESCO, the Newfoundland government, and Parks Canada had reserved seats in the front row. Helge and Arvid, however, had to settle for the back row, where no one took the slightest notice: he who had discovered the settlement and led the expeditions of excavating the findings. My father was furious.

However, a very different reception greeted them a few years later in August 1985, when the museum at L'Anse aux Meadows was to officially open. My parents were invited as honorary guests, and even though my mother feared the worst, she agreed to go. This time the trip was paid for and they were given the reverence they deserved. A plaque in their honour was also unveiled along the pathway between the houses.

But what touched Helge and Anne Stine the most was how much the local people shared their sincere joy over having found the discovery. Many had themselves taken part in the excavations and therefore felt a part of the team. Now, they hoped that the museum and the tourists coming in could provide an income that otherwise was disappearing with the declining cod stocks. Already that summer, over fifteen thousand long-distance travellers had come to visit the place, and residents had plans for a souvenir shop, places to stay, and similar other features just outside the park's boundaries.

Anne Stine and Helge in front of the reconstructed houses at L'Anse aux Meadows. Photo by Finn E. Strømberg/Aftenposten/Scanpix.

Why the great shift in attitude towards my parents? Helge believed it was due to a change of directors at Parks Canada. Most likely, too, the government of Newfoundland had acquired more control over the site. As we saw in the previous chapter, the premier was very concerned about the "looming crisis" that national management of the area by Parks Canada could possibly cause. It was evident now that certain public figures had gained control of the situation and wished to acknowledge my parents with the thanks and praise they deserved.

Anaktuvuk Pass Forty Years Later

When Helge left Alaska in 1930, he exchanged letters with his friends there for a few years, but then all grew quiet. He often thought about the people and the place, and his film and slides from Anaktuvuk Pass were for many years the basis for his lectures that he gave around Norway. My father felt that it was a protected place on earth, protected from "civilization" that is. But he later sensed this was no longer the case, partly because I had visited Anaktuvuk Pass in 1967 and had been able to tell him about some of the changes that had occurred. When I was there, several families still lived in hide tents or turf huts, but others now had modern houses. The children went to school, but the caribou were still an important part of their existence.

Simon Paneak's family were happy to see me, but I felt that some of the younger people believed that Helge had depicted them as too primitive and uncivilized in his book *Nunamiut*, now published in English. I never mentioned this to Helge so as not to hurt him. It was the nature of his book to focus on the old, traditional culture rather than newer influences. Those teenagers, however, probably remembered little of what life had been like back then.

Still, it was a wonderful surprise when on Christmas in 1988 he received a telephone call and heard a voice saying, "Hello, this is from Anaktuvuk Pass." The man on the other end was Grant Spearman, curator for the local Simon Paneak Museum, named after Helge's old hunting companion who had now passed away. Suddenly the world seemed a much smaller place. The reason for the call was that when the museum was established, someone remembered that a Norwegian had lived there long ago – a person who wandered around with a camera and tape recorder. "Do you have anything from Anaktuvuk Pass that we could use in the museum?" Spearman asked. "Yes, lots," replied Helge.

That is how Grant Spearman came to Norway in March 1989, along with Roosevelt Paneak, Simon and Susie's four-year-old son when Helge was there. It was a moving encounter and most touching as we watched Roosevelt's reaction when he saw Helge's film from 1949. He now lived in a town with a school, clinic, airport, church, and museum. The film transported him back to a land far away, back to his childhood and nomadic way of life that he had almost forgotten, back to all those loved ones who were now gone. Tears ran down his cheeks.

Helge gave the museum copies of all the films and all his pictures as well as the original recordings of the taped songs and legends. Because Helge had been so incredibly interested in their old culture, the Nunamiut were now able to retrieve parts of their lost history, stored in

Norway. My father now had the pleasure of reciprocating the kindness and hospitality that he was so generously given.

Helge was invited to the official opening of the Simon Paneak Museum on 5 October 1989, almost exactly forty years after he had first landed in Anaktuvuk Pass. Years earlier, when we had asked him if he wanted to travel there again, he had said no. He wanted to remember the place as it had been. However, now the situation was very different. He was to be guest of honour and felt he couldn't refuse. Besides, the opening of the museum was a special occasion and he very much wanted to pay tribute to his good hunting friend. But now he was nearly ninety years old, and it was a long trip. His son-in-law Edwin accompanied him as his personal physician and his thirteen-year-old grandson Eirik was an eager assistant.

The changes in Anaktuvuk Pass made it nearly unrecognizable to Helge. In Prudoe Bay, north of the mountains, rich oil deposits had been discovered in 1968. This led to the construction of the pipeline that runs through Alaska, north to south, a little east of Anaktuvuk Pass, providing employment for a few young people as well as an annual share of oil revenues for everyone in Alaska. No great fortune, but enough to help build a new house.[8] There was a grocery store with a decent selection of foods and a new school with teachers who spoke only English. At the same time, caribou hunting was now limited to one animal per person once a year during an allotted hunting season.[9]

As permanent residents and consumers of store-bought food, they no longer lived by the seasons of the year, or the landscape, or the caribous' ways. Now it was modern technology in the form of snowmobiles and better rifles that determined the hunt. Only one shaggy sled dog remained. Still, the caribou held one last influence; to disappear forever from Anaktuvuk Pass. Something that recent reports have now indicated to a certain extent.

Helge shook his head; the mountains were the only thing that remained unchanged in Anaktuvuk Pass. Of all his old friends, only Susie (Umealaq), Simon Paneak's wife, was still alive. It was a warm-hearted reunion. Helge had a red silk scarf he had bought for her a long time ago, but never got around to sending it. He now gave it to her in person. The museum was opened with a traditional drum dance. The ceremony was to primarily honour Paneak, but Helge too was honoured as one who had largely contributed to the collection.

World Travels

Alaska was not the only place Helge visited in his old age. After his expeditions were over, my father's desire to travel still remained strong. In 1984, both my parents travelled to Botswana, Africa, where my family and I were living for two years. My husband Edwin was working as a district medical officer in the small village of Molepolole. Despite their age, my mother and father agreed to a safari and to sleeping in tents. All went well until an elephant wandered into our camp one night. As its trunk brushed against my parents' tent, my mother sat up terrified. My father just gave it a whack to shoo it off. For Helge, with his keen interest in people and other cultures, Bostwana was a great experience. For my mother, she had had enough of safaris.

A few years after the Africa trip, Helge was invited by his friend and SAS airlines lead navigator, Einar Sverre Pedersen,[10] on a trip to Hobart, Tasmania, in Australia to unveil a statue of Roald Amundsen, the Norwegian who was the first to reach the South Pole. Then in 1993, Helge was invited by the Science Academy in Beijing, China, to hold a lecture about his research on Vinland and the discovery at L'Anse aux Meadows. The two-week journey, accompanied by journalist friend Arvid Bryne and grandson Eirik, included a cruise on the Yangtze River and visits to major tourist attractions. Whether my ninety-three-year-old father was the oldest person ever to climb the Great Wall of China I do not know. But I am sure he wasn't far off the record.

18 OLD AGE

As Helge grew older, he also grew milder – not so stubborn, adamant, or as self-centred. He discovered things around him to which he had not previously given much attention. When his youngest granddaughter Marit was born in 1987, he would trudge the 40 metres down the hill to our house to visit. He kept track of the hours she was awake and enjoyed the little life unfolding before him. For her baptism, he gave a cheque for her education fund. "You know," he said, "she might not remember me, so I would at least want her to know that this came from me."

One of the disadvantages of having lived as a freelancer was that my father's retirement fund was poor. He managed to save some of the money he had earned from his book *The Land of of Feast and Famine*, but inflation had dramatically reduced what once seemed to be a large sum. He always thought that he had to save for old age. It was a relief, therefore, that toward the end of their lives both he and Anne Stine were awarded honorary lifetime grants from the Norwegian government. The modest amount they received for this meant that every year he had to write a report about the scholarly work he had completed during the previous year, not an easy task after turning ninety. Even the day before he turned one hundred he received an official letter requesting an outline of his future research plans. Nothing big, mind you, just a formality.

Eventually, his writing waned, his vision grew worse, his hand grew shakier, and he tired more quickly. But his thoughts were clear and he still personally answered each and every letter he received. And he still had the great pleasure of having many young Norwegian adventurers come to visit him and seek his advice. Each sat in Helge's living room in front of the fireplace telling him of their plans and in return received good advice and encouragement. My father, though, did not fully understand the point of just reaching a pole or a summit of a high mountain. For him, it was the people and wildlife of the Arctic that interested him most. However, he did understand the power of adventure, gusto, and enthusiasm that motivated these young people.

As his knees worsened after he turned ninety-five, his life became more sedentary. He could sit and browse through his own books, especially those about Vinland, and happily reminisce over his life's greatest achievement: "my discovery" as he called it.

As Anne Stine aged, she became increasingly more agitated. She often returned to Lillehammer and to her memories, especially those including her brother Tycho that she could not let go. Sometimes, it felt like her childhood memories were more important to her than we were, those of us still alive. She talked about all the summers at Maribuseter that she never had while she lay scraping at the site at L'Anse aux Meadows. She talked about all the dinners she had made for Helge and all the other things she could have done with her time instead.

Quite spontaneously, she would get in her car and take off for the mountains to spend the day at her beloved cabin Maribuseter. She didn't really enjoy being alone with her memories up there, but it was difficult to find any friends to join her. They too had grown older and had grandchildren and family retreats of their own. My children and I tried to juggle between being with Helge and Anne Stine at two different locations: one by the sea and the other in the mountains. But we were all pressed for time and busy with our own demanding lives.

Anne Stine could not bear to watch Helge grow more and more frail, nor could she cope with the responsibilities of such a condition. Despite being eighteen years younger than him, she could not expect many more active years herself and she felt restricted before her time. Helge was no longer her youthful hero, but an increasingly elderly man who required care. Tending to an aging spouse was never on her mind when, at the age of seventeen, she wrote her fan letter to him.

As Helge's ability to involve himself with other issues gradually lessened with age, "his discovery" became more and more important to him. Anne Stine, on the other hand, became increasingly more sensitive and intolerant of anything to do with L'Anse aux Meadows due to the various conflicts they had to endure. The L'Anse aux Meadows discovery became a topic the two could not discuss and therefore created an enormous rift between them. The major forces that had contributed to this, Parks Canada, along with Bengt Schönbäck and Birgitta Wallace, and Aage Roussell in Denmark, inflicted much more than just academic damage. The conflicts caused this vulnerable but highly competent woman to experience much sadness at the end of her life.

What did give my mother pleasure in her old age, besides her grandchildren and her work with the Oseberg Viking Ship textiles, was doing traditional Norwegian decorative painting called *rosemaling*. Once a week she had a "thank goodness day" when she attended her *rosemaling* course, where she also made new friends. In retrospect, she was most likely very depressed during these years. On top of all this, there was one last "storm" in the waiting: a spirited media debate between Helge and another well-known Norwegian, explorer Thor Heyerdahl.

Our Friend Thor

It was inevitable that they would meet. A country as small as Norway does not foster many famous men who live at the same time. Helge was known for his explorations and then the discovery of the Viking settlement in Canada. Thor Heyerdahl was internationally recognized for proving that it was possible to cross the Pacific Ocean on a raft, the *Kon-Tiki*, in 1947.

Besides both being explorers, however, they shared other common links. Anne Stine knew Heyerdahl's mother, Alison, and his first wife, Liv, who was from Lillehammer. Helge also had connections with Heyerdahl through the Authors' Union, the Explorers' Club, as well as through Gyldendal, the Norwegian publisher they both worked with. When Heyerdahl moved to Oslo with his second wife, Yvonne, the Ingstads and Heyerdahls soon became part of the same circle of friends.

That Helge and Heyerdahl would become friends, however, was not as predictable. Helge's statement about his father-in-law – "There wasn't enough room for two chiefs in one house" – also seemed to apply to Heyerdahl. The friendship was based on an unspoken agreement that each held to his own "house" and did not foray into the other's area of interest. Helge in his youth had surely dreamt of going to a Pacific Island, but that part of the world was certainly nothing he would pretend to be

Thor Heyerdahl. Photo from Gyldendal Archives.

an expert on. He also knew that Heyerdahl had not spent time in the Arctic and was no expert on Viking expeditions. In this sense, the two men were not "contenders" nor, as Helge assumed, disrespectful enough to step into the other's area of expertise.

Helge also thought highly of Heyerdahl, whose adventures had much in common with his own. He was also impressed, perhaps even a little envious, of his ability to handle the press and create publicity and income out of every little thing he did. Helge himself was not as adept at doing this and often chose to prioritize his time in other ways and waited to comment about something until he was absolutely sure he had something to show. Helge never really had much to say about Heyerdahl's theories other than mumbling once in a while that he perhaps drew some bold conclusions based on insufficient grounds. For Helge, it was far more important to scrutinize the research than to drum up easy publicity.

Once, the two even travelled together, along with their wives Anne Stine and Yvonne, in August 1966 to the International Congress of Americanists conference in Mar del Plata, Argentina, where they both presented their work. Afterwards, I met the four of them there and we all travelled together to Bolivia, Lake Titicaca and Machu Picchu in Peru, and then to the pyramids in Mexico. Heyerdahl, who knew these areas well, was our guide, and Anne Stine later thought this trip was one of the greatest experiences in her life.

Thor and Yvonne eventually moved to Italy, and their contact with my parents became less frequent. Christmas letters were sent and received, and a few telegrams were exchanged when Heyerdahl again crossed the oceans on a raft, this time the *Ra I* across the Atlantic Ocean. But after this, Helge and Thor had little contact with each other.

An Unexpected, Unfriendly Surprise

After several years of quiet between the two friends, an eruption suddenly occurred.[1] On 23 June 1995, the main Norwegian newspaper *Aftenposten* published an interview with Heyerdahl, along with Swedish geographer Per Liljeström, presenting his new theory that Christopher Columbus had been on a journey to Davis Strait between Greenland and Baffin Island in 1477 and knew that land existed in the west. The theory included a Portuguese connection to Greenland, that the Portuguese had possibly landed there and forced the inhabitants to become slaves. This would explain the mystery of the vanishing Norse people from Greenland.[2]

Helge was initially stunned over Heyerdahl's comments and perceived his conjectures into the mystery of the Norse people in Greenland to be an enormous betrayal and breach of trust in their friendship. Not that anyone can have a monopoly of a research field, but to have a person "mess with somebody else's place in such a shoddy way; and even worse by a friend!"

Anne Stine was completely crushed. She had managed to overcome the attacks from the Danes and all the fuss with Parks Canada to now have to enter a new debate, and this time with a friend. "I can't take it anymore!" she almost shrieked. My father was just very quiet for several days. "You see, I could crush him with my arguments," he told me, "but he has been a good friend." Initially, Helge chose not to respond. Eventually though he changed his mind and then spent a large portion of the summer on writing a counter-argument, a factual response to what my father perceived as "Thor's erroneous and loosely founded allegations." Helge also realized that Heyerdahl, with his international renown, could be falsely supported for his thinly based theories. This in turn could have undermined the valid scientific work in Newfoundland that Helge and Anne Stine worked so hard on, and for so many years. Plenty of quasi-scientists with casual theories about Viking voyages and unsubstantiated Viking findings in North America might gladly embrace Heyerdahl's theories, Helge thought.

At the same time, Helge felt that he was getting old and could not bear to get involved as he did when he was younger. He thought it was important to say what he needed to say, formidably and factually, once and for all.

A refute written by Helge was printed in *Aftenposten* on Sunday 8 October 1995 that proceeded to disprove Heyerdahl's assertions point by point. A key argument was that Heyerdahl claimed that Christopher Columbus sailed to Greenland in February, reasoning that this was the safest time of the year to journey due to the fewer number of icebergs. Helge responded that this assertion was absurd. During the winter (which included February), both drift ice and pack ice often lay kilometres from land, making all travel by sea impossible. Helge said, "Ships would have been crushed if they had dared to sail in ... this reveals so much ignorance about Arctic conditions that comments are unnecessary."[3]

Helge was also in complete disagreement with Heyerdahl concerning a Portuguese connection to Greenland. According to Heyerdahl, the oldest surviving map of Portuguese geographic discoveries, called the Cantino map (from 1502), depicted two Portuguese flags on a contour of eastern Greenland. Heyerdahl supported a theory that the Norse settlements here could have been completely emptied by a sudden and unexpected slave ship from Portugal. Helge explained that there was no such evidence whatsoever that supported this claim. Furthermore, Helge pointed out the important fact that the Portuguese flags on the Cantino map are drawn on the eastern part of Greenland, far from the verified settlements in western Greenland.

Following Helge's article in the newspaper, a couple of more posts were made between the two men, but then Helge had had enough. He ended his last article by writing, "I can understand that Liljeström (collaborative partner on project) and Heyerdahl disliked that my earlier report revealed that they had no knowledge about the Norse settlements that lay on the western coast of Greenland, whereby the basis of their dramatic descriptions of the Norse Greenlanders's fate evaporates, but one can wonder about their methodology.[4]" After this my father approached professor of archaeology Christian Keller and said, "I am too old and can't continue this, now you have to take over, but keep my name out."[5] It was the first time in Helge's life that he gave up on a case he believed was important.

Keller kept his promise to Helge and continued the debate, together with historian Per Norseng, in which they wrote an article and submitted it to *Aftenposten*. The article was denied publication with the editorial explanation: "We don't print critique against Heyerdahl and the Monarchy," which Keller later remarked was "an interesting sequence." A shorter version of the article was later printed in another Norwegian newspaper, *Verdens Gang*, with the title "Heyerdahl Is Bluffing."[6] And with that, the debate continued.

Another alarming part of this story is that Keller and several other scholars and scientists who presented counter-arguments to Heyerdahl's theory in the ensuing debate received letters from the attorney firm Wiersholm, Mellbye & Bech warning them that they would "pursue the matter legally with consequences of a financial and nonfinancial nature."[7]

Heyerdahl perhaps never really understood how his actions affected Helge, and I prefer that explanation. Much of what Heyerdahl wrote suggests that he could not have read Helge's two historical accounts of the Norse settlements in Greenland and the Vinland voyages, as he never referred to their contents.[8] Another less pleasant explanation is that he reckoned Helge was too old to refute his theory with counter-arguments.

Regardless, in 1999 Heyerdahl and Liljeström published a book titled *No Borders* in which they expounded on these theories, including the idea that Vinland was "the area from Hudson Strait to St. Lawrence Bay and Long Island,"[9] in other words the largest part of the eastern coast of North America. Ironically, Heyerdahl sent a copy of his book to Helge signed: "To my old friend Helge who together with his wife Anne Stine changed the history of the world by proving that Vinland lay where the

Sagas indicated." Helge read the book thoroughly and on nearly every page he marked it with question marks, exclamation points, notes, and coffee stains.

It is quite strange that Heyerdahl never made any effort to contact Helge regarding his Vinland theories. It would have been a natural, friendly courtesy to have contacted Helge before the first article in the newspaper, or during the years that followed. The only time the two men met following the controversy was at a dinner at the Norwegian Royal Palace in March 1999. As recipients of the Grand Cross of St Olav, both were often invited to official dinners, state visits, and other such events of national importance. Helge had stopped attending such functions some years earlier. However, when Nelson Mandela made an official visit to Norway as the first president of the new South Africa, Helge wanted to attend to honour the great statesman. Attending such events at the age of ninety-nine was courageous of the old trapper. I accompanied him to help.

Heyerdahl also came to this particular event with his third wife, Jacqueline. Helge and Heyerdahl were seated far from each other at the table, but after dinner all the guests gathered in the adjacent hall. When Heyerdahl showed no sign of coming over to greet us, Helge asked me to follow him over to where Thor stood. It was a very brief, terse reunion as these two old friends did not really have much to say to each other. When we returned home that evening, Helge said to me, quite satisfied with himself, "I think he appreciated that we went over and said hello to him."

Anne Stine's Last Year

At the beginning of 1997, my mother increasingly began to ail. She had always been thin but was now eating even less and beginning to grow gaunt. No matter what delicacy we dished up, we couldn't tempt her to eat. What we didn't know then, and what she chose not to tell us, was that sometime earlier that fall she had been to the dermatologist to remove a large dark mole that had appeared on her shoulder. Whether a biopsy had been performed, or if the doctor told her it was malignant, or she guessed it herself, none of us knows. I only discovered the scar after she died and we never located the doctor whom she had visited.

As the year progressed, she steadily declined but still refused to go to the doctor, until June, when lumps appeared under her arm and on her neck. Biopsies were taken and results confirmed malignant melanoma, which had spread. She was to return to the specialist after the summer holidays but by then had decided not to pursue treatment. It was not easy for those of us who loved her and wanted her to at least try something. What we did know was that if such cancer started to spread chances of survival were almost zero. That is how she got her own way: no more doctor's appointments and no medical treatment, only time to live her life as well as she could, for as long as she could.

First, we all went to our family cabin on the southern coast of Norway, thereafter to the mountains and Maribuseter with granddaughter Marit and me. Her best friend Barbro from Sweden stopped by, and as we sat with our backs propped against the wall soaking up the sunshine, each with a glass of sherry, we could almost pretend that nothing was wrong. On the way home from Maribuseter we took a side trip to see the old farm Bårdsetbakken where she and Helge had lived during the Second World War and where I spent my first year as a baby. We had never before visited the place. When we finally found our way there, the house had been renovated and was freshly painted, so Anne Stine didn't recognize the place at first. But as we wandered around, memories came flooding back of a good period in life, for both her and Helge, despite the chaos in the world around them. Those times could very well have been their best years together.

The nineteenth of October, my birthday, was the last day Anne Stine was able to make it down to the living room at Brattalid. Afterwards, she remained in her old canopy bed on the second floor and lay there so beautifully, greeting everyone who stopped in to say goodbye. She was not in pain and it was almost as if she radiated happiness. She had found peace and I think she was completely happy. Perhaps for the first time in her life she felt as if she were the centre of everyone's love and attention.

On her nightstand was a picture of Helge with his pipe and cap. He had put it there with the inscription *To my dear wife from your Helge.* He was not able to make it up the stairs to see her as often as he would have liked. "Imagine, he was the man in my life," she proudly said to her friend who had come to say goodbye. "Isn't he wonderful and handsome? I took that picture when we were in Greenland."[10]

She refused any intravenous food or fluids, and near the end she wrote on a piece of paper, *I want to die as soon as possible.* On 6 November, she died peacefully in her sleep.

Old Helge

Being on his own was not easy for Helge. He never thought he would outlive his wife, who was eighteen years younger. He was now so physically feeble that it was no longer possible for him to live on his own, but a nursing home was out of the question. He would live at Brattalid as long as he possibly could, preferably for the remainder of his days.

With the help of public home care, my children, and myself, we were able to come to an arrangement that worked, more or less. Having Helge at home allowed friends and young adventurers to more easily visit. Eventually though, another category of people began to show up: those who wanted to say that they had met Helge Ingstad before he died, and those who very much wanted his autograph. Sometimes he thought this was nice, other times bothersome.

Helge's brother Kaare, who lived until 1999, had also lost his much younger wife and lived on his own about an hour away. Even though it was not easy for them to see each other, they often spoke on the telephone. My father explained to his brother the technical finesse of canes with spiked tips for navigating on the snow and ice, and walkers on wheels to prevent broken bones, and suggested to Kaare to move his bed downstairs to avoid the stairs. Helge's expertise and focus had changed with his advancing years.

As Helge approached his one hundredth birthday, there was ever-increasing media coverage leading up to the event. In celebration of the milestone, his Norwegian publisher Glydendal published the collected works of all his books. In the many interviews in the newspapers and on radio, Helge was continually asked the same question: How did he manage to live to be a hundred years old? He began to detest that question and would reply that it was because he had stopped smoking, but neglected to add that he didn't do that until he turned 85.

We celebrated the day of his birthday like we always did, exactly like Anne Stine would have done, with a beautifully arranged buffet of Christmas foods and an open house for friends and family. Early morning on 30 December 1999, large bouquets of flowers began to flood in from a number of highly distinguished people such as the king and queen and the prime minister, among many others. Helge was overwhelmed. After a long and pleasant day with people streaming in and out of the open house, and when Helge thought the party was over, a surprise awaited.

King Harald V congratulates Helge on his one hundredth birthday during a celebration at the Norwegian Academy of Science and Letters. Photo by Berit Roald/Scanpix.

The Norwegian Society for the Conservation of Nature (Naturvernforbundet) had earlier announced a torch parade for him starting at the local city train stop and up the street to his house in the woods north of the city. Well over one hundred people arrived at Helge's door – a sea of lit ceremonial torches. Everyone was invited in and the house was chock full of guests in his living room, who then began to sing and play traditional Norwegian songs. Helge was deeply moved.

Three weeks later, on 22 January, the Norwegian Society of Science and Letters (Det Norske Vitenskaps-Akademi), of which Helge was an honorary member, arranged a celebratory lunch for him with the king of Norway and selected guests. It was an incredibly grand event.

Being a centenarian proved a challenge for Helge in several ways. He had little patience for all the comments about how wonderful that he was "still looking so well." He was fit and healthy, in spite of his worn-down knees, and wanted to be treated as such, not like someone who should have been bedridden, or even dead.

One day, Helge received a telephone call from his alma mater in Bergen, Katedralskolen. They said that they wanted to put his name on a plaque in the hallway along with Nordahl Grieg and other famous pupils and afterwards have a reception with several invited guests. Helge replied that he thought that would be nice and looked forward to attending the event. A little embarrassed, the caller explained that the hanging of the plaque and reception would be held after his death. Helge was quite amused when he related the story, and we agreed that his granddaughter Marit and I would attend the ceremony on his behalf.

At his birthplace in Meråker, officials wanted to arrange an annual dogsled race and called to ask if the event could be named the "Helge Ingstad Memorial Race." Helge made them smile when he politely reminded them that he was still very much alive. It was then called the "Helge Ingstad Honorary Race" until long after he passed away. It was a challenge for my father to be one hundred years old and relatively healthy, but made to feel pushed to the side. For the most part, though, Helge had a good sense of humour about it all.

Leif Eiriksson's One Thousandth Anniversary Celebration

The year 2000 marked the thousandth anniversary of Leif Eiriksson's arrival in North America. A large celebration was planned by Norway, Iceland, the US, and Canada with the main attraction being a Viking exhibition that the four countries had collaborated on. In Norway, little happened. But in the US and Canada, the event was highly celebrated. Planning for it began a few years earlier when researchers from Washington, DC, who were most responsible for the exhibition, travelled to and around the Nordic countries and various museums.

L'Anse aux Meadows, of course, played a central role in the celebrations, and several photographs from the excavations and copies of both the spindle whorl and ring-headed pin were to be exhibited. People from the exhibition committee came to talk with Helge, but beyond this there seemed to be no further plans to incorporate him into the celebrations.

It was primarily Parks Canada and Birgitta Wallace, who the committee seemed to think represented L'Anse aux Meadows.

That is, until Eva Bugge, head of the Norwegian Foreign Affairs Cultural Department took up the issue. The Foreign Department was partly funding the exhibition, and she took the time to visit Helge and discuss the issue with him. Most likely she had heard about the problems with Parks Canada and everything else that Helge and Anne Stine had to contend with. Not long after, an invitation from the Foreign Department arrived asking Helge to be their guest of honour at the opening of the exhibition in Washington, DC, on 29 January 2000. Travel expenses would be covered and include "a comfortable class," and he could take along the people he wanted to help him.

At the time, Marit, Eirik, and I were in Berkeley, California, on a sabbatical leave, but I had daily contact with Helge. "Are you really going to travel to the opening of the exhibition?" I asked quite doubtful. "Of course," he almost snorted, and so the planning began. Helge would travel with the help of a medical student from Norway and the rest of us would travel from Berkeley to meet him in DC. The Foreign Department had arranged for us to stay at one of the finest hotels in the city where we must have occupied nearly half a floor. We each had a large room and shared a lovely living room that we used to meet with journalists and the like. Helge truly felt like an honoured guest, and the rest of us basked in his limelight.

On the opening day, 20 April 2000, Helge was placed on a large stage along with Norwegian King Harald and Queen Sonja and President Bill Clinton and his wife Hillary, the latter being the high patrons of the exhibition. After careful consideration, Helge concluded that he would not read his speech himself as he was afraid that his voice would not carry, so he asked me if I would. It was an incredible feeling to stand beside him on that stage and read his words, which I knew he would have liked to have spoken himself.

Later that day, the Norwegian embassy arranged for a news conference back at the hotel. A woman journalist from a major newspaper interviewed him and they had a long and pleasant conversation. When Helge afterwards asked her if he could receive a copy of the interview, the woman replied, somewhat embarrassed, that, no, it would be for his obituary. Helge felt a little crestfallen at the thought that this was the reason why most of the reporters were there.

The day after, we had lunch at the White House together with several dignitaries. Helge seemed to be quite unaffected by it all as he had been there before with President Lyndon B. Johnson on the proclamation of "Leif Erikson Day." But for the medical student and I, after being screened as necessary helpers, it was a fascinating experience.

When Helge, along with his helper, flew back to Norway the day after, it is safe to say that he was worn out. But he was very happy with the trip and grateful to Eva Bugge and the Foreign Department for making such wonderful arrangements.

Helge Dies

The trip to Washington, DC, was Helge's last expedition. He never quite regained his physical strength after the journey and became noticeably frailer, but he thought it was absolutely worth it. He could not travel any more but was quite pleased to have me represent him at the opening of the same exhibition in both New York and Ottawa that year. At all these places, I read the same speech from the opening and relayed greetings from Helge.

The rest of the year was quiet and uneventful for Helge as he was no longer very mobile. One of the most pleasant events was in July with the birth of his great-grandson Max. It gave Helge much to think about – the new generation was arriving, while he himself was about to depart.

His one hundred and first birthday was celebrated as usual with an open house and many good friends of all ages who stopped by. But it seemed we were all thinking the same thought: this could surely be his last.

One final event, which Helge managed to wait for, was held on 25 January 2001. Good friends Arne Skouen and Arvid Bryne spent several years organizing funding for a sculpture of Helge and Anne Stine to be placed outside the Viking Ship museum in Olso. The artist, Nils Aas, had been to visit Brattalid several times, including when Anne Stine was still alive.

The big day arrived and Helge reluctantly agreed to take along a wheelchair to the event. It began with a reception in the Viking Ship hall, where a few speeches were held. Afterwards, the crowd went outside for the unveiling of the statue, which was conducted by the Norwegian King. It was a beautiful monument, and Helge sat in his wheelchair in

Helge sits gazing at the monument of Anne Stine and himself outside the Viking Ship Museum in Oslo. The inscription under their names reads, "They discovered the Vikings' America." Photo by Heiko Junge/Scanpix.

front of the sculpture for a good long while. When we later drove him home, quietly from the back seat he said, "Now I have nothing more to look forward to."

A few weeks later, Helge's health began to deteriorate. He fell out of bed one night, knocked himself, and was unable to get up from the cold floor where he lay. We agreed with a doctor that he would stay at a nursing home for a couple of weeks to recover. Helge didn't like the place one bit. "You have no idea what it's like to be here," he said to me when I visited. The evening before he was to return home, he started coughing horribly and having pains on his left side. A young doctor was summoned and after a quick check said that Helge was fine. The next morning, the day Helge was scheduled to come home, I was awakened with a telephone call from the hospital. Helge had pneumonia and was taken to the hospital.

Several years prior to this, I had tried to prepare myself mentally for my father's death. I actually thought that Helge would die peacefully in his sleep, in bed or in a chair just like his father Olav had done. But in reality, his deathbed was very different from anything I had ever prepared myself for. When I got to the hospital, Helge didn't know who I was. He imagined that he was sailing down rivers, fighting his way through ice and large bodies of water, and holding back large boulders that were about to fall on him. I should have guessed that he would not go so easily. When he finally died on 29 March, he was utterly exhausted from struggling against those imaginary forces of nature.

I called Arvid Bryne and asked him to notify the press. The next day the radio and newspapers announced, "Helge Ingstad died peacefully in his sleep at [the hospital]." Why is it that everyone is expected to die "peacefully"? Is it not just as well to die fighting, especially for someone whose life was lived with the motto "There is always a way out"?

Helge was given a state funeral and buried at Ris church in Oslo not far from his home. The king and queen were present, Prime Minister Jens Stoltenberg gave the eulogy, and the famous Norwegian TV personality Erik Bye read what Helge called his farewell poem, "Snow Will Fall." The church was filled to the rafters with people and beautiful flowers, including a wreath from Thor Heyerdahl.

19 LEGACY

Helge cared about his legacy. He wanted to be remembered as a person who had created something meaningful in life. Anne Stine was more modest and far less concerned about any legacy. For her, it was important to be warmly remembered by those to whom she was closest. However, although she never really expressed it, she would have liked future generations to acknowledge what she had accomplished at L'Anse aux Meadows.

Ingstad Mountain

It pleased Helge greatly to have his name on that beautiful mountain in Anaktuvuk Pass, Alaska, whether or not it was officially on any map. However, thanks to the initiation and drive of one enthusiastic woman by the name of Gerd Hurum, Ingstad Mountain was put on the map. Hurum, who had been in the Norwegian resistance during the Second World War and was an indispensable secretary for Thor Heyerdahl when planning and completing the *Kon-Tiki* expedition, later became a secretary at the Norwegian consulate in Montreal, Canada. This is where she first met Helge and heard about the mountain. Hurum took it upon herself to research the issue and send letters to Knut Vollebæk, the Norwegian ambassador in the US at the time. Officially naming a place cannot occur until five years after the person's death. Therefore, the matter of naming Ingstad Mountain had to sit and wait a few years. Unfortunately, Hurum passed away without ever seeing the results of her tireless lobbying.

On 17 April 2006, however, the US Board on Geographic Names unanimously gave the 1,487-metre-high mountain the name Ingstad

Ingstad Mountain in Alaska. Photo by Grant Spearman.

Mountain. On 10 September of the same year, a large group of people, including Ambassador Vollebæk and his wife, myself and my son Eirik, as well as a number of residents of Anaktuvuk Pass gathered together to celebrate the great event.[1] The local village council had previously been presented with the case to name the mountain but officially gave their approval during the naming ceremony; those in the village had always used that name.

Afterwards, a large party was held in the gymnasium with traditional drum dancing, something the Nunamiut were particularly proud of because they were top winners of this in national competitions. In the middle of the room, in front of all the dancers, was perched a mammoth skull with great tusks. It had emerged from the permafrost when the ground shifted due to climate change and melting.

Teachers had asked the schoolchildren to interview their grandparents about what they remembered of Helge's time there in 1949–50. These stories were printed and posted on the wall along with the children's drawings. The teachers said that the assignment had created great interest and led to several discussions about the old days. Some of the schoolchildren were grandchildren and great-grandchildren of Helge's old friends, and some of the older people had been children themselves during his time with them.

On behalf of the Norwegian Foreign Department, Helge's grandson Eirik had enlarged some of his grandfather's old pictures and made an exhibit of these, which were later given to the village. At the naming ceremony, these photographs were hung on the wall in the gymnasium; some people recognized relatives who had passed away or even themselves as children.

Off in the distance, Ingstad Mountain lay surrounded in autumn colours crowned with a ring of fog. It was also very visible from the museum, where a plaque with the mountain's name was erected on a stand and unveiled by Ambassador Vollebæk. A remarkable feeling pervaded both the place and event, and I felt that Helge, Simon, Susie, and all the old ones who had died were now with us, just like the Nunamiut tale of how the dead can invisibly be present.[2]

L'Anse aux Meadows Legacy

What kind of legacy did Helge and Anne Stine leave behind at L'Anse aux Meadows? In Norway, they are clearly recognized as those who found and excavated the ruins. But in other countries and in some academic circles, various groups continue to promote their own work and interests in the discovery.

Danish archaeologists still cling to their version of the discovery at L'Anse aux Meadows. An obituary for Jørgen Meldgaard in 2007 read: "In 1958 [Meldgaard] traveled to Newfoundland with the Vinland Sagas in his hand and proved the likely place of the Norse settlements. The site was later excavated as a global sensation by Norwegian Helge Ingstad who thanked Meldgaard for disclosing the find."[3] As discussed earlier, this was not an exact account of the events.

In the long run, Thor Heyerdahl was far less harmful to the Vinland research than Helge had feared. One reason was that Heyerdahl's own death in 2002, a year after Helge's, put an end to the debate. Another reason was that Heyerdahl focused so much on the whimsical in his debate that scholars stopped taking him seriously.

Another, much more dangerous, factor affecting the legacy of my parents' work at L'Anse aux Meadows was Parks Canada and Birgitta Wallace, who systematically minimized Helge's, and especially Anne Stine's, efforts, in both scientific and mainstream publications, and in their reorganization of my mother's initial exhibition at the site.[4] Wallace wrote about the site as if it were she and Parks Canada who were responsible for the bulk of the excavation work. Anne Stine's and Helge's work on the excavations and the story of their discovery were only briefly mentioned in Wallace's writings. In long discussions about the possible uses of the houses, she never mentions any of Anne Stine's analyses.[5] The house drawings that Wallace used are identical copies of Anne Stine's drawings from her 1977 book[6] and the artifacts – the ring-headed pin, spindle whorl, hearths, and other items – are marked on Wallace's drawings without any information indicating that these were found under Helge's expedition with Anne Stine as head archaeologist.[7] Wallace's articles are used as reference by academicians in the most recent (and, by implication, most important) publications in the field. This is one way of intentionally "confiscating" another's work. One wonders what became of scholarly ethics.

In 2008, I was in Iceland attending a conference and travelled to Keflavik. There in the airport departure hall I discovered to my utter amazement two commemorative plaques with text about the Viking voyages to North America. On the one was the cover of the Viking book from the one thousandth anniversary exhibition celebrated in 2000. On the second plaque, written in both Icelandic and English, were the names of the most "important" people involved in the L'Anse aux Meadows excavations: "Helge Ingstad, Kristian Eldjárn and Birgitta Wallace revealed 8 structures of the Icelandic Viking Age type." That it was Helge, with help from George Decker, who found the ruins, was not presented. The fact that it was Anne Stine who "revealed the 8 structures" is also never mentioned.

I later found out[8] that these plaques had been part of the large travelling Viking exhibition during the one thousandth anniversary celebrations and were purchased by Iceland after the event. In other words, this text wandered around North America wherever the exhibition was shown.

How would my parents have reacted if they had seen these? Anne Stine would of course have been upset and sad; Helge would have been furious. But I also think my mother would have said that she had been right in that she had "wasted seven summers freezing at L'Anse aux Meadows instead of spending time at [her beloved cabin] Maribuseter."

However, the most important part of my parent's legacy at L'Anse aux Meadows is revealed in the feelings of the people who live there. The Newfoundland government began making amends for the treatment of Anne Stine and Helge over the years. That helped. The honorary doctorate degrees and naming of the buildings at Memorial University at St John's were the first visible signs of efforts to commemorate their work. The unveiling of the plaque with their names at L'Anse aux Meadows was another.[9] Part of this acknowledgment derives from the fact that local officials now understand the potential of the Vinland tourist attraction and its financial benefits for the province. The Norse ruins at L'Anse aux Meadows are the first of their kind[10] in North America and have provided Newfoundland an entirely new identity, both nationally and internationally.

In a Google search asking the question "Who discovered the Vikings' Vinland site?" the majority of responses name Helge and Anne Stine as those who indeed discovered the old Norse settlement at L'Anse aux Meadows.

Returning to L'Anse aux Meadows

I had a feeling something was happening between Parks Canada and the Newfoundland government, but was not sure what that was. The first time I returned to L'Anse aux Meadows after my last visit there in 1963 was in July 2000 when I was invited to attend the one thousandth anniversary celebration at L'Anse aux Meadows. Together with my daughter Marit, we were met at the St Anthony airport by Newfoundland's minister of tourism Charles Furey, who welcomed us with a big smile. Quite unexpectedly, he led us to a waiting helicopter that took us the rest of the way to L'Anse aux Meadows. Forty years after my first visit and on a beautiful sunny summer day,[11] I flew across the area looking down on the shimmering sea and scattered icebergs farther north toward Belle

Isle. On the road below, a long queue of cars and campers were headed in the same direction as us. Off the coast of L'Anse aux Meadows, several large cruise ships lay anchored.

When we landed, our old friend Lloyd Decker, son of Big Chief, was there to welcome us along with his daughter Loretta, who was now a guide at the museum. Several of the Colbourne children, now of course adults, were also there. Of those of the older generation whom I first met at L'Anse aux Meadows, only Job Andersson and mother Colbourne were still alive. It was so wonderful to see all of them and a pleasure that Marit could meet them.

The village was the same, and now had forty-four residents. It had been incorporated into the park's boundaries, which the people there were moderately happy about. A couple of incidents were quite unfortunate: one occurred when Lloyd Decker was reported to the police for driving his father's coffin over the meadows to the burial site; second, the surrounding islands, where the locals previously collected eggs and hunted seabirds, were now a protected area. However, most people could live with this, as local bed and breakfast establishments, as well as the museum, now provided work and income for L'Anse aux Meadows residents.

In 1992 the Canadian federal minister of Fisheries and Oceans declared a moratorium on cod fishing in the areas along Newfoundland and the Labrador coast. This was obviously a disaster for the small communities whose incomes were heavily based on fishing. The residents at L'Anse aux Meadows unanimously agree that if it had not been for the Viking ruins, this entire area would have been deserted. They thank Helge and Anne Stine for preventing that from happening.

An estimated seventeen thousand people attended the one thousandth anniversary celebration in L'Anse aux Meadows in June 2000. Many prominent people came: the premier of Newfoundland Brian Tobin, Iceland's prime minister Ólafur Ragnar Grímsson, Greenland's governor Jonathan Motzfelt, and many other officials from Newfoundland, Canada, and Scandinavia. There were guided tours of the excavated house sites and of the lovely new museum buildings situated on the marine terrace on the other side of Black Duck Brook. A few sites have been reconstructed and re-enactors dress in Viking clothes to greet the tourists.

My suspicion of something underlying the relationship between the nationally managed Parks Canada and the local Newfoundland government was confirmed when I again visited L'Anse aux Meadows a few months later the same year. I was confidentially told to take a look at the official book Newfoundland had released in connection with the one thousandth anniversary titled *The Millennium Book of Newfoundland and Labrador*. When I opened the book, to my great surprise, I found a full-page picture of my mother and father. I was even more astonished when I discovered that an entire 29 out of 119 pages were devoted to their work at L'Anse aux Meadows and included a discussion of the conflict with Parks Canada and confirmed clear support for Helge and Anne Stine. This section turned out to be written by a man named Edward Roberts, a very revered man in Newfoundland who was previously both a former cabinet minister and lieutenant-governor of the province of Newfoundland and Labrador. He also had visited Norway and Helge in 1999. This was in many ways an instance of Newfoundland making amends.

In the spring of 2002 I was once again back in L'Anse aux Meadows in connection with the Norwegian King Harald and Queen Sonja's state visit in Canada. Again, the Norwegian Ministry of Foreign Affairs made great efforts to honour my parents. A duplicate sculpture with Helge and Anne Stine, the same as outside the Viking Ship museum in Olso, had been created and transported to L'Anse aux Meadows. King Harald did the honours of unveiling it on a windy, freezing day (not exactly the best aspect of L'Anse aux Meadows) with thick pack ice out in the bay and rain coming down sideways. The statue, however, was duly unveiled and the warmth and affection that were shown to us from the local population were noticeable by everyone. They rejoiced to see Helge and Anne Stine back at L'Anse aux Meadows.

The area will always have an important place in my family's life. L'Anse aux Meadows brought with it many problems and sorrows that influenced my young life, but also many good memories. The greatest pleasure for both Anne Stine and Helge, and for myself, was getting to know the wonderful people who have lived and still live at L'Anse aux Meadows. And, not least, it is satisfying to know that what we discovered has come to mean something positive for them and the area, now and in the future. Every year, approximately thirty thousand people come from afar to visit the museum and ruins. For those who live there, they no longer need to worry that fishing is not a viable living. They now have other opportunities and do not have to leave.

During Christmas 2009, I received a card from Loretta Decker, Big Chief's granddaughter. The card had a picture of the torchbearers for the Winter Olympics in Vancouver, British Columbia, when they visited L'Anse aux Meadows on their journey through Canada. On the back it read:

Dear Benedicte,
I can't help but think about your parents and my dad on these occasions. If they could only see the world's attention and veneration that L'Anse aux Meadows is experiencing. Both our families will forever be proud of the credit of starting this wonderful story.
All good, Loretta

In July 2010, I again received a nice greeting from Loretta. This time it was an invitation on behalf of Parks Canada to attend the fiftieth anniversary of the meeting between Helge (and me) and George Decker at L'Anse aux Meadows that led to the discovery of the ruins. I must admit that I initially was skeptical about going. Months of reviewing the old correspondence with Parks Canada in connection with this biography made me quite unsure whether officials in the organization even wanted a representative from the Ingstad family there. But I decided to go, along with my daughter Marit, and it proved to be a good choice. We were greeted like royalty and made to feel very welcome. Parks Canada's pleasant new director praised Anne Stine and Helge in his speech, and I told about how we first found the ruins. In the evening, there was a large bonfire on the beach and a fireworks display. The relationship with Parks Canada ended well this time.

But the best part was to experience yet again the warmth and friendship that poured forth from so many people there. For me and my family, L'Anse aux Meadows will always be a very special and cherished place.

AFTERWORD

I am at Maribuseter alone for a few days in June 2003. I did not intend to come on my own, but everyone else who was planning to come couldn't, for one reason or another. It is the first time I am here on my own, and the silence is almost overwhelming. I am far from any other people. The radio batteries are used up, my watch is broken, the solar batteries are depleted from lack of sunshine, and my cellphone has gone dead. The fog is thick over the valley and conceals any sign of the farms down by the lake below that I normally see in the distance. An old German shepherd, two horses out grazing on the grass surrounding the cabin, and a computer with a low battery are the only things keeping me connected to the present.

But I don't feel alone. There are plenty of memories here. Not far away, my Uncle Tycho's memorial stone, my grandparents, Eilif and Louise, lay buried, and now also Anne Stine. A mountain birch grows up from these graves, quite large now and leaning towards a stone that marks the spot just a few metres from the large memorial stone for Tycho. Several years ago, the tree divided into two strong trunks, one for Eilif and one for Louise. It was now forming a third branch, one for Anne Stine. A little strange to think that this tree is absorbing its nourishment from the earth where my nearest and dearest now lie. I pat the stone and place a few flowers on the ground when I walk past.

Silence can be quite overwhelming when you are all alone. Some people eventually learn to love it, as Helge learned to love the solitude in the wilderness. "It is only with other people that loneliness stirs," he wrote in a poem. The way I knew my father, I am convinced he truly meant that.

I remember when, not long after Grandma Louise's death, my mother tried to be here on her own. The loneliness and memories were all too powerful for her. This was evident when we later arrived at Maribuseter only to find that she had fled to the village as fast as she could and left an unmade bed and half-eaten meal on the table. She would otherwise never have done that.

We smiled about it at the time, my husband Edwin and I, in our unexperienced youth. Why did I only understand her now? Why didn't I come up here with her more often? Well, I had more than enough to do with a husband, children, work, and taking care of my father during the summer vacations so she could have some time free. However, it does no good to stand by a grave and weep. But it is a pity that a person only really understands their parents after they are gone, or until he or she experiences something similar in life.

Helge had no intention of being buried up at Maribuseter; even dead he did not want to stay long at her family's place. This is how in the end they separated. She is in the mountains, and he (together with my late husband Edwin) is in Oslo. They both believed in life after death, so perhaps my parents are finally blissful, together under the Pole Star.

A FAREWELL POEM BY HELGE
No wreaths on my grave
for there will come a time
when deep within me I will know
that the time I have is near.
And that last way in
to what lies beyond
is all a part of life.

I will harness my dogs to the sled
mush to a wind-blown knotted birch
to the edge of the tundra
to a tree I know well.

I will sit down beside it
feel its rough bark
be close to another life

which has struggled to break through
struggled to survive
just as we
have braced the icy cold winds.

And then night will fall
the starry sky will appear
my familiar roof from years in the snow
marvellous vaulting bustling planets
created by the one who created me.

So I lay my head to rest
against that old tree
with thanks for the good life I had.
Snow will fall.[1]

A WORD OF THANKS

There are many who deserve a word of thanks in helping me to write this biography of my parents. First and foremost, I would like to thank my grown children for supporting me and the work on this biography for yet another year, as well as reading the manuscript and providing comments along the way. But not only to them, but also to my grandchildren this book is dedicated. In this way, our family history continues through the generations.

I have had many good helpers, but one of the most important has been Christian Keller, who has guided me safely through the historical and archaeological chapters, and who has even piqued my interest in becoming (finally) interested in Norse history and archaeology. Likewise, Hans Fredrik Dahl has read and provided comments on the chapters about the war. My late Uncle Ole Henrik Moe senior has read and made comments on the chapters about Anne Stine's childhood and youth. My good friend Per Fugelli has read the entire manuscript at an earlier stage and provided comments. I wholeheartedly thank all of these people.

Thank you also to Thòrarinn Eldjàrn, who provided me with a copy of his father's, Kristian Eldjàrn's, journal from the L'Anse aux Meadows expedition, and to Thelma Dogg Robertsdottir, who translated it from Icelandic to Norwegian. Thank you also to Lyder Marstrander, who has allowed me to include his father's, Sverre Marstrander's, Vinland file in the Ingstad archives. A special thank you to Edward Roberts, who helped me to locate important archives in Newfoundland. The late Robert Paine is also remembered with thanks for his patience in helping me find answers to a number of questions concerning Newfoundland.

I also would like to thank helpful archivists at the National Library in Iceland, the library at Memorial University at St John's in Newfoundland,

the University of Fairbanks in Alaska, the Regional Archives in Opp-
land, Norway, and the University Library in Oslo.

Others who also need to be sincerely thanked for various forms of
information and help are: Jim Allen, Kirsti Berug, Arvid Bryne, Eva
Bugge, Bjørn Bækkelund, Arne Emil Christensen, Adolf Fridriksson,
Lisbet Grut, Sigrid Kalland, Terje Kristoffersen, Jon Vegard Lunde, Kjell
Smedsaas, Merete Taksdal, Bjørn Økern, and the helpful people in Øvre
Rendalen and at Sølensjøen.

A special thank you too to Janine Stenehjem, who has done much
more than just translating. Also to Shani Pearson for her keen eye for
detail in help with editing the English drafts and to James Leahy, copy
editor of the final English manuscript.

My great appreciation for those who have contributed funding for this
book project include: the Norwegian Non-Fiction Writers' Organization
(Norsk faglitterær forfatter- og oversetterforening), NORLA (Norwegian
Literature Abroad), Oslo county's cultural stipend from 2008, Eckbos
Legat, and the Arts Council of Norway, which previously helped fund
the collecting and archiving of my parents' remaining letters, documents,
and papers. Thank you again to Paul Sporsheim, who conducted this
work. Without that organization and overview, it would have been impossible to have written the second half of this book.

Last but not least, a special thanks to Ingrid Ryvarden, my editor at
Gyldendal Publishers for her much-appreciated suggestions for condens-
ing the two Norwegian books into one English version; and to Mark
Abley, editor at McGill-Queen's University Press, who showed interest
in the English translation of the book, for his patience and kind words
during the time it took to finish the work.

Benedicte Ingstad

NOTES

INTRODUCTION

1 Part of the many conversations with Helge that were recorded between the summers of 1999 and 2000.

CHAPTER ONE

1 Taken from recorded conversations during summer 1999.
2 As written by Helge in an introduction of an incomplete autobiography.
3 He also took courses in university library archiving and later published a few judicial articles and collected material for an Ingstad genealogy book.
4 *Bergen bys historie* (Bergen city history, vol. 3: *A City Society in Development, 1800–1920*, ed. Anders Bjarne Fossen [Bergen: Universitetsforlaget, 1982]). Registered population figures were 76,959 in 1900 and 84,330 in 1910.
5 Ibid.
6 *Amtmann* (district governor) was the highest-ranking civil servant in the county. From 1919, the position was retitled *Flykesmann*.
7 The description of Helge's childhood and youth is based primarily upon recorded interviews conducted during the years 1999 and 2000. Helge's brother Kaare also wrote several pages of notes and stories about the boys' childhood when Helge thought about writing an autobiography. These were used to supplement and check the interviewed material from Helge.
8 From recorded conversations summer of 1999.
9 G.C. Rieber AS was one of Bergen's largest and oldest businesses. It was established in 1879 and was based on processing hides, leather, and shoe wear. It quickly grew to be one of the largest of its kind in the north with affiliated stores in many other Norwegian towns. E. Ertresvaag, contributing writer, "Et bysamfunn i utvikling" (A City Society in Development), *Bergen bys historie*, vol. 3.
10 Taken largely from a note that Helge himself wrote in conjunction with the beginning of an autobiography.

11 Olav Ingstad was president of Christiania Football Club in 1889. In 1894, he suggested establishing a national association for football and in 1934 he was named a lifetime honorary member. *Norwegian Football Association Anniversary Issue* (Oslo, 1927), 15, 17, 19.

12 From recorded conversations, 1999.

13 Tuberculosis is not exclusively a lung disease but can afflict any organ in the body. Interview with Professor Gunnar Bjune.

14 From recorded conversations, 1999.

15 This poem has never been found despite a thorough search in Hugin archives by the school's students and teachers. Nor is there a copy in Helge's archives. But the story has been confirmed from various sources.

16 From recorded conversations, 2000.

17 Several years later Helge met history professor Sverre Steen in the Norwegian Science Academy, who also had "The Bishop" as a teacher and agreed that he was a good man who understood his students.

18 http://europeana1914-1918.eu/en/europeana/record/08607/URN_NBN_no_nb_video_5717.

19 A detailed description of the fire was written by Helge's brother Kaare and is filed in the Ingstad archives.

20 Hardangervidda encompasses an area of approximately 8,000 km^2.

21 This paragraph is widely based on Helge's own notes in connection with a draft of his autobiography.

22 Wild reindeer in Scandinavia are closely related to but slightly smaller than North American caribou.

23 This and all other quotes used from Helge's journal of his Hardanger trips can be found in Ingstad archives, E-0003.

24 Ingstad archives, E-0003.

25 Written by Helge while at university, around 1920, translated by J.K. Stenehjem.

26 He later took up smoking the pipe again and never quit until he was eighty-five years old.

27 Ingstad archives, E-0001. Helge kept and filed all correspondence he received as well as copies of many letters he sent which are now filed in the Ingstad archives. Helge's father also kept most letters received from Helge, which are also filed in the Ingstad archives.

28 From recorded conversations, 1999.

29 Letter from Kaare to Helge, October 1932. Ingstad archives, E-0001.

30 The local story was that this was how he toughened himself up to spend time in Canada. It is doubtful, however, that Helge had any such plans at the time to intentionally train for such difficult conditions.

31 Interview with Helge in membership magazine *Sverre*, no. 1 (1972).

32 Ingstad archives, E-0002.

CHAPTER TWO

1 The most important sources for this chapter are Helge's narrative accounts that were recorded between 1999 and 2000 as well as his book *The Land of Feast and Famine*, translated by Eugene Gay-Tifft (Alfred A. Knopf, 1933). *Pelsjegerliv: Blandt Nord-Kanandas Indianere* (Gyldendal Norsk Forlag, 1931).

2 http://edmonton.ca/city.../population-history.aspx.

3 Ingstad, *Land of Feast and Famine*, 3–4.

4 Dene people, also known as the Athabaskan peoples, are an indigenous group who live in Canada's Northwest Territories.

5 From Helge's journal, 24 December 1926. Ingstad archives, FA-001.

6 Hjalmar Dale went to Canada under the name Hjalmar Nilsson, or just Hamar, which was most likely an English simplification of Hjalmar. He later changed his name to Hjalmar Hammer.

7 H. Ingstad, "En villmarkens sønn" (Son of the Wilderness), in *Ingstads beste* (Oslo: Gyldendal Norsk Forlag, 2005). First published in the magazine *Hjemmet*, no. 44 (1936).

8 Undated notes written in connection to receiving the news about Dale's death. Ingstad archives, FA-0002.

9 Ingstad, *Land of Feast and Famine*, 4.

10 Ibid., 5–6.

11 Ibid., 8.

12 Ibid., 17.

13 From Helge's journal, 21 June 1927. Ingstad archives, FA-0001.

14 Ingstad archives, FA-0001.

15 On the map of the Northwest Territories, a small river that runs into Snowdrift River, Ingstad Creek, was named after Helge.

16 From this time onward, he begins to write his journal in English.

17 In order to use the sleds across the ice since the dense forests were impossible to get through.

18 Ingstad, *Land of Feast and Famine*, 51–2.

19 Ibid., 72.

20 *Vinterliv i Nord-Canadas villmark. En humoristisk beretning om en kinkig opplevelse*, in *Hjemmet*, no. 1 (1939). Also published in Ingstad, *Ingstads beste*.

21 Ingstad, *Land of Feast and Famine*, 90.

22 Ingstad archives, DA-0001: "I travelled from Reliance 18 Feb. 1929, stayed for three days with the Indians at Artillery Lake and then travelled to Thelon and further down the river by canoe to Baker Lake. I stayed here for 6 weeks. At Schultz Lake I met Hoare (game warden) who guided me further. In the spring, I returned to Beaverly Lake and remained there for two years. From here and down, there were only Eskimos. But they don't

venture further up than Beaverly Lake as they are afraid of the forest. Hoare travelled further for a month with Knoks then on to Reliance. Knoks followed. That time when Helge had his worst attempt towards the Thelon I was not far away, only half-a-day journey away. There were numbers of caribou around where I was. I travelled back to Beaverly Lake, around the shoreline and up towards Chesterfield Inlet and stayed there for six weeks. At that time, there was plenty of fox but then they disappeared. I then travelled south and settled by Lake Athabasca. From 1932, no new trappers came to the land. I met Antoine at Thelon in April after Helge had left in March. Clasen, Jansen and Jo Nilsen are now prospecting at Bear Lake."

23 Ingstad, *Land of Feast and Famine*, 145.

24 Information about Snowdrift in the 1930s was acquired from Kristen Olesen in conversations with elderly local residents. I thank her for the information.

25 The place was relocated due to an invasion of caterpillars.

26 Helge's journal, Ingstad archives, FA-0001.

27 Also part of the Dene who live in the northern boreal and Arctic regions of Canada. The Dene speak Northern Athabaskan languages.

28 Ingstad, *Land of Feast and Famine*, 182.

29 Ibid., 168–9.

30 Ibid., 193–4.

31 Ibid., 206.

32 Eileen Lake.

33 From the short story *Til Thelons kilder. En jule-tids sledeferd med Nord-Canadas indianere* (To the Sources of Thelon: A Christmas-Time Sled Trip with the Northern Canadian Indians). The place of publication is unknown.

34 Translated by J.K. Stenehjem.

35 Ingstad, *Land of Feast and Famine*, 238.

36 Ibid., 240–1.

37 Helge's letters were not saved.

38 Olav most likely meant that indigenous relatives of a potential in-law would expect an amount of support and share of assets.

39 Ingstad, *Land of Feast and Famine*, 291–2.

40 Ibid., 330.

41 Ibid., 331.

42 Ibid., 332.

43 Christiania was renamed Oslo in 1925.

44 He touches upon this subject briefly in *The Land of Feast and Famine* (*Pelsjegerliv*) and again in his books on East Greenland and Svalbard, and also in his stories from his time with the caribou-eating Nunamiut in Alaska.

45 Ray Mears, *The Real Heroes of Telemark: The True Story of the Secret Mission to Stop Hitler's Atomic Bomb* (London: Hodder and Stroughton, 2003), 111–13.

46 Ibid., 113.

CHAPTER THREE

1 Ingstad archives, DA-0001.

2 Ibid.

3 journals.cambridge.org/article_S0032247400042340.

4 Several quotes and information were obtained from *En avlyst fangstekspe-disjon* and *Eirik Raudes Land*, Ingstad archives, DA-0001, unless otherwise noted.

5 Helge had written and asked to meet him. Hoel sent a positive reply 9 September 1930.

6 This was assumed to be Gustav Smedal.

7 *Karmøybladet*, 24 October 2007.

8 Ida Blom, *Kampen om Eirik Raudes Land. Pressgruppe-politikk I Grøn-landsspørsmålet 1921–1931* (Oslo: Gyldendal Norsk Forlag, 1973), 174, writes that Helge's expedition was arranged the year after (1932) by private funding. This was only partly true. The main reason Helge was able to arrange the expedition was because he was employed (and therefore paid) by the Norwegian government as governor.

9 Aleksandra Mikhajlovna Kollontaj was minister for the Soviet Union in Norway in 1922–26 and 1927–30. She had a similar position in Sweden in 1930–45. *Aschehoug og Gyldendals Store Norske Leksikon* (Oslo: Kunnskapsforlaget, 1980).

10 Ingstad archives, FB-0003.

11 Telegram from the Justice Dept. to Governor Ingstad, 11 July 1932. Ingstad archives, FB-0001.

12 Ingstad archives, FB-0003.

13 King Haakon VII was Danish born and called Prince Carl of Denmark until 1905, when Norway gained independence from Sweden. Haakon VII became the first king of Norway.

14 Helge Ingstad, *East of the Great Glacier*, translated by Eugene Gay-Tifft (Alfred A. Knopf, 1937), 17. *Øst for den store bre* (Oslo: Gyldendal, 1935).

15 Newspaper clipping from an unknown newspaper. There is no date but it was clearly published a short time before the *Polarbjørn*'s departure. Ingstad archives, FB-0001.

16 Helge Ingstad, *Landet med de kalde kyster* (Oslo: Gyldendal, 1948), 260–1.

17 Ingstad archives, FB-0003.

18 A letter from Helge to carpenter Marthinsen, Storgt. 38, Oslo, dated 4 July 1932, shows that in exchange for building "9 huts made of wood" Marthinsen was paid 13,000 Norwegian kroner, excluding material.

19 Ingstad, *East of the Great Glacier*, 93.

20 Ibid., 155–6.

21 Ingstad archives, FB-0005.

22 Ibid.

23 Piotr Migoń, *Geomorphological Landscapes of the World* (New York: Springer, 2010), 227.

24 Ingstad, *East of the Great Glacier*, 215–16.

25 Ibid., 221.

26 Ibid., 228.

27 Ibid.

28 Ibid., 229–30.

29 Ingstad archives, FB-0003.

30 Both the coded and deciphered notes are stored in box FB-0003 in Ingstad archives.

31 Ingstad archives, FB-0003.

32 Ingstad, *East of the Great Glacier*, 269.

33 Today called Centre Party.

34 Blom, *Kampen om Eirik Raudes Land*, 59–60.

35 Ingstad archives, DA-0001.

36 Ibid.

CHAPTER FOUR

1 From Svalbard's national song. H. Ingstad, *Spor I sneen*, translated by J.K. Stenehjem (Oslo: Gyldendal, 2002).

2 Ingstad archives, DA-0002.

3 Letter to Mrs Nansen's brother, Herstein Sandberg, 4 September 1933.

4 4 September 1933, Ingstad archives, DA-0001.

5 14 September 1933, Ingstad archives, DA-0001.

6 The preceding journey description is based on Helge's own notes. Ingstad archives, DA-0002.

7 Recorded conversation, July 1999, Ingstad archives.

8 H. Ingstad, *Siste båt* (Oslo: Gyldendal, 1948).

9 Recorded conversations, summer 1999.

10 H. Ingstad, *Landet med de kalde kyster* (Oslo: Gyldendal Norsk Forlag, 1948), 239–40.

11 Ingstad archives, DA-0001.

12 Ingstad, *Landet med de kalde kyster*, 259.

13 This section is adapted partly from an article of the same name whose origins are unclear. The article elaborates more on the occurrences than does the similarly titled chapter in the book *Landet med de kalde kyster*.

14 This section is partly based on a manuscript for an unknown weekly magazine and is somewhat more extensive than the chapter titled "Gjennom storm og mørke" (Through Storm and Darkness) in the Svalbard book, *Landet med de kalde kyster*.

15 Neither the book chapter nor the article mentions anything about Helge becoming seriously ill during this trip. The version that I tell here is correct and was provided to me by Helge.

16 Ingstad, *Landet med de kalde kyster,* 314.

17 Undated telegram in Ingstad archives, DA-0002.

18 Dated 14 February 1935. In the private collection of the Ingstad family.

19 There was still a certain stigma associated with the disease, but, most importantly, it could be contagious if left untreated.

20 Ingstad archives, DA-0003.

21 Tore Sørensen, "Sysselmannen på Svalbards vanskelige barndom" (The Governor Position of Svalbard's Difficult Childhood), *Svalbardposten,* no. 50, 22 December 2000.

CHAPTER FIVE

1 Letter to his parents, 20 December 1936, Ingstad archives, FD-0001.

2 He was offered $400 for the article if they printed it and $100 dollars whether or not it was accepted.

3 It was not unusual at the time that nameless rivers and mountains were given names of white people who had been there. It was also known in Canada that Helge had written *The Land of Feast and Famine (Pelsjegerliv).*

4 Letter to his parents, Ingstad archives, FD-0001.

5 Letter to his parents, 13 February 1937, Ingstad archives, FD-0001.

6 Recorded conversations, 1999.

7 Population of Phoenix, Arizona, in 1930: 48,118. http:/www2.census.gov/ prod2/decennial/documents/10612963v3p1cho2.pdf. In 1940, its population was 65,414. http:/www.2.census.gov/prod2/decennial/documents/ 33973538v2p1ch5.pdf.

8 Descriptions in this section are based directly, and indirectly, on journal notes that Helge sent home to his parents for safekeeping. Ingstad archives, FD-0002.

9 Letter dated 9 June 1937, Ingstad archives, FD-0002.

10 Ingstad archives, FD-0005.

11 Ingstad archives, FD-0002.

12 Ibid.

13 Told to his father Olav in a letter dated 9 June 1935. Ingstad archives, FD-0001.

CHAPTER SIX

1 Today scholars have concluded that Native Americans in the American southwest and the northwestern part of Mexico, including the Navajo and Apache, speak an Athabaskan language like the Dene's. It is believed this

language connection indicates a migration of these peoples from the north to the south.

2 Ingstad archives, FD-0002.

3 This description is taken from a letter Helge wrote home to his parents dated 2 August 1937. Ingstad archives, FD-0001.

4 Ingstad archives, FD-0005.

5 Letter dated 3 October 1937, Ingstad archives, FD-0003.

6 Journal notes, 13 August 1937, Ingstad archives, FD-0003.

7 Helge held a theory that the Navajo and Apache peoples were originally Caribou Eaters who had wandered south as one tribe before they divided into different nations. Scholars now say that Athabaskan peoples *did* migrate south from Alaska and Canada and split into several distinct groups, including the Apache and Navajo.

8 Journal entry, Ingstad archives, FD-0002.

9 Ibid.

10 http://www.biography.com/people/geronimo-9309607?page=2.

11 H. Ingstad, *The Apache Indians: In Search of the Missing Tribe*, translated by Janine K. Stenehjem (Lincoln and London: University of Nebraska Press, 2004), 30–1. *Apache-Indianerne: Jakten på den tapte stamme* (Oslo: Gyldendal Norsk Forlag, 1939.

12 Ibid., 31.

13 Ibid., 30.

14 Ibid., 77.

15 Letter dated 12 October 1937, Ingstad archives, FD-0002.

16 Ingstad, *The Apache Indians*, 78.

17 Letter dated 5 October 1937, Ingstad archives, FD-0002.

18 G. Goodwin and N. Goodwin, *The Apache Diaries: A Father-Son Journey* (Lincoln and London: University of Nebraska Press, 2000).

19 Letter dated 10 October 1937, Ingstad archives, FD-0004.

20 Letter dated 4 October 1937, Ingstad archives, FD-0004.

21 Among other things, after contact with anthropologist Morris Opler.

22 Ingstad archives, FD-0002.

23 Dated 16 October 1937, Ingstad archives, FD-0003.

24 Dated 11 November 1937, Ingstad archives, FD-0002.

25 Ingstad, *The Apache Indians*, 98.

26 Ibid., 104.

27 Ibid., 113–14.

28 Ibid., 132.

29 Ibid.

30 Journal entry, 23 December 1937, Ingstad archives, FD-0005.

31 Ibid.

32 Ibid.

33 Letter dated 22 February 1938, Ingstad archives, FD-0003.

34 Letter dated 17 February 1938, Ingstad archives, FD-0003.

35 Ingstad archives, FD-0003.

36 He is referring to the so-called "Night of Broken Glass" in Germany on 9 November 1938.

37 Not until many years later, in 2004, after Helge had died, was the manuscript accepted by the University of Nebraska Press after certain linguistic alterations of the manuscript by his anthropologist daughter. Finally, the term "wild" Apaches was changed to the "free" Apaches.

38 Another critical voice arose when the book was first published. Norwegian immigrant Odd Halset, whom Helge had met in Arizona, wrote a somewhat seething post in the *Nordic Journal* in which he accused Helge of falsifying history.

39 The Norwegian newspaper *Dagbladet*, 20 June 1940.

40 Letter from Normann Andersen dated 3 July 1937, Ingstad archives, FB-0001.

41 Letter dated 26 October 1937, Ingstad archives, FD-0002.

CHAPTER SEVEN

1 From an unfinished manuscript Anne Stine began about her childhood in Lillehammer.

2 Conversations with L. Forfang on 23 February 2001.

3 Eilif worked on a doctoral degree in copyright law, which most likely would have been groundbreaking work, but died before he was able to finish it.

4 In the early 1900s, Anders Sandvig, a local dentist, began collecting objects from the old Norwegian farming culture that was in the process of disappearing. He also bought, deconstructed, and then rebuilt old buildings in his own garden in Lillehammer, which were later moved to a large plot that became the open-air museum.

5 Bjørnstjerne Bjørnson was one of Norway's, and Europe's, most important writers in the second half of the 1800s. He was quite prolific and his work includes novels, short stories, plays, and poetry. In addition to this, he was also a journalist, commentator, theatre director, and political activist.

CHAPTER EIGHT

1 Notes for an autobiography.

2 Roald Amundsen and Fridtjof Nansen were the most famous and celebrated polar explorers in Norway at the time.

3 Louise had briefly met Helge at a ball when she was younger, and Helge's sister Gunvor worked as an assistant to Anders Sandvig for a period at Maihaugen.

4 Werner von Grünau, *Die letzten Inseln* (Leipzig: Paul List Verlag, 1937).

5 Dated Lillehammer, 3 March 1939.
6 Anne Stine and Helge met Werner and his wife on two occasions. Once they visited them during a trip through Germany, and the second time was when Werner and his wife visited Norway. Werner named his oldest son Tycho.

CHAPTER NINE

1 H. Ingstad, *Nedtegnelser fra krigens utbrudd i Norge*. In *Ingstads beste: høydepunkter fra et eventrylig liv* (Oslo: Gyldendal Norsk Forlag, 2005).
2 Approximately 200 km northeast of Lillehammer.
3 Recorded conversations from summer 1999. In the Ingstad archives.
4 The stories about the war experiences are partly obtained from recorded conversations from summer 1999 and partly from an introduction to a book about the war that Helge had begun but was not able to finish.
5 The Administrative Council was the civilian governing body in the German-occupied part of Norway from 15 April to 25 September 1940.
6 Ingstad archives, G-001.
7 Description from the Administrative Council dated 18 April 1940. Ingstad archives, G-001.
8 From Helge's journal, 4 September–11 October. Ingstad archives, G-0003.
9 During the Second World War, Sweden maintained a policy of neutrality.
10 A letter dated 25 April from Helge to his father about the wedding.
11 From Eilif's speech to Anne Stine at her wedding on 21 May 1941; not in the archives but in the family's possession.
12 Later letters reveal that this "thingy" was a large salmon.
13 "White Buses" was an operation run by the Swedish Red Cross and the Danish government in the spring of 1945 to rescue Scandinavian concentration camp inmates and return them home. The term "white buses" originates from the buses having been painted white with red crosses to avoid confusion with military vehicles.
14 The stories about Bårdsetbakken are based partly on Anne Stine's own written narratives for a draft of an autobiography.
15 From Anne Stine's unfinished draft of an autobiography.

CHAPTER TEN

1 Eilifsen was a policeman who was shot because he declined to arrest a few young girls who had refused community services that were demanded of them by the Germans. See H.F. Dahl, *Vidkun Quisling. En fører for fall.* (Oslo: Aschehoug, 1992), 445–57.
2 Many considered Nasjonal Samling (National Unity Party) to be a Norwegian version of the Nazi Party. Most refused to co-operate with it in any way.
3 Helge wrote down the interviews he had with Quisling.

4 Later, Helge wrote a comment in pencil on his typewritten manuscript: "The end written in a slightly infatuated mood due to seeing a condemned prisoner's despair. I am not at all that now. Quisling has committed a crime against his country and it is terrible what he has done."

5 Helge's interview with Quisling.

6 Quisling *was* found guilty of embezzlement, murder, and high treason and was executed by a firing squad at Akershus Fortress in Oslo on 24 October 1945. So strong was the effect of Quisling's betrayal on Norway that the word "quisling," even in English, is now synonymous with the term "traitor" and "collaborationist."

7 The death penalty in Norway was reinstated after the Second World War as military criminal punishment, later abolished in 1979 and constitutionally prohibited in 2014.

8 Taped interview from the summer of 1999. Available in the Ingstad archives.

9 Personal communication, local historian Jon Vegard Lunde, Lillehammer.

10 From Helge's letter to his father, reprinted in Y. Ustvedt, *Den varme freden – den kalde krigen. Det skjedde i Norge 1945–52*, vol. 1 (Oslo: Gyldendal, 1978), 147.

11 Helge's interview with Saatvedt.

12 Personal communication with local historian Jon Vegard Lunde, Lillehammer.

13 In his conversations with me, Helge refused to say who this was, but answered my question by saying "It is unimportant now."

14 Bernt Balchen was a pioneer polar aviator, navigator, aircraft mechanical engineer, and military leader. He helped establish Det Norske Luftfartselskap (DNL) (the Norwegian Airline Company), which began commercial Europe–US airline flights across the North Pole. DNL later merged with Danish and Swedish airlines to become Scandinavian Airlines. In 1931, Balchen was aviator mechanic for Amelia Earhart and helped modify her plane for her solo transatlantic flight.

15 Helge's letter to Balchen.

16 Helge's letter for reallocation of grant money.

17 Letter dated 18 August 1950. Not in the archives.

CHAPTER ELEVEN

1 At that time, there was discussion among ethnographers whether Inuit had come from Asia or whether the culture had developed independently in North America. The most accepted theory is that Inuit have Asian DNA.

2 During the period Helge was there, the Nunamiut people used mostly their Inuit names but also had English names which they often used in combination with their Inuit name as a last name. That is why Helge often discusses

Simon Paneak with his Inuit name Paneak as a last name and his wife as Umealaq. Later he refers to them as Simon and Susie Paneak and their children by their English names.

3 Son George was born while Helge was there and later Simon and Susie also had two more children, Allen and Alice.

4 N.J. Gubser, *The Nunamiut Eskimos Hunters of Caribou* (New Haven and London: Yale University Press, 1965).

5 J.M. Campbell, ed., *In a Hungry Country: Essays by Simon Paneak* (Fairbanks: University of Alaska Press, 2004).

6 Simon Paneak was born in 1900 and died in 1975.

7 According to Campbell, *In a Hungry Country*, these were not coincidental, unknown places, but places from previous journeys they knew where various resources could be obtained.

8 Gubser, *Hunters of Caribou*.

9 Campbell, *In a Hungry Country*.

10 In 1898, the first 1,280 domestic reindeer were introduced to Alaska from Siberia. The project was only moderately successful. The reindeer tended to escape and mix with the wild caribou. The Inuit were more interested in hunting than herding. Until 1920, it was not permitted for anyone other than indigenous peoples to raise reindeer. When this law was changed, two brothers named Lomen introduced several thousand more reindeer. They also brought Sami people and reindeer from Norway to teach Inuit to herd; around 1929 about 600 Sami and Inuit were employed for this purpose (Gubser, *Hunters of Caribou*). In 1940, the Lomen brothers sold the animals to the state and they were transferred to Nunivak Island where a herd still exists.

11 H. Ingstad, *Nunamiut: Among Alaska's Inland Eskimos*, translated by F.H. Lyon (London: Unwin Brothers, 1954), 59. *Nunamiut: Blant alaskas innlandseskimoer* (Oslo: Gyldendal, 1951).

12 Ingstad archives, FR-002.

13 Ingstad, *Nunamiut*, 181–2.

14 Ingstad, *Alaska's Inland Eskimos*, 88.

15 From Helge's journal, 10 September. Ingstad archives, FE-0005.

16 Ingstad archives, FE-0002.

17 They were called this because they came from the place called Killik River.

18 Wolverine fur does not gather frosty icicles in the cold and that is why it is used this close to the face.

19 Ingstad, *Alaska's Inland Eskimos*, 201.

20 This description of Christmas is based on Helge's journal entries (Ingstad archives, FE-0005); H. Ingstad, "Jul hos Alaskas innlandseskimoer" (Christmas with Alaska's Inland Eskimos), *Julehelg* 31 (Oslo: Dreier, 1952); and H. Ingstad, *Blant Alaskas innlandseskimoer* (Together with Alaska's Inland Eskimos), 191–3.

21 Letter to Anne Stine dated 30 December 1949. Privately owned by family, not in archives.

22 Based on an unpublished note. Ingstad archives, FA-0003.

23 Ingstad, *Alaska's Inland Eskimos*, 208.

24 Ibid., 209.

25 Ibid., 252.

26 Ibid., 253.

27 I had the opportunity to go through these archives while attending the naming ceremony of Ingstad Mountain in 2006.

28 In 1952, Paneak worked for Professor Lawrence Irving to help catch and register birds. As a means of thanking Paneak, Irving took him and his sons Raymond and Roosevelt to a conference in the south to present the results.

29 Campbell, *Hungry Country*.

30 Gubser, *Hunters of Caribou*.

CHAPTER TWELVE

1 The Norwegian newspaper *Aftenposten*, 8 July 1950.

2 A Dr. philos. degree can be taken without previous education in the relevant subjects. Therefore, Helge could possibly have gotten a Dr. philos. degree in the subject that was then called ethnography if he had prioritized it.

3 This was later edited into a CD by composer and musicologist Sigvald Tveit. H. Ingstad, E. Groven, S. Tveit, *Songs of the Nunamiut: Historical Recordings of an Alaskan Eskimo Community* (Oslo: Tano-Aschehoug, 1998).

CHAPTER THIRTEEN

1 According to the Sagas this occurred "14 or 15 winters before Christianity was introduced to the island," which means 985 or 986. H. Ingstad, *Landet under Leidarstjernen* (Oslo: Gyldendal, 1959).

2 Dale Mackenzie Brown, *The Fate of Greenland's Vikings*, Archaeological Institute of America, 28 February 2000, archive.archaeology.org/online/features/greenland/.

3 H.C. Gulløv, ed., *Grønlands forhistorie* (Copenhagen: Gyldendal, 2004).

4 Saga scholars believe this story to have been later made up.

5 For the one-thousand-year celebration of Leif Eiriksson's discovery of America in 2000, a replica of Thjodhilds church was built at Brattahlid at Østerbyd in Greenland.

6 DNA tests now confirm that these two folk groups did not intermix.

7 Ingstad, *Landet under Leidarstjernen*, 36.

8 The description of Greenland is based partly on Anne Stine's journal and partly on what Helge wrote in *Landet under Leidarstjernen* (*Land under*

the Pole Star). I myself visited Brattahlid in September 2009 and could therefore also elaborate with my own impressions.

9 I have chosen to use the Saga's place names, as Helge does in his book, and have included current Greenland place names in parentheses.

10 Gulløv, *Grønlands forhistorie*, 249.

11 Ingstad, *Landet under Leidarstjernen*, 440–1.

12 Sandnes was excavated by the Danish archaeologist Aage Roussell. Roussell, "Sandnes and the Neighbouring Farms," *Meddelelser om Grønland* 88, no. 2 (1936).

13 Ingstad, *Landet under Leidarstjernen*, 444–6.

14 Letter dated 27 October 1954, not filed in the archives.

15 Ingstad, *Landet under Leidarstjernen*, 514–21.

16 Like the story described in Niels Egede's diary. He was the son of Hans Egede, lived from 1710 to 1782, and spoke the language of the Inuit fluently.

CHAPTER FOURTEEN

1 P.B. Taylor, "The Hønen Runes: A Survey," *Neophilologus* 60, no. 1 (January 1976): 1–7.

2 Ibid.

3 There was also an earlier version in the so-called Hauksbok from approximately 1350.

4 Rev J. Sephton, *Eirik the Red's Saga* (Gloucestershire, UK: Dodo Press, 2009).

5 Abstracts from the Sagas are taken from the translation of A. Holtsmark, *Vinland det gode. Av Eirik Raudes Saga og en saga om grønlendingene* (Oslo: Fabritius & sønner, 1964).

6 *Mark* means forest or woods in the old Norse language.

7 He is also mentioned in the *Grønlandssagen*, but plays a smaller role in relation to Eirik Raudes' children.

8 This is told only in *Grønlandssagen*.

9 This date is chosen because this was the day that the first group of organized immigrants from Norway (Stavanger) landed in New York in 1825 on the ship *Restaurasjonen*.

10 Leif Erikson Day was proclaimed a "Day of Observance" by the US Congress in 1964. It was first recognized by Lyndon B. Johnson, who invited Anne Stine and Helge to the White House as guests of honour for the first official announcement.

11 W.A. Munn, *Vineland Voyages: Location of Helluland, Markland and Vinland* (St John's: St John's Daily Telegram, 1930).

12 V. Tanner, "De gamla nordbornas Helluland, Markland och Vinland," *Budkavlen*, vol. 20 (Åbo: Foreningen Brage og Åbo Akademi, 1941), 58.

13 Ibid., 1.

14 He leans towards Fridtjof Nansen's theory in *Nord i tåkeheimen* that stories about grapes, thus the changing interpretation of the name, were introduced at a later date by Saga printers' contacts with other Europeans, especially the Irish.

15 Tanner, "De gamla nordbornas," 21.

16 Ibid., 31.

17 *Hóp* is also defined as a "land-locked inlet still influenced by tides." R. Williams, *Icelandic-English Glossary of Selected Geoscience Terms*, pubs.usgs.gov/of/1995/of95-807/geoicelandic.html.

18 H. Ingstad, *Vesterveg til Vinland* (Oslo: Gyldendal Norsk Forlag, 1965), 111–12.

19 Including G. Storm, *Studier av Vinlandsreisene, Vinlands geografi og etnografi* (Copenhagen, 1888).

20 http://www.mysteriesofcanada.com/newfoundland/beothuk/.

21 http://anthropology.uwaterloo.ca/ArcticArchStuff/dorset.html.

22 This organization had been established to improve living and health conditions for fishermen. Shocked by the widespread poverty and the almost total lack of health services, Grenfell collected funds and was later joined by several doctors to establish a hospital in Battle Harbour, Labrador. Eventually, a number of health centres, staffed by nurses, were also established along the coast and the headquarters moved to St Anthony in 1901. Various measures were also initiated to provide the population with alternative sources of income when fishing failed. A handicraft project is still running, but an attempt at domestic reindeer herding failed after a few years. Dr Grenfell continued to work in Newfoundland and Labrador until his passing and remains a legendary figure in the area.

23 This was seventeen years before the World Health Organization had its famous Alma-Ata meeting that established the slogan and campaign "Health for All by the Year 2000." This campaign promoted primary health care supported by a referral system at various levels, not unlike the Grenfell Mission had during the 1960s.

24 Colin Archer was a Scottish naval architect and shipbuilder from Larvik, Norway. His parents emigrated to Norway from Scotland in 1825. He was known for building safe and durable ships, including the Fram, used in both Fridtjof Nansen's and Roald Amundsen's polar expeditions. https://en.wikipedia.org/wiki/Colin_Archer.

25 Clayton Colbourne is now a guide at the museum at L'Anse aux Meadows.

26 Not much later, in 1964, the Gannet Islands became a wildlife reserve and in 1983 were designated the Gannet Islands Ecological Reserve, now open only to a few scientists due to its sensitive nature. Canadian Department of Environment and Conservation, http://www.env.gov.nl.ca/env/parks/wer/r_gie/.

27 A.S. Ingstad, *Det nye land med de grønne enger* (Oslo: Gyldendal norsk forlag, 1975).

CHAPTER FIFTEEN

1 Roussell later claimed to have been misquoted by the press and said that his statements were a defensive reaction to claims that the Danish National Museum had done nothing to search for Vinland.
2 Newspaper clippings are filed in the Ingstad archives, FF-0013. Letters from this section are filed in FB-0014.
3 Dorset culture was a palaeo-Eskimo culture that came before Inuit in Arctic North America and Greenland. We talk about three phases in this culture: the early phase that began around 500 B.C., the middle that started around A.D. 800 and the last phase around A.D. 1000–1500. http://en.wikipedia.org/wiki/Dorset_culture.
4 Among others, *Stavanger Aftenblad*, 11 May 1960.
5 The letter is written on blue carbonless copy paper and is filed in Ingstad archives, FB-00014.
6 J. Meldgaard, "Fra Brattalid til Vinland," *Naturens Verden* (December 1961): 353–8.
7 It has since been argued that Meldgaard at this meeting mentioned to Helge where he was going to dig. Helge denied that such was the case, but it is of little importance since Helge found the ruins at L'Anse aux Meadows at the beginning of August 1961, that is, the year before.
8 C. Koch Madsen and M. Appelt, *Meldgaard's Vinland Vision* (Copenhagen: National Museum of Denmark, 2010).
9 *Montreal Star*, 4 October 1961.
10 Script of cassette tape L-0285 in Norwegian Broadcasting Channel archives. Files from DRA archive 3013, cuts 6 and 7.
11 See note 1.
12 *Aftenposten*, 11 November 1961, evening issue.
13 *Berlingske Tidende*, 11 November 1961.
14 *Politiken*, 10 November 1961.
15 For the future, it may be useful to set up a timeline for the main events concerning the conflict with the Danes. Everything can be documented through archival footage and quoted newspaper references:
1953: Helge visited Copenhagen. Obvious first meeting with Meldgaard. Pleasant conversation that mostly revolved around questions about Norse ruins in West Greenland. Vinland question also discussed.
1955: Letter from Meldgaard in which he informs Helge that his plans for a Vinland expedition in 1955 have been postponed to the following year. Helge responds and says his own expedition probably will be later

than that. He wishes him good luck and says that there is no competition between them.

1956: Meldgaard travels to Newfoundland on a one-man expedition. Says later that he explored bays west of Cape Bauld.

1958: Meeting in Copenhagen. Meldgaard informs Helge about his journey and says (according to Helge's notes) that he has explored the coast from the northern tip and southward along the east coast of the "long tongue" in Newfoundland. Is this correct, or a deliberate cover-up, or has Helge misunderstood? Says he has seen something that he will look into in the future.

1959: *Landet under Leidarstjernen* comes out in Norwegian. Here, Helge presents his theories (based partly on Tanner and the Stefanson map) that Helluland had to lie on Baffin Island, Markland along the coast of Labrador, and Vinland in Newfoundland's northern tip.

1960: Summer. Helge and Benedicte are in Newfoundland. Find promising ruins at L'Anse aux Meadows. According to the locals, no others from outside the area had been there and previously seen them. The find was kept secret.

1960: Late autumn. Helge is in Copenhagen for the launch of *Leidarstjernen* in Danish. Meeting with Meldgaard in which two Danish journalists afterwards claim to have heard Meldgaard tell Helge where he should look. Neither Meldgaard nor Helge recall this when asked. At this point the ruins have already been found, but not disclosed.

1961: Late October. *Halten* expedition arrives home after sailing along the Newfoundland and Labrador coast and first excavations at L'Anse aux Meadows. The findings are published as "promising finds of Norse ruins" at a press conference in New York on 13 October. On 9 November, the full-page newspaper story with a claim from Roussell that the Danes had found the ruins first. The controversy breaks loose. Meldgaard publishes in December an article about his 1956 trip in which he clearly says that what he found was a landscape that matched the Saga descriptions, not ruins. He repeats in several newspaper interviews and on radio that he has never set foot in L'Anse aux Meadows. Roussell does not give up and the battle continues.

16 It is said in a letter from Premier Smallwood to Raymond Gushue, dated 17 January 1962, that Linton is the son of "one of the greatest American archaeologists." This could possibly be Professor Ralph Linton and so may explain the authority that was associated with his letter. However, it has not been possible to confirm this. The letter from Premier Smallwood is in Memorial University's archives and a copy in the Ingstad archives, FF-0039.

17 The original is kept in the archives at Memorial University, St John's, Newfoundland. A copy is located in the Ingstad archives, FF-0039.

18 See note 15.

19 Attempts to find an American photographer named David Linton on Google have not been successful. For the record, I perused the archives of the former manager of the National Museum of Iceland, later president, Kristian Eldjàrn, who presumably must have had some contact with Danish archaeologists, but did not find any traces of Linton.

20 Letter from R. Gushue to I. Whitaker, 1962. Original is kept in the archives at Memorial University of Newfoundland and a copy in the Ingstad archives, FF-0039.

21 Letter dated 19 February 1962 from Sir Mortimer Wheeler to president of Memorial University, R. Gushue. Original is kept in the archives at Memorial University of Newfoundland and a copy in the Ingstad archives, FF-0039.

22 Letter to Dr Raymond Gushue from R.A. MacKay, Carleton University, Ottawa. Ingstad archives, FF-0039.

23 Ingstad archives, FF-0049.

24 Letter from Anne Stine to her mother, Louise, dated 9 July 1962. Not in the archives but in family collection.

25 Eldjàrn was later named Iceland's third president (1968–1980).

26 Eldjàrn's son Thòrarinn Eldjàrn kindly lent me a copy of the journal his father kept during the expedition at L'Anse aux Meadows and gave permission to use it. The journal was translated from Icelandic to Norwegian by Thelma Dogg Robertsdottir.

27 Recorded conversations summer 1999. In the Ingstad archives.

28 From Anne Stine's journal for 1960–61. Ingstad archives, H-0003.

29 Radiocarbon dating was conducted by the laboratory at the Norwegian University of Science and Technology, NTNU.

30 In *Land under the Pole Star* Helge mentioned the possibility that a more southerly Vinland could also exist. He discarded this theory in subsequent publications. He didn't rule out, however, that the Norse seafarers could have taken detours farther south on their journeys.

31 Eldjàrn's journal. See note 26.

32 Eldjàrn writes "1962" here but either he recorded it incorrectly or G. Decker conveyed it mistakenly in that the year was 1962 when the quote was made.

33 Eldjàrn's journal. See note 26.

34 A few years later, they found the other half of the stone in the river below. They dammed the river temporarily, steering it into a new direction.

35 Iron was a vitally important resource to Vikings, for farm tools and equipment, for shipbuilding and repair, and weaponry. The Norse in Greenland depended on imports of iron, mostly from Norway and Iceland.

36 Report by Henry B. Collins to Dr Carmichael dated 22 October 1963. The original is in Memorial University archives with copies in Ingstad archives, FF-0039.

37 Statement by Dr Junius Bird, curator of archaeology, American Museum of Natural History. The original is in Memorial University archives with copies in Ingstad archives, FF-0039.

38 Eldjàrn's journal. See note 26.

39 Letters of this correspondence are filed in Memorial University archives with copies in Ingstad archives, FF-0039.

40 Ingstad archives, DA-0011.

41 It appears from correspondence between Whitaker and Eldjàrn that Whitaker understands "Scandinavian." Among other things, Eldjàrn writes a letter to him in Danish. Maybe he had studied or stayed for a period in Denmark?

42 The question was repeated in a new letter, 7 September 1964.

43 Letter in Danish dated 16 June 1954. The original is in Memorial University archives and a copy in Ingstad archives, FF-0039.

44 Letter from Premier Smallwood dated 5 June 1964. Ingstad archives, DA-0011.

45 A.S. Ingstad et al., *The Discovery of a Norse Settlement in America: Excavations at L'Anse aux Meadows, Newfoundland 1961–1968* (Oslo: Universitetsforlaget, 1977).

46 Draft of a letter to Premier Smallwood, undated. Ingstad archives, DA-0011.

47 Letter is dated 16 June 1964 and is filed in Memorial University archives and a copy in Ingstad archives, FF-0039.

48 Ingstad archives, FF-0039.

49 The formal correctness of this could possibly be questioned.

50 It is not found anywhere in the surviving archival material to suggest that sponsorship funds had been used for purposes other than expenses for the expeditions. Helge and Anne Stine, in other words, worked all those years without any form of compensation.

51 H. Ingstad, *Vesterveg til Vinland* (Oslo: Gyldendal Norsk Forlag, 1965).

52 F. Mowat, *Westviking: The Ancient Norse in Greenland and North America* (Toronto: McClelland and Stewart/Boston: Little, Brown Company, 1965).

53 *Evening Telegram* (St John's), 5 February 1964.

54 A stick is inserted in the hole in the wheel, and by setting it to rotate, like a top, wool is twisted around, spinning the yarn into threads.

55 Letter dated 29 December 1965.

56 K.A. Seaver, *Maps, Myths and Men: The Story of the Vinland Map* (Stanford, CA: Stanford University Press, 2004).

57 Helge received a medal from the British Royal Geographical Society and several other honorary degrees in Norway, Canada, and the US. He was an honorary member of the Norwegian Academy of Science and Letters. He also held honorary doctorates at the University of Oslo, Memorial University of Newfoundland in Canada, and at St Olaf College in Minnesota. He was awarded the Grand Cross of the Royal Norwegian Order of St Olav (in

1991; previously Knight 1st class in 1965 and Commander in 1970), Knight of the Order of Vasa, and was presented with the Norwegian Red Cross Badge of Honour for his efforts in Finnmark during the Second World War. For her efforts, Anne Stine Ingstad received numerous awards and honours, including the Franklin L. Burr Award from the National Geographic Society (1965), the Wahlberg medal from Svenska för Sällskapet Anthropologie och Geography (1967), and the Patron Medal from the Royal Geographical Society in London (1991). She was a member of the Norwegian Academy of Science and Letters in 1990 and became an honorary doctor at Memorial University, St John's, Newfoundland, in 1979 and at the University of Bergen, 1992. In 1979, she was appointed a Knight of the 1st Class Order of St Olav and a Commander in 1991.

58 From Anne Stine's journal, 28 August 1968. Ingstad archives, FF-0010.

59 Ingstad archives, FF-0010.

60 V. Hreinsson et al., *The Complete Sagas of Icelanders (Including 49 Tales)*, vol. 1 (Iceland: Leifur Eiriksson Publishing, 1992).

CHAPTER SIXTEEN

1 Ingstad archives, FF-0031.

2 Ingstad archives, DA-0014, FF-0010.

3 Ingstad archives, FF-0031.

4 In 1963, Anne Stine received CAN$2,000 from the Newfoundland government, but this appears to be the only time she received anything.

5 Other members included Dr Thor Magnusson, director of the National Museum in Reykjavik, Dr Bengt Schönbäck in Stockholm, Dr Leslie Harris, dean of Faculty of Arts and Sciences, Memorial University of Newfoundland, Dr W.E. Taylor, director of the Museum of Man in Ottawa, and John H. Frederick, head of the Research Department at the National Historic Sites Services in Ottawa.

6 Letter from Helge to Vice-Director Bennett dated 1 March 1972. This is kept in Sverre Marstrander's Vinland files, which are kept along with the Ingstad archives.

7 Edward Roberts was at the time leader of the Liberal Party, which was in opposition. Since he had been a Member of Parliament for northern Newfoundland for several years, he had, besides a general interest in history, a special interest in L'Anse aux Meadows.

8 The sequence of events in the following is based on a letter from Anne Stine to the director of Parks Canada, Pat Thomson, dated 14 September 1976. It is filed in the Ingstad archives, FF-0031.

9 Official minutes of the meeting of the International Research Advisory Committee, 14 April 1975. Located in Professor Sverre Marstranders files included in the Ingstad archives.

10 Ibid.

11 Ibid.

12 Letter from Helge to Director P.A. Thomson, dated 18 February 1976. Ingstad archives, FF-0031.

13 Ibid.

14 Ingstad archives, FF-0033.

15 Ibid.

16 Dated 14 September 1976. Ingstad archives, FF-0031.

17 Letter from Anne Stine to director for Parks Canada, Pat Thomson, dated 14 September 1976. Ingstad archives, FF-0031.

18 Ibid.

19 Ibid.

20 Letter from James G. Canning, clerk of the Executive Council, to Premier Frank D. Moores, 12 October 1976. Reprinted in J.R. Red Thoms, *Our First Thousand Years* (St John's, Newfoundland: Stirling Communications International, 2000).

21 Letter from Premier Frank D. Moores to James G. Canning, clerk of the Executive Council, dated 19 October 1976. Reprinted in Thoms, *Our First Thousand Years*.

22 See, for example, B.L. Wallace, *Westward Vikings: The Saga of L'Anse aux Meadows* (Historic Sites Association of Newfoundland and Labrador, 2006). This book, which serves as a kind of official presentation of the park and ruins, does present Anne Stine and Helge as the ones who discovered the site and first excavated it. But in the further presentation of the site, no mention is made of Anne Stine's work on the excavations, discoveries, and scientific discussions so that the unaware reader easily gets the impression that it is Parks Canada that has stood behind the most important elements. Such lack of references is highly remarkable in scientific circles. Nor are there references to Helge's historical discussions.

23 He justifies this in an appendix to the second edition of Anne Stine's 1977 book, *The Discovery of a Norse Settlement in America: Excavations at L'Anse aux Meadows, Newfoundland from 1961 to 1968*, vol. 1 (Oslo-Bergen-Tromso: University Publisher, 1977).

24 A.S. Ingstad et al., "The Norse Settlement at L'Anse aux Meadows Newfoundland: A Preliminary Report from the Excavations from 1961 to 1968," *Acta Archaeologica* 41 (1970).

25 A.S. Ingstad, *Det nye land med de grønne enger* (Oslo: Gyldendal, 1975); published in English as *The New Land with the Green Meadows* (Historic Sites Association of Newfoundland and Labrador, 2000).

26 J. Doig, "Storm over Ungava. An Embattled Maverick's Long Quest to Rewrite Canada's History," *Anthropological Journal of Canada* 21 (1983).

27 Including Dr Bill Taylor, who also participated in the excavations at L'Anse aux Meadows.

28 Correspondence regarding this issue is kept in the Ingstad archives, H-0003.

29 Ingstad, *The Discovery of a Norse Settlement in America*, 146.

30 R.E. Lee, "Radiocarbon and L'Anse aux Meadows Dating," *Anthropological Journal of Canada* 20, no. 3 (1982): 9–15; R.E. Lee, "L'Anse aux Meadows – Can There Really Be No Doubt?" *Anthropological Journal of Canada* 20, no. 4 (1982): 18–32; R. Lee, "LAM – More of the Same!" *Anthropological Journal of Canada* 20, no. 3 (1982): 29–31; M.F.D. Farmer, "Drop Spindles and Norse Weaving," *Anthropological Journal of Canada* 20, no. 3 (1982): 22–5; G.F. Carter, "Questions. L'Anse aux Meadows Radiocarbon Dates." *Anthropological Journal of Canada* 20, no. 3 (1982): 5–7.

31 Edward Roberts had kindly given me a copy of this correspondence.

32 Mowat dedicated his book *The Farfarers* to Thomas Lee.

33 This article could not be located, but several sources independently have told me about it.

34 Personal email correspondence with Sigrid Hillern Hansen Kalland, dated 28 January 2010.

CHAPTER SEVENTEEN

1 Helge's 1977 speech, "NO to the European Common Market," Ingstad archives, E-0050.

2 http://www.neitileu.no/aktuelt/medieklipp/helge_ingstad.

3 Ingstad archives, E-0052.

4 *Nationen*, 13 October 1979.

5 I have not succeeded in getting this confirmed for sure, but one family book shows that Skjervøy, at the time she was born, was predominantly populated by Coastal Sami and that Eilertine Jensen grew up as a foster child of the minister.

6 Ingstad archives, E-0052.

7 Letter from Professor Sverre Marstrande dated 5 January 1980, located in Marstranders files in the Ingstad archives.

8 The amount given to all those who have resided in Alaska for at least a year, regardless of age, ranges between US$1,200 and 1,500 per year.

9 This quota can vary from year to year.

10 He developed a method of navigation in the Arctic and over the North Pole, which meant that SAS was the first airline to offer scheduled flights from Europe to Asia across the North Pole.

CHAPTER EIGHTEEN

1 For an outsider's assessment of this debate, see Roar Skolmen, *In the Shadow of the Kon-Tiki* (Oslo: N.W. Damm & Son AS, 2000), 246–58.

2 *Aftenposten*, 23 June 1995.

3 *Aftenposten*, 8 October 1995. Helge's counter-argument to Thor.

4 *Aftenposten*, 8 January 1996.

5 Personal conversation with Christian Keller.

6 *Verdens Gang* (*vg*), 4 September 1999.

7 Including a letter to Christian Keller from Andreas Mellbye, dated 8 March 2000.

8 In the book *Ingen grenser* (*No Limits*), Heyerdahl refers to the findings of L'Anse aux Meadows, but the (humble) knowledge he demonstrates on the matter might as well have been picked up at the conference in Argentina in 1966. Neither Helge's nor Anne Stine's books are referred to in the bibliography.

9 *New York Times*, "Science," 19 January 2000.

10 Personal conversation with Anne Marie Weideman.

CHAPTER NINETEEN

1 Besides this day, there was also a two-day symposium, "The Helge Ingstad Symposium on Arctic Change," at the University of Fairbanks. Both the symposium and unveiling ceremony at Anaktuvuk Pass were supported by the Norwegian Embassy in Washington, DC.

2 H. Ingstad, *Nunamiut: Blant Alaskas innlands-eskimoer*, 150.

3 Meldgaard's obituary, *Politiken*, 18 March 2007.

4 B.L. Wallace, *Westward Vikings: The Saga of L'Anse aux Meadows* (St John's: Historic Sites Association of Newfoundland and Labrador, 2006).

5 The "unfortunate" House F that Anne Stine believed Parks Canada had destroyed, was presented by Wallace as a repair yard for boats, while Anne Stine justifies why it must have been a house for living in. It is interesting to note that House F in today's L'Anse aux Meadows has been rebuilt as a house next to the ruins.

6 See, for example, A.S. Ingstad et al., *The Discovery of a Norse Settlement in America: Excavations at L'Anse aux Meadows, Newfoundland from 1961 to 1968*, vol. 1 (Oslo-Bergen-Tromso: University Publisher, 1977), 26; and B. Wallace, "L'Anse aux Meadows: Gateway to Vinland," *Acta Archaeologica* 61 (1990): 175.

7 This occurred in 1990 when they were both alive.

8 Email correspondence with William W. Fitzhugh, director of the Smithsonian's Arctic Studies Center, senior scientist at the National Museum of Natural History, and co-editor of *Vikings: The North Atlantic Saga* (National Museum of Natural History and Smithsonian Institution Press, 2000).

9 On my last visit there in 2013 the plaque had been removed by Parks Canada.

10 The work of archaeologist Patricia Sutherland, still in progress, indicates that Vikings may have built an outpost on Baffin Island, now called Nanook.

11 29 July 2000.

AFTERWORD

1 Extract from the poem *"Sne vil falde – et avskjedsdikt"* ("Snow Will Fall – A Farewell Poem") by Helge Ingstad, translated by J.K. Stenehjem.

APPENDIX

Publications in English by Helge and Anne Stine Ingstad

The publications in this list refer to the latest publisher. The references in the Notes refer to first publisher. Some of the books have been published successively at two different publishers.

BY HELGE INGSTAD

Land of Feast and Famine. Translated by E. Gay-Tifft. Montreal and Kingston: McGill-Queen's University Press, 1992.

East of the Great Glacier. Translated by E. Gay-Tifft. New York: Alfred A. Knopf, 1937.

The Apache Indians: In Search of the Missing Tribe. Translated by J.K. Stenehjem. Lincoln and London: University of Nebraska Press, 2004.

Nunamiut: Among Alaska's Inland Eskimos. Translated by F.H. Lyon. W.W. Norton, 1954.

and Elijah Kakinya and Simon Paneak. *Nunamiut Stories*. Translated by K. Bergsland. Alaska Native Language Center and University of Alaska Fairbanks for the North Slope Borough Commission on Inupiat History, Language, and Culture, 1987.

and Eivind Groven and Sigvald Tveit, eds. *Songs of the Nunamiut: Historical Recordings of an Alaskan Eskimo Community*. Oslo: Tano-Aschehoug, 1998.

Land under the Pole Star: A Voyage to the Norse Settlements of Greenland and the Saga of the People That Vanished. Translated by N. Walford. New York: St Martin's Press, 1966.

Westward to Vinland: The Discovery of Pre-Columbian House-Sites in North America. Translated by E.J. Friis. London: Jonathan Cape, 1969.

The Norse Discovery of America, vol. 2. Translated by E.S. Seeberg. Oslo: Norwegian University Press, 1985.

and Anne Stine Ingstad. *The Viking Discovery of America: The Excavation of a Norse Settlement in L'Anse aux Meadows, Newfoundland.* New York: Checkman Books, 2001.

"Vinland Ruins Prove, Vikings Found the New World." *National Geographic Magazine,* November 1964. Microsoft Encarta 2009. Microsoft Corporation.

BY ANNE STINE INGSTAD

"The Norse Settlement at L'Anse aux Meadows Newfoundland: A Preliminary Report from the Excavations from 1961 to 1968." *Acta Archaeologica* 41 (1970): 109–54.

The Discovery of a Norse Settlement in America: Excavations at L'Anse aux Meadows, Newfoundland 1961–1968, vol. 1. Translated by E.S. Seeberg. Oslo: Norwegian University Press, 1977.

The New Land with the Green Meadows. Translated by J.K. Stenehjem. Historic Sites Association of Newfoundland and Labrador, 2000.

INDEX

territory 145–6; wars, 146, 149–54, 158
Arizona, 138–68, 146–7, 150–2, 155, 160, 167–8, 170, 171, 222, 225, 337, 379
archaeology, 317; pre-Columbian, 336, 349
Arctic, 26, 83–5, 91–4, 96, 112, 110, 126, 133, 137–9, 141, 155, 157, 161; community, 116, 123, 132; darkness, 116; explorer/researcher, 61, 87; fox, 96, 118; hare, 75; ice, 98; islands, 95, 111; Ocean, 40, 105, 111, 116, 301; ships, 114; tundra, 54
Arctic Institute, Copenhagen, 320
Archer, Collin, 297, 299
Argentina, 390
Artillery Lake, 58–9
Åsgårdstrand, 179
Asia, 156, 228, 349
Askim, 113
Associated Press, 165
Åsvaldsson, Thorvald (father of Eirik the Red), 263
Athabasca: River, 49; nation, 64; tribes, 157. *See also* Native Americans
Austmanna Valley, 270
Australia, 385
Authors' Union, 219, 255, 388
Avignon, 39

Bacerac, 160
Bærum, 9
Baffin Island, 262
Baker Lake, 62
Balchen, Bernt, 167, 187, 223, 237
Balestrand, 207
Bang, Hans Hvide, 329, 336
Bårdsetbakken, 209, 211, 217–18, 394

Bårdsson, Herjulf, father of Bjarni Herjulfsson, 280, 358–9
Bårdsson, Ivar, 272
Beardsley, Tony, 345
Barentsburg, 112, 119, 121, 122–4
Barren Grounds (lands), 41, 54, 68, 74–5, 143, 280, 358–9
Bassøe, Johannes Gerckens, 114
Bat Lake, 43–4
Bavispe River, 160
Be-do-ja. *See* Victorio
Beijing, 385
Beksadian, Mr, 91
Belle Isle, 287, 307, 307–8, 319; Strait of, 262, 287, 288–9, 298, 301
Benedicte, Greenland expedition ship, 264–8
Bennett, Peter H., 362
Bergen, 3, 7–25, 30–4, 45, 60–1, 72, 76, 78, 83, 86, 99, 107, 112, 118–19, 128–30, 139, 168, 169, 189–90, 209, 210, 211, 216, 248, 262, 276, 397
Bergensfjord, 128, 311
Bergens Tidende, 166
Bergsland, Einar, 256
Bering Sea, 227–8
Berlin, 189
Berlingske Tidende (Aftenavis), 315
Bessastadir, Icelandic presidential residence, 357
Big Chief. *See* George Decker
Bikaner. *See* Sing, Karni, Maharaja of
Bill(y), cowboy, 141; foreman, 142
Bird, Junius, 336, 342, 344, 345, 352, 361, 433
Bird, Peggy, 345
"Bishop," teacher, 21–2
Bjerknes, Vilhelm, 11
Bjoreia, River, 27–8
Bjørgvin, 272, 287
Bjørnson family, 180

Clark, trapper, 69
Clearwater River, 49
Clinton, Bill and Hillary, 398
Clyde River, 359
Colbourne, family, 303, 305, 312, 352, 362, 407
Colesdalen, 120-1
Collins, Henry, 336, 340, 342
Colorado, 146
Colorado Springs, 138
Columbus, Christopher, 285, 321, 390-1
Common Market, 376-7
Copenhagen, 316-17, 319, 330, 351, 369
Coppermine River, 48-9, 53
copyright law, 4, 178
cowboy, 15, 17, 41, 136, 138-47, 169, 222, 300, 337
Crook, George, 149-150

Dale, Hjalmar, 45-7, 56, 62, 86, 99, 106, 108
Danes, 78, 84-5, 87-8, 92-4, 102, 106, 265, 315-16, 322-4, 326-7, 330-3, 391
Decker, George (Big Chief), 292-4, 303, 305, 312, 329, 333-4, 337, 344-5, 362, 405, 407, 409
Decker, Lloyd, 303, 345, 350-1, 407
Decker, Loretta, 409
Decker, Mae 303, 345, 351
Deering, 227
Denmark, 80, 84-5, 88-9, 92, 105, 133, 145, 203, 265, 315, 318, 362, 374, 388
Denver, 138
Department of Interior: Alaska, 223; Northwest Territories, 60
Devold, Hallvard, 89
Dingwall, 289
Disko Bay (Nordseta), 263
Doric, ship, 39, 40

Dorset culture, 290, 317, 319, 337, 357, 373. *See also* Inuit
Dostoevsky, Fyodor, 21
Douglas, Arizona, 155-6, 160, 164, 167
Dripping Spring Valley, 139

East Fork, 146, 148, 151
Eckhoff, Nicolay, 336, 358
Edmonton, 40-1, 43, 45, 49, 53, 76, 77, 87
Egede, Grethe, 267
Egede, Hans, 267
Egypt, 108, 185, 381
Eileen Lake, 54-5
Eilifsen, Gunnar, 216
Einarsfjord, 268
Einarsson, Torvard, 268
Eirik (Thorvaldsson) the Red, 132, 136, 216, 261, 263-4, 266, 268, 270, 280-5; Freydis, daughter, 263, 266, 268, 283-4; Thjodhild, wife, 263, 266; Thorstein, son, 263, 270, 282-3, 285, 289; Thorvald, son, 263, 267, 282
Eirik Raudes Land, 89, 92-4, 102, 104, 106, 261; governor of, 92, 94-5, 102, 104-7
Eiriksfjord (Tunulliarfik), 263, 265-6
Eiriksson, Leif (Leiv), 40, 132, 261, 263-8, 270, 280-5, 285, 289, 312, 331, 336, 357, 359; anniversary celebration, 397-9
Eldjàrn, Kristian, 330- 6, 339-42, 357, 370, 405
Ellingsen, Alf, 18
Elverum, 195, 277-8, 296, 323
Engerdalen, 133
England, 113, 205, 209, 211, 217, 274, 276, 327, 339, 349
English River, 309
Epaves Bay, 286, 304, 307
Espedalen, 180

correspondence with Helge, 130, 184, 186–7, 184–8, 249, 189–90, 192, 207, 225; courtship and marriage, 171–2, 187, 191, 206–7; death and legacy, 393–4, 402, 404–10; engaged to Werner, 188–192; at Elverum, 277–9; in Germany, 189–90; liberation, 213; on life after Vinland, 375–6, 380–82, 386–90; losing Tycho, 108, 211, 216–17; in Paris, 186, 191; trip to America, 221–5; trip to West Greenland, 264–9; and the war, 202–4; on work at L'Anse aux Meadows, 296–313, 329–57, 360–74; as young and romantic, 195

Ingstad, Helge, 4–5, 13–17, 253; activism, 376–9; becomes author, 78–81, 113–14; boyhood, 7–31; building Brattalid, 219–21; and chess, 4; conflict with Danes, 315–24; correspondence with Olav, 34, 38, 166, 207; cowboy life, 134–43; finds "Vinland," 275–96; in France, 38–9; goes west, 133–8; governor of Eirik Raudes Land, 84–110; with Icelandic archaeologists, 330–4; as lawyer in Levanger, 34–72; new "storms," 360–74; and Nunamiut, 225–52, 256, 382–4; old age, death, and legacy, 386–409; and Parks Canada, 350, 361–3, 365–70, 381–2, 388, 390, 398, 405–6; peace work and Quisling, 213–19; Pine Point, 73, 258–9; search for "free" Apaches, 144–71; and Siberia 91, 100, 122–3, 134, 137, 181, 208, 223, 241; as student, 31–4; and Svalbard, 111–32; and Thor Heyerdahl, 388–93; as trapper in Canada, 39–77; trip to America, 221–5; trip to "Helluland," 357–9;

war and Red Cross, 193–21; West Greenland and Norse settlements, 261–74; on work at L'Anse aux Meadows, 296–314, 324–60; as world traveller, 385

Ingstad family: Benedicte, daughter, 14, 220, 249, 253–54, 302, 409, 414; Dorothea, grandmother (born Greve), 32; Eirik, grandson, 258, 376, 384–5, 398, 404; Emil, uncle, 32; Gunvor, sister (married name Trætteberg), 4, 8, 14, 20–2, 33, 36, 77–8, 211, 255; Kaare, brother, 4, 9, 12, 14, 16–17, 34, 77–8, 83, 92, 99, 114, 130, 141, 168, 171, 205–7, 221–4, 337, 395; Marcus, grandfather, 4, 9, 32; Marit, granddaughter, (married name Teige), 128, 376, 386, 394, 397–8, 406–9; Olav, father, 4, 8–17, 20–3, 32–3, 38, 51, 60–2, 72, 78, 106–7, 136, 154, 216, 241, 274, 276, 401; Olga, mother, grandmother (born Qvam), 8, 11, 13, 61, 119, 136, 211, 216

Ingstad Mountain, 402

International Research Advisory Committee, 360, 363, 365–6, 368, 381–2

Inuit, 61–2, 100, 228–9, 230–1, 240–1, 256, 263–4, 267, 269–70, 272, 296, 305, 358–9. See also Dorset culture

Iqaluit, 262, 358

Ireland, 132

Irgens, Judge, 130

Isèp, Dene hunter, 67

Isfjorden, 111–12, 119, 121

Italy, 108, 390

Ivittuut, 263, 265

Jacobsen, Arne, 95–7, 108, 118

Lockhart River, 60
Lom, 178
London, 113, 205, 220
Longyearbyen, 112, 114–28, 130–1, 185
Los Angeles, 166–7, 221
Lund, Bureau Chief, 128
Lund, Kristine, 119
Lutselk'e, 62
Lynx Lake, 55, 69

MacKay, R.A., 328
Mackenzie River, 46, 62
Maihaugen, 178, 181, 207
Mandela, Nelson, 393
Marlow, Anton, 131, 171
Mar del Plata (Argentina), 390
Maribuseter, 180–1, 187–8, 191, 207, 210, 217, 225, 265, 269, 277, 324, 357, 387, 394, 406, 410, 411
Markland, 274, 281, 283, 285, 287–8, 309, 357, 359
Marlow, Wolmer Tycho, 131, 171
Marstrander, Sverre, 362, 364–5, 369, 381
Martens, Odd, 23–5, 27–31, 34, 77, 88, 113, 171, 131, 207, 297–9, 301, 303, 310
Märtha, Crown Princess of Norway, 102, 205
Maursetseter, 28
McCray, Director of Indian Affairs, 158
McKay, trapper, 69
Mehren, Herman, 113
Meldgaard, Jørgen, 295, 316–28, 333–4, 351, 404
Memorial University, Newfoundland, 13, 290, 327–30, 339–41, 362, 372, 406, 413
Meråker, 8, 397
Mexico, 138, 146–7, 160–1, 168, 390

minerals: search for, 41, 73, 138, 140, 158, 163, 228; Pine Point 73, 258–9
Minnesota, 349–50, 356
Mjøsa Lake, 173, 209
Moe, Anne Stine. See Ingstad, Anne Stine
Moe, Eilif, 4, 173–88, 192, 195, 203–4, 207–9, 211–12, 218, 220, 225, 254, 265, 410
Moe, Louise, 173–4, 176–88, 192, 209–10, 212, 218, 220, 225, 254, 256, 265, 277–8, 311, 324, 375, 410–11
Mole, Ole Henrik, 176–7, 183, 188, 203, 208–9, 431; at Sachsenhausen, 211–17, 231
Mole, Tycho, 174–81, 183, 185, 188–9, 194, 202–3, 207–10; death and memorial, 211–12, 216–17, 279, 375, 387, 410
Molepolole (Botswana), 385
Montagnais. See Native Americans
Montreal, 39, 40, 77, 85, 298, 358, 402
Moore Trading Post, 43
Moores, Frank D., 367–8
Moose Lake (Elgsjøen), 55, 57–60
Mora, Ididro, 161–5
Moreni, Gildardo, 161
Morgenstierne, minister, 135
Mormons, 163
Moscow, 91
Motzfelt, Jonathan, 407
Mount Baldy, 146
Mozambique, 39
Munn, William, 285–8, 292, 295, 320, 332
Museum of Cultural History, Oslo, 365
Museum of Natural History. See American Museum of Natural History

230, 233, 248, 256, 259–61, 264,
271–2, 274, 279, 288, 296–7, 307,
311, 317, 324, 332, 335–7, 339,
341–2, 344, 347–9, 353–4, 362,
365, 370, 373, 375–80, 383–4,
388, 393, 396–9, 404, 408; central,
8; eastern, 27, 31; German occupation of, 81, 110, 134, 193–213,
218, 377; history, 84–5, 275, 280;
Little Norway pilot training centre
in Canada, 181; mountains (*see
also* Hardangervidda), 10, 23, 259,
283; northern, 95, 131, 260; southern, 3; western, 7, 45–6
Norwegian Council of Arctic Administration, 87, 89
Norwegian Forest Museum (Skog-
bruksmuseet), 277, 279
Norwegian Polar Navigation, 259
Norwegian University of Science and
Technology (NTNU), 340
Norwegians Worldwide (Nordmanns-
forbundet), 135
Nova Scotia, 289, 312
Nunamiut, 26, 227–52, 256, 260,
379, 393, 403–4; history 230–2
Nuuk (Godthåp), 262–3, 267, 269,
270
Nygaardsvold, Johan, 128
Nygardsen, the "hermit" of Sølens-
jøen, 193, 195

Økern, Bjørn, 368, 414
Olav V, king of Norway, 102, 349
Olav Haraldsson, king of Norway,
283
Olsen, district governor, 12
Olsen, Magnus, 275
Omre, Arthur, 255
Opler, Morris, 157
Order of St Olav, 350
Orkney Islands, 132, 262, 276

Oslo, 8–9, 15, 31, 77, 79, 83, 85,
91–2, 95, 109, 113–14, 169, 173–4,
178–9, 185, 187, 195–6, 198–200,
203–4, 206, 208, 211, 213–14, 216,
219–20, 255, 259, 262, 276–7,
315, 356, 364–5, 375, 378–9, 388,
400–1, 411; fjord, 221, University
of, 227, 257, 349–50, 370. *See also*
Christiania; Kristiania
Østerbygd. *See* Greenland
Ottawa, 328–9, 366–7, 399
Øverland, Arnulf, 255

Paddon, physician at Grenfell
Mission, 295
Palmer, Anna, 152–3
Pamioq Island, 372
Paneak family, 231, 234; museum,
383–4; Roosevelt, 230, 383; Simon,
230–6, 238, 239–43, 245–6, 249–
51, 383; Umealaq (Susie), 230, 238,
240, 243, 283, 384
Pangnirtung, 358
Paris, 38, 114, 130, 147, 186, 191
Parks Canada, 360–3, 365–70,
381–2, 388, 390, 398, 405–6,
408–9
Pedersen, Einar Sverre, 259, 385
Pedersen, Ole Crumlin, 362
Petrè, Rolf, 329–30
Phoenix, 138–9, 145, 165, 224, 337
Phresi, Dene woman, 65, 70
Pikes Portage, 54, 59, 74
Pine Point. *See* minerals
Pisissarfik, 269
Pistolet Bay, 285–8, 292, 312, 320,
333–4
Platou, Carl, 106
Point Barrow, 236, 250
Point Hope, 228
Polarbjørn, expedition ship, 94–5, 97,
108–9

Prudoe Bay, 259, 384
Puddefjord, 16

Quebec, 298–301, 372
Quebec City, 298
Quisling, Vidkun, 110, 134, 196,
  205–6, 214–16
Qvam, Eilertine Marie (born Jensen),
  31, 379
Qvam, Olga Marie. *See* Ingstad
  family, Olga

Radiocarbon datings, 336, 340
Rail S Ranch, Arizona, 139
Raleigh, 292, 321, 333–4
Red Bay, 286, 301
Red Cross, Norwegian, 197–202,
  208; Swedish, 205
Rendalen, 193
Rennes, 217
Reykjavik, 13, 262, 330
Rieber family, 15; Mrs, 17–18;
  Rieber's man, 15–17, 61
Roberts, Edward, 363, 373, 408, 413
Rolloff, Aagot. *See* Lindeman
Roosevelt, Franklin D., 134
Rørholt, Arnold, 197–8
Round-up of cattle, 141–3
Rousseau, Jacques, 372
Rousseau, Jean Jacques, philosopher,
  169
Roussell, Aage, 315–16, 321–4,
  327–8
Ruge, Otto, 196
Russia(n), 9, 22, 90; coal mining, 112,
  115, 119, 121–5, 181, 205, 208;
  government, 134, 168; music, 124,
  143; people, 126. *See also* Soviet
  Union
Rusten. *See* Rieber family
Royal Canadian Mounted Police
  (RCMP), 48, 59, 60, 62

Saatvedt, Arne Braa, 218–19
Sachsenhausen, 208, 211, 217
Saga, 257, 261, 263–4, 267–76, 279–
  91, 294–5, 298, 301–2, 307–10,
  312, 320–1, 332, 336, 343, 346,
  357–9, 393, 404; of Eirik the Red,
  280, 283; of the Greenlanders,
  280–1, 283, 359
Salater, Kristian, 35
Salt River, 51
Sami, Norwegian indigenous people,
  183, 260, 378–80
San Carlos, 145–6, 150, 157, 222
Sandberg, Edwin, 375, 384–5, 411
Sandbu, Guttorm Gjesling, 177–8
Sandemose, Aksel, 255
Sandnes (Norse farm in Greenland),
  270, 289
Sandvig collection friends, 178
Sandviken, 14
San Fransiscus Hospital, 199
Satin-tuè, 68
Scandinavia(n), 39, 89, 109, 178, 361
Schönbäck, Bengt, 363–8, 388
Scoresby Sund, 84, 89, 91–2, 102–3,
  104–5, 110
Scotland, 132, 259, 276
Seattle, 227, 250
Seaver, Kirsten, 349
Second World War, 4, 81, 110, 170–
  79, 181–9, 265, 377, 394, 402
Sellie, John, 43–5, 47
Sept-Îles, 299–300
Seter (mountain farm), 24, 27–8. *See
  also* Maribuseter
Shanghai, 78
Shearer, Douglas, 167
Shetland Islands, 132, 262, 264, 276
Ship Cove, 292
Shorty, cowboy, 141
Siberia, 90–1, 100, 122–3, 134, 137,
  181, 223, 241; railway, 208

Sienequita, 160
Sierra Madre, 151, 154, 156–8,
    161–6
Sinding-Larsen, Henning, 213
Singh, Karni, Maharaja of Bikaner,
    338
Skálholt map, 288
Skaugum, 213–14
"Skipper." See Sørnes, Paul
Skjåk, 218, 256
Skjøtingen, 36
Skoglund, Sverre, 126–7
Skouen, Arne, 3, 399
Slave River, 48, 51, 53–4
Smallwood, Joseph R., 325, 327, 340,
    351
Smedal, Gustav, 93, 103–5, 107
Smithsonian Institute, 336, 342
Smyrill, John, Bishop, 268
"Snippen," 3, 10
Snorre, first European born in Amer-
    ica, 285, 346
Snowdrift, 53–4, 57, 60–2, 69, 72–3,
    76; River, 53–4, 62, 72, 74
Søderberg, Swedish linguist, 287
Sognefjord, 207
Sølensjøen, 193, 414
Sonja, Queen of Norway, 370, 398,
    408
Sonora, 157, 160–1; Desert, 138,
Sørnes, Paul ("Skipper"), 297, 299,
    301, 303, 307, 309, 311–2
South Pole, 80, 97, 146, 319, 325,
    385
Soviet Union, 90–1, 119, 132, 134,
    137, 308. See also Russia(n)
Spearman, Grant, 383, 403
Spitsbergen, 111, 115–17, 126, 139
Stalin, Joseph, 122
St Anthony, 286, 291–2, 294, 296,
    305, 312, 321, 329, 347, 351, 353,
    406

State Department, Washington, DC,
    223
Stavanger, 375
Stavangerfjord, ship, 134, 224–5
Stavern, 19
Stèfanson, Sigurdur, 320
Stenberger, Mårten, 352–4
Stilla (near Alta in Norway), 379
St John's, 318, 413
St Lawrence River, 40, 298
Stockholm, 90, 106, 169, 178, 205–6
St Olav College, 350
Stoltenberg, Jens, 401
Storbråten, Jo, 256
Store Norske Spitsbergen Coal Com-
    pany, 115, 131
Storhøliseter, 180
Strait of Belle Isle, 262, 287–9, 301
Straitsview, 305
Straumsey, 284. See also Belle Isle
Straumsfjord, 284, 287, 298, 301,
    309
Sulheim, Lars, 178
Sunnmøre, 15, 268, 297
Superstition Mountains, 140, 143
Svalbard, 95, 97, 100, 105–18, 128–
    32, 135, 169, 171, 184, 187, 208,
    221, 262; book, 133, 218–19; oil,
    259; treaty, 119
Svarstad, Hans Undset, 225
Sweden, 9, 80, 89–90, 207, 329, 330,
    352, 376, 394
Swedish Society for Geography and
    Anthropology, 90, 169
Sweet, Pamela, 292

Taipa, Apache scout, 147, 149, 150,
    222
Tanner, Väinö, 285, 287–8, 292, 295,
    301, 320–1, 332
Tau, Max, 178, 188–9
Tau, Renate, 289

Winnipeg, 40
Wolf Valley, 103–4
Women's Defense League, 203
Wyse, William, 328

Yahnozah, Apache, expedition
  member, 158–66

Yale University Press, 349
Yarmouth, 289
Yugoslavia, 141, 143
Yukon, 41, 229, 231